Modern

their character and influence

Revolutions

H. R. Cowie

Nelson

An International Thomson Publishing Company

Melbourne • Bonn • Boston • London • Madrid • Mexico City • New York • Paris • Singapore
Tokyo • Toronto • Albany NY • Belmont CA • Cincinnati OH • Detroit MI

Nelson I(T)P®
102 Dodds Street
South Melbourne 3205

Nelson I(T)P® *an International Thomson Publishing company*

First published in 1996
10 9 8 7 6 5 4 3 2 1
05 04 03 02 01 00 99 98 97 96

National Library of Australia
Cataloguing-in-Publication data

Cowie, H.R. (Hamilton Russell).
Modern Revolutions: Their character and influence.

Includes index.
ISBN 0 17 009156 2

1. Revolutions—History. I Title.

321.094

Edited by Maryanne Lynch
Designed by Erika Budiman
Maps and diagrams designed by H. R. Cowie
drawn by Alan Laver, Shelly Communications (maps); Post Typesetters (diagrams)
Cover designed by Deborah Gilkes
Cover photographs: Camera Press (Lenin, Castro), David King collection (Mao),
Réunion des Musées Nationaux (Napoleon), the Photo Library/Hulton Deutsch (Marx).
Typeset in 11/13pt Bembo by Post Typesetters, Brisbane, QLD
Printed in Singapore by Kin Keong Printing Co. Pte. Ltd.

Nelson Australia Pty Limited ACN 004 603 454 (incorporated in Victoria) trading as
Nelson ITP.

introduction

Common to all revolutions is a stated desire to build an improved society. Equally common to all such attempts is a degree of 'shortfall' between the hope and the attainment. Basic also to most revolutions is a striving for a group identity—as a nation liberated from the intrusions and interferences of other nations, or as a society released from burdens imposed by an anachronistic and exploitative authority.

Modern Revolutions examines the key revolutions of Modern History. Emphasis is given to the varying explanations that can be made of the causes of these revolutions, and students are encouraged to develop critical responses to the evidence presented. The aim of such an approach is to encourage in students a view of History as comprising both evidence from the past and questions arising from present day society.

Accordingly, each chapter is introduced by theme questions, to which students are expected to construct their own answers. Extracts from primary and secondary sources offer diverse views of the events described, and additional interpretative questions are posed. At the same time the information necessary to an understanding of the events, and their social and theoretical underpinnings, is supplied in succinct form.

Modern Revolutions aims to provide the knowledge base upon which students of History can expand their understanding of the world around them and of how widespread social, political, economic and/or religious changes occur.

table of contents

acknowledgments

The author and publisher would like to gratefully credit or acknowledge permission to reproduce photographic and cartoon material:

The Australian, p. 160: AAP Photo Library, pp. 158, 162, 252; Australian Picture Library/Bettmann, pp. 159, 166–8, 185, 213, 218, 221, 225; Camera Press, pp. 129, 136, 194, 209, 240, 246–7; Cooee Historical Picture Library, pp. 17, 81; David King Collection, pp. 96, 140, 142, 145, 191, 199; Freer Gallery of Art and Arthur M. Sackler Gallery Archives, Smithsonian Institution, photographer Hsun-ling, p. 177; Harlingue-Viollet, p. 181; The Mansell Collection, pp. 9, 46, 49, 56, 80, 86, 98; Mary Evans Picture Library, p. 14, 35; People's Liberation Army Office, p. 197; Peter Newark's Pictures, pp. 27, 32, 58; Punch Library and Archive, p. 143; Queensland Newspapers/Mac Vines, p. 157; Réunion des Musées Nationaux, p. 65; Roger-Viollet, pp. 45, 57, 63, 92; Nicholas Rothwell/*The Australian*, p. 169; Sporting Pix/Popperfoto, pp. 36, 110, 118; the Photo Library/Hulton Deutsch, pp. 50, 85, 109, 183; Pattrick Zachmann/Magnum Photos, p. 227.

The author and publisher would like to credit or acknowledge permission to reproduce text, maps, diagrams and charts:

The Age, p. 161, 4 October 1990; William Ashley, p. 15, *The Economic Organisation of England: An Outline History*, Longman, Green and Co., 1949, pp. 154–5; R.E. Bonachea and N.P. Valdes (eds), pp. 238–9, *Revolutionary Struggle 1947–58*, MIT Press, 1972, pp. 217–21; *China Daily*, p. 223, 18 August 1986, p. 220, 21 August 1986; Mikhail Gorbachev, p. 156, *Perestroika: New Thinking for Our Country and The World*, HarperCollins Publishers, London, 1987, pp. 34–5; H. Johnson, p. 135, *The Socialist Sixth of the World*, Victor Gollancz, London, 1939, pp. 15–16; E. Lyons, p. 141, *Assignment in Utopia*, George Harrap, NY, 1938, pp. 279–80; J. Mirsky, p. 224, *The Bulletin*, 26 July 1983; L. Namier, p. 11, *Vanished Supremacies: Essays on European History, 1812 to 1918*, Harper Torchbooks, 1963, p. 22; *Quotations from Chairman Mao Zedong*, pp. 207, 210, Foreign Languages Press, Beijing, 1967, pp. 24, 177; *Time*, p. 219, 25 September 1978; Mok Chiu Yu and J.F. Harrison (eds), pp. 226–7, *Voices from Tienanmen Square: Beijing Spring and the Democracy Movement*, Black Rose Books, Montreal, 1990, pp. 47–53; p. 18, reprinted with the permission of A.P. Watt Ltd on behalf of Michael Yeats; C.V. Wedgwood, p. 257, *William the Silent*, Jonathan Cape, 1944, p. 224; M. Williams, pp. 190, 198, *The East is Red: The Chinese, A New Viewpoint*, Sun Books, Melbourne, 1969, pp. 18, 35.

Every effort has been made to trade and acknowledge copyright holders. Where the attempt has been unsuccessful, the publisher welcomes information that would redress the situation.

MAPS

DIAGRAMS

chapter one

The End of Obedience: Challenging Authority in the Modern World

Whereas recognition of the inherent dignity and of the equal and inalienable rights of all members of the human family is the foundation of freedom, justice and peace in the world,

Whereas disregard and contempt for human rights have resulted in barbarous acts which have outraged the conscience of mankind, and the advent of a world in which human beings shall enjoy freedom of speech and belief and freedom from fear and want has been proclaimed as the highest aspiration of the common people . . .

Now, therefore, The General Assembly

Proclaims this Universal Declaration of Human Rights, as a common standard of achievement for all peoples and all nations, to the end that every individual and every organ of society, keeping this Declaration constantly in mind, shall strive by teaching and education to promote respect for these rights and freedoms and by progressive measures, national and international, to secure their universal and effective recognition and observance, both among the peoples of Member States themselves and among the peoples of territories under their jurisdiction.

Declaration of the General Assembly of the United Nations Organisation, New York, 10 December 1948

The predominant emphasis in the statement above is that all human beings have rights. We take this for granted today. Yet the concept of individual rights is a very recent phenomenon in History. It is the major feature of what is often termed the 'modern world'.

To begin a study of modern revolutions, we need to pose several key questions:

Theme Questions

➣ What features, particularly in societies of European origin, justify the description 'modern'?

➣ If European societies had achieved a measure of stability for thirteen centuries under the feudal system, what influences operated to alter them and produce their 'modern' features?

➣ What features and ways of life distinguish the modern world from the medieval and ancient worlds?

➣ What brought about the changes that created these differences?

➣ What basic disagreement about the features of society has made the modern age one of fearful conflict and violent revolution?

➣ Has humankind gained benefit from the revolutions of the modern era?

I ANCIENT AND MEDIEVAL TIMES

In the European view of History, we live in the modern era, with a period known as the 'Middle Ages' sitting between modern and ancient times. These divisions cannot be measured scientifically; they are a matter of opinion.

What Europeans call 'ancient times' spans the period from the emergence of city civilisations *circa* 3000 BC to *circa* AD 480. The complex organisation of cities was a product of humanity's ability to divide tasks into specialised functions. Before cities could grow, specialist farmers had to be able to produce food in quantities beyond their own subsistence needs. Other people then could do jobs other than farming, and builders, stone masons and craftsmen could develop city amenities. Hence, the first city civilisations usually developed in fertile river valleys.

Once groups of people specialised in one productive activity, they needed to be able to exchange their produce for supplies of other resources (for example, food and shelter). While this occurred in the earliest societies in the form of barter (exchanging goods or services), the idea of a divisible currency (coinage or some other easily carried symbol) later evolved. Such a system eventually became a feature of all human societies.

With the enlargement of small communities into cities came the need for management, or control. In many ancient civilisations powerful military leaders assumed this function, although some communities of ancient Greece attempted democracy—government by the people or their elected representatives. Control was embodied in rules, or laws. To perpetuate and spread knowledge of such laws, a written language was needed. Different civilisations developed such records in different ways.

Once production of goods was well established, trade with other communities could begin—as a means of exchanging surplus goods for scarce products. Overland trade routes opened communications. Eventually shipbuilding and navigation skills made it possible to trade by sea.

As the wealth from trade created resources that became the envy of other communities, the ancient civilisations were forced to develop military strength to protect themselves. Having attained military power, they were also likely to seek conquests. Many ancient civilisations—European, Asian, African and American—conquered and dominated neighbouring territories. **Imperialism** (the practice of acquiring and administering an empire) was a characteristic of the ancient world.

People's need for faith was fulfilled by religious practices, and grandiose buildings were erected in the cities for their observance. These temples, together with royal palaces and tombs, were often the most lavish of the architectural achievements of ancient civilisations. Religious leaders usually sponsored literacy through the recording of events on clay, stone or paper. From these written records people in modern times have been able to learn about events and practices in ancient civilisations. It is this written evidence that distinguishes historic times from prehistoric times.

Imperialist greed eventually corrupted and over-extended many of the ancient empires, and one by one they fell to marauding bands of destroyers. The name of one such group, the Vandals, we still use as a word for destroyers. The Western Roman Empire was gradually dismembered by attacks by Germanic tribes from the north, and finally Rome itself was vanquished in AD 476 by the Visigoths. Although the Eastern Roman Empire survived, governed from Constantinople in the eastern Mediterranean, this date is sometimes used to indicate the end of ancient times.

The Medieval Period and the Feudal System

Historians refer to the period from *circa* AD 470 to 1450 (approximately one thousand years) as the **medieval period**, or the Middle Ages. The word 'medieval' is formed from two Latin words, *medius* (middle) and *aevum* (age). The word was coined by Western scholars during the revival of learning called the Renaissance (*circa* fifteenth century AD). The present-day use of the word is historically significant because it is evidence of the continued influence of the language of ancient Rome (Latin) and of the sense of superiority of the Renaissance scholars. The very use of the term 'middle' indicates that the period referred to was regarded as less important than the eras that preceded and followed it—the classical age of antiquity and the Renaissance respectively.

As the Roman rule of law collapsed, 'barbarian' raids reduced most of the peoples of Europe to a state of fear and uncertainty in which they could not even be assured of harvesting the next crop. In such an atmosphere, the vital relationship between progress and security became evident. If a society lacks security, people can live only at the barest level of subsistence. Any improvement to property, or any advancement in scale of production, is worthless if the house is likely to be plundered or the produce stolen. In these circumstances the common person is most in need of security and is therefore willing to seek protection at almost any cost.

In this condition of insecurity, a supreme warrior, or 'king', was likely to establish control over a wide area, and then reward his major helpers with grants of land. These 'lords' or 'barons' owed the king a 'fee', or payment of loyalty and service, in return for their grant of land, which was known as a *fief*. The lords, in turn, granted the use of strips of land for farming to the peasants, who thus also in effect held a fief, and were required to pay a fee for both the use of the land and the protection they received.

The Latin term for this type of contract (in which the payment of a fee in return for a service or privilege was the dominant feature) was *feodum*. From this word the term 'feudal' evolved to describe this form of organisation of society. The **feudal system** was thus a product of the condition of insecurity that developed as the Roman Empire crumbled away and the rule of law collapsed.

In this 'fee paying' system the lords paid their debt of allegiance and loyalty to the monarch by providing soldiers in times of emergency. The feudal lord constructed a fortified stronghold, or castle, and maintained a core of trained soldiers, some of whom became lesser lords or knights. The common people made their homes and farmed their land alongside the castle. In return for the lord's protection and land, they formed themselves into fighting bands in time of war, worked on the lord's domain for several days of the week without wages, and gave everything they had, if necessary, to pay his ransom charges if he were captured by enemies.

A well-defined class distinction that was simultaneously a class inter-dependency developed between the aristocratic landowners and the uneducated peasantry. Apart from a few skilled craftsmen and some officers and stewards of the lord, there was no significant **middle class** in the feudal world.

In this feudal system the person owing the fee to his superior was the 'vassal' of that overlord. The barons were the vassals of the king, and the peasants were the vassals of the barons and lords. The condition of **vassalage** ensured obedience. Each vassal was expected to be loyal to the overlord and ultimately to the king, who ruled by 'divine right', deriving his power from God. There was no concept of individual liberty in feudal society.

The Role of the Christian Church

While secular (earthly) authority in medieval Europe was vested in the feudal lords, spiritual authority was exercised by the Christian Church. Headed by the pope in Rome, and 'universal' in its application ('catholic' means universal), the Catholic Church was the major force that bound western Europeans together. In eastern Europe another branch of Christianity, calling itself the Orthodox ('correct') Church, fulfilled the same function. The Orthodox Christians claimed to be the direct successors of the church founded by Jesus of Nazareth and St Paul.

The true strength of the Church in the Middle Ages was its resilience and usefulness at the

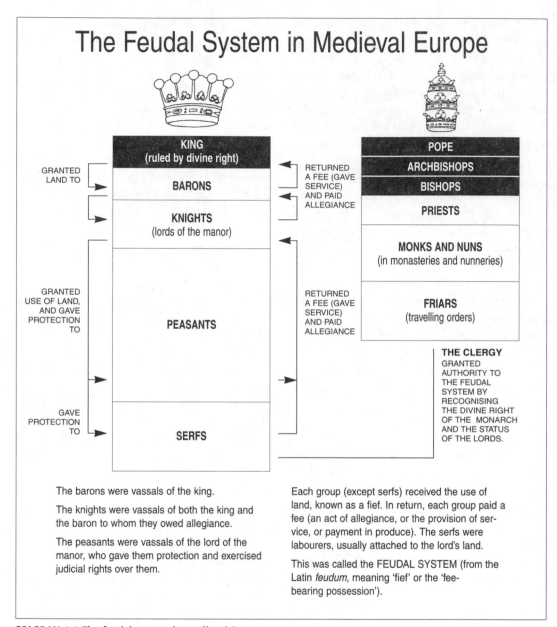

The Feudal System in Medieval Europe

KING (ruled by divine right)
BARONS
KNIGHTS (lords of the manor)
PEASANTS
SERFS

GRANTED LAND TO

GRANTED USE OF LAND, AND GAVE PROTECTION TO

GAVE PROTECTION TO

RETURNED A FEE (GAVE SERVICE) AND PAID ALLEGIANCE

RETURNED A FEE (GAVE SERVICE) AND PAID ALLEGIANCE

POPE
ARCHBISHOPS
BISHOPS
PRIESTS
MONKS AND NUNS (in monasteries and nunneries)
FRIARS (travelling orders)

THE CLERGY
GRANTED AUTHORITY TO THE FEUDAL SYSTEM BY RECOGNISING THE DIVINE RIGHT OF THE MONARCH AND THE STATUS OF THE LORDS.

The barons were vassals of the king.

The knights were vassals of both the king and the baron to whom they owed allegiance.

The peasants were vassals of the lord of the manor, who gave them protection and exercised judicial rights over them.

Each group (except serfs) received the use of land, known as a fief. In return, each group paid a fee (an act of allegiance, or the provision of service, or payment in produce). The serfs were labourers, usually attached to the lord's land.

This was called the FEUDAL SYSTEM (from the Latin *feudum*, meaning 'fief' or the 'fee-bearing possession').

DIAGRAM 1.1 The feudal system in medieval Europe

The feudal system was essentially a 'fee paying' system. Members of each class held a *feudum* (a fee-bearing posses-sion), and had to pay a fee to the overlord from whom they had obtained it, or who owned it and had given permis-sion for its use. People in each class were vassals to a powerful person in the class above them. Feudalism established a system of law, order and defence, but created a very rigid class structure, in which it was almost impossible for an individual to move from one class to another. It was not until the English Revolution of 1688 and the French Revolu-tion of 1789 that the feudal system was openly challenged, and broken, by the champions of a new order.

local level. The monasteries, the impressive ruins of which can still be seen in many parts of Europe, must be regarded as the greatest human achievement of the medieval world, not for their architecture alone, but for their value in terms of human service. They were the schools, universities, hospitals and churches of the period. The monks maintained and nurtured the priceless heritage of classical Greek and Roman culture. The European medieval monasteries, in preserving the cultural links with classical antiquity, made a significant contribution to the world we live in today. In the twentieth century many people of many nations live in societies that have adopted the customs and culture of one small continental peninsula, Europe.

The Church's monopoly of learning made its scholar monks and office-bearing priests objects of awe and veneration. The priests held the power of communication between ordinary people and God, and could withdraw this right from offenders. People excommunicated by the Church were cut off, unable to gain forgiveness of their sins, and were therefore destined to suffer eternal damnation. Church services stressed the might and majesty of God. Everyone, from powerful barons to peasants, acknowledged the authority of the Church, which controlled people's minds and allowed no independence of thought.

Europe was theoretically united in a great Christian entity known as the Holy Roman Empire, or 'Christendom'. Spiritual authority was held by the pope, and secular authority by whichever one of the feudal kings held the title of 'Holy Roman Emperor'.

II FEATURES OF MODERN SOCIETY

The Renaissance
During the fifteenth century European society came under new influences and, in part, broke from the 'static' conditions of the previous thousand years. The period has come to be known as the Renaissance, or 'revival of learning', because there developed a great revival of interest in the art, sculpture and literature of the classical past. In this period we can begin to see some of the characteristics of the modern world.

Any such revival, however, depends on people with the inclination, and the leisure, to devote to cultural interests. In the years following the Crusades (the attempts by Christian monarchs between AD 1096 and 1291 to recapture Jerusalem and the Holy Land from Islamic control), trade with the East had created wealthy merchant classes in the Italian city-states. These classes thirsted for knowledge. Travel had broadened minds and awakened a sense of curiosity about the wider world. Moreover, the development of the printing press in the fifteenth century greatly expanded the opportunities for the spread of knowledge. The educational activities in the monasteries continued, but concern for learning was now developing in a secular city-dwelling group, a group that had emerged as a result of the practice of investing capital in the search for profit from commercial ventures.

The Age of Discovery
The search for knowledge expanded from the desire to learn more about the past (as was manifested in the Renaissance) into a search for knowledge of the other parts of the world. Europe is but a tiny fraction of the global land surface, and in the fifteenth century Europeans knew very little about the rest of the world and about the civilisations, of greater age and complexity than their own, that existed in India and China.

In the Age of Discovery European society expanded its knowledge of the non-European world on a scale hitherto unequalled. By 1487 the Portuguese navigator Bartholomew Dias had discovered that it was possible to sail around the southern tip of Africa; by 1498 countryman Vasco da Gama had used this new sea route to visit India. Meanwhile, in 1492 Christopher Columbus, a Genoan sailor working for Ferdinand and Isabella, the joint monarchs of Spain, pioneered the sea route to the Americas by sailing westward across the Atlantic. Although Columbus thought he was opening a new sea route to China and the East, he had discovered what became known as the 'New World'. In 1522 a Spanish crew, which had left Spain in 1519 under the leadership of Ferdinand

Magellan, completed the first circumnavigation of the world.

In a few decades European navigators had opened up a vast area of land and ocean to explore, exploit and colonise. The centuries that followed were to witness the 'Europeanisation' of these territories on an immense scale.

The Reformation

The new sense of enquiry ultimately weakened the authority of the Church. The papacy, the symbol of Christian unity in Europe, lost prestige through splits, scandals and bad leadership. Some of the fifteenth-century popes seemed to be more concerned with secular matters than with their spiritual responsibilities. The role of the Church as a leading influence in society was coming under challenge. One of the main sources of criticism and discontent was the practice of selling 'indulgences', by which Church officials provided guarantees of salvation in return for large donations to Church funds.

The long-accepted dominance of the papacy was now regarded as an irksome intrusion upon personal rights, particularly by the merchant classes and the secular-minded princes and aristocrats of central and northern Europe. This animosity towards the papacy and the Roman Catholic Church culminated in the great upheaval in European society that we now know as the Reformation. At first, concerned and earnest Christians sought to achieve reform within the Church, but the unrest eventually led to division.

In 1517 Martin Luther, a German professor of theology, provided the critical step towards separation when he publicly rejected the Church's teaching that human beings could achieve salvation only through the agency of the priesthood. He proclaimed that people could seek their own communion with God through faith and prayer. For this defiance of the authority of the pope, Luther was excommunicated from the Church, but he found protection among the princes of northern Germany, many of whom were only too eager to break from papal authority. The 'protest' had produced Protestantism.

Another Reformation (sometimes called the Counter Reformation) later took place within the Roman Catholic Church, which rectified many of the malpractices that had developed. But the disagreement had shattered the illusion of the religious unity of Europe. Christendom was divided between a Protestant north and a Roman Catholic south, and it was also potentially divided between those who professed religious beliefs and those who denied them—the secularists. Even more significantly, the Reformation provided an example of defiance of long-established authority, a precedent for later revolutions.

Cities, the Bourgeoisie and the Proletariat

Most of the key features of the modern world—mass production under a factory system; capitalist investment; status based on wealth rather than birth; a literate population; the involvement of the people in the political process—have developed in cities. In the Middle Ages the majority of towns were small, existing only to serve adjacent rural districts. It was the growth of cities, largely as a result of the trading activities generated by the new contacts with the East opened up by the Crusades, that made possible the emergence of most of the features of society that we now associate with the modern world—mass production under a factory system, capitalist investment, distinctive class roles, and expanded educational opportunities.

As the need for day-to-day protection from robber bands diminished, towns spread outside the protective walls of the feudal community. The increased trade with other cities and other cultures resulted in the emergence of a new class, the 'middle men', who did not manufacture a product, but dealt in the sale and purchase of goods. They were merchants rather than craftsmen, men of the towns, or *bourgeoisie* as the French named them, and as a new class they represented a growing force for change in the way society was organised. As their wealth increased and they became economically powerful, they naturally wanted a say in how society was organised and regulated. Under the feudal system the bourgeoisie had no role and no status.

Expanded trading also encouraged an increase in cash dealings rather than the barter system. This created greater buying power, and allowed large sums of capital to be invested in schemes for large-scale production. Mass production of goods often drove individual craftsmen out of business and into wage-earning jobs, in which they lost much of their dignity as individuals. A basic division developed in the cities between investors (the bourgeoisie) and the wage-earners (the proletariat)—a class rivalry that was to become bitter animosity in later years, when the effects of the Industrial Revolution accentuated their differences.

The Age of Reason

The changed conditions of society brought new attitudes of mind. For centuries European men and women had been fettered by custom and tradition. They accepted practices and beliefs without question. Their capacity to think creatively had been largely negated by the authority of the Church, which claimed the right to interpret the teachings of God. But this monopoly on opinion and interpretation was broken during the Reformation.

People in modern European society, building on the liberation of thought brought about by the Renaissance and Reformation, believe that human beings are endowed with the gift of reason. They should therefore be able to control their own destiny, rather than be told by another authority what to believe and what to do.

From the fourth century to the seventeenth century, educational activity in Europe was mainly based on two pillars of conformity: the classical tradition and the fixed teachings of the Church. By contrast, the **secular** strand of learning that had been growing among the bourgeoisie flowered in the eighteenth century

in a great age of intellectual discovery called the *Enlightenment*, or the *Age of Reason*. The leaders of this new movement emphasised seeking reasons, criticising existing practices, analysing problems and finding solutions. Through constant questioning and enquiry, they believed, human beings could seek the truth, and the individual could be freed from the bondage of tradition and superstition based on ignorance. All established practices and malpractices—economic, social and political—were regarded as being open to improvement or reform through the application of rational investigation.

The Age of Reason produced within European societies influential **anti-clerical** and anti-aristocratic groups dedicated to change. They wanted the individual to be free from the restraints on thought, religion and commercial enterprise imposed by the Church and the monarchy. They wanted a new society based on rational principles rather than tradition.

The Rights of the Individual

In the critical atmosphere generated by the Enlightenment, it was inevitable that if God could be questioned, so could the divine right of monarchs. The bourgeoisie were dissatisfied with the financial authority of the monarchy and resented the established systems of privilege through which administrative positions were dominated by members of the **aristocracy**. They demanded a share in the functions of government.

This raised the question of the rights of the individual. For centuries both rulers and their subjects had believed that within a society a person was born to a particular 'station' in life, and that it was the duty of the individual to accept the obligations associated with that station. The feudal system had institutionalised and perpetuated this belief. A person served the wider community and obeyed 'superiors'—the feudal lord and the priest.

Among the enterprising bourgeoisie of France and England, however, were free-thinking intellectuals who claimed that individuals should enjoy freedom, and that governments should exist to provide that freedom. The best-known statement of this argument was presented in John Locke's *Two Treatises of Government* (1690), in which it was claimed that people were endowed with reason and with natural rights, and that the true function of government was not to impose laws upon the people but to discover what the laws of nature were and to protect and preserve the natural rights of the people.

Although the bourgeoisie were not seeking to establish **democracy** as we know it (they did not think it appropriate to entrust the **franchise** to the uneducated masses), they were seeking to release the individual from many long-established restrictions. They claimed that people should be liberated from the ignorance forced upon them by strict adherence to the rules of the feudal system; from the bondage of superstition and fear imposed by the Church; from the injustice of classifying persons into classes of privilege through the accident of birth; and from the restrictions imposed on private enterprise by inefficient local and monarchical authorities.

The Nature of Modern Society

Largely as a result of the Agrarian and Industrial revolutions, the modern world is strikingly urban in nature. Hundreds of millions of its peoples live in cities of over 50 000 inhabitants. The world carries a population far greater than ever before, and a large proportion of these peoples live in cities of staggering immensity.

In the eighteenth century European society was predominantly rural; 90 to 97 per cent of the population lived in a country environment. Even in England, where industrial development and the growth of cities occurred earlier than in most of the other nations of Europe, the percentage of the population in cities exceeded the rural population only after 1851. In 1789 no city in Europe was as large as Sydney or Melbourne today. London, with 1 000 000 people, was smaller than present-day Melbourne, while Paris, with 500 000—the agent of change in the Western world—was smaller than present-day Brisbane.

The establishment of factories in which mass-production techniques could be applied meant that workers had to be located nearby. This resulted in the building of large suburbs. In the decades before government regulations ensured minimum standards of space allocation and health facilities, these suburbs usually offered very poor accommodation, earning the derogatory title of 'slums'.

The crowding of the proletariat into the slum areas generated many social problems. As educational opportunities for the children of the poor were at first minimal, most people were locked into low-earning occupations, with many families barely surviving above what we now call the poverty line. Disease and malnutrition were rife. The workers were generally grossly exploited under a system in which they worked long hours for low pay.

Once the proletariat were concentrated into suburbs, however, they were open to political indoctrination. Seeking a fairer distribution of wealth, and an improvement in social services, once armed with the vote they became in turn likely advocates of **socialism** and supporters of proposed remedies for the inequalities in society.

The city was also the wealth and power-base for the middle class, who claimed the political power previously exercised for centuries by the landed aristocracy. Thus, in the newly industrialised cities the newly emergent classes of the proletariat and the bourgeoisie faced each other in rivalry.

The medieval world was one in which only a tiny minority of people engaged in the luxury of travel. Most villages, with their surrounding agricultural land, were almost self-sufficient. The majority of people never travelled beyond the confines of their local district; they were born, lived and died within sight of their parish church. The modern world is one in which communication facilities have increased beyond the wildest dreams of the people of the eighteenth century. Trade has taken men and women to the farthest corners of the globe, and travel, from city to city as well as between

An artist's impression of life in a nineteenth-century British slum. While some children roll on a rubbish heap, others nearby play with a dead rat. An old lady looks through the same heap of rubbish for food, which she puts in her apron. A baby lies on the filthy ground to the right. This sketch was subtitled: 'A Court for King Cholera' (a disease). What message was the artist attempting to give?

nations, has become part of the modern way of life. The world, in the sense of time taken for travel, is 'getting smaller'.

Living standards have also improved. While it must be clearly remembered that even today millions of Asians and Africans are struggling merely to exist, many a middle-class family of the twentieth century enjoys a standard of living that would have been beyond the dreams of avarice entertained by a nobleman of the Middle Ages. Perhaps of all the features that differentiate this age from the preceding centuries, the Industrial Revolution is the most significant. In the brief span of the last two centuries humankind has achieved, and is continuing to achieve, technological advances of immeasurably vaster significance than their predecessors accomplished in the twelve thousand years

since societies emerged in a Neolithic culture.

With town or city life as the major social environment, with higher living standards and accelerated technological progress, it is natural that greatly increased education opportunities have also developed in the modern age. It may well be that future historians will call our age the Age of Literacy—the period of human historical development in which, for the first time, a significant percentage of the world's population attained the ability to read and write.

This new level of literacy, however, has meant that the general populace can be more readily persuaded to accept new views on the nature of society and the purpose of government. A working class gathered into cities is more easily indoctrinated and more readily organised for group action than a scattered peasant class. The French and Russian revolutions, for example, were both launched by activist groups based in cities in which conditions were ripe for change. Indeed, the city, as a centre for debate on the desirability and need for change, has been a major component in many of the revolutions of the modern world.

Class distinctions generated by the inequalities of wealth resulting from the capitalist system have generated heated debate on the merits and defects of capitalism and proposals that capitalism should be displaced by a better way of organising society and distributing wealth—that is, socialism or communism. The modern world has been, and no doubt will continue to be, an age of debate and disagreement, crisis and conflict.

Differing Concepts of the Nation

Another source of conflict in modern society has been the contest between opposing views on the nature of society and the place of the individual within it. The American Declaration of Independence claimed that governments are 'instituted among men' to ensure the 'Life, Liberty and . . . Happiness' of individuals. If a government fails to ensure the liberty of individuals, the Americans claimed that 'the people' had a right to 'alter or abolish' it. In this line of thought, governments exist to serve individuals. Nations founded on such a principle are called 'liberal democratic' in character.

A contrasting opinion on the nature of the relationship between the individual and the nation is that the individual should subordinate his or her interests to the needs of a larger cause. This theory was partly derived from the teachings of Jean-Jacques Rousseau (1712–78), who argued that governments should reflect the 'general will' of the people. It was reinforced by the teachings of philosophers such as the German professor Heinrich von Treitschke (1834–96), who preached that 'the individual must realise the unimportance of his own life compared with the common weal'.

From this concept of the responsibilities of the individual there arose the totalitarian view of society which attained its political manifestation in one-party regimes. Communist one-party states demanded that the 'freedom of the individual' should be curtailed in the interests of class loyalty—the cause of the proletariat. At the other end of the political spectrum, in extreme capitalist (right-wing) one-party dictatorships, such as those of Fascist Italy and Nazi Germany in the 1930s, similarly totalitarian regimes stressed that the individual was to find his or her true destiny in subordinating their own interests to those of the State.

Most of the major political revolutions of the modern world have been mounted as a means of advancing one or the other of these major causes—either the liberal (and later the democratic) cause or, on the other hand, the interests of a 'unified group'. Two major types of the latter can be identified: the aggressive nationalists, such as the Fascists of Italy or the Nazis of Germany, and the determined proletarians, such as the communist parties of the USSR and the People's Republic of China.

Large-scale conflict among these three main groups can be seen as a major feature of the modern world—conflict between the Western liberal tradition and the nationalist totalitarian loyalty; conflict between the nationalist **fascist** ideology and communist totalitarianism; conflict, in turn, between Western liberal societies and communist regimes.

chapter two

The Nature of Modern Social and Political Revolutions

Revolutions are usually preceded by periods of high intellectual achievement and travail, of critical analysis and doubt, of unrest among the educated classes, and of guilt consciousness in the rulers: so it was in France in 1789, in Europe in 1848, and in Russia in 1917.

L. Namier, *Vanished Supremacies*, Penguin, Harmondsworth, 1962, p. 35

In current everyday speech we frequently come across the use of the word 'revolution'. We hear of 'revolutions' in such areas as transport, communications, marketing, fashion and even sports administration and the associated television rights. In the study of History however, we need to define the term more carefully. Indeed, for historians **revolution** has a specialist meaning. It is applied to extreme changes in society, that is, in the ways a particular society organises its economic and political activities, distributes its wealth, and makes decisions that affect the way of life of the people.

Students of History can thus distinguish between social revolutions and political revolutions. A social revolution can occur without there necessarily being a major change in the way the society is governed. A political revolution, however, implies the overthrow of a particular form of government and its replacement by another form of government which is radically different. Such a change can occur without physical violence and bloodshed. In many instances, however, political revolution has involved the use of violence. What is common to both forms of political revolution is the emergence of a newly dominant set of beliefs, upon which the new government bases its claim to authority. A successful political revolution, therefore, is likely to be the catalyst for a social revolution.

To continue our study of modern revolutions, we need to concentrate on several key questions:

Theme Questions

➤ Are there features or developments which can be identified as 'necessary conditions' for the onset of a revolution?

➤ In the event selected for special study, what influences can be seen to have weakened established economic and political practices to the extent that a revolution became possible?

➤ Are there identifiable common features in the causes and consequences of several of the major revolutions of modern times?

I THE ECONOMIC REVOLUTION

Politics (the activity of government) is derived from the Greek word *polis* (the city). All politics involve the control of finances, because all community facilities, particularly the means of defending the city or nation, require the collection and disbursement of funds. The management of finances is in turn related to methods of production and to the distribution of goods and services. Production is influenced by who owns the **factors of production** (land, labour and capital). Government policies can change the nature of this ownership. Similarly, wealth can be very unevenly distributed between the privileged and the poor. Government action can alter the character of this distribution. Thus, economic and social objectives can be discerned in all modern political revolutions.

THE AGRARIAN AND INDUSTRIAL REVOLUTIONS (LATE 18th TO MID 19th CENTURY)

Agrarian Revolution	Industrial Revolution
Greater profits from raising animals for WOOL and MEAT than from crop-growing	Riches from trade with colonial possessions and other nations provided CAPITAL for investment
Enclosure of land previously used in strips for crop-growing by peasants	Success of the COTTON industry (cheap labour in both growth and manufacturing and large markets)
Specialist animal breeding and rotation of crops to provide winter fodder for animals	INVESTMENT in other industries (iron, steel, railways, shipbuilding, manufactured goods); aided by • canals, railways for transport • steam power for traction and factories
Less demand for labour in rural areas—fewer positions for younger people	Growth of FACTORIES for large-scale production
To cities in search of employment	Heavy urban concentrations of labourers seeking wages from factory work. Slums built close to factories. Growth of large CITIES and ports
CLASSES	CLASSES
ARISTOCRACY Still wealthy because of land ownership	BOURGEOISIE (middle class) Wealthy from investments in commerce and industry
PEASANTS Still poor, diminishing in numbers	PROLETARIAT Poor, crowded into slums. Nothing to sell but their labour. Earning low wages because not yet protected by awards and trade unions.

DIAGRAM 2.1 The Agrarian and Industrial revolutions

The changes in the use of the land and of productive resources resulted in changes in the class structure.

The Agrarian and Industrial Revolutions

For over one thousand years (from *circa* AD 450 to the fifteenth to eighteenth centuries), European society functioned practically unchanged under the feudal system. Land was owned by the monarch or his most powerful secular or ecclesiastical office-bearers (barons and bishops respectively). The right to use the land was allocated to others in return for service or payments. The teachings of the Church cemented the concept of the divine right of kings, and so for centuries virtually no influences for change were operative. The emergence of a new trading and investing class—the middle class—and the seventeenth-century defiance of the Church's authority in the movement known as the Reformation introduced two factors that eventually facilitated extreme change.

Beginning in western Europe *circa* 1760, a rural (agrarian) revolution, characterised by significantly improved methods of growing crops and breeding livestock, and an industrial revolution, featuring vastly expanded factory production of manufactured goods, together initiated great changes in social organisation which eventually affected the whole world.

Owners of capital, seeking expanded profits, invested their wealth in new ventures. In so doing, they displayed enterprise. A French term, *entrepreneurs*, which means 'enterprisers', was used to describe the members of this capitalist class. Because most of these investors were city-dwelling businessmen instead of rural-based, landowning aristocrats, they were additionally known by another French term, the *bourgeoisie*, or 'men of the cities'.

The combined effects of the ensuing industrial, economic and technological changes constitute the most rapid transformation of working and living conditions in the history of humanity. Because these changes were so rapid and so profound, the term 'revolution' has been applied, no doubt to indicate the parallel between these great economic and social changes and the political changes initiated by the French Revolution of 1789.

Several decades of rapid economic and social changes occurred before commentators began using the term 'revolution' to describe their effects. It is generally agreed that this description was not used until the 1820s. But if by 'revolution' we mean a sudden change in accepted practices, a deep upheaval with staggering consequences, an overthrow of established methods, then this was the greatest revolution of them all. It affected all aspects of human society—politics, art, culture, economics, religion, education, standards of living and methods of warfare.

Almost every major development in modern world history has grown out of the Industrial Revolution: the conflicting philosophies of free enterprise and socialism; the promotion of nationalism through improved communications and education; the altered social structure and the problems associated with it; the changes in government resulting from extended political responsibility; the vast cities and the amazing communication networks of the twentieth century. From the affluence it created, the conquering bourgeoisie has risen to dominance, but similarly the industrial **proletariat** (the wage-earners) has grown to challenge that dominance.

The industrial changes can be described as a revolution because they were not simply adaptations of or improvements upon existing techniques of production. All manufacturing enterprises had hitherto been dependent on muscle power (human or animal) or the harnessed forces of wind or running water. Through the inventions of steam power, electricity and the internal combustion engine, people broke age-old limitations on their productive capacity. Whereas under the domestic system individual workers had produced marketable products by hand within their own homes, the combined effects of new inventions and the aggregation of capital for investment made possible the erection of factories.

Under the factory system new sources of power could drive machinery, allowing the utilisation of techniques of mass production. New methods of business administration and marketing also emerged.

The newly developed techniques of mass production characteristic of the Industrial Revolution necessitated the design and construction of large buildings called 'factories'. This caused a decline in the rate of use of the 'domestic system', under which small-scale production, usually of textiles, had been achieved in cottages. In the factories large numbers of workers could be held under supervision for long periods each day. In most cases they were severely overworked and underpaid.

Political repercussions followed. The investing classes wanted governments to encourage business activity by cancelling tariff barriers and customs regulations to facilitate freedom of enterprise and the operation of the 'laws' of supply and demand. This attitude to the role of government came to be known by another French term—*laissez-faire*—meaning 'let things be', or allow commercial activity to function with a minimum of restrictions. In the absence of regulations, however, the wage-earners were vulnerable to exploitation. This principle is still an issue today, with some businesses asking governments to allow deregulation so that employers can negotiate working conditions directly with employees.

The Economic Revolution can be defined as the process by which, through the application of large-scale private investment, the adoption of the factory system of production and the employment of new techniques and inventions, the productive capacity of a nation or nations was rapidly increased beyond previously accepted limitations. The term 'Economic Revolution' is perhaps preferable to the more usual 'Industrial Revolution' as it suggests that the change was not only in techniques of industrial production, but in investment and commerce as well.

It is probably most useful to regard the Economic Revolution as encompassing:
- a revolution in methods of manufacturing—the Industrial Revolution;
- a revolution in commercial and marketing methods—the Business Revolution; and
- a revolution in food production—the Agrarian Revolution.

This great economic revolution fostered a political revolution. The bourgeois class, the

The significance of great inventions to the emergence of the 'factory system', 1914

HISTORICAL CONTEXT: By 1914 British historians were in a position to review and evaluate the key features of the great changes that had made Britain the strongest industrial power in the world.

This historian analyses the key part played by important inventions and, in effect, states the well-known principle: 'necessity is the mother of invention'.

Source: **W. Ashley, *The Economic Organisation of England; an Outline History*, Longman Green, London, 1914, pp. 154–5**

The cotton 'factory' was so much the most striking example of the new conditions, that 'factory system' is on the whole the most expressive term to describe the new organisation. But of course the essential feature of the phenomenon is the aggregation of a body of workpeople in one workplace, drawn together by the necessity of attendance upon power machinery, and directed by capitalist employers. This was to be seen in the coalmine and in iron or engineering works just as much as in the textile factory.

Undoubtedly it was the necessary outcome of the great mechanical inventions. Of these there may be distinguished two parallel series—one in the textile sphere and one in the allied spheres of coal, iron, and steel.

It is well to bear in mind in studying them . . . the three conditions of invention. There must be, first, the discovery of a new principle for the accomplishment of some mechanical task. That principle may be discerned centuries before the idea is actually realised, because the other two conditions are absent. Secondly, a method of construction must

be invented by which the principle can be carried out. And thirdly, a strong practical purpose must present itself, for which the new mechanism is urgently needed. Thus in the history of the steam engine, the business motive was furnished by the desire to get rid of the water which began to trouble coal miners as shafts became deeper; and in the textile series, the business motives were, first, the desire to get abundant cotton yarn in order to supply the recently improved handlooms, and then the desire to improve the loom still further in order to make rapid use of the now cheapened and abundant yarn.

Throughout, the growth of population, and the improvement of transportation (by turnpike roads, canals and later by railways), accompanied the progress of manufactures. It is impossible to say that either was simply the cause or the effect of the others. All three stimulated and promoted one another.

QUESTIONS

1 Which two conditions made necessary the 'aggregation of a body of workpeople in one workplace'?

2 What was the significance of the direction by 'capitalist employers' in the development of the factory system?

3 The author cites three conditions which must operate conjointly if a great invention is to have widespread application. What are they?

4 Which three developments characteristic of the Industrial Revolution are claimed to have 'stimulated and promoted one another'?

originators and the products of the Economic Revolution, reached for political power as a means of consolidating and expanding their economic power. In England they gained political power gradually, without violent upheaval, but in France the change was sudden and involved bloodshed and war. This is the

event usually referred to as the French Revolution of 1789–1815.

A political revolution of French origin and an economic revolution of English origin together initiated an overall transformation of society that ultimately engulfed the world, changing the relative composition of rural and urban sectors of each population, and ultimately producing an urbanised world.

II THE POLITICAL REVOLUTIONS

Although it can be convincingly argued that the Economic Revolution has been the most influential occurrence in modern history, many historians would claim that the major political revolutions—particularly the French Revolution of 1789–1815 and the Russian Revolution of 1917—are of greater significance.

The political revolutions are more tangible evidence of a society breaking down, and can generally be more readily assessed as revolutions than can economic changes extending over many decades. Before we study examples of major political revolutions of the modern era, it will be valuable to identify the key features of what we mean by the term 'revolution' in the political sense.

The term 'revolution' connotes a concept of 'revolving' or turning around. To use an analogy from geometry, it is perhaps most fruitful to imagine a turn of 180°, so that a completely opposite position has been attained. Observers would claim that some revolutions eventually involve a 360° turn, in which conditions eventually return to the status quo.

A political revolution can be defined as a sudden (sometimes violent) overthrow of a government and its replacement by another government of drastically different form, character and policy. Key features of modern political revolutions include many of the following characteristics:

- the existing form of government (often called the *ancien régime* or 'old order' after the example of France in the 1780s) has lost effective control of the nation, generating a 'guilt consciousness in the rulers';

p. 11

- significant groups within society are no longer willing to tolerate the existing conditions and are prepared to take drastic action because of an extreme deterioration in their basic living conditions;

- a campaign for drastic change in society has been waged by an influential thinking group—an intelligentsia—creating 'high intellectual achievement and travail' . . . 'critical analysis and doubt' . . . and 'unrest among the educated classes';

p.

- these agents for change have exerted a great deal of effort in arousing the populace through propaganda, and this backing (popular support) provides the weight of influence for the overthrow of the established order;

- a group of activists is determined to force the issue and take action in defiance of the government;

- after the *ancien régime* is overthrown, a permanent change is made in constitutional and political practices, that is, the methods by which the nation is governed;

- a 'new order' is promised for the future, and the people are asked to make sacrifices in order to ensure its attainment;

- a major alteration is effected in the relationships within society between classes and groups. A previously dominant class is usually supplanted by a new group seeking dominance for itself. This process is often described as a redefinition of the ruling elite;

- the reconstruction of society is itself sometimes referred to as 'the revolution', and its permanence is assured through the statement of a new ideology—a set of beliefs that were the justification for the act of seizing power and which now become the official creed. Loyalty to this new creed is expected and demanded, and a new political language is developed to express and explain it;

- the new ideology is then realised, or implemented, in new institutions and practices, and constant reference is made to the leaders of the revolution, dead or alive, as the true interpreters of this ideology.

It is often argued that revolutions became both possible and probable in the modern era because the medieval concept of absolute monarchy ordained by God was destroyed by the secularisation of the concept of authority.

Before secularisation took hold, a revolt against monarchical authority was not only extremely difficult to inspire or organise, but was also an act of sacrilege. The Reformation was the movement which made possible a challenge to the previously dominant power of the Roman Catholic Church. Secular rulers now governed their principalities without Church sponsorship. Instead, they sponsored the Reformed Church (or Protestantism) within their own territories. In the long term this secularisation process made challenges to authority more attainable.

Further, once dissent emerged as a possibility, and the printing press facilitated (from *circa* AD 1460) the dissemination of opinions among an educated portion of the populace, the possibility of action against an existing government was more likely than in the days when the combination of superstition, ignorance and illiteracy held the mass of the people in thrall.

In some instances (as in the Tienanmen Square protest in Beijing in 1989) a rebellion may occur as an act of defiance against a government. The terms 'insurrections' and 'uprisings' are also used to describe such events. If such an act of defiance does not succeed in overthrowing or displacing the government, it does not usually acquire the label of a revolution. Some rebellions, of course, result in the overthrow of a government and thus attain the description of a revolution. What distinguishes a revolution from a rebellion is the *extent* of the change brought about. In a revolution there is a fundamental alteration in the nature and the purpose of the exercise of political power, and this inevitably brings social and economic changes as well.

In our study of the causes and consequences of revolutions, we should ponder the reasons why it becomes possible for the unarmed and helpless populace of an authoritarian society to overthrow a monarch or governing group which has command of the army and police. By the use of terror and repression, such a government would seem to be able to hold the

The term 'modern revolutions' evokes images of violence on the streets, and the camera has made possible the recording of many memorable scenes. This photograph, usually alleged to be a portrayal of street action in St Petersburg in 1917, is one of the best known. It captures the essential truth that in most revolutions the masses of the people are involved in acts of violence, and this ensures a high level of danger to their lives.

The Nature of Modern Social and Political Revolutions

people in subjugation indefinitely. Revolution therefore becomes possible when, after a government has failed to satisfy the needs and wants of the population, it also loses some of its ability to suppress them. This may be because sections of the armed forces have been won over to a new ideology and are prepared to switch allegiance, or because an external power intervenes.

Revolutions frequently result in a 360° rather than a 180° turn. The overthrow of one set of oppressive masters can lead to the emergence of another. After World War II, most of the people in the central and eastern European nations were eager to support the establishment of socialist governments. They wanted liberation from imperial and capitalist control. But the revolutions produced one-party governments in which a new ruling élite—the Communist Party hierarchy—was just as oppressive as the former imperial capitalist class.

The Irish poet W.B. Yeats cynically described this process:

The Great Day

Hurrah for revolution and more cannon shot!
A beggar upon horseback lashes a beggar on foot.
Hurrah for revolution and cannon come again!
The beggars have changed places, but the lash goes on.

Jeffares, A.N. (ed.), *W.B. Yeats: Selected Poetry*, Macmillan, London, 1962, p. 190

chapter three

The Revolution in the American Colonies

Oh! thus be it ever, when freemen shall stand
Between their loved homes and the war's desola-
tion!
Blest with victory and peace, may the heaven res-
cued land
Praise the Power that hath made and preserved
us a nation,
Then conquer we must, for our cause it is just,
And this be our motto: 'In God is our trust'.
And the star-spangled banner in triumph shall
wave,
O'er the land of the free and the home of the
brave.

An extract from the National Anthem of the United
States of America, written by Francis Scott Key,
1814

A rebellion began in 1775 against both the British monarchy and rule by an unrepresentative and remote parliament. The location of this insurrection was a group of colonies that had been established by British settlers on the Atlantic coast of the North American continent over the period from 1607 to 1733.

Simmering discontent against the regulations imposed by the British government resulted in some of the colonists taking up arms and forming semi-official military groups known as militia. Mostly farmers and town tradesmen, the members of the militia were alternatively called 'minutemen' (because of their readiness to fight at a minute's notice).

On 19 April 1775 British troops advancing to confiscate a stockpile of arms were confronted by colonial minutemen at Lexington, Massachusetts. Suddenly a shot rang out; followed by a large-scale exchange of gunfire. The colonists, British subjects, had taken up arms against the soldiers of King George III. The American author Ralph Waldo Emerson later described this first shot as 'a shot heard around the world'.

The actions of the minutemen had launched a revolution; the first of a series of revolutions of the modern era. The 'shot' was to be heard again in Paris in 1789, in numerous European cities in 1848, in St Petersburg in 1917, and in Moscow in 1991.

Theme Questions

➤ What were the main sources of grievance irritating the British settlers in the American colonies?
➤ Why did the level of discontent rise to the point where the settlers took up arms against British rule?
➤ What was the significance of the victory of the rebels?

➤ To what extent can the range of changes instituted be legitimately termed a revolution?

I THE PRE-REVOLUTIONARY ORDER

Most of the British subjects who had crossed the Atlantic to settle on the North American continent over the period 1607–1775 were people of independent attitudes. They had left Britain to begin a new life in a 'new' continent. In many instances the major motivation behind their emigration was a desire for religious freedom. In Britain the Church of England was the established Church—virtually a branch of the government—and many dissenters (non-Anglicans) wanted to live in a different sort of society.

Other motivations also operated. Some settlers sought a less rigid society, with fewer class distinctions. Others were enterprising adventurers who hoped to prosper in the new colonies. After the colonies had been established the British government sent convicts across the Atlantic to serve terms of imprisonment before being released. All these trends contributed to the growth of societies that were inclined to defy directions from the mother country.

By 1750 there were thirteen British colonies on the North American continent, with a population of over 2.5 million, of whom half a million were either black slaves imported from Africa or their descendants. Each of the colonies had a form of local government but the overriding laws and regulations were established and enforced by the parliament of Great Britain, which met in Westminster, London.

Up till the 1750s Britain had had to contend with a major European rival in North America—France. The French had established colonies in what today is called Canada, and by pushing up the St Lawrence River had established a series of inland outposts behind the northernmost British colonies. Rivalry between the French and the British—with each

nation scheming to get help from Indian tribes—generated many skirmishes and conflicts in the frontier zones adjoining the colonies.

The Seven Years' War 1756–63

During the 1750s a complicated war in Europe between a Franco–Austrian alliance and Prussia spread to the overseas colonies. Over a seven-year period Britain, allied to Prussia, fought against the French in both India and Canada. The results were disastrous for France. A decisive British victory at Plassey in India (1757) marked the beginning of a century of British dominance on that sub-continent. In Canada the British achieved an equally emphatic military victory over French forces at Quebec. By the 1763 Treaty of Paris, King Louis XV of France ceded 'New France' (the French-claimed territories in North America) to Britain.

The British colonists in North America had profited considerably from the Seven Years' War with France. Gone were the French forts which had held up progress into the Mississippi Valley region; gone too were the French agents who had incited Indian tribes to resist English settlers. The colonies enjoyed the protection of the English navy and Britain was a guaranteed market for American goods. Yet, within twenty years the colonies fought for and won their independence from British government. How did this situation come about?

The Existing System and the Challenge to Authority

The British victory over France in the Seven Years' War had been attained at great cost to the nation and to its taxpayers. The large British navy was costly to maintain, and thousands of troops had been equipped, transported, and sustained.

The British parliament naturally expected the British subjects in North America to bear some of this cost. A system already existed for this to be effectively achieved. It was known as the mercantilist policy. Under this policy,

Map 3.1

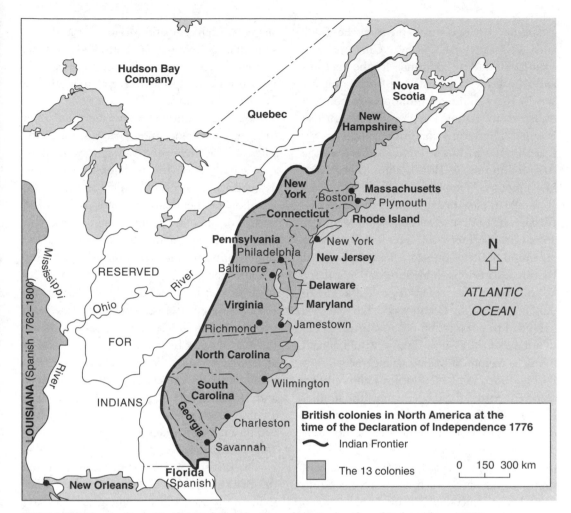

MAP 3.1 British colonies in North America at the time of the Declaration of Independence 1776

Representatives of thirteen of the British colonies on the Atlantic coast of North America were the signatories of the 1776 Declaration of Independence. The British colonists in Canada did not participate in this action. The original British settlement had been at Jamestown, Virginia, in 1607. The French and Dutch also moved into North America—the French at Quebec and the St Lawrence River Valley, and the Dutch at New Amsterdam (now New York). In 1620 the 'Pilgrim Fathers', a group of Puritan Christians, arrived from Europe in the *Mayflower*, and settled in Plymouth, in what became the State of Massachusetts. This was the first British settlement on the northern Atlantic coast, later call New England.

The new nation proclaimed by the Declaration was restricted in the west by French settlements and the Indian Frontier, beyond which the British army had declined to offer protection. The Spanish still possessed Florida in the south. There was little evidence at the time that these thirteen small colonies would grow to become a great power.

established by legislation known as the Trade and Navigation Acts, Royal Charters were awarded to trading companies for the transport and sale of merchandise. Each such company was in effect granted a monopoly to conduct trade in an assigned region of the British Empire. The return condition, however, was that all trade had to be conducted within the British Empire, in British ships. The Royal Navy provided the necessary protection.

In effect, as with any other 'ism', **mercantilism** was both a set of beliefs (an ideology) and a series of practices. The beliefs were an extension of the unquestioned assumption that British institutions were superior to others. Within what was sometimes called a 'closed empire' system, the British way of life was to be extended to colonies on other continents. All members of the British Empire would benefit from the reciprocal trading arrangements.

The practice of mercantilism ensured that colonies existed for the benefit of the mother country. Ideally they were meant to supply raw materials the mother country could not produce itself. For this reason the British government favoured tropical colonies capable of supplying products such as tobacco, cotton, sugar, tea and spices, which could not be grown in a temperate climate like that of Britain. In a reciprocal arrangement, the colonies provided a market for British manufactured goods.

At each stage of exchange the government could levy taxes on the produce, this being, at the time, the major means by which governments raised revenue. Income tax was yet to be introduced. Goods from the colonies were landed in Britain, so that all trade could be monitored and taxes levied, and only then were the goods re-exported to other colonies or, if a surplus emerged, to other European nations. A rigid system of embargoes locked foreign nations out of this trading process.

The mercantilist system also encompassed strict regulations concerning the use of shipping within the trade of the British Empire. Not only did ships have to be British-owned, but the majority of crew members had to be British subjects. Such regulations boosted the British shipbuilding industry and ensured that the nation always had at call a large reserve of trained seamen capable of serving in the Royal Navy in times of war.

In a direct contrast to the later theories of 'free' or open trade among nations, the advocates of the mercantilist system wanted to reduce trading activities with foreign nations to as small a scale as possible. This intention was based on a belief that the wealth of the world was fixed, and that Britain would best assure its own wealth by denying to other nations the opportunity to increase their share in the world's trade.

British leaders were convinced that British colonists were very fortunate to be participants in the mercantilist system. Instead of being threatened week by week by the likelihood of attacks by foreign powers, the colonists prospered under the protection of the Royal Navy and British soldiers. Instead of unrelenting anxiety about the sale of their produce, they had guaranteed markets in the mother country and other British colonies.

The British government therefore expected the British colonists in America to bear a fair share of the costs of maintaining the navy and the soldiers necessary for the security and protection of the settlements. During the Seven Years' War (which the colonists called the 'French and Indian War'), the colonists had been extremely alarmed by the threat to their territories posed by the Indian tribes recruited as allies by the French, and indeed by the French themselves. Without the help supplied by the British navy and army, the colonists could have been killed, injured and dispossessed. Yet, when the war was over the colonists reverted to their earlier practice of evading taxation by systematically subverting the British trading regulations. Smuggling was a common practice, even among prominent citizens. To counter this subversion, the British government resolved to tighten up the procedures for extracting taxation payments from the colonists.

In each of the colonies the citizens were

represented in locally elected assemblies. Both voters and candidates for election had to fulfil property qualifications—that is, they were required to own or rent property of a specified value. Although not 'democratic' in the modern sense, these assemblies nevertheless expressed local public opinion.

Real power, however, lay with the British crown and the British parliament, thousands of kilometres away on the other side of the Atlantic. Communication between the colonies and London was extremely slow. A delay of six months between a despatch and the receipt of a reply was the norm. Yet it was the British parliament that passed the major legislation affecting the colonists—the trade and navigation laws, and the taxation laws. In the colonies a British governor and British admiralty courts enforced these regulations.

To the parliamentarians in London, all this seemed eminently reasonable: after all, were the colonists not all British subjects? And did they not all participate in the benefits of the mercantilist system? The British ruling classes were incapable of regarding the distant colonists as equals. It was expected that the colonists would simply accept their 'fortunate' status and obey the laws set by the British parliament.

By the late 1760s the colonists were reaching a point of frustration with this arrangement. To them, the local assemblies were the real source of authority for government. They wanted these assemblies to exercise control over more than local affairs, and were ready to challenge the authority of the British parliament.

II REVOLUTIONARY IDEAS AND LEADERS

By the 1770s some of the British colonies in America had been established for more than 150 years. In this time a form of society had evolved that was very different from that of the mother country. In England life seemed stable, fixed and unchanging. Each social group knew its place, the Church was strong, government was by the chosen few, and the majority did not question the authority of the privileged governing class.

In America, however, most people lived within a stone's throw of the forest. True, there were rich and poor in America—powerful men who lived like noble Englishmen and poor servants, slaves and workers. But the great, unsettled frontier always beckoned. In England most poor people only dreamed of owning land; in the American colonies there was always cheap land to be had, and, as a result, a more open, independent society developed. It was not a particularly rich society, and life on the frontier was not easy, but America had been settled by people willing to suffer rough conditions in exchange for a society more free and more tolerant than England could offer. They also were more ready to envisage and actively seek changes in society than those who had remained at home.

Another factor generating discontent was related to the particular form of economy that had developed in the Americas. The major productive efforts were directed to goods for export—cotton, tobacco, forest products, furs and sugar—and these activities produced an energetic populace who were prepared to challenge existing practices. Rather than seeing themselves as beneficiaries of the mercantilist system, as the British would have them believe, they resented the restrictions it imposed. They particularly wanted to be able to trade with the French, the Dutch and other nations, and were angry that the British regulations prevented them from doing so. The answer as they saw it was to break away from British control. In this attitude lay the seeds of revolutionary action.

Implicit in all the claims made by the American colonists was an assertion that they were entitled to the same rights and privileges as English citizens. If Englishmen could only be taxed by a legislature of their own elected representatives, such should also be the case for citizens in English colonies. Ironically, the taxation policies of the British parliament forced the colonists to seek these rights through secession from the British Empire.

As is the case with most revolutionary movements, the influence of a vocal minority was significant in the American independence movement. Strongly motivated individuals in turn are usually instrumental in forming committees or organisations to promote the cause in which they are most concerned. Several pro-revolutionary groups, with names such as the Sons of Liberty and the Committees of Correspondence emerged in the American colonies. Equally effective as a means of challenging British authority were the smuggling organisations which encouraged evasions of the customs duties.

From these activities there emerged key individuals who spoke, wrote and campaigned for independence from Britain. Samuel Adams (1722–1803) was a driving force behind the Sons of Liberty organisation, headed the protest against the 'Boston Massacre' in 1770, and Sect. III organised the 'Boston Tea Party' in 1773. Paul Revere (1735–1818) stimulated a spirit of protest through the propaganda effect of his cartoons and engravings. In the early 1770s journalists in the colonies frequently published articles proclaiming the need to break away from British control. Three other leaders of the independence movement—George Washington, John Adams and Thomas Jefferson—became the first three presidents of the new nation, the United States of America.

The spirit and style of the protesting individuals reflected the claims for individual liberties being made in European society in the Chapter 1 Sect. II same period. It was perhaps significant that it was a pamphlet published by a visiting Englishman that was the most persuasive influence on the American revolutionary attitude of mind. Thomas Paine (1739–1809) did not arrive in the American colonies until 1774. In 1776 he published a pamphlet, *Common Sense*, which argued for full independence.

Paine stated a case for the independence of the colonies in plain, forthright language that could be understood and applauded by all independent-minded colonists. His pamphlet presented in popular form the philosophy of

natural rights that was later embodied in the Declaration of Independence.

Paine's exposition appealed to colonists fed up with the burden of complex regulations. He called for a minimum level of government interference in human activities, describing government 'in its best state . . . but a necessary evil; in its worst state, an intolerable one'. He attacked monarchy as an absurd form of government and portrayed it as a form of tyranny. Separation from Britain, claimed Paine, would avoid the likelihood of the colonists becoming embroiled in wars between European powers, and would make possible the opening up of world markets to American trade. This argument stressed the apparent disadvantages of being involved in the mercantilist system, whilst neglecting to point up the advantages.

Common Sense painted a rosy picture of a self-sufficient, independent republic that could assure the prosperity and liberty of its citizens. So receptive were the colonists to Paine's line of reasoning that the pamphlet sold 100 000 copies within three months, and close to 400 000 copies in all. It was one of the most influential publications of the century, and is credited with providing the final impetus towards the declaration of independence by the American colonists six months after its publication. Its enormous popularity was a manifestation of the depth of the conviction among rank-and-file colonists that their liberties could best be secured in a republic, in which a democratically elected president, rather than an **hereditary monarch**, would be the source of governing authority. In the democratic society they yearned for, true egalitarianism could only be achieved by the removal of royal authority. Paine stressed that the word 'republic' implied the public interest, or 'the good of the whole'.

Another important influence upon the public opinion in the colonies was the deeply religious outlook of the majority of the colonists. Many of their forebears had come to the colonies to seek freedom of worship. They belonged to Christian denominations which rejected ecclesiastical hierarchies and formal and ritualised religious practices. The monarch of England, as head of the Church of England, an institution in which archbishops and bishops negated egalitarian principles, symbolised the very religious standards many colonists held in suspicion. These sentiments bolstered the assertions that a republic could better ensure their liberation from the 'old order'.

III THE CRISES LEADING TO REVOLUTION

From their dissatisfaction with the regulations imposed upon them by the British parliament, the American colonists moved at first to a state of rebellion, and then to a revolution which established a radically different form of society. It should also be noted that many thousands of colonists did not support the revolution, choosing to remain loyal to the British crown and parliament.

Key Events Provoking a Spirit of Rebellion

After the Treaty of Paris (1763) which ended the Seven Years' War, the British government passed the Proclamation Act of the same year. This drew a line on the map—often referred to as the Indian Frontier, along the crest of the Appalachian Mountains. Concerned that they could be faced with administrative responsibilities too vast to handle, the British decreed that colonial settlement should not proceed west of this line. The colonists were angered by this event, regarding it as a restriction on their opportunities.

Applying the policy that the colonists should share in the costs of paying for the war debts and for the ongoing expenses involved in defending and administering the Empire, the British government imposed several taxes. The major taxes were customs duties on imported goods and a 'Quartering' tax, which required the colonies to contribute to the cost of 'quartering' (accommodating) British soldiers.

Many of these taxes were evaded. Large-scale smuggling for example, was in many instances condoned by prominent citizens. Seeking a tax that could not be easily evaded, the British government introduced (in 1765) a Stamp Act, which called for the payment of a stamp duty on all paper products, legal documents, contracts and newspapers. Such an act had been operative in Britain itself for over seventy years, and the measure did not seem unreasonable to the parliamentarians in London.

The Stamp Act outraged the colonists, rich and poor alike, and proved to be the affront which united them in defiance of the British government. The Virginia Assembly proposed that the colonists should pay no taxes except those approved by their own assembly, and called for a rejection of the British tax, justifying their position with the slogan 'No taxation without representation'.

Such was the level of anger that the individual colonies agreed to meet in a Stamp Act Congress (October 1765) in order to plan common action. Nine of the thirteen colonies sent representatives, and these colonies jointly declared that 'no taxes ever have been, or can be constitutionally imposed on them, except by their respective legislatures'. They further declared that the Stamp Act had 'a manifest tendency to subvert the rights and liberties of the colonists'. The Stamp Act Congress was significant in that it was the first inter-colonial meeting summoned by colonial initiative, and as such marked a major step towards common action from the colonists as 'Americans' (as proposed by one of the delegates) rather than as representatives of the individual colonies. It may be regarded as the opening move in the steps towards revolution.

In response to the vociferous colonial opposition to the Stamp Act, the British parliament repealed it in 1766, but immediately reasserted its claim to be able to impose taxes upon the colonists by passing a Declaratory Act defining its right to make laws for the colonies 'in all cases whatsoever'. The British parliament had rescinded a law it could not enforce, but was not surrendering the constitutional principle of the sovereignty of parliament.

From the British point of view, the actions of the parliament were eminently reasonable. Concessions were being made to the colonists, in a spirit of extreme generosity. There was no doubt in the minds of the parliamentarians that the colonists should bear their share of the costs of defence, having benefited significantly from the defeat of the French and the removal of the threat of French conquest. Yet the parliament was accepting a rate of taxation for the colonists much lighter than that borne by British citizens. It was claimed in one government estimate that the average American colonist's tax burden was only sixpence a year, while the average annual tax burden on the British taxpayer was 25 shillings—fifty times higher. Moreover, these taxes were not being imposed by a tyrannical monarch, as had been the case in the reign of Charles I in the seventeenth century, but by a duly constituted sovereign parliament.

The parliament therefore renewed its efforts to collect taxes by imposing import duties on goods that were needed in the American colonies, such as lead, glass, paper, paint and tea. These duties, together with the apparent military supervision imposed by the conspicuous presence of British soldiers ('redcoats'), continued to inflame colonial sentiment.

The colonists' reaction was the adoption of a 'non-importation' policy—an unofficial but effective practice of refusing to buy British goods. This protest was enormously effective. In the year 1768–69, the value of purchases of British goods in the American colonies fell by 33 per cent. In some colonies the protest was even more effective. By 1769 the colonists of New York had cut their imports to only 14 per cent of what they had been in 1764. The British attempt to coerce the colonists had proved to be counter-productive, with massive losses of revenue the result.

Instead of recognising the folly of its policies, the British parliament stepped up its attempts at coercion. It further outraged the colonists by threatening to close down their local elected assemblies unless they accepted and endorsed British taxation policies, and additionally declared that offenders who resisted the policies would be taken across the Atlantic to London for trial. All this led to the expansion of cries of 'resist tyranny' from the colonists.

In March 1770, in the city of Boston, tensions escalated into violence. Different versions of the incident emerged, but it seems that a lone British sentry outside the Customs House was taunted by a group of colonists. Other soldiers came to his aid, a scuffle developed, shots were fired, and five Bostonians were killed.

Expanding this unfortunate incident into a focal point of crisis, the Sons of Liberty organisation labelled it the 'Boston Massacre'. Paul Revere, an engraver, published a representation of the incident portraying British troops as firing upon helpless citizens. Such a portrayal served to inflame the general public.

In a mixed response of concession and perseverance, the British parliament repealed all the customs duties except one, retaining that on tea 'as a mark of the supremacy of parliament'. Again the British parliamentarians displayed an inability to understand the major sources of the colonists' grievances. This so-called 'concession' generated more tension and defiance.

In 1773 the British government granted the British East India Company the right to sell taxed tea directly to the American colonists. This would have made tea cheaper than previously, but it threatened the lucrative trade in smuggled tea. The pro-independence groups in the colonies urged a boycott of the tea, saying that the new British rules were yet another example of tyrannical regulations imposed by a distant parliament, and an indication that the British intended to introduce trading monopolies to favour their big commercial companies. In December 1773 a group of colonists, disguised as Indians, boarded an East India Company ship in Boston Harbour and dumped large quantities of tea into the harbour. This action was applauded by the opponents of the British regulations, and widely acclaimed as the 'Boston Tea Party'.

The 'Boston Massacre' of 1770: an engraving published in a Boston journal by Paul Revere, a leading opponent of British rule. This artist's version of the event serves to highlight the problematical nature of pictorial evidence. The engraving shows a well-disciplined platoon of British troops callously firing into a group of respectable citizens, at short range and in broad daylight. The British authorities, however, claimed that the shots were fired at night, after a small group of British soldiers were taunted, abused, and pelted with missiles by a large, drunken and disorderly mob. The published version was, naturally, very effective as propaganda against the British administration.

From the British viewpoint, the colonists had engaged in outrageous acts of defiance against reasonable expectations that they should bear some of the costs of their own defence and administration. After having backed down and offered concessions on many previous occasions, the British now decided that they had to insist on conformity. In 1774 the British parliament introduced the Coercive Acts. Boston Harbour was to be closed until the destruction of the tea was paid for, and more troops were sent to the colonies to enforce obedience to the regulations.

These acts (labelled the 'Intolerable Acts' by the colonists) escalated the tensions and virtually ensured a rebellion. Many of the colonists declared that they had been subjected to military rule. Such an opinion was reinforced even in individual households by the British governors' insistence that soldiers would be billeted in people's homes where necessary.

The assemblies of Virginia and Massachusetts declared that the Coercive Acts were an assault on the liberties of all colonists. A congress of all the colonies was called for, and met in September 1774, with twelve of the thirteen colonies represented. British intransigence had now generated another phenomenon—a willingness among the hitherto relatively uncooperative colonies to work together. It was a necessary step towards the concept of a separate nation.

Collectively, the colonies next proclaimed a boycott on all trade with Britain—a total denial of the mercantilist system—and declared that only their own assemblies could levy taxation. They also proclaimed that all of the British parliament's acts since 1763 had violated the rights of 'Americans' (a significant distinction), and further claimed the right to form and arm militia forces. At this stage they did not deny the authority of the monarch and actually petitioned King George III to respond to their grievances.

The British government, declining to yield on the principle of the supremacy of the Westminster parliament, chose the colony of Massachusetts as a test case, and in February 1775 declared it to be in a state of rebellion. The British had now embarked on the impossible project of attempting to subjugate 2.5 million people in a distant continent. They were yet to learn that they could attempt to exert authority but that it was impossible to govern an unwilling community of this size.

High levels of emotion and numerous calls for 'liberty from tyranny' now prevailed in the colonies. In early 1775 news reached the British commander-in-chief, General Thomas Gage, that colonists in Concord, Massachusetts, were stockpiling gunpowder and military stores. The farmers and townsfolk of that region had trained themselves into a militia of 'minutemen'. Gage despatched troops to confiscate this cache of arms. Paul Revere, a passionate advocate of independence, rode his horse through the night to warn the colonists of the approaching troops (a deed later immortalised in a poem by Longfellow).

At a town called Lexington, on 19 April 1775, the British soldiers and the minutemen exchanged shots. Who fired first, American or British, remains unresolved, but eight colonists were killed, and the patriots were able to depict the incident as a brutal attack upon civilians. Additional skirmishes ensued at Concord, and in the next few days 247 British soldiers were killed. The first blood of the American War of Independence had been shed. This was the 'shot heard around the world'.

While all the colonies were abuzz with the sensational events at Lexington and Concord,

---

SOURCE 3.1
Patrick Henry claims 'We must fight' and cries 'give me liberty or give me death!', March 1775

HISTORICAL CONTEXT: Patrick Henry (1736–99) was a lawyer and politician in the colony of Virginia. In some of his court cases in the 1760s, in defence of colonists who had defied British regulations, he had gained fame from his eloquent pleas for natural rights. His most famous speech, which inspired many colonists to take up arms against British rule, was delivered to delegates to a Virginian convention in March 1775. It concluded with the stirring call: 'give me liberty or give me

death!' Several versions of the speech were subsequently published, with no guarantees of their total accuracy.

Source: The Virginia Gazette, 18 March 1775, reprinted in M.C. Tyler, Patrick Henry, American Statesman, Boston, 1887, pp. 140–43

This is no time for ceremony. The question before the House is one of awful moment to this country. For my own part I consider it as nothing less than a question of freedom or slavery.

. . . I have but one lamp by which my feet are guided; and that is the lamp of experience. I know of no way of judging of the future but by the past. And judging by the past, I wish to know what there has been in the conduct of the British ministry for the last ten years to justify those hopes with which gentlemen have been pleased to solace themselves and the House? Is it that insidious smile with which our petition has been lately received?

. . . Ask yourselves how this gracious reception of our petition comports with these warlike preparations which cover our waters and darken our land. Are fleets and armies necessary to a work of love and reconciliation?

. . . These are the implements of war and subjugation; the last arguments to which kings resort. I ask gentlemen, sir, what means this martial array, if its purpose be not to force us to submission? Can gentlemen assign any other possible motives for it? Has Great Britain any enemy, in this quarter of the world, to call for all this accumulation of navies and armies? No, sir, she has none. They are meant for us: they can be meant for no other. They are sent over to bind and rivet upon us those chains which the British ministry have been so long forging.

. . . Let us not, I beseech you, sir, deceive ourselves longer. Sir, we have done everything that could be done to avert the storm which is now coming on. We have petitioned; we have remonstrated; we have supplicated; we have prostrated ourselves before the tyrannical hands of the ministry and parliament.

. . . If we wish to be free—if we mean to preserve inviolate those inestimable privileges for which we have been so long contending—if we mean not basely to abandon the noble struggle in which we have been so long engaged, and which we have pledged ourselves never to abandon until the glorious object of our contest shall be obtained, we must fight! I repeat it, sir, we must fight! An appeal to arms and to the God of Hosts is all that is left us!

They tell us, sir, that we are weak; unable to cope with so formidable an adversary. But when shall we be stronger? Will it be the next week, or the next year? Will it be when we are totally disarmed, and when a British guard shall be stationed in every house?

. . . Sir, we are not weak, if we make a proper use of the means which the God of nature hath placed in our power. Three millions of people, armed in the holy cause of liberty, and in such a country as that which we possess, are invincible by any force which our enemy can send against us. Besides, sir, we shall not fight our battles alone. There is a just God who presides over the destinies of nations; and who will raise friends to fight our battles for us. The battle, sir, is not to the strong alone; it is to the vigilant, the active, the brave. Besides, sir, we have no election. If we were base enough to desire it, it is now too late to retire from the contest. There is no retreat but in submission and slavery! Our chains are forged! Their clanking may be heard on the plains of Boston! The war is inevitable and let it come! I repeat it, sir, let it come!

It is in vain sir, to extenuate the matter. Gentlemen may cry peace, peace—but there is no peace. The war is actually begun! The next gale that sweeps from the North will bring to our ears the clash of resounding arms! Our brethren are already in the field! Why stand we here to idle! What is it that gentlemen wish? What would they have? Is life so dear, or peace so sweet, as to be purchased at the price of chains and slavery? Forbid it, Almighty God! I know not what course others may take; but as for me, give me liberty, or give me death!

QUESTION

Many of the statements in Henry's speech are indications of the motivations for the actions by the American colonists in seeking independence.

Study each of the extracts below in the column under the left-hand heading. In the column under the right-hand heading, write your response.

Assertions or aspersions made by Patrick Henry	The grievance or suspicion, held by the colonists, of which this is evidence
1 . . . it is nothing less than a question of freedom or slavery	Britain intends to hold the colonists in a condition of servitude
2 I wish to know what there has been in the conduct of the British ministry in the last ten years to justify . . . hopes	
3 Are fleets and armies necessary to a work of . . . reconciliation?	
4 . . . these are implements of war . . . the last arguments to which kings resort	
5 . . . to bind and rivet on us those chains which the British ministry have been so long forging	
6 . . . an appeal to arms and to the God of Hosts is all that is left to us	
7 . . . when a British guard shall be stationed in every house?	
8 . . . we have no election. If we were base enough to desire it, it is now too late to retire from the contest. Our chains are forged!	
9 Is life so dear, or peace so sweet, as to be purchased at the price of chains and slavery?	

Source 3.1

the Second Continental Congress assembled in Philadelphia (10 May 1775). The delegates had been inspired to a spirit of defiance by a widely reported speech by a Virginian lawyer, Patrick Henry, in which he had proclaimed: 'the war is inevitable and let it come! . . . Is life so dear, or peace so sweet, as to be purchased at the price of chains and slavery? . . . I know not what course others may take; but as for me, give me liberty, or give me death!'

Even with the acts of rebellion and the accompanying deaths, a declaration of independence was not necessarily inevitable. The congress declared they were loyal subjects of the king and sent George III what was called an 'olive branch' petition. But the king refused to receive such a petition from a group of colonies which he declared to be in a state of rebellion.

In January 1776 Thomas Paine's pamphlet *Common Sense* was published, and so captured the mood of the colonists that it was read by or to almost every adult in the colonies. Paine's pamphlet not only hardened the colonists' determination to proclaim independence, but poured scorn on the principles of monarchy, divine right and hereditary succession of authority. Such was its effect that it ensured not only a declaration of independence but the proclamation of a republic.

In June 1776 the Continental Congress proclaimed that the colonies 'are, and of right

Sect

SOURCE 3.2
Thomas Paine writes to encourage the claims by the American colonists for independence, 1776

HISTORICAL CONTEXT: Thomas Paine (1739–1809) arrived in the American colonies from England in 1774. In January 1776 he published a pamphlet, *Common Sense*, which argued the case for independence from Britain and for the republican form of government. The pamphlet attracted a huge readership, and was influential in generating a widespread emotional and intellectual commitment to the independence movement. Five months after its publication, the colonists issued the Declaration of Independence.

Source: **T. Paine, *Common Sense: Addressed to the inhabitants of America*, Philadelphia, 1776, pp. 10, 18, 19, 20, 22–3, 28–9 passim**

Mankind being originally equals in the order of creation, the equality could only be destroyed by some subsequent circumstance; the distinctions of rich and poor may in a great measure be accounted for. . . . but there is another and greater distinction for which no truly natural or religious reason can be assigned, and that is the distinction of men into kings and subjects. Male and female are the distinctions of nature, good and bad the distinctions of heaven; but how a race of men came into the world so exalted above the rest, and distinguished like some new species, is worth inquiring into, and whether they are the means of happiness or of misery to mankind.

In the early ages of the world, according to the scripture chronology, there were no kings, the consequence of which was there were no wars; it is the pride of kings which throws mankind into confusion. . . . The nearer any government approaches to a republic, the less business there is for a king . . . Of more worth is one honest man to society, and in the sight of God, than all the crowned ruffians that ever lived.

As much has been said of the advantages of reconciliation, which, like an agreeable dream, has passed away and left us as we were, it is but right that we should examine the contrary side of the argument and inquire into some of the many material injuries which these colonies sustain, and always will sustain, by being connected with and dependent on Great Britain.

. . . I have heard it asserted by some that, as America has flourished under her former connection with Great Britain, the same connection is necessary toward her future happiness and will always have the same effect. Nothing can be more fallacious than this kind of argument. We may as well assert that because a child has thrived upon milk that it is never to have meat, or that the first twenty years of our lives is to become a precedent for the next twenty. But even this is admitting more than is true; for I answer roundly that America would have flourished as much, and probably much more, had no European power had anything to do with her. The commerce by which she has enriched herself are the necessaries of life and will always have a market while eating is the custom of Europe.

. . . I challenge the warmest advocate for reconciliation to show a single advantage that this continent can reap by being connected with Great Britain. I repeat the challenge; not a single advantage is derived. Our corn will fetch its price in any market in Europe, and our imported goods must be paid for, buy them where we will.

But the injuries and disadvantages we sustain by that connection are without number, and our duty to mankind at large, as well as to ourselves, instruct us to renounce the alliance; because any submission to or dependence on Great Britain tends directly to involve this continent in European wars and quarrels and sets us at variance with nations who would otherwise seek our friendship and against whom we have neither anger nor complaint. As Europe is our market for trade, we ought to form no partial connection with any part of it. . . .

Europe is too thickly planted with kingdoms to be long at peace; and whenever a war breaks out between England and any foreign power, the trade of America goes to ruin because of her connection with Britain. *The next war may not turn out like the last; and should it not, the advocates for reconciliation now will be wishing for separation then, because neutrality in that case would be a safer convoy than a man-of-war. Everything that is right or natural pleads for separation. The blood of the slain, the weeping voice of nature cries, "'Tis time to part."*

. . . America is only a secondary object in the system of British politics. England consults the good of this country no farther than it answers her own purpose. Wherefore her own interest leads her to suppress the growth of ours in every case which does not promote her advantage or in the least interferes with it.

QUESTIONS

1 Although Paine suggests that distinctions between rich and poor can be 'accounted for', he asserts that there is another distinction that is not natural. What is this distinction?

2 What linkage does Paine identify between kings and wars?

3 How does Paine counter the claim that the prosperity of the American colonies is dependent on maintaining the connection with Britain?

4 According to Paine, a continued connection with Britain means disadvantages to the Americans. What are they?

5 Why might Paine have used the expression 'the weeping voice of nature' to bolster his claim that it was 'time to part'?

ought to be, independent states'. Finally, on 4 July 1776, the official Declaration of Independence, written by Thomas Jefferson and amended by others, was published. The congress opened all American ports to foreign trade and began negotiations with France for military assistance. The rebellion had escalated into a revolution.

An artist's impression of the occasion of the signing of the American Declaration of Independence, on 4 July 1776. It stated that 'all men are created equal, that they are endowed . . . with certain inalienable Rights [and that] . . . Governments derive their just powers from the consent of the governed'. What effect has the artist striven to achieve, and how effective has he been?

SOURCE 3.3
The British colonists in North America make the Declaration of Independence, July 1776

HISTORICAL CONTEXT: Fighting had broken out between British soldiers and rebellious colonists in the American colonies in April 1775. The Continental Congress, an assembly of delegates from the thirteen colonies, appointed Colonel George Washington as commander-in-chief of American forces in June 1775. This was the act of an independent nation, but twelve months passed before a declaration of independence was issued, partly because some of the colonies' delegates continued to argue in favour of reconciliation.

The Declaration was issued on 4 July 1776. This date is still celebrated as the national day of the United States of America. Thomas Jefferson, the principal author (and later the third president of the USA), stressed the principles of 'natural rights' in the compilation of the statement.

The Declaration proclaimed to the world that all persons have rights of which they cannot be deprived, and that governments should work to protect those rights. The only justifiable source of a government's power was 'the consent of the governed'. A validation for revolution was also stated, in that it was declared that if any government failed in this responsibility, the people were entitled to 'alter or abolish it'.

Source: Revised Statutes of the United States, Congress of the USA, Washington, 1878

When in the Course of human events, it becomes necessary for one people to dissolve the political bands which have connected them with another, and to assume among the Powers of the earth, the separate and equal station to which the Laws of Nature and of Nature's God entitle them, a decent respect to the opinions of mankind requires that they should declare the causes which impel them to the separation.

We hold these truths to be self-evident, that all men are created equal, that they are endowed by their Creator with certain unalienable Rights, that among these are Life, Liberty and the Pursuit of Happiness. That to secure these rights, Governments are instituted among men, deriving their just powers from the consent of the governed, That whenever any Form of Government becomes destructive of these ends, it is the Right of the People to alter or to abolish it, and to institute new Government, laying its foundation on such principles and organising its powers in such form, as to them shall seem most likely to effect their Safety and Happiness.

. . . when a long train of abuses and usurpations, pursuing invariably the same Object evinces a design to reduce them under absolute Despotism, it is their right, it is their duty, to throw off such Government, and to provide new Guards for their future security.

We, therefore, the Representatives of the United States of America, in General Congress, Assembled, . . . do solemnly publish and declare, that these United Colonies are, and of Right ought to be Free and Independent States; that they are Absolved from all Allegiance to the British Crown, and that all political connection between them and the State of Great Britain, is and ought to be totally dissolved; and that as Free and Independent States, they have full Power to levy War, conclude Peace, contract Alliances, establish Commerce, and to do all other Acts and Things which Independent States may of right do.

QUESTIONS

1 What motive might have led to the composition of the first paragraph?

2 What is the meaning of the term 'unalienable rights'?

3 According to the Declaration, what is the function of a government?

4 According to the Declaration, governments do not derive their powers from God, but from 'the consent of the governed'. What does this mean?

War and International Recognition

The War of Independence raged for five more years. Many of the colonists did not support the rebellion. At least 30 per cent of the population proclaimed their continuing loyalty to the British crown. Of this group, about 100 000, proclaiming themselves 'United Empire Loyalists', opted to emigrate from the new nation. Approximately 37 000 of them went into Canada, while the remainder journeyed to the Bahamas, the West Indies, or back to Britain itself.

There were other obstacles to the success of the Revolution. George Washington, the commander of the colonial militia, experienced great difficulty in keeping his volunteer troops in the field. Many of them regularly left the ranks to go home to their families.

The British also had problems. The redcoats suffered continuous harassment from the civilian population. It was not possible for the British soldiers to know just who their opponents were. The unpopularity of the soldiers was increased by the introduction of Hessian (German) mercenary soldiers, who eventually constituted over 30 per cent of the British army. This added to the American perception that foreign military rule was being imposed.

It was extremely difficult for the British commanders to maintain military operations in such a hostile environment. In 1778 the French monarch afforded recognition to the United States of America as an independent nation, and declared war on Britain. There was a substantial irony in this development, as the French monarchy was far more authoritarian than the **constitutional monarchy** of Britain, and did not in spirit support the principles of democracy espoused in America. The motives of the French were predominantly self-seeking, and more related to taking the opportunity to attack Britain than to condoning revolution. Nevertheless, the recognition of the new nation by the most powerful monarchy in Europe placed its status beyond question or doubt.

When the British finally realised that they had no hope of winning the war, they sought a settlement. This was achieved in the Treaty of Paris in 1783, in which Britain acknowledged the independence of the thirteen American colonies and their status as a nation.

By 1787 another Constitutional Convention had agreed upon a constitution to unite the thirteen former colonies. The resultant innovation became another feature of the American Revolution. The convention established a bicameral (two-house) parliament, or congress, together with a set of 'checks and balances' through which the executive, the legislature and the judiciary could complement and moderate one another to ensure no element in the governing process could dominate another. Finally, in 1789, George Washington was inaugurated as the first president. A fledgling nation—destined to become the world's greatest superpower—had been born.

IV THE SIGNIFICANCE OF THE REVOLUTION

The Declaration of Independence not only announced the birth of a new nation. It also proclaimed a set of principles for the nature of government and the source of a government's

George Washington (1732–99), first president of the independent United States of America. A self-taught soldier who had gained military experience in campaigns against the French and the Indians, he was appointed commander of the armed forces of the new nation in 1775. In matters of strategy he excelled, winning so much respect that when the new constitution took effect in 1789 he was elected as the first president of the new nation. He served two terms (1789–97), and his wise and dignified style of administration was important in validating the American Revolution and establishing the reputation of the new nation.

authority that have been of continuing influence throughout the nineteenth and twentieth centuries. This achievement highlights the fact that a revolution is something greater than a war for independence. Most definitions of revolution stress that it means more than a rebellion; it implies a set of far-reaching changes. Such changes encompass political, constitutional, ideological and social values, together with the associated practices.

The Declaration constituted a major revolution in the history of humankind in that it put forward and established a new claim—that governments exist to ensure and protect the rights of individuals, and that if they fall short in this

attainment, then the people have the right to change the government. The source of the authority of a government was said to be 'the consent of the governed', not an award of authority from God. The American Revolution was the first of the modern revolutions directed against both an hereditary monarch and a traditional regime.

The course of the Revolution demonstrated the far-reaching effects of 'mind set'. The British sense of superiority over the colonists was all-pervading. The British authorities continued to insist on this principle when virtually every attempt to enforce it cost the British nation both revenue and goodwill. Every action was counter-productive to the maintenance of the prosperity and integrity of the British Empire. In over a decade of acrimonious dispute the British government never sent a delegate across the Atlantic to discuss the source of the grievances, or to ascertain what was destroying the relationship between the mother country and the colonists and how it might be saved. Nothing disturbed the assumption that the British possessed the right to demand obedience. And so they lost the American colonies.

This successful revolution was the first practical rejection of the 'old order' in European politics—the breakthrough in the struggle against privilege and traditions. It gave reality to the principles of individual liberty, freedom of speech, freedom of belief and limited government—the idea, as Jefferson put it, that 'that government is best which governs least', making a minimum encroachment upon the rights of the individual in commerce or in society. It raised the hopes of revolutionaries in Europe, sending back into European society men like the French aristocrat the Marquis de Lafayette, who, despite his privileged upbringing, fought for democratic principles during the American Revolution and later played a key role in the 1789 French Revolution.

Another, more cynical and more materialist, explanation of the course of events was that the major motivation driving the American colonists was not the high ideal of liberty but a

Thomas Jefferson (1743–1826), third president of the United States of America. In 1776 he was the principal author of the Declaration of Independence, one of the most influential documents in the history of modern revolutions. It has been quoted by many other revolutionary leaders ranging from Ho Chi Minh of Vietnam to Fidel Castro of Cuba. Jefferson served as president from 1801 to 1809.

desire to escape from the restrictive policies of the mercantilist system. Advocates of this school of thought see economic self-interest as the key to events. The expressions of principles and ideals were, to their minds, mere propaganda. Historians are indeed duty-bound to address alternative explanations, and some truth may reside in this interpretation.

The American Revolution was, significantly, a successful nationalist revolution against the principle of government from a distance. It showed that colonial peoples would almost certainly develop a sense of independence and nationalism based on their sense of attachment to their own environment, even if they had been voluntary emigrants from the mother country in the first place and continued to speak the same language. The success of the Americans gave hope to subject and colonial peoples everywhere, and foreshadowed the emergence of nationalism as one of the great controlling forces of History.

Although the Revolution was a denial of British authority, the spirited actions of the colonists won widespread admiration in the English-speaking world, and later in other societies. Lord Chatham (the former William Pitt, 'first minister' from 1756–61) memorably expressed this sentiment in the British parliament on 20 November 1777 when he declared: 'If I were an American, as I am an Englishman, while a foreign troop was landed in my country, I would never lay down my arms—never, never, never.'

In stating that 'all men are created equal' and that governments derive 'their just powers from the consent of the governed', the Declaration of Independence defined essential democratic principles in universal terms, and thus issued a challenge to all autocrats and despotic governments. The 'Rights of Man' had received practical application.

The independence so proudly proclaimed had, moreover, been won by armed revolution. This, too, was justified in the Declaration of Independence, which asserted that if any government denied the people their just freedoms, they had the right to 'alter or abolish it' and to 'institute new government'. These sentiments introduced an age of revolution, in which many an uprising against rule by a dominant minority was to find justification in the theory thus stated.

Finally, in another challenge to the old regimes of Europe and the wider world, the new nation of the United States of America put aside the custom of a hereditary monarchy and instituted a form of **republican government** under an elected head of state. Such has been the steady expansion of this concept that it seems likely that Australia will eventually join the large number of modern nations that have followed the example of the USA.

The adoption by the USA of the federal form of government—with powers shared between State governments and a central government with limited defined spheres of responsibility—marked another new line of thought in practical politics. This was further proof that the old order could be broken and new methods attempted. This innovation, too, has been adopted in many nations of the world, Australia again included.

Of further international significance was the fact that both the houses of Congress were elected by the people from candidates nominated by the people. The Senate was a States' house, not a house of privilege based on property qualification or any other distinction. Never before had a legislature been created in a large modern nation in which all branches (in this instance, both houses) were composed of elected representatives of the people. Further, the executive authority was vested in a president, elected by an Electoral College which also derived its authority from the people. As the Declaration of Independence had stated, the institutions of government were to derive their just power from 'the consent of the governed'.

The principles established by the American Revolution have had a continuing effect. Even in the USA itself, it became evident in the early nineteenth century that the high ideals expressed in the Declaration of Independence were not being fulfilled in relation to women and to black Americans. In 1848 a national women's convention voted that the Declaration of Independence should have stated that 'all men and women are created equal'. Similarly, the leader of the civil rights movement in the 1960s, Martin Luther King, consistently and regularly quoted from the Declaration to justify his demands for civil liberties and equality in society for black citizens.

A demonstration of the universal applicability of the principles of the American Declaration of Independence was provided when Ho Chi Minh, leader of the Vietnamese independence movement, used the same words on 2 September 1945 to claim separate identity for his nation. In an ironic reversal of roles, the USA later became involved in a protracted war from 1960 to 1975 over the issue of which government was to rule over an independent Vietnam, and tragically found itself supporting a losing cause against what proved to be majority opinion.

MAJOR EVENTS LEADING TO THE FORMULATION OF THE AMERICAN CONSTITUTION

1756–63	The Seven Years' War, in which Britain and Prussia as allies, gained an ascendancy over France and Austria. In North America it was known as the 'French and Indian War'.
1764	The Sugar Act (an attempt to collect taxes from the colonists on imported molasses)
1765	The Stamp Act
1766	Repeal of the Stamp Act
1766	The Declaratory Act (asserting the British parliament's right to legislate for the colonies)
1767	Revenue Act (imposing duties on specified goods)
1770	The 'Boston Massacre'
1773	The 'Boston Tea Party'
1774	The Coercive Acts
1774	The First Continental Congress (twelve of the thirteen colonies represented)
1775	Massachusetts declared, by British parliament, to be 'in rebellion' Battles of Lexington and Concord (first organised armed rebellion) War of Independence began Battle of Bunker Hill
1776	Publication of Thomas Paine's *Common Sense* Declaration of Independence
1778	France entered the war as an ally of the USA
1779	Spain entered the war as an ally of the USA
1781	Last battle (Yorktown) of the War of Independence
1783	Treaty of Paris (in which Britain recognised the independence of the USA)
1789	A new constitution, establishing the federal form of government for the United States of America, was drafted and ratified
1789	George Washington inaugurated as the first president of the USA

chapter four

The Political and Cultural Revolutions in France 1789–1815

Come, children of the fatherland,
The day of glory now is here;
. . . To arms, citizens, form your battalions,
Let us march, Let us march!

. . . What seeks this horde of slaves,
Of traitors and conspiring kings?

. . . What! shall these foreign cohorts
Make the law in our homes?
What! shall these hireling phalanxes
Throw our proud warriors down?

. . . Sacred love of fatherland,
Guide, sustain our brave avengers;
Liberty, dear Liberty,
Fight with thy defenders!
That victory under our flags
Shall hasten to thy noble call . . .

Extract from *Marche des Marseillois* (or *La Marseillaise*)

The date 1789 is still used by many historians as the identifiable starting point of the 'modern world'. This reveals a political rather than a social criterion of judgement. If one examines the effects of the Industrial and Agrarian revolutions, one could argue for a different starting point.

Such a claim about an event in France also reflects a European-centred attitude to 'the world' and to the nature of development and change. Nevertheless, there is no doubt that what is known as the French Revolution was one of the greatest upheavals in modern history, whose effects spread over all Europe and eventually throughout the world. It split opinion in Western society, being regarded as either a disaster or a triumph; people were forced to declare themselves for or against it. Its impact could not be ignored.

Theme Questions

➤ What were the features of the *ancien régime* (old order) in France before the Revolution, and why was it vulnerable to displacement and overthrow?

➤ Why is the French Revolution almost universally regarded by historians as being of great importance?

➤ What were the key ideas, ideals and proposals for change that triggered off the Revolution?

➤ What effects did the Revolution exert upon the political and social organisation of France?

➤ How did the Revolution affect the other nations and other peoples of the world up to and including the present day?

Chapters 1 & 2

I THE *ANCIEN RÉGIME*

It is significant that '*ancien régime*'—the French term for the 'old order'—has become the term used for any pre-revolutionary order. Only fifty years before the Revolution, the *ancien régime* of France had appeared to be so stable and permanent that it could last forever.

Absolute Monarchy

France had been the most powerful and influential monarchy in Europe during the seventeenth and eighteenth centuries. In common with most European monarchs of the time, the kings of France believed that they ruled by divine right (the will of God). Chinese emperors of the same period were convinced that they ruled by the 'mandate of heaven'—a similar concept. As the authority of the monarch was virtually unlimited, this form of government was called absolute monarchy. The loyalty of the people was totally directed towards the monarch rather than the nation. In fact, the concept of 'the nation' did not exist. France was a monarchy, and all administrative agents derived their authority from the monarch.

Absolute monarchy reached its highest peak in France under the flamboyant and extravagant King Louis XIV, who reigned from 1643 to 1715. Louis XIV acted as his own first (prime) minister, assuming effective as well as ceremonial power. The kingdom was ruled virtually as a personal fiefdom, and even though the landowning aristocracy enjoyed extraordinary privileges and wealth, they were denied any effective voice in policy-making.

Louis XIV revelled in his power and prominence. As a means of displaying his grandeur, he built a lavish palace at Versailles (near Paris), the most spectacular in Europe. Many monarchs of Europe later attempted to match or surpass Versailles. Louis XIV became known as *la Roi Soliel* (the Sun King) implying that his benevolent presence cast a blessing upon his subjects. He was the personification of the absolute monarch, constituting a role model for the other monarchs of Europe.

Despite the apparently assured status of King Louis, the feudal principle that kings ruled by divine right had already been challenged in England during the seventeenth century. A monarch, Charles I, had been deposed and executed in 1649, and for eleven years the country was in effect governed as a republic under a 'Lord Protector', Oliver Cromwell. In 1660 the British monarchy was restored under Charles II, but his successor, James II, was deposed by the parliament in what the British called the 'Glorious Revolution' on the grounds that it had been achieved without bloodshed.

To replace James II, a joint monarchy (William III and Mary II) was proclaimed in 1688. These monarchs held office, not by divine right, but by the will of parliament. Their powers were defined and limited in a Bill of Rights. These events in Britain created a prototype of a constitutional (limited-power) monarchy—a precedent that was to be of great significance during the momentous events in France between 1789 and 1792.

The Social Order in France

Within the *ancien régime* in France, society was regarded as having been organised into three 'estates' or class divisions.

The First Estate was made up of the office-bearers of the Roman Catholic Church. Their status was indicative of the indissoluble connection between the monarchy and the Church, which bestowed its blessing upon the concept of divine right. The power of the Church was additionally entrenched by the royal decree that only Roman Catholics held full civil rights.

The Church was immensely wealthy. It has been estimated that it owned 10 per cent of all the land of the kingdom. Enhancing this wealth, the officers of the Church collected a tax (the *tithe*), usually representing one-tenth of the annual income of all the common people. If a peasant was unable to pay the tithe in coinage, he was expected to pay it in 'kind' (that is, produce).

The upper clergy lived lives as luxurious as those of the powerful nobles. The priests of the lower clergy, who did not enjoy the trappings of wealth, were closer in spirit and lifestyle to the common people, and sympathetic to the need for reforms to improve their condition.

The Second Estate was the class of the aristocratic landowning nobility. Although they owned more than 20 per cent of the land of the kingdom, they made up only one per cent of the population. In theory the king delegated much of his authority to the nobles, whose ancestors in earlier times had received their huge estates in return for providing the monarch with armed forces in time of need. In return, the nobles had been exempted from taxation. They were in fact, the major tax-collecting authorities.

In the seventeenth century, during the 'golden age' of French supremacy, Louis XIV had gathered all effective governing power into the hands of the monarchy, leaving the nobility their privileges but little effective power. Thus,

A French cartoon portraying 'the burden of the Third Estate' (the peasantry) under the *Ancien Régime*. The three characters in this illustration represent the three estates. The globe is the kingdom of France. Around the circumference of the cartoon the publisher offers an 'explanation of the allegory', which reads 'The Third Estate bears alone the weight of the Kingdom, under which he sags; a Noble, instead of easing the burden, adds to the weight by leaning on it; the Priest seems to want to help but only uses the tips of his fingers.'

1 What is the significance of the *fleur-de-lis* symbol on the 'burden'?

2 What impression is the artist seeking to create in his portrayal of (a) the noble; (b) the clergyman?

3 What is the message the cartoonist is trying to convey?

although politically France had become a centralised monarchy, socially and economically it was still operating on the feudal 'pyramid' structure. Because the nobles controlled tax collections, insufficient income reached the king. The obvious remedy was for the nobility to surrender some of their revenue to the monarch.

Through the **parlements**, or hereditary law courts, the nobility could block royal decrees and thus exercise some restraint on attempts to alter the status quo, but they lacked the power to initiate policy and were determined not to surrender any of their feudal privileges without receiving a compensating increase in political influence. The aristocrats used their influence, in fact, to prevent even the modest reforms the king and his advisers wished to apply, not because they opposed all of these reforms but because they resisted any means by which the power of the monarch might be further increased.

The Third Estate was, in theory, all the remaining people of the kingdom other than the clergy and nobility. In reality there were four other classes within this category—the bourgeoisie, the peasants, the town artisans and the poverty-stricken unemployed in both urban and rural communities.

The middle class, or bourgeoisie (a French term for 'men of the towns', meaning prosperous city-based salary- or profit-earners), constituted the most potent force for change in French society. Owning 25 per cent of the land and the commercial capital, they were a class growing in social influence every year, particularly in the key cities and ports. These men were the trading and investing class of the towns, together with men of the educated class such as lawyers, doctors and teachers. A further source of bourgeois influence emanated from supporters within the nobility, many of whom were in fact recently ennobled bourgeoisie.

All the ramifications of the feudal system were regarded by the bourgeoisie as intolerable intrusions upon the liberty of the individual. They resented the taxation they paid, the trade barriers that restricted their activities as merchants, and the codes of privilege that denied them entry into the government service. They wanted a new structure of society in which rewards would flow to enterprise and merit, and an economy in which the principles of capitalism could flourish.

However, while the bourgeoisie wanted changes in society, they did not desire a complete political upheaval. In many instances they had lent money to the government, and they wanted to be repaid. Many bourgeois investors desired a constitutional monarchy, with efficient financial and trading systems, as a replacement for the inefficient absolute monarchy of the *ancien régime*.

The category of the Third Estate also included the peasants—the vast bulk (67 per cent) of the population of France. Few peasants owned their own lands. The majority were tenants of the nobility or, in some cases, of bourgeois landowners. The landowners distributed portions of their estates to peasants, who thus had the opportunity to use land which they did not own. On the land they could grow crops and graze livestock, but they had to pay for this concession with services and taxes, either making themselves available as soldiers or unpaid labourers, or surrendering a large percentage of their produce to the overlord. As decades passed, many lords demanded a cash payment instead of, or as well as, the payments in produce. Many peasants were extremely discontented with these enormous taxation and service burdens.

In addition to the heavy feudal dues, payable to the local overlord, the peasant was taxed by the Church through the tithe, and by the monarch through the *taille* (a tax on value of the land and house) and the *gabelle*, a tax on salt. Further unpaid labour on public works (*corvée*) was often demanded of them. Many historians estimate that the peasants paid from 70 to 80 per cent of their income in taxes.

Despite their oppressed condition, the peasants were the source of the wealth of the kingdom. Agricultural produce constituted 75 per cent of the Gross National Product. Much of this, of course, emanated from the manors of the nobility, largely farmed by the peasantry paying their dues in unpaid labour.

Yet another group existed (or barely survived) in France in the 1780s, officially part of the Third Estate, but large enough to constitute a separate class altogether. They were the landless and the unemployed. While many of the peasants may have been wretched and oppressed, at least they had the produce of their soil on which to survive. But in the France of 1786 there were over 4 million individuals whose subsistence was not assured for even one month. Many of these vagrants flocked into towns and cities on a seasonal basis, looking for work. They were a desperate and dangerous pool of discontent.

All these class divisions were regarded by the king, the clergy and the nobility as permanent, but forces of change were brewing up a momentous upheaval.

II REVOLUTIONARY IDEAS AND LEADERS

Despite (or perhaps because of) the condition of absolutism that was established by King Louis XIV and maintained under his successors, Louis XV and Louis XVI, there emerged in France a climate of opinion demanding greater freedoms for the individual. This intellectual emphasis was a component of the movement widely called the Age of Reason or the Enlightenment.

The thinkers whose publications contributed to the Enlightenment based their work on the proposition that humankind's capacity for mental initiative was so great that the people were capable of working out systems of government better than those imposed upon them by tradition. It was claimed that humanity possessed the capacity for self-management and self-government.

In the seventeenth century René Descartes (1596–1650) had promoted the use of reason by his assertion *Cogito ergo sum* ('I think, therefore I am'). To him, people justified their existence by questioning and doubting. Descartes initiated a rational approach to philosophy, one of tracing effects from causes.

The French philosophers (*philosophes*) of the eighteenth century greatly popularised this movement towards intellectual freedom, and so promoted a challenge against tyranny of any kind. There came a great demand for individual freedom in religion, in social standing, and in the conduct of commerce. The writings of the *philosophes*, particularly Voltaire, Montesquieu and Diderot, attracted widespread attention from literate groups. In the years 1751–72 these French leaders of the Enlightenment published the most famous of all their works—the *Encyclopédie* or *Dictionnaire raisonné des Sciences* (The Great Encyclopedia) in which it was proposed to subject all institutions of society to rational explanation.

The Scope of the Challenge

The *philosophes* of late eighteenth-century France were staunch advocates of the principle of government by consent—yet they lived in a nation that was ruled by an absolute hereditary monarch. They advocated freedom of the individual and the promotion of talent—yet France was a society devoted to the privileges of the Church hierarchy and the aristocratic nobility. There was a great demand for a trading system freed from the limitations imposed by **tariffs** and local taxes—yet France, like most of Europe, was still inhibited by parochial (local) restrictions arising out of the feudal system.

The individual mind, the *philosophes* claimed, should be free to think, to criticise, to doubt—yet they faced a Europe enslaved by the ignorant traditionalism of the Middle Ages, and by superstitious fear of 'hellfire and damnation'. And while they claimed that humankind could search, through intellectual enquiry, for a rational order in society, Church teaching stressed that people could only improve themselves through the forgiveness of sin. The *philosophes* therefore regarded the Church as a barrier to intellectual and social progress.

The activities of the *philosophes* created a reforming state of mind in the active, literate

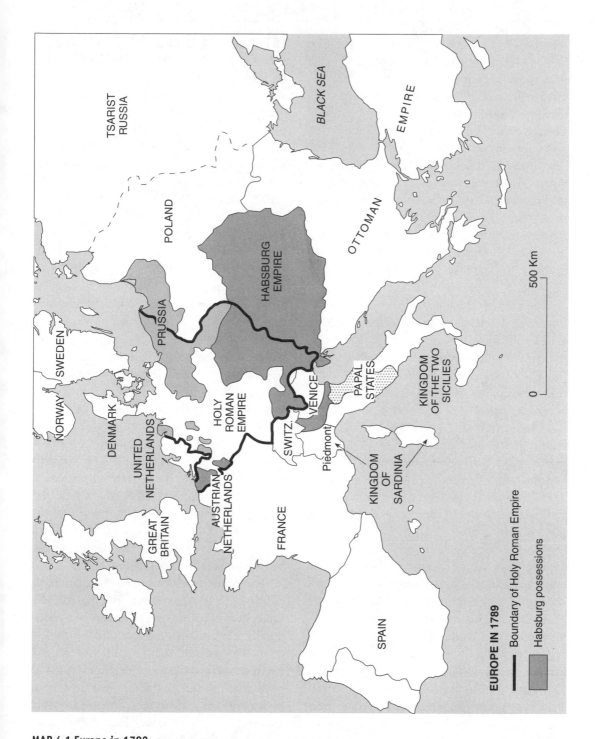

MAP 4.1 Europe in 1789

In 1789, before the French Revolution, Europe was subdivided into numerous principalities, dukedoms and monarchies, almost all of which were governed by absolute monarchs. France was the most prominent and powerful monarchy. Germany did not exist as a nation, but most of the Germanic peoples were loosely associated in the Holy Roman Empire, which contained more than three hundred principalities and kingdoms, together with about fifty cities. The Habsburg Empire, which contained many national groups, dominated central Europe; the Tsarist and Ottoman (Turkish) empires between them dominated all the nationalities of eastern and southern Europe.

members of society. There was a surging demand for the emancipation of the individual from the political tyranny of absolute monarchy, the intellectual dominance of the Church, and the social inhibitions of the feudal system. Voltaire attacked the corruption in Church and government, whilst Montesquieu demanded constitutional limitations to the power of the monarchy. Rousseau rejected the authority of the monarchy altogether and claimed that sovereignty rested in the people. The form of government, he asserted, should reflect the 'general will' of the people and should be the product of a 'social contract' between the people and the government.

The scope and immensity of the new opinions almost certainly ensured that the change in European society, when it came, would be violent and all-encompassing. It was perhaps fortunate for the advocates of the new order that a first challenge to the old principles came from across the Atlantic, in the form of the American Declaration of Independence (1776). This stated that 'all men are created equal', and that governments derive 'their just powers from the consent of the governed'. The principles thus stated were phrased in universal terms, and constituted a challenge to all autocrats and despotic governments. The 'Rights of Man' had received practical application.

The new nation of the United States of America placed aside the custom of a hereditary monarchy and instituted a republican form of government. This was to be a significant example for the 'Old World' (Europe). The American Revolution, moreover, had been achieved by armed rebellion. This too was justified in the Declaration of Independence, which asserted that if any government denied the people their just freedoms, they had the right to 'alter or abolish it' and to 'institute new government'. These sentiments introduced an age of revolution, in which many an uprising against rule by a dominant minority was to find justification in the theories thus promoted.

Source 3.3

III THE CAUSES AND STAGES OF THE FRENCH REVOLUTION

As with all complex events in History, there were many causes of the French Revolution, some long-term, and some 'triggering' factors particular to the year 1789.

One of the most quoted statements on the reasons for the outbreak of the rebellion that escalated into revolution was that of Joseph Weber, a foster brother of the deposed Queen Marie Antoinette. Weber was reported as recognising three primary causes—'the disorder in the finances, the state of mind, and the war in America'. He went on to state that the character of King Louis XVI, and the way he responded to events, must rank as a fourth primary cause.

Weber's reference to the 'disorder in the finances' was an acknowledgment that it was the bankruptcy of the monarchy that opened the door to defiance of the king's authority. Indeed, the greatest single 'trigger' of the revolution was the economic crisis, which forced the monarchy to open up a debate about possible changes. Although the monarchy had been subject to criticism, the established patterns of administration and oppression might well have endured had not the sheer inadequacy of the revenue collection system forced the monarch to consider drastic action. An economic crisis was the prelude to a political revolution.

The 'state of mind' was also critical. Drastic change to centuries-old established practices is unlikely to occur unless the leaders of a rebellion have an alternative system under consideration. This mental condition can only prevail if much debate and discussion has occurred. The *philosophes* of the Enlightenment had contributed significantly to this climate of opinion challenging absolute monarchy.

The 'war in America' to which Weber referred was the American War of Independence, by which the American colonies, with French military aid, had won their independence from the British crown. The French participation was of critical significance to events in France because the enormous associated

Sect

costs precipitated the financial crisis of the monarchy. Additionally, the success of the Americans provided the French people with strikingly significant precedents—an established order had been overthrown by a popular uprising, and the Declaration of Independence had formally stated that governments 'derive their just powers from the consent of the governed'. The prime demand of the American revolutionaries had been 'no taxation without representation'.

The institution of monarchy had been spurned by the American colonists, who adopted the republican form of government. They had stressed that the principle of inherited authority wielded by a privileged family was contrary to the public interest. Their head of state was to be an elected president—a practical application of authority being derived from the 'consent of the governed'. Moreover, through the French monarchy's decision to help the infant United States of America in its war against Britain, many French soldiers and sailors had brought ideas of republicanism, self-government and individual liberties back to French society. The French monarchy had aided the American revolutionaries primarily as a means of embarrassing the traditional opponent of France (Great Britain), but in a supreme irony had dealt itself a 'double whammy'. It had generated both a financial crisis and encouraged a set of revolutionary ideas.

The character of Louis XVI also figured prominently in Weber's list of 'causes'. The character of his queen, Austrian-born Marie Antoinette, was equally significant. Louis XVI was well-meaning but weak-willed and vacillating; Marie Antoinette was strong-willed but impulsive. When the crises came, the king and queen acted with imprudence and poor judgement. Had they possessed a deeper understanding of events, the crisis might have been limited in scope, and perhaps could have resulted in a transition to a constitutional monarchy.

Weber's concise analysis omits another major causative factor: the desperate plight of millions

Sans Culottes du 10 Aoust 1792 de la République Française

A sketch, dating from the French revolutionary period, of a *sans-culotte*. During the French Revolution much of the agitation was said to be a search for reform on behalf of the *sans-culottes* (literally, those without fancy trousers). Their lack of knee breeches, or fancy trousers, was used as a symbol of their poverty. Later the term was used to refer to revolutionaries in general, particularly the extremists. In the period of the Reign of Terror the *sans-culottes* dominated the city of Paris, imposing their will on the members of the National Convention.

of peasants, and the even more critical situation of the landless vagrants and the unemployed masses in the towns. Between 1715 and 1789 the population of France had increased from 18 million to 26 million. Land was a fixed resource. Thousands could not find work in the rural regions. As a result hordes of nomadic malcontents were forced into the towns. In 1788–89 conditions worsened when a severe economic crisis followed poor harvests in 1788. High prices for bread and basic foodstuffs, and widespread unemployment and destitution, accentuated the crisis.

When the monarchy reached total bank-ruptcy in 1789, the numerous causes of dissatis-faction combined to influence events towards revolution. The nation at large was seething with discontent: thousands of creditors to whom the monarchy owed debts were desper-ately worried; the bourgeoisie were angry at the threat that their taxes might be increased without a corresponding decrease in the privi-leges of the nobility; the poor harvests and high prices produced intense bitterness amongst the peasants and town labouring classes; and the nobility, fearful that the monarch might lose control of the situation, were clamouring for some means of exercising power themselves.

The Four Stages of Revolution

The French historian Georges Lefebvre, in *The Coming of the French Revolution* (Vintage Books, New York, 1947), argues that four 'revolutions'

emerged from the upheavals that began in 1789: the aristocratic revolution, the bourgeois revolution, the popular revolution and the peas-ant revolution.

The aristocratic revolution can be regarded as the stage in which the critical series of changes was initiated. King Louis's finance ministers, Calonne and Necker, had attempted to meet the financial crisis by proposing that the nobility should submit to taxation. The aristoc-racy, whilst largely willing (reluctantly) to acknowledge this necessity, were determined to use the crisis as a means of regaining the politi-cal power their forebears had lost under Louis XIV. They therefore persuaded the king to re-convoke the Estates-General, an assembly which had not met since 1614.

By the old formula there were to be three 'houses' or 'estates', of equal voting power. The First Estate was to represent the clergy, the

An artist's impression of the convocation of the Estates-General of France, meeting on 5 May 1789 for the first time in a century and a half. Six weeks later the Third Estate broke away to declare itself the National Assembly, thus defying the authority of the king and launching the French Revolution.

1 Who would have commissioned an artist to draw this picture, and what would be the resultant expectation?

2 Who or what is the focus of all attention?

3 Of which condition is this evidence?

4 What overall effect has the artist achieved?

Second Estate the nobility, and the Third Estate the 'common' people. The nobility and clergy hoped to use their combined voting power to effect an alteration in the political power structure in order to reduce the authority of the monarch. They also hoped to sustain and safeguard their privileged positions in society. This was the attempted 'aristocratic revolution', the main aim of which was to achieve an efficient administration under a monarchy with limited powers.

The bourgeoisie, however, regarded the calling of the Estates-General as an opportunity to exercise their vastly increased social and economic influence. As the educated class, they constituted most of the representation of the Third Estate. On 17 June 1789, after the Estates-General had gathered, the Third Estate, in alliance with some liberal-minded nobility and clergy, broke away from the three-estate assembly and formed what they called the 'National Assembly', a body claiming to represent the whole nation.

Louis XVI attempted to check further developments by closing their assembly hall, but the dissidents defied the order to disband. Meeting in an indoor tennis court, they swore the famous 'Tennis Court Oath' that they would resist dissolution until a constitution had been established. It was significant that the oath

Source 4.1

SOURCE 4.1
The Third Estate of the French Estates-General proclaims itself a National Assembly and refuses to disband, 17 June 1789

HISTORICAL CONTEXT: When King Louis XVI of France called the Estates-General in June 1789, he expected that the combined voting power of the First Estate (the clergy) and the Second Estate (the aristocracy) would function to prevent too radical a change in the political organisation of the monarchy.

On 17 June 1789, however, the representatives of the Third Estate broke away from the Estates-General and, meeting in an indoor tennis court, declared themselves to be a 'National Assembly'. Defying the king's authority, they resolved not to disband until a new constitution had been established. This act of independence really marked the beginning of the French Revolution.

Source: **Declaration of the National Assembly, Versailles, 20 June 1789**
The National Assembly, considering that it has been summoned to establish the constitution of the kingdom, to effect the regeneration of public order, and to maintain the true principles of monarchy; [declares that] nothing can prevent it from continuing its deliberations in whatever place it may be forced to establish itself; and, finally, that wheresoever its members are assembled, there is the National Assembly;

[The Assembly also] decrees that all members of this Assembly shall immediately take a solemn oath not to separate, and to reassemble wherever circumstances require, until the constitution of the kingdom is established and consolidated upon firm foundations; and that, the said oath taken, all members and each one of them individually shall ratify this steadfast resolution by signature.

QUESTIONS
1 What was the significance of the change of name, adopted by the breakaway Third Estate, in calling itself the 'National Assembly'?
2 What expressions within the statement are evidence that the members of the assembly did not at this stage plan to establish a republic?
3 What expressions within this statement provide clues to the type of government the members of the assembly planned to establish?
4 What is implied by the reference to the need to 'effect a regeneration of public order'?

acknowledged a commitment to maintain the 'true principles of monarchy'. To emphasise that they were no longer dependent upon a royal summons, the deputies further declared that wherever they were gathered they constituted the National Assembly. The king's will had been defied—a bourgeois-led political revolution had begun.

A major ingredient in the volatile brew of revolutionary emotions that boiled up in June–July 1789 was the king's own sense of obligation to his subjects. In specifying the process by which each local district was to elect representatives to attend the Estates-General, King Louis XVI authorised the drawing up of *cahiers* (statements of grievances). This elicited 25 000 'wish lists' of reforms, generating a powerful nation-wide expectation that a host of changed conditions could and would be promptly provided as a result of the momentous meeting of the Estates-General.

From this great collection of desired reforms a rallying call for the Revolution now emerged. It was *Liberté, Egalité, Fraternité* (Liberty, Equality, Fraternity). This motto was later to be proclaimed in all corners of Europe and the wider world. Its meaning, however, was not as simple as might first appear, because the motto was of bourgeois origin. The 'liberty' thus advocated was the outgrowth of the demand for the freedom of the individual. It encompassed the desire for freedom in economic endeavour (free enterprise), freedom of expression and freedom from arbitrary authority. The 'equality' envisaged was not at first a claim that all men were equal, but that all men should enjoy equal opportunity in society so that talent may be rewarded and promoted, and that all men should by right enjoy equality before the law. In 'fraternity' we find the proposition that all men are brothers, but this concept was soon modified to brotherhood within the nation, with resultant pride in the title 'citizen' and the acceptance of the view that this sense of brotherhood was to be found in the service to the nation. This interpretation of 'fraternity' was later used to foster aggressive nationalism.

By late June 1789, conditions and emotions were now momentarily suitable for the establishment of a constitutional monarchy similar to the British model, with the king widely expected to surrender some of his powers to a legislative body which would be representative of many classes in society but which would not in any sense be democratic. The reform-minded nobility and the bourgeoisie, with capital invested in trade, commerce, production and government loans, did not desire a comprehensive or far-reaching destruction of existing institutions, but they promoted four key demands:
- equality before the law and equal justice for all classes;
- the opening of careers to talent;
- freedom of speech and freedom of enterprise and internal trade;
- a fair distribution of tax responsibility.

This opportunity to establish a constitutional monarchy based on a limited-franchise parliament was lost because of the entry into the revolutionary process of the mass of the people. This was the 'popular revolution' referred to by Lefebvre—the involvement of the populace. The urban masses of Paris, rendered desperate by the extreme hardships of famine and the exorbitant price of bread, organised themselves into a force of protest, motivated by a determination to achieve reforms in their own interest. To them, the clergy, nobility and bourgeoisie were all self-seeking privileged classes who had to be challenged.

During the latter weeks of June and the early weeks of July 1789, suspicions and rumours swept Paris. Louis XVI was suspected of simply allowing the National Assembly a temporary existence while he organised a mercenary army, including foreign soldiers, to crush the uprising. On 14 July 1789 the working-class people of Paris, who in April 1789 had already staged large-scale riots against employers who had attempted to reduce wages, stormed the Bastille, a medieval fortress in Paris that had been used as a prison. Although the mob liberated only seven prisoners, the act was of greater significance than any event in French history.

The newly self-constituted National Assembly, pictured at the indoor tennis court in which the assembly members took an oath never to disperse until they had given France a constitution. This was the first great revolutionary action of 1789, because it was in defiance of the king's wishes, and it constituted an assembly not summoned or authorised by the monarch.

The Bastille symbolised absolute monarchy—the people captured it, murdered its governor, and literally demolished the building stone by stone. To this day 14 July, Bastille Day, is the French national day.

After centuries of oppression and neglect, the masses had emerged as a potent force in political decision-making. By their decisive intervention they proclaimed that they were no longer anybody's property, and that no lasting political settlement could be achieved without due consideration of their needs and rights. From July 1789 it was not possible for lawyers and constitutional theorists to make decisions about institutions of government without due consideration of the wishes of the populace. Indeed, during the decade 1790–1800 many critical decisions were made while the masses were literally shouting their demands from the very doorsteps of the legislative chamber, intimidating the parliamentarians into taking actions in fear of their lives.

In the rural areas of France (in which the bulk of the kingdom's population resided) the long-oppressed peasants quickly followed the example of their Parisian cousins and stormed what were sometimes called the 'forty thousand bastilles'—the lavish and ornate *châteaux* (mansions) of the nobility. This was what Lefebvre referred to as the 'peasant revolution'. Just as the Bastille had symbolised absolute monarchy in Paris, the châteaux symbolised the gross inequalities of wealth in the rural areas. These monuments to the riches of the nobility also housed the documents detailing the tax commitments of the peasants. Excited by the promise of liberation and opportunities for revenge, the peasants destroyed manorial records and attacked the families of cruel landlords.

There were thus virtually three revolutions in France in 1789: a revolution within the Estates-General; a municipal revolution in the city of Paris and the provincial towns; and a revolution in the countryside. The first was a political revolution concerned with the governance of the nation. The second was a claim by the cities and towns to be able to control their own municipalities, to elect their own office-bearers, and to free themselves from monarchical taxes. The third was a revolution of the peasantry against their aristocratic overlords. These three simultaneous developments collectively destroyed the power of the aristocracy, who, having been the source of the drive to reduce the power of the monarchy, ironically became the first casualties of the Revolution.

A 'New Order' to Replace the *Ancien Régime*

The outbreaks of violence having generated great alarm among the aristocracy and the royal family alike, King Louis XVI reluctantly assumed an air of co-operation with the National Assembly. The mob uprisings were thus useful to the bourgeois leadership of the assembly, as these events served to convince the king that unless reforms were provided, chaos could ensue. At this stage many of the bourgeois leaders still held the belief that if reforms could be effected quickly, order could be restored under a constitutional monarchy.

The National Assembly acted quickly. The burdens of the feudal system, which had

An artist's impression of the storming of the Bastille, Paris, 14 July 1789. The date of this event is France's national day. The fortress, standing in the heart of Paris, housed only a handful of prisoners, but it symbolised the power of absolute monarchy. In the assault soldiers of the royal regiments joined with the protesters—the critical moment in a revolution. The people captured the fortress, murdered its governor, released the prisoners, and literally demolished the building stone by stone. What impression is the artist striving to create?

prevailed for more than one thousand years, were abolished on 4 August 1789. In one stroke this action removed—on paper at least—most of the grievances of the middle and lower classes. The feudal régime was totally abolished, all feudal dues were cancelled 'without indemnification' (compensation) to the former holders, and all 'offices' (positions of authority) were deemed to be available to all citizens without distinction of birth.

On 27 August 1789 the National Assembly then issued the Declaration of the Rights of Man and the Citizen, a statement similar in some ways to the American Declaration of Independence but more significant in that it emanated from the leading nation of Europe. The authors asserted that the major cause of corruption of governments and 'public miseries' was the neglect of, or contempt for, the 'rights of man'. Under the authority of the 'Supreme Being' (the revolutionaries' attempt to humanise God), the assembly declared that all men were born free and equal in rights, and that the function of government was to preserve the natural rights of the citizen (which significantly included the right to own property). All sovereignty was said to be derived from the nation—an application of Rousseau's principle of the 'general will'. The law, in fact, was said to be the expression of the general will, and was deemed to be the 'same for all', whether it protected or punished.

This Declaration of Rights thus constituted a total break from the past. In the *ancien régime* authority had been derived from God and the king, and the common people were basically items of property, charged with the duty of being obedient in the fulfilment of their duties. They had no rights. Now it had been asserted that all people were free and equal, that sovereignty rested in the 'general will' of the people as a nation, and that all persons had rights they could not lose.

Already in England, by the 1689 Bill of Rights, a precedent of restricted or constitutional monarchy had been set, but the French formula for the nature and operation of a soci-

ety prescribed a far greater scope for individual freedom than had the English system. Whereas class distinctions still prevailed in England, they had now officially been abolished in France.

As the year 1789 drew to a close, many citizens of France thought that the revolution had been achieved and that a new and glorious era had dawned. Writing in a publication called *Les Annales Patriotiques* (31 December 1789), an enthusiastic bourgeois journalist proclaimed that 'the glorious year' had witnessed the overthrow of the 'pompous Clergy', the termination of the power of the 'proud Nobility', and the end of a government of 'frightful memory'.

In the next year (1790), the National Assembly moved to make permanent the displacement of the power of the clergy. Anti-clerical feeling was strong amongst the revolutionaries, principally because the upper clergy had been corrupt and excessively wealthy. The assembly confiscated the Church's property and put it to sale by auction, with the land largely passing into the hands of the class that could afford to buy it—the bourgeoisie. The assembly declared that priests were to take an oath of loyalty to the nation, and that bishops and priests were to be elected by the people. This decision offended thousands of parish priests and devout Roman Catholics, who felt their loyalty was to God and the pope.

A 'new order' had been created. The statements of principles issued by the revolutionaries of France constituted a challenge to all the absolute monarchs of Europe and the rest of the world. A new formula for the organisation of society had been established. The world would never be the same again. But the fulfilment of the apparently noble principles of liberty and choice was to involve enormous struggle and suffering both in France itself and all other communities which aspired to the enjoyment of their liberating influence.

The Consolidation of the Revolution

As will be seen in the study of other revolutions, once launched, revolutionary change is

SOURCE 4.2
The National Assembly abolishes feudalism, 4 August 1789

HISTORICAL CONTEXT: Most of the grievances of the lower classes of France in 1789 stemmed from the demands placed upon them by the thousand-year-old feudal system. Under this system each person holding or using land was a vassal of his immediate overlord, having duties but no rights. For the lower classes the burden of paying feudal dues and taxes to both the Church and the monarchy was incredibly oppressive. The bourgeoisie regarded the feudal system, with its myriad of local tariffs and obstructions to trade, as an obstacle that had to be removed if a free-enterprise trading system had any chance of being established.

Source: **Declaration of the National Assembly, Versailles, 4 August 1789**

. . . The National Assembly completely abolishes the feudal regime. It decrees that, among the [feudal] rights and dues . . . all those originating in real or personal serfdom, personal servitude, and those which represent them, are abolished without indemnification.

. . . Tithes of every kind and dues which take place thereof, under whatever denomination they are known and collected, . . . are abolished, subject to the devising of means for providing in some other manner for the expenses of divine worship, the maintenance of ministers of religion, relief of the poor, repairs and rebuilding of churches and parsonages, and for all establishments, seminaries, schools, colleges, hospitals, communities and others, to the maintenance of which they are now assigned . . .

. . . Pecuniary privileges, personal or real, in matters of taxation are abolished forever. Collection shall be made from all citizens and on all property, in the same manner and in the same form; and means of effecting proportional payment of all taxes, even for the last six months of the current year, shall be considered.

. . . Since a national constitution and public liberty are more advantageous to the provinces than the privileges which some of them enjoy, and the sacrifice of which is necessary for the close union of all parts of the realm, all special privileges of provinces, principalities, . . . cantons, cities, and communities of inhabitants, whether pecuniary or of any other kind, are declared abolished forever, and shall be absorbed into the law common to all Frenchmen.

. . . All citizens, without distinction of birth, are eligible to any office or dignity, whether ecclesiastical, civil or military.

QUESTIONS

1   What is meant by the abolition of 'personal servitude'?

2   Explain the expression 'without indemnification'.

3   What system is being cancelled by the statement that 'tithes . . . are abolished', and which institution would have been weakened as a result?

4   What social services are, however, acknowledged as having been supported by tithes, and will in future need some other source of funding?

5   What is being significantly altered by the declaration that 'pecuniary privileges . . . in matters of taxation are abolished forever'?

6   What characteristic of modern nation-states is being forecast by the fourth of the clauses printed here?

7   What long-practised principle is being abolished by the fifth of the clauses here?

SOURCE 4.3

The National Assembly proclaims a Declaration of the Rights of Man and the Citizen, 5 October 1789

HISTORICAL CONTEXT: This Declaration in effect claimed that most of the problems of French society had been the product of a neglect of the rights of the individual. It constituted a major break from the past. Under the *ancien régime* authority was derived from God and the monarch. Common people had duties and obligations, but no rights. Now it was being claimed that all individuals had rights, and that the 'source of sovereignty' was the nation, and that law should be the expression of the 'general will'. A new definition of the relationship between citizens and the government had been proclaimed, reflecting similar claims in the American Declaration of Independence.

Source: **Declaration of the Rights of Man and the Citizen, National Assembly of France, Versailles, 5 October 1789**

The National Assembly recognises and declares, in the presence and under the auspices of the Supreme Being, the following rights of man and citizen.

- *Men are born and remain free and equal in rights. Social distinctions can be based only upon public utility.*
- *The aim of every political association is the preservation of the natural and imprescriptible rights of man. These rights are liberty, property, security, and resistance to oppression.*
- *The source of all sovereignty is essentially in the nation; no body or individual can exercise authority that does not proceed from it in plain terms.*
- *Liberty consists in the power to do anything that does not injure others; accordingly, the exercise of the natural rights of each man has no limits except those that secure to the other members of society the enjoyment of these same rights. These limits can be determined only by law.*
- *The law has the right to forbid only such actions as are injurious to society.*
- *Law is the expression of the general will. All citizens have the right to take part personally, or by their representatives, in its formation. It must be the same for all, whether it protects or punishes.*
- *No man should be accused, arrested, or held in confinement, except in cases determined by the law, and according to the forms which it has prescribed. All who promote, solicit, execute, or cause to be executed, arbitrary orders, ought to be punished, and every citizen called upon, or apprehended by virtue of the law, ought immediately to obey, and renders himself culpable by resistance.*
- *The unrestrained communication of thoughts and opinions being one of the most precious Rights of Man, every citizen may speak, write, and publish freely, provided he is responsible for the abuse of this liberty, in cases determined by the law.*
- *Every citizen has a right, either by himself or his representative, to a free voice in determining the necessity of public contributions, the appropriation of them, and their amount, mode of assessment, and duration.*
- *The right to property being inviolable and sacred, no one ought to be deprived of it, except in cases of evident public necessity, legally ascertained, and on condition of a previous just indemnity.*

QUESTIONS

1 What is meant by the 'Supreme Being', and what might be the reason this wording was chosen?

2 What new principle is implied by the declaration that social distinctions can be based only on 'public utility'?

3 Which two clauses specifically reject one of the major principles later advocated by supporters of socialism?

4 What previously unquestioned principle is being rejected in the assertion that 'all sovereignty lies essentially in the nation'?

5 The definition of 'natural rights' encompasses a basic principle of 'equality'. In what sense?

6 Which clause indicates a principle directly derived from the writings of Rousseau?

7 What is the procedure, frequently practised under absolute monarchies, that is prohibited by the wording of the seventh clause?

8 What 'freedom' is being guaranteed by the eighth clause?

9 What is common between the expression of the ninth clause and the independence campaign waged by the British colonists in the American colonies?

Source 4.1

difficult to stop. Nevertheless, in the years 1789–91, the bourgeois leaders continued to work to achieve the revised 'constitution of the kingdom' to which they had committed themselves in the Tennis Court Oath. In this way they hoped to consolidate the reforms achieved and restore stability.

The new constitution was proclaimed in September 1791. Elections were held, the National Assembly was disbanded, and a new parliament with a new name—the Legislative Assembly—took office in October. Already discrepancies could be observed between the high ideals of the Declaration of the Rights of Man and the decisions of the framers of the new constitution. The franchise having been limited to men paying a reasonable amount of direct taxation, the poorer working classes were excluded from the privilege of the vote. Yet had it not been declared that all men were 'equal in rights'? In effect the bourgeoisie had used their position of influence to ensure that the uneducated masses, whom they regarded as 'irresponsible', could not exercise political power. They had in fact created a new privileged class.

New political parties emerged in the Legislative Assembly, and it is from where they sat in this assembly (on the left and right) that we derive our present-day classification of political parties or factions. Thus we speak of the 'Right' (the more conservative or reactionary groups) and the 'Left' (those advocating reform or radical change and generally representing the less privileged classes).

Meanwhile, the attacks on the châteaux had resulted in a widespread exodus from France, as many noblemen fled to England, Austria and other European kingdoms in fear of their lives. Most of these *emigrés* (exiles) became involved in plotting a counter-revolution. They gained a sympathetic hearing from the German princes and the Austrian emperor, the brother of Queen Marie Antoinette.

Within France rumours quickly spread that the emigrés and their foreign supporters were about to invade France and crush the Revolution. Thus, to be an emigré was to be labelled an opponent of the Revolution.

At this point in the sequence of events, the actions of King Louis XVI became immensely important. Had he co-operated wholeheartedly with the bourgeois plan to establish a form of constitutional monarchy, he might have saved both himself and the monarchy. But in June 1791, even before the new constitution had been proclaimed, the king and queen, wishing to break free from their virtual imprisonment by the mob, attempted to escape in disguise to Austrian territory (in what is now Belgium). They were recognised and captured at Varennes, a town north of Paris. This action aligned Louis XVI with the hated emigrés and, together with his proclamations in opposition to the Church reforms, led to his being branded as an enemy of the Revolution. The attempt to establish a constitutional monarchy, dependent as it was upon a co-operative and largely passive figurehead monarch, was doomed even before it was completed. It was now apparent that further radical changes in the constitutional form of government would ensue.

War, Republicanism and Terror

By 1792 it was obvious that France would be invaded by Prussian and Austrian troops intent on restoring the power of the monarchy. Public feeling against traitors and emigrés intensified, uniting the general populace in a frenzy of patriotic fervour. Aggressive elements in the Legislative Assembly declared that if there was to be a war it would be one in which the French nation would export the benefits of the Revolution to the oppressed peoples of the world. The peoples of Europe would destroy the monarchs. Thomas Paine, the English democrat who had been influential in the American Revolution, and who now had become a naturalised French citizen, declared that all 'nations' would become allies of the French people, while every 'court' would be its enemy. He wrote: 'it is now the case of all peoples against all kings'.

In August 1792, all faith in the king having been destroyed or abandoned, the assembly 'suspended' the monarchy. To be truly patriotic now meant being republican. Massacres of suspected royalists increased. Emotional commitment to 'the nation' was proclaimed the duty of every citizen. Large sections of the working classes, both urban and rural, poured their energies into the defence of the Revolution. A group of volunteers from Marseilles brought with them a revolutionary song, the *Marseillaise*, which captured the determination of the people to defend their hard-won liberties against foreign invasion or treachery from within. A translation of part of the stirring marching song, which became the French national anthem, refers to 'traitors and conspiring kings', and to the threat of 'foreign cohorts' making the laws in France. Contempt for the mercenary soldiers of the invading monarchs was expressed in the term 'hireling phalanxes'.

At the Battle of Valmy, on 20 September 1792, to the astonishment of most of the rest of Europe, a French army largely made up of bedraggled, untrained revolutionary zealots defeated the professional soldiers of Prussia and Austria. Here was a military victory of staggering significance—a group of individuals had found in 'the nation' a common cause powerful enough to weld them into a fearsome fighting force. Until this time men had fought either for a feudal lord or king, or for payment. The Frenchmen at Valmy fought voluntarily for a cause. After Valmy, every Frenchman who bore arms looked upon himself as a champion of the cause of liberty and an enemy of tyrannical despotism. The German philosopher Johann Goethe, accompanying the Prussian soldiers as an observer, made the evaluation that 'from this place and this time forth commences a new era in world history'.

On the very next day the French monarchy was abolished, for the battle was seen as a defeat of the attempt to achieve a royalist restoration. France was declared a republic, and the highest rank within it was that of 'citizen'.

Public agitation now demanded the election of another parliament. The Legislative Assembly, with its limited franchise, was now replaced by a new assembly, the National Convention, elected on manhood suffrage. The revolutionary movement thus passed out of the hands of the bourgeois advocates of constitutional monarchy. France now embarked on an experiment in full democracy, with the masses in control.

Louis XVI, now officially known as 'Citizen Capet' (his family surname), was voted guilty of treason and was executed in January 1793. In the convention Danton exclaimed, 'Come all the kings of Europe against us and we will hurl at their feet in defiance, the head of a king.'

The National Convention embarked on a radical reform programme. With the Parisian populace exerting a threatening influence, the Jacobin Party (an extreme **left-wing** party) became the dominant force. As royalists from Austria, Prussia, Britain, Holland and Spain continued to attack, France became a 'nation in arms'. Conscription for military service (the *levée-en-masse*) was introduced. The nation now demanded as full a measure of obedience and service from its citizens as had their former feudal lords.

Under the threat of invasion, and in the

An artist's impression of the women's march on the Palace of Versailles. In October 1789 a shortage of bread sparked off a protest march by the women of Paris. Over 8 000 women walked the 18 kilometres to Versailles. They had already hanged a baker from a lamppost for selling bread under its stated weight. Some women declared that they would kill the queen, Marie Antoinette.

1 What means has the artist employed to portray the anger and determination of the women?

2 What revolutionary symbols has the artist used?

3 There are scales on the banner in this picture. What did they represent?

4 What might have been the motivation for the women to carry this sort of banner when marching to Versailles?

5 Two other symbols on display are the 'liberty tree' and the *bonnet rouge* (the red revolutionary bonnet). What is the purpose of each of these symbols?

The execution of the former Louis XVI on 21 January 1793. Having been retitled 'Louis Capet', the ex-king was convicted of treason against the nation, and put to death on the guillotine.

1 Why would the executioner be displaying the severed head?

2 What is the significance of the two objects held high on poles (probably pikes) on the right?

3 Who are occupying the positions closest to the execution platform?

4 What might this suggest regarding the public's attitude to this event?

extremity of war, effective executive power came to be concentrated in fewer and fewer hands. A feature later to be observed in other revolutions now emerged. In the name of 'preserving' the revolution which had been staged to win liberty, equality and fraternity an organisation emerged which in fact suppressed individual liberties. The Jacobin Party, through a small executive which named itself the Committee of Public Safety, and which claimed to be protecting the Republic from counter-revolution, now instituted what became known as the 'Reign of Terror'.

All the features of a totalitarian police state now emerged, with the forces of the government geared to insist upon a form of unquestioning military patriotism. All sorts of actions could be condemned as 'unpatriotic' and deemed to be a reason for the death penalty.

Such 'crimes' included 'spreading false news', 'seeking to inspire discouragement', and 'impairing the purity of the Revolution'. Any person suspected of supporting the monarchy, or accused of maintaining aristocratic connections, could be convicted of treason and executed on the guillotine.

Thousands of 'traitors' were executed both in Paris and provincial cities. Even to disagree with the Jacobin Party was a capital offence. Twenty-two elected deputies representing the Girondins (a provincial political party) were among those guillotined. In present-day terms this was equivalent to a government killing off troublesome members of the opposition. The hypocrisy of all these killings in the name of 'liberty' was vividly summarised in the cry of one of the victims, Madam Roland: 'O Liberty, what crimes are committed in thy name?'

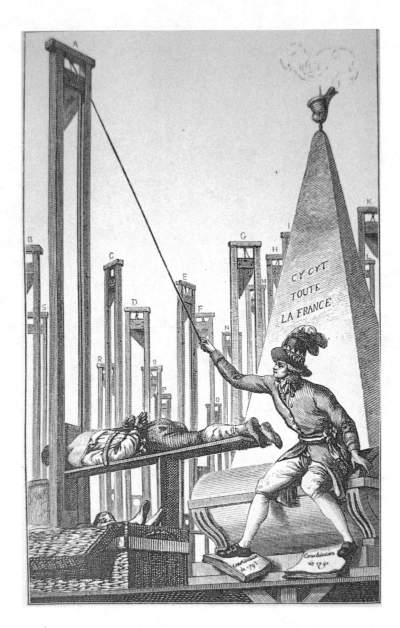

Maximilien Robespierre (1758–94), the brilliant leader of a radical group of revolutionaries called the Jacobins, was the dominant figure during the Reign of Terror. In this cartoon, among a forest of guillotines working overtime, Robespierre has run out of victims, so he executes the executioner. The alphabetical labels on the guillotines are meant to represent the groups of politicians or sections of society who, having been identified as opponents of Robespierre and the Jacobins, have been executed. At the top of the obelisk labelled 'Here Lies All France', a liberty bonnet, upside down, has been spiked, and converted into a cremation chimney. Robespierre is portrayed as trampling all over the constitutions of 1791 and 1793.

1 What might the artist have intended by not showing any living person other than Robespierre?

2 What is the significance of the 'forest' of guillotines and their identification labels?

3 Explain the artist's probable intentions in his presentation of the liberty bonnet in this fashion.

4 What is the purpose of the positioning of the constitutions?

5 What ideological position is being challenged by the cartoon, and what message does it provide about the likely conduct of revolutionary leaders?

During the 'war dictatorship' Maximilien Robespierre, a leading figure in the Jacobin Party, acquired almost dictatorial powers. Over 20 000 'enemies of the republic' were executed in the name of democracy during the Reign of Terror.

The 'war emergency' eventually became 23 years of war, which ultimately affected peoples all round the world. The French claimed that they were ready to 'export' liberty. They offered their assistance to all those wishing to recover their liberty from royal despotism.

The additional significance of the Reign of Terror was that it provided another example of a revolution 'devouring its own'. This time it was the bourgeoisie who were the main victims of a movement they thought they had brought under their own control, only to discover that the raw violence of the Parisian masses could exercise more decisive political power than speeches and resolutions. The Reign of Terror marked the period of ascendancy of the *sans-culottes* (literally, those without fancy trousers, or in other words the unprivileged ones). It was the supreme example of how hatred for all things privileged could organise the previously underprivileged into a deadly force.

The Emergence of the Forces of Counter-revolution: the Directory

In 1795 a coalition of moderate forces, in reaction against Jacobinism, deposed the Jacobins and pushed a revised constitution through the National Convention. The right to vote was again restricted, more so in fact than had been the case under the constitution of 1791. Executive power was placed in the hands of a group of five men called the Directory. In effect, forces representing the bourgeoisie had regained power.

This ended the period of Jacobin dominance. The experiment in 'extreme democracy' was terminated, but it left an enduring legacy. The term 'Jacobin' became the most effective 'scare word' or 'smear word' of the nineteenth century. Any working-class movement, in Britain or mainland Europe, that appeared to

threaten the position of privileged persons was rapidly labelled as 'Jacobin' and thereby portrayed as a menace to stability.

In its turn, however, the Directory failed to win popularity because it was opposed by both the democratic republicans and the groups within France who now desired a royalist restoration. The administration was corrupted by racketeers and profiteers. The wars resumed, and although some outstanding military successes by the young general Napoleon Bonaparte brought France some prestige in 1796–97, by 1799 setbacks and defeats suffered by other military leaders had brought the Directory into disrepute. The French countryside fell into disorder, and there were royalist uprisings in the provinces.

In seeking to prevent a resurgence of mob rule, the Directory was forced to rely more and more upon the army, and the key figure in the army was Napoleon Bonaparte. His successes had made him a national hero.

In 1799 the Directory finally collapsed, and the powers of government were placed in the hands of a Consulate of three, of whom Bonaparte was first consul. France accepted this trend almost without reservation; the new constitution providing for the placement of executive power in the hands of the Consulate was given overwhelming approval in a nationwide **plebiscite**. The 'general will' had been consulted and had approved a return to what was virtually one-man rule.

Continuing the trend back to a concentration of authority, another plebiscite (in 1802) approved Napoleon's appointment as consul for life. In 1804 he assumed the title of emperor. The republic for which so much blood had been shed had been abandoned—France was again ruled by a powerful monarch. The difference lay, however, in the fact that it was a monarchy based on merit and the exercise of the 'general will' rather than on unquestioned application of the principle of divine right and hereditary authority.

Though it may have appeared that the wheel had turned full circle from absolute monarchy, through extreme democracy and back to autocracy, Napoleon was actually dedicated to ensuring the fulfilment of many of the aims of the Revolution, particularly those related to the reform of the law, the modernisation of the economy, and the abolition of feudal privileges. In fact he boasted, 'I am the Revolution'.

IV THE COUNTER-REVOLUTION

In revolutionary movements the most publicised events are usually the prominent acts of defiance or the decisive acts of change. The less colourful acts of resistance to the revolutionary changes receive less attention in newspapers, film and television, novels and even history books themselves. Thus, books on the American Revolution do not dwell on the fact that 100 000 colonists, calling themselves United Empire Loyalists, rejected the Revolution and journeyed to Canada and to other British colonies in order to continue life under the British crown.

Similarly, during the first decade of the French Revolution (1789–99) many thousands of French citizens opposed the radical changes to society and government occurring in Paris. Much of this opposition stemmed from the fact that at the outbreak of the Revolution, approximately 82 per cent of the rural population of France were devout Roman Catholics. They resented the extreme anti-clericalism and anti-Christian policies of the revolutionaries in Paris.

Extreme measures were proposed by the Revolutionary assemblies to destroy the power and wealth of the Church. The decrees of 1789 abolishing all privileges referred to the clergy as much as to the aristocracy. On 2 November 1789 the National Assembly decreed the seizure of all ecclesiastical property. The property passed into national ownership, to be sold off to cancel the massive national debt. This action sparked off a heated debate, because the original Declaration of the Rights of Man had declared the ownership of property to be 'inviolable'. To rationalise this action, the assembly declared that the Church had only been holding such properties in 'trust' for the nation.

Even more radical actions against the Church were perpetrated in the proclamations of the Civil Constitution of the Clergy, on 12 July 1790, and the so-called 'Oath Law' on 27 November. These laws demanded that the clergy take an oath of allegiance to the national constitution, and made provision for the clergy to be elected by all citizens, whether they were Catholics or otherwise. Predictably, the pope denounced these attempts to nationalise Christianity. Almost all members of the office-bearing clergy and more than half of the parish clergy refused to take the oath of loyalty to the constitution.

The assault on the Church forced millions of devout Catholics to choose between the Revolution and the Church. Combined with a strong feeling in the provinces that the city-dwellers of Paris were attempting to control their lives, this emotion generated a defiance of the decrees of the new government. This was one of the sources of the counter-revolution, which emerged in many of the provinces of France.

Long-established loyalty to the monarchy was also not easily suppressed. The accusations of the Parisian revolutionaries that the emigrés were plotting to reverse the trend of events were accurate. Thus the combined effects of royalist sentiment, Roman Catholic zeal, and provincial antipathy to 'rule from Paris' fuelled counter-revolutionary activities.

The first significant outbreak of violence resulting from counter-revolutionary action occurred in Nimes, in southern France, on 13 June 1790, during elections for the new Revolution-established district and departmental councils. In the demonstrations and protests against the new government, many hundreds of people lost their lives.

The most prolonged and best publicised episode of resistance to the Revolution, particularly after the declaration of the Republic in 1792, occurred in La Vendée, a coastal region in mid-western France. The area was economically stagnant, with the predominantly

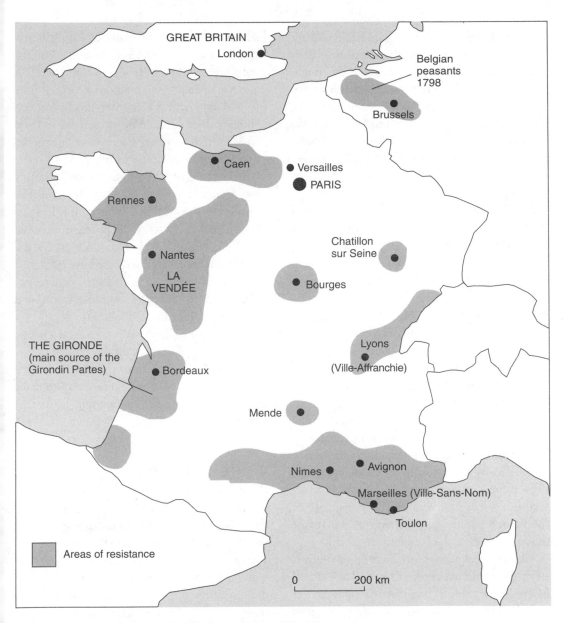

MAP 4.2 Areas of resistance to the French Revolution 1793–99

If a reader of French History concentrates on the events in the capital city, Paris, during the period 1789–99, one could get the impression that the major decisions made there enjoyed majority support. From the year (1793) of the execution of the monarch, however, many citizens of France were in opposition to the policy-makers and power-brokers in Paris. In many regions and provincial cities citizens rose up against the Parisians. Many were royalists, protesting against the Republic. Others were devout Roman Catholics, protesting against the new non-Christian, quasi-religious 'Cult of the Supreme Being'. In all the regions offering resistance to the directions from Paris, terrible acts of repression were conducted. Many thousands of resisters were executed by the army of the Republic, particularly in the region called La *Vendée* where royalist sentiment had remained strong. A 'Catholic and Royal' army was raised to resist the Revolution. It was sustained by arms and money from British sympathisers. This army held out for months against the forces of the Republic. Several cities, in particular Lyon, Toulon and Marseilles, also defied the Paris-based government during the Jacobin period, and suffered severe punishments in consequence. For six years regional forces continued to oppose the major decisions associated with the Revolution.

(and largely illiterate) peasant population resistant to new philosophies whilst remaining profoundly loyal to the monarchy and the Church. They rejected the attempt to establish a civil constitution for the clergy. The major uprising against Parisian rule occurred in 1793, and was savagely suppressed by Jacobin forces. Thousands of citizens were slaughtered in La Vendée, where to be declared an opponent of the Republic was effectively a death warrant. In a particularly gruesome approach to the task of suppressing opposition, the Jacobin forces resorted to mass drownings in the River Loire. Reputable historians estimate that at least 2 000 and perhaps even 48 000 persons were thus drowned (many of these 'executions' were carried out at night). It is difficult to discern any difference in sheer inhumanity between these mass drownings and the Nazi-decreed gas executions of Jews during World War II.

Another uprising in La Vendée broke out in 1795, supported by emigrés operating from British bases. The region was not totally pacified until 1801, when Napoleon Bonaparte, as first consul, enforced military discipline whilst simultaneously negotiating the Concordat with the pope, which re-established Roman Catholicism as the religion of the majority of the French people, and thus appeased many of the opponents of the Revolution.

Other focal points of counter-revolution were the southern cities of Lyon, Toulon and Marseilles. In June 1793 an anti-Jacobin faction seized control of these cities, defying the edicts issued from Paris. What followed was virtually a civil war, as Republican armies marched south to attack the dissidents as if they were foreign enemies. Lyon, France's second largest city, was besieged for several weeks, then subjected to vicious punishment. The homes of 'the rich' were destroyed, and executions carried out every day for months. At one stage the Jacobin forces resorted to mowing down masses of 'counter-revolutionaries' with cannon shot. The city itself was punished by having its name cancelled, being officially labelled '*Ville Affranchie*' (liberated town). A column was erected, stating: 'Lyon made war on Liberty: Lyon is no more'. At Marseilles similar punishments were inflicted. It was also renamed: as *Ville-Sans-Nom* (town without a name)! The price of supporting a counter-revolution was chillingly demonstrated by the carnage in Lyon and Marseilles—further examples of outrageous crimes committed in the name of liberty.

A feature of the counter-revolutionary movements was their diversity. In Lyon the defiance of the National Convention in Paris was primarily a matter of the bourgeoisie resisting the extreme regulations decreed by the Jacobins, whereas in La Vendée the resistance came from a coalition of peasants, priests, ex-nobles and royalists, all claiming continued adherence to Roman Catholicism.

Throughout the decade of radical change (1789–99), large sections of the French populace resisted the reforms of the Revolutionary governments in Paris. A counter-revolutionary element thus became an ongoing feature of French society.

V THE CULTURAL REVOLUTION

In the French Revolution we can observe the emergence of a phenomenon that was to reappear in later revolutions; namely, the claim that a 'new order' was being created, with a 'new man' or 'citizen' as its embodiment. Such was the scale and code of standards of this claimed reconstruction of society that it can reasonably be labelled a **cultural revolution**.

The most important formula for the process of creating this new culture was the attempt to achieve a de-Christianisation of society. The Church was dismantled, its property was confiscated, its monasteries and nunneries were closed, and its clergy were forced to accept a civil constitution. Churches were converted to 'temples of reason'. This institutionalised secularisation of society marked the suspension of the very elements that had bound French society together for centuries. Napoleon's 1801 Concordat (reconciliation) with the pope reversed many of these decisions, but an extreme erosion of the fabric of society had occurred.

The abolition of the monarchy was almost a natural corollary to the de-powering of the Church. If God's authority could be challenged, was not a monarch even more vulnerable? If divinity was no longer recognised, the divine right of kings was but a fantasy. So emerged the French Republic, ostensibly existing for the public good rather than the fulfilment of a monarch's wishes, with authority stemming from the 'general will' rather than from God.

With the new culture there came a new set of symbols and expressions. The revolutionary motto—liberty, equality, fraternity—was the precursor to other slogans. The new flag, the tricolour, combining the red and blue of the city of Paris with the white of the Bourbon royal family, was originally meant to signify the union of the people with their king in the

Three of the major symbols of the Revolution are portrayed in this sketch. The 'liberty tree' symbolised a new life and a new beginning. Most towns in France planted or identified a 'liberty tree', which became the focal point for gatherings or celebratory dances (as shown here). On the tree can be seen numerous examples of the tricolour (red, white and blue) cockade, the colours of which are to this day still displayed on the flag of France. Originally the white represented the Bourbon monarchy, while the red and blue were the colours of the city of Paris. The tricolour therefore dates from the early days of the Revolution, when the expectation was that a limited-power monarchy would be established within the reform movement. The dancers are all very obviously *sans-culottes*, being dressed in ostensibly ragged clothing. On the head of one of the dancers, on the top of the tree, and on the building in the distance, there is displayed the *bonnet rouge* (red cap), also known as the liberty bonnet or the Phrygian cap. This symbol dates from Greek and Roman times, having derived its name from Phrygia, a province of Greece. It can be seen on Roman coins on which freed slaves are shown receiving such a bonnet as a mark of their emancipation. When King Louis XVI was forced to abdicate, his humiliation was compounded by having to wear such a red cap instead of the crown.

months when the hopes for reform lay with the prospect of a constitutional monarchy. It survived into the days of the Republic to become permanently established as a 'people's flag'.

Both the name *sans-culottes* and the class thus described became another symbol of the Revolution. Likewise the liberty cap, a conical-shaped red cap (the *bonnet rouge*), sometimes called the Phrygian cap after an ancient Greek and Roman predecessor, was an almost universally displayed uniform favoured by the *sans-culottes*. Eventually it became the official symbol of the Revolution, seen on town halls, coins and stamps right through to twentieth-century times.

Of major significance during the first decade of the Revolution, although perhaps less remembered today than the tricolour or the cap, was the symbolism of the 'liberty tree'. In almost every town in France, a liberty tree was planted in a political ceremony commemorating the birth of the new era. It has been estimated that some 62 000 such ceremonies were conducted. These trees created a gathering point for Republican ceremonies and anniversary celebrations.

Perhaps the most memorable attempt by the revolutionaries to signify that they had launched a totally new era was their introduction of a new calendar. This discarded the dating of years from the estimated year of the birth of Christ, and instead proclaimed that year one began on 22 September 1792, the date of the proclamation of the Republic. Further to stress the change, the seven-day week was abandoned, with ten-day periods called *décades* substituted, and the 365-day year was divided into twelve months of thirty days each, with the 'extra' five days at the end of year devoted to festivals and holidays. The thirty-day months were given new names, representative of the seasonal weather patterns. Thus the first month (beginning in the former September) was named *Vendémiaire* (vintage—the time of grape gathering), the next *Brumaire* (mist), the third *Frimaire* (frost) . . . and so on. The use of the calendar did not survive the heady days of the Revolution. On 1 January 1806, under the Napoleonic regime, France returned to the use of the Gregorian calendar (as established by Pope Gregory XIII in 1582), to match the rest of Europe. The French had learned that no nation could be an island in time!

Another feature of the 'new order' which emerged from the reforms of Revolutionary France was the metric system of measurement and the associated decimal monetary system. The essentials of the system are derived from a recommendation by the French Academy of Sciences to the National Assembly in 1791. The metre, or unit of length, was to be a one-millionth part of a quadrant of the Earth measured along a meridian of longitude. A kilometre ('kilo' means a thousand) is a thousand metres. The gram, the basic unit of mass, was to be equal to the weight of one cubic centimetre of water. As with the revolutionary calendar, the metric system of measures and weights was a deliberate step of departure from the *ancien régime*. Unlike the calendar, the metric system spread around the world and is used in Australia today.

VI NAPOLEON: TRUE REVOLUTIONARY OR DICTATOR?

As noted in Section III, it is alleged that Napoleon Bonaparte, even after having himself declared emperor and thus in effect restoring the monarchy, claimed: 'I am the Revolution.' By this he meant that under the stability his reign ensured, the major gains of the Revolution were consolidated and therefore assured.

In 1790 the English writer Edmund Burke published a deeply thoughtful work entitled *Reflections on the French Revolution*. In it he argued that although the French revolutionaries had destroyed the long-established forces of cohesion in society—the monarchy, tradition and the Church—they would not be able to build a new stable society on the basis of rationalism and the rights of the people, for these principles were too vague, unstable and variable. They would mean different things to different people. In such conditions therefore, Burke claimed, there would be no truly substantial source of authority, and a military dictatorship was therefore almost inevitable.

This prediction was fulfilled in France. By 1799 the Directory had collapsed, and the government was placed in the hands of a Consulate of three. The effective ruler of France was the first consul, Napoleon Bonaparte, a thirty-year-old general. Between 1796 and 1799 this dashing young Corsican had become the idol of France. Through his much publicised military successes and what must have been a rare ability

Napoleon Bonaparte (1769–1821), was born on the French island of Corsica. He acquired a reputation as a military genius as a result of many impressive victories over the enemies of Revolutionary France in the period 1796–1801. He also gained a reputation as a domestic administrator, holding the position of first consul from 1799. On 2 December 1804 he proclaimed himself emperor of the French, taking the crown from the hands of Pope Pius VII and placing it on his own head as a symbolic enthronement of a 'self-made' emperor. The French Revolution, which deposed a hereditary monarch, had produced an emperor in his place.

to lead, enthuse and organise other men, Napoleon had risen to the status of the only true national hero.

Seemingly almost desperate to embrace a charismatic leader, the French people accepted Napoleon virtually without reservation. After all the years of turmoil, of rebellion, revolution and counter-revolution, with associated loss of lives and fluctuating expectations from 'the government', the people yearned for stability and security. The new constitution providing for the placement of executive power in the hands of the Consulate was given overwhelming approval in a nation-wide plebiscite. The 'general will' had been consulted and had approved a virtual dictatorship.

In 1802 another plebiscite approved Napoleon's appointment as consul for life; in 1804 he assumed the title of emperor, having ensured that the pope was present to bestow the blessing of legitimacy on the new office. At the crowning ceremony on 2 December 1804 Napoleon took the crown from the hands of the pope and placed it on his own head as a symbolic enthronement of a 'self-made' emperor. The republic for which so much blood had been shed was no more—France was again ruled by a powerful monarch. The difference lay, however, in the fact that it was a monarchy based on merit and the 'general will', rather than on 'divine right'.

Domestic Administration under Napoleon

The qualities of planning, organisation and leadership ability that had earned Napoleon his reputation as a general served well to ensure efficient management of domestic affairs. When he came to power in 1799, France desperately needed stability and unity. The finances were in disarray, and trade was in jeopardy because of fluctuating prices and an insecure currency. The new laws for which much of the revolutionary effort had been exerted were still not codified. Divisive quarrels still rent the nation—large numbers of royalists were in a state of armed rebellion and Roman Catholics

PHASES OF POWER-CONCENTRATION DURING THE FRENCH REVOLUTION AND THE NAPOLEONIC PERIOD

Year	Absolute, or autocratic, power	Aristocracy in power	Bourgeoisie dominant	Proletariat dominant
1788	Louis XVI **ABSOLUTE MONARCH**			
1789		Estates-General called First and Second Estates dominant	June: Third Estate forms **NATIONAL ASSEMBLY**	
1790				
1791			**LEGISLATIVE ASSEMBLY**	
1792				Monarchy abolished **NATIONAL CONVENTION**
1793				Louis XVI executed Jacobins dominant
1794				Committee of Public Safety Reign of Terror
1795			**THE DIRECTORY**	
1796			Napoleon's victories in Italy	
1797			Napoleon defeats Austria	
1798			Nelson defeats Napoleon's fleet	
1799			**THE CONSULATE** (Napoleon First Consul)	
1800			Code Napoleon	
1801			Concordat with pope	
1802	Napoleon appointed Consul for Life			
1803				
1804	Napoleon crowned **EMPEROR**			
1804				

DIAGRAM 4.1 Phases of power-concentration during the French Revolution 1789–1805

The French Revolution began when all three classes of society resolved to use the calling of the Estates-General as an opportunity to reduce the power of the absolute monarch. Once the monarch was deposed, power passed quickly to the bourgeoisie, and then to the extreme left (the Jacobin-led proletariat). The excesses of the Reign of Terror caused widespread disillusionment with the Jacobins, and power was then reconcentrated into fewer hands, under the Directory and the Consulate. In a classic display of the search for secure, stable rule, the French then established Napoleon Bonaparte as first consul, then as consul for life, and finally as emperor.

were alienated by the anti-clerical activities of the Republican leaders in the 1790s.

Napoleon analysed and attacked these problems as he would have dealt with an impending series of military encounters. He brought order and purpose to the administration of France, centralising administrative power in his own hands and delegating provincial affairs to prefects answerable directly to the first consul. Taxation was entrusted to agents of the central government. The Bank of France was established to stabilise the currency. New codes of law civil, penal and commercial were formulated into the *Code Napoleon*, ensuring equality before the law and bestowing a sense of permanence on the gains of the Revolution.

In addition to imposing efficiency upon the civil administration of France, Napoleon also had to face the task of restoring nation-wide cohesion. While fervent republicans had adopted the concept of loyalty to 'the nation' instead of to the monarch, many royalists and Catholics had rejected this new focal point. Under Napoleon's administration the royalists ceased their armed rebellion, and a considerable number in time accepted Napoleon as a substitute monarch. The emigrés were encouraged to return to France and were guaranteed citizenship. The thousands of devout Roman Catholics, whose loyalty to the Church had led them to abandon emotional attachment to France during the years of anti-clericalism under the Republic, welcomed the Concordat with Pope Pius VII in 1801. By its conditions it was again possible to be both a devout Roman Catholic and a loyal French citizen.

Napoleon also discerned that the egalitarianism of the early Revolutionary years had removed a motivational feature of human behaviour: the desire for recognition of effort and achievement. He had always encouraged his soldiers with the policy that every private soldier had a field marshall's baton in his knapsack; that is, all could win promotion.

On the national scale Napoleon reintroduced, through his Legion of Honour, a system of awards and distinctions. To the critics who claimed this destroyed the philosophy of equality, Napoleon replied that equality still prevailed in the opportunity to win the awards. In 1815 he stated: 'My motto has always been: a career open to all talents, without distinction of birth.' As a military leader Napoleon understood the force of sentiment; he fully realised that the French loved honours and coveted glory. He gave honours to loyal persons and made them even more loyal, and he unified the nation around a new belief in promotion by merit and a fierce national pride in the glory of the success of French arms.

Under the rule of Napoleon, the centralised efficiency of the administration, the nation-wide uniformity of law, the new education system under the supervision of the University of France, and the improved roads and bridges all helped to reunify the nation.

Napoleon's Foreign Policy

In the first decade of the Revolution the French revolutionary troops, claiming to be fighting for 'all peoples' against 'all monarchs', won many victories over less motivated troops. Supported by a nation-wide conscription system (the *levée-en-masse*), the French armies ranged over Europe from 1796, achieving amazing successes under the leadership of Napoleon. By 1812 Napoleon controlled almost all of Europe. Vast territories had been added to France itself, other areas were under Napoleon's 'protection', while relatives and friends of Napoleon sat on thrones at his behest. Monarchies that had tried to defeat him on land—such as Prussia, Austria and Russia—had been defeated by the seemingly invincible general and his zealous troops. At sea, against the British navy, he did not enjoy similar success.

As the now vanquished princes and monarchs of the numerous German and Austro-Hungarian principalities and kingdoms had not necessarily won the affection of their subjects, Napoleon in the early years of his conquests was often hailed as a liberator. In theory he brought the benefits of the Revolution to the peoples of Europe in the form of the abolition of feudalism and the termination of legal inequalities and privileges. But as the first expressions of euphoria died down, and as the French liberation became the French occupation, and the French demanded taxes from their conquests and imposed new princes and monarchs upon them, anti-French sentiment flourished.

The ending of feudalism released the Europeans from their parochial loyalties, and a sense of broad national identity was able to develop among such peoples as the Germans, Italians and Spaniards. Even if their princes and monarchs professed to be co-operating with Napoleon, the common people usually refused to do so. The French occupying forces became the hated enemy against whom this sentiment could be directed.

In all his military ventures there was one opponent Napoleon could not defeat: Britain. Once the combined French–Spanish fleet had been destroyed at the Battle of Trafalgar (1805), Napoleon lacked the sea power he needed to match Britain. He therefore attempted to destroy Britain economically through the 'Continental System', by which all European ports under his control were to be closed to British goods. Britain responded with a counter-blockade.

It was in his attempt to enforce the Continental System, which in turn had grown from his obsession to destroy Britain, that Napoleon overreached himself. To punish European cities and monarchs who refused to co-operate, he rushed armies all over Europe.

The spirit of nationalism, one of the creations of the French Revolution, turned against Napoleon. The Spanish people, for instance, endured incredible atrocities and hardships, but never ceased to oppose the French with courage, passion and determination. In the countryside they formed *guerrilla* (little war) bands to harass and upset the French. The so-called Peninsular War (on the Iberian Peninsula, south of the Pyrenees Mountains) became an enormous drain upon Napoleon's resources.

The emotional power of outraged British

and Russian nationalism, however, provided the major forces that brought about Napoleon's downfall. When the Tsar of Russia failed to co-operate in the enforcement of the Continental System, Napoleon invaded Russia in 1812 with half a million men. The prolongation of the campaign and the associated problems with supplies, the Russian policy of withdrawing whilst destroying supplies, and the deadly cold of winter all combined to highlight the folly of the venture. The Russian people were determined, in their national pride, to resist the French oppressor. When the French troops finally withdrew, only twenty thousand pitiful survivors of the *Grande Armée* had survived the combined enmity of the Russian winter and Russian nationalism. The legend of Napoleonic invincibility on land had been destroyed.

The British people, meanwhile, escalated the effort to end the French militaristic dominance of Europe into a national concern. In the early years of the French Revolutionary wars the main anti-French sentiment in Britain had been from the aristocracy, who saw that their privileged positions could be threatened if similar events occurred in Britain. The common people of Britain were not at first disposed to become involved in a war against France. In 1797, in fact, the Royal Navy had been paralysed by mutiny. But as Napoleon's ambitions became clear, the whole nation rallied to the cause. The British foot soldier, as well as the 'tar' (the British navy's typical sailor), became one of the instruments of Napoleon's destruction, firstly in Spain and Portugal, and later in France and at Waterloo in 1815 (where Prussian troops also played a critical part). Napoleon was ultimately destroyed by the immeasurable force which had at first been his greatest source of strength—nationalist zeal, wielded against him rather than in his cause.

Napoleon's Place in the Revolution

Although Napoleon brought France to ruin, and through the excessive ambition of his campaigns destroyed the basis of French supremacy in Europe, he is revered in France to this day as

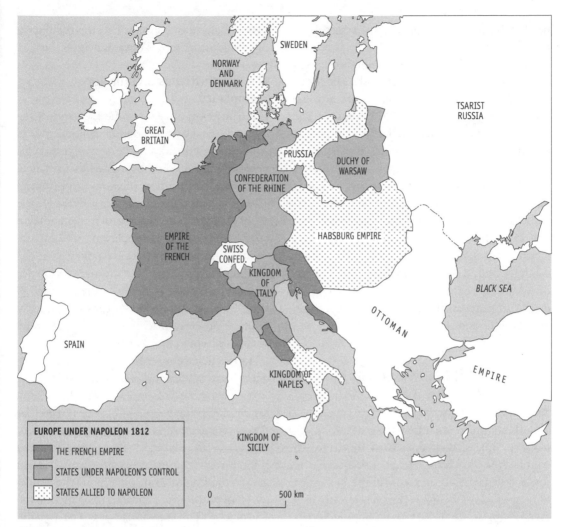

MAP 4.3 Europe under Napoleon 1812

By 1812 Napoleon dominated Europe. The French Empire, under his direct rule, extended north to Denmark, encompassing all of present-day Belgium and Holland. It also included much of the Italian peninsula. In addition, the temporary Kingdom of Italy, the Confederation of the Rhine and the Duchy of Warsaw were, in effect, puppet states. Wherever French control extended, the influences of liberalism (the striving for individual liberties) and nationalism (the desire for separate national identity) were extended and reinforced.

the greatest Frenchman in history. Perhaps this is because, in the extraordinary range of his achievements, he pleased almost all French citizens in one way or another.

His conquests, his colourful exploits and the legend of the superiority of the French troops filled the people with Gallic pride. Napoleon unified the nation in many other ways. The bourgeoisie approved of his administration because he provided a bulwark of order and stability, established orderly commercial, market-

ing and currency conditions, and made permanent the policy of promotion by merit. To the peasants Napoleon was a security against the restoration of feudal privileges and a guarantee that they would retain the land. To the emigrés he was the means by which they were permitted to return safely to France. To the Roman Catholics he was the instrument of an agreement which, while not wholly satisfying, enabled them to be simultaneously loyal to the pope and the nation. Even among some of the royalists he was grudgingly accepted as a substitute for a monarch.

Under Napoleon France was not, however, a democracy. He was not the embodiment of the democratic strand in the revolutionary process. Rather, Napoleon fulfilled the aims of the bourgeois revolutionaries by providing an orderly, efficient, stable economy in which the capitalist system could function without the encumbrances of feudalism. The laws he introduced were liberal in spirit, but he ruled in an authoritarian framework. By using the 'general will' concept as a device for authorising totalitarian control, he established a precedent that was to be followed by dictators in the twentieth century. He proved that to many peoples despotism is acceptable if it feeds national pride and provides social stability and order.

VII THE OUTCOME AND INFLUENCE OF THE REVOLUTION

The Revolution was many different things to many people. Its effects varied from city to countryside, and from northern France to the south. Nevertheless, in terms of the metaphor of a revolution being a '180 degree' turn—establishing some diametrically opposed positions from those previously operative—much can be noted. In another sense we can almost identify a '360 degree' turn, especially in the installation of an emperor. Significantly, too, the Revolution extended its influence beyond France, eventually reaching all corners of the globe.

An evaluation of the significance of the changes brought about during the Revolution involves the identification of the aims of the revolutionaries, and judgement on the extent to which they were attained. Both 'democratic' and 'liberal' aspirations became influential forces in European society as a result of the Revolutionary period. In the early stages of the Revolution the liberals and democrats were united in their efforts to achieve an alteration of the old order, yet the nineteenth century was to witness a split between these two groups because the liberals opposed further moves towards democracy.

The Revolution as a Claim for 'Democracy'

If the principal purpose of the Revolution was the attainment of 'full' political democracy as an application of the idea of the 'sovereignty of the people', then it could be argued that it failed. Only one constitution of the period (that of 1792) provided for manhood suffrage. If the theory of the 'sovereignty of the people' is taken to its logical conclusion, the masses should influence and decide policy. But the period of Jacobin rule, with its use of violence and terror, largely discredited the concept of 'rule by the masses' as a means of attaining political progress, placing this principle under suspicion both in France and abroad.

In the half-century that followed, extreme democracy was generally regarded with fear and suspicion by the propertied classes. In Britain, for example, the events in France during the Revolutionary period left a profound distrust of working-class activities. The excesses of the Jacobin regime aroused deep feelings of alarm among the English bourgeoisie, and the confiscation of property in France terrified the English aristocracy. The influential classes of Britain, therefore, found cause enough to regard the French Revolution as a disaster of the highest order. These reactions against full political democracy delayed the evolution of political reform in many nations.

Nevertheless, the principle of the 'sovereignty of the people' had won its followers, and an historical force had been set in motion. Repercussions were to ensue in later generations and on all continents. The 1854 Eureka Stockade incident in Australia, with its republican overtones and its insistence that workers should fight for their rights, is but one example of the global spread of the principles of the French Revolution.

A new era had begun, based on the dual example of the American and French revolutions, in which it was established that the citizenry of a nation held the right to abolish any form of government it found oppressive, and to institute new forms of government better suited to guaranteeing their 'natural rights'.

The revolutions had effected a transformation in the position of a person in society. In place of the obligations and duties characteristic of the feudal structure, the individual could now claim inalienable rights.

The Revolution as an Assertion of Republicanism

The establishment of a republic had not been one of the primary aims of the revolutionaries. A form of constitutional monarchy was the widely preferred option in the early years. Three years of turmoil and manoeuvre elapsed before the power-brokers in Paris achieved the abolition of the monarchy and the declaration of a republic.

After the Republican administrations had failed to achieve stability and order, the French people returned to the monarchical form of government (or at least they accepted it when it was imposed upon them), firstly under Napoleon I as an emperor (1804–14), then under the restored Bourbon monarchs (1814–30), and later under the House of Orleans (1830–48). Another short-lived republic functioned from 1848 till 1852, to be succeeded by yet another substitute monarchy in the form of the 'Second Empire' of Napoleon III (nephew of Napoleon I), which lasted until 1870.

In a type of 'delayed action' effect, the republican form of government (with an elected rather than an hereditary head of state) finally became established in France in 1870, prevailing until the present day after having undergone several revisions in constitutional design. The American and French republics have served as an example for many other republics in Europe and the wider world, although it should be noted that to this day France's immediate neighbours to both the north and south (Belgium, the Netherlands and Spain) have retained the monarchical form of government, as has Canada, the immediate neighbour of the USA.

Many of the new nations that emerged from the post–World War II dissolution of the former colonial empires also adopted the republican form of government, and in the 1990s the prospect that Australia might follow suit has become a topic of active and lively debate. This debate can be seen to be a direct consequence of the American and French revolutions.

The Destruction of Privilege

Through the momentous 1789 declarations abolishing feudalism and proclaiming the rights of the citizen, together with that abolishing the monarchy (1792), the French revolutionaries destroyed the power and prestige of both the previously privileged aristocracy and the monarchy. The theories of 'legitimacy' (that some people of some classes were 'born to rule' as legitimate leaders) and of 'divine right' had suffered grievous blows from which they never recovered. The principle of 'consent of the governed' was now destined to replace the accident of birth as the basis of ruling power. The republican and anti-monarchic features of the Revolution eventually prevailed in French society. Royal authority was discredited, and the 1815 restoration of the monarchy did not endure, being doomed to suffer modification in 1830 and extinction in 1848.

Source 4.2

Source 4.3

The Reduction in the Authority of the Church

Through the revolutionary proclamations of the Civil Constitution of the Clergy, and the confiscation and sale of Church lands, the Roman Catholic Church lost its dominant position in French society. In effect society was largely de-Christianised and secularised. For Protestants and Jews, the deconstruction of the Roman Catholic Church marked a new era of civil egalitarianism and freedom of worship. Many loyal Roman Catholics, however, who might otherwise have supported the political reforms of the Revolution, were alienated from the Revolutionary regimes by the anti-clerical actions of the Republic.

This division in French society lasted until 1801, when Napoleon I, seeking greater national cohesion, concluded a Concordat (agreement) with the papacy. By the Concordat Catholicism was again recognised as 'the religion of the majority of Frenchmen', liberty of worship was guaranteed, and a new set of bishops was appointed. Nevertheless, through Napoleon the government nominated the bishops, and the stipends of both bishops and clergy were State-controlled. Thus, although Napoleon partially restored the status of the Church, it was unable to regain the position of power and influence it once exercised in French society.

Social Change through Revolution

Having used armed rebellion and the defiance of authority as the means of displacing the apparently impregnable *ancien régime* in 1789, the French people reverted to this method on several more occasions. It could be argued that a tradition of seeking political and social change through revolution had been established. France was again embroiled in revolutions in 1830, 1848 and 1871. As recently as 1958, during the domestic turmoil emanating from opposing views on how to deal with the claims by the Algerian people for independence, France was again threatened with revolution. Another crisis in May 1968—largely a student-led protest against the government's economic policies—demonstrated this tendency of the French to resort to insurrection.

It is perhaps this national characteristic that has caused the more conservative elements among the French people to revert to authoritarian rule as a safeguard of stability. Examples of such reactionism can be seen in the period 1852–70 under Napoleon III, and again, in modern times under General de Gaulle (president 1958–69), who ruled in effect as a 'modified' emperor, but one whose authority was based on 'talent' rather than 'legitimacy'.

The Revolution as an Assertion of 'Liberalism'

The aims of the bourgeois leaders of the Third Estate of 1789, as expressed in the Tennis Court Oath, were to retain the monarchy and to establish a constitution upon 'firm foundations'. The primary aim of the middle-class revolutionaries was not the attainment of democracy; for them the Revolution was fundamentally a movement for the creation of a stable, efficient business community free from the restrictions imposed by a feudal system and an absolute monarch. They wanted a State organised in their own interests, in which they would be free to engage in trading and investment activities on a large scale. The bourgeoisie's commercial aims were effectively expressed as *laissez-faire* and *laissez-passer*—respectively 'let things be' (or 'let them act'), and 'let things pass'. In combination these expressions indicated the desire of the bourgeoisie for a 'free-trade' society, in which buying and selling could function without inhibitions. In the *ancien régime* these principles had been denied by the effects of scores of local tariffs and regulations which restricted trade and cancelled out the opportunity to reap dividends from investment.

Because the feudal regulations and taxes had been the product of class-based allocations of authority, the bourgeois revolutionaries desired the abolition of the practice of privilege (which had hitherto reserved positions of administrative influence for the nobility) and the termination of the power of the Church. Thus, their 'revolution' was both secular and commercial in spirit.

Expressed in political terms, the bourgeoisie's objective was **liberalism** rather than democracy. They wanted a society in which control was exercised by representative institutions rather than by a despotic monarchy, but in which the right to vote was to be limited to property-owners with a vested interest in stability of government. Among the 'freedoms' they sought was freedom from mob rule. Awarding the franchise to the masses was not a policy supported by the middle classes.

Most of these objectives, except for the functioning of representative institutions, were achieved under Napoleon. An efficient economy was established, within which trade and investment were facilitated in the interests of the trading class. The Church lost property and suffered a reduction in its power and position. A secular society, able to function without Church sponsorship or approval, was successfully established. The abolition of privilege was accomplished through the application of the principles of equality before the law, equality of tax burdens and promotion through talent rather than inheritance. Napoleonic France was virtually a bourgeois-dominated society. This French-initiated example of the attainment of political supremacy by the bourgeoisie through the implementation of liberalism was to be the outstanding feature of nineteenth-century Western Europe.

The Cultural Revolution

From the great range of reforms in Revolutionary France a greatly changed culture emerged. A new political vocabulary, a series of reformed constitutions, a new social order, a redefined role for 'the citizen', the diminution in the authority of the Church and a new loyalty—to the nation rather than to the feudal overlord—all conjoined to effect a virtual cultural revolution.

The Modern Centralised State

Feudalism, being essentially parochial in the attitudes it fostered and the barriers to trade it erected, had been an obstacle to the efficient organisation of France as an economic unit. The modern economic revolution therefore required, as a prelude, alterations in the management of society to encourage large-scale investment, the key to all economic expansion. The abolition of feudalism and the establishment of a centralised control of trade, taxation and banking—all results of the Revolution—contributed to the later economic changes.

Under the civil administration of Napoleon, an example of the modern nation-state was established and consolidated. The abolition of privilege, justified in the interests of a more efficient society geared to the promotion of talent, was accomplished through the enforcement of the principle of equality before the law and through a just distribution of taxation burdens. The large estates were distributed to the peasant classes, who thus obtained, through land ownership, an interest in preserving the new administration and opposing further moves towards mob rule.

The application of central (capital city) power to eliminate local obstacles to trade and investment generated new problems. It was demonstrated that even when acting in the name of 'liberty', a powerful central government could erode personal freedoms. If, as was the case of France in 1792, external enemies conducted warfare against the State, the spectacle of the nation at war under centralised control carried ominous portents for the future. For example, the French Committee of Public Safety presented the first example of the deliberate mobilisation for war of a whole nation, with conscription being introduced and enforced. This centralisation of power resulted ultimately in the seizure of political power by the one group which proved consistently stronger than the mob—the army—and led to military dictatorship under Napoleon. This example of quasi-totalitarian rule was followed later in other nations and on other continents.

It was also shown that if the 'condition of war' was prolonged, so too could the claim of the State that extreme challenges required extreme sacrifices from the people. In the French Revolution–Napoleonic era, the protracted twenty-year period of warfare virtually established militaristic values and a readiness to respond to the 'call to duty' as normal conditions.

The French Revolution and European Nationalism

An all-pervading opinion among the citizens of France in the exciting and terrifying years of 1789–92 was that they were pioneers in a new era, as exemplified in the new political institutions and the new calendar. These events engendered within the French people a sense of pride in their status as 'citizens' and in the nation as a community.

Under the Bourbon kings France had been the most powerful and influential monarchy in Europe, but the people themselves had not felt involved. Now a new sense of destiny prevailed: France was to be the instrument by which the captive masses of the world were to be liberated. This sense of pride was vividly exhibited in a French newspaper in 1792: 'The people are going to remain in permanent insurrection until the perfect establishment of universal liberty. How glorious it is to be French!'

With the abolition of the monarchy and the proclamation of a republic in 1792, the centuries-old loyalty to the monarch as overlord was replaced by loyalty to the nation. The 'fraternity' component of the revolutionary motto was applied to the concept of a 'brotherhood' of citizens within 'the nation', acting as the instrument of Rousseau's concept of the 'general will'. The French Revolution astonished Europe with the spectacle of a populace thinking and acting independently of its traditional governing class.

Moreover, the 1789 Declaration of the Rights of Man and the Citizen had made the Revolution a world force. It promised a new form of society based on reason, to supplant the traditional bonds of obedience to overlords and submission to the dictates of an unchanging system.

However attractive the concept of the rights of citizens seemed to be, it soon became apparent that with the new rights there came new obligations. The survival of the nation and the defeat of the military attacks from the monarchies intent on destroying it demanded a new loyalty and a new obedience. The 'motherland in danger' was a rallying cry that could be used to justify the placing of emergency powers in a few hands. The rule of the Committee of Public Safety during the Jacobin period, as we have seen above, was nothing less than a one-party dictatorship. People who attempted to exercise their individual rights to oppose its policies risked being branded as traitors. The threat to the nation was also used to justify the *levée-en-masse*—conscription for military service. The masses had a new master, just as powerful as the old, whose demands were based on passionate appeals to new allegiances rather than to traditional obligations.

Two divergent concepts of 'the nation' developed from different interpretations of the revolutionary motto: 'Liberty, Equality, Fraternity'. To the bourgeois lawyers and merchants who dominated the processes of change in the halcyon days of 1789–90, the new national character was best achieved within a 'liberal' political system. The 'liberty' they advocated was a product of the emphasis during the Enlightenment on the freedom of the individual. It encompassed the desire for freedom of expression, freedom from Church domination of the institutions of society, and most significantly, freedom from arbitrary controls on economic effort (that is 'free enterprise' or *laissez-faire* in commerce). The bourgeoisie wanted a society in which control was exercised through representative assemblies rather than a despotic monarchy, but in which the right to vote was to be limited to those with a vested interest in the stability of the economy. Most of these objectives, except for the operation of representative institutions, were in fact achieved under Napoleon.

To the bourgeoisie 'fraternity' suggested brotherhood within the new legal and commercial framework, with paths of promotion open but with a class structure still operative. This was the formula for a capitalist nation, and it was accepted by both the middle class and the peasants (once they had become landholders after the break-up of the feudal estates) after 1792.

A different concept of 'the nation' evolved among the urban poor and wage-earners. It derived its basic characteristics more from folk-lore and emotion than from logic or commercial priorities. Years of neglect and oppression, years of enduring ill-treatment as 'non-persons', contributed to a massive upsurge of excitement among the lower classes. While they were perhaps uncertain about the liberty and equality they were to enjoy as citizens, they knew they had broken the apparent permanence of the *ancien régime*, and they became imbued with the urge to carry the benefits of the new liberty to their fellow unfortunates in other lands.

Other national groups were affected by the French passion for 'the nation'. For the first few years of the Revolution 'fraternity' carried the connotation of 'brotherhood of all men' (women not being considered in the sloganeering). But as the French transformed themselves from liberators to oppressors, other European national groups (for example, the Spanish, the Germans and the Russians) found a new source of brotherhood in common hatred of France. The French in their turn, converted the 'brotherhood of man' into a sense of loyalty to France in its stand against its enemies.

Emotional demands for bravery and devotion in the cause of nationalism contributed to the acceptance of the view that people best find their destiny in the group effort. This line of teaching, very close to that of many religions, was being turned to the interests of what was practically a new religion, devotion to the motherland. Thus was developed the strand of nationalism that later reappeared with the emergence of nationalist totalitarian dictatorships, which subverted democracy whilst claiming that they were instruments of the 'general will'.

Support for the Revolution

In the early years of the French Revolution many intellectuals and supporters of reform responded enthusiastically to the exciting developments. The declarations and reforms appeared to be a great victory for the forces of reason over tradition and class privilege. Many of the responses expressed exalted optimism in the expected advantages of the 'new era' that

---

SOURCE 4.4

An English historian reviews the significance of the French Revolution, 1918

HISTORICAL CONTEXT: This summation, published 129 years after the outbreak of the French Revolution, is an indication of the extent to which the changes it wrought influenced historians and commentators on public events in the English-speaking world.

Source: **P.A. Brown, *The French Revolution in English History*, Cass, London, 1918, pp. 28–9**

The spectacle was amazing; more striking than a similar change would have been in any other state of Europe. The French monarchy had been to all appearance, the strongest and the least malleable of political institutions . . . The great military achievements of the monarchy, and its powerful hold upon national institutions, Church, Nobility, and Army, had filled the imagination with a sense of impregnable solidity. Now all had come toppling to the

ground at the summons of the people's representatives.

The Revolution was therefore a notable encouragement to all who believed in change and the power of human endeavour. All reformers rejoiced.

QUESTIONS

1 What does the writer mean by judging the French monarchy of 1789 as having been the 'least malleable' in Europe?

2 What were perceived as the three pillars of the monarchy in France, and which class would have dominated those institutions?

3 Who had brought these institutions 'toppling to the ground'?

4 Why might 'all reformers rejoice'?

5 What was likely to be the frame of reference of this author, given that he was a graduate of an English university?

SOURCE 4.5
Edmund Burke warns of the likely adverse effects of the French Revolution, 1790

HISTORICAL CONTEXT: Among the expressions of euphoria sparked off by the reforms of the French Revolution, there were counter-balancing warnings. One of the influential individuals expressing misgivings about the nature of the Revolution was an Anglo-Irish intellectual, Edmund Burke. Although Burke had supported the American Revolution, acknowledging it as having occurred within the 'normal' process of change, he condemned the French Revolution because he believed its reforms were too radical, marking too sudden a departure from established practice. Burke believed that stability in government was dependent upon gradual reforms, achieved without too great a break from traditions. He asserted that the current generation should work to conserve the achievements of previous generations. From his arguments there emerged the 'conservative' approach to political practices.

Source: **E Burke, *Reflections on the Revolution in France*, London, 1790**
The [1688] Revolution [in Britain] was made to preserve our ancient indisputable laws and liberties, and that ancient constitution of government which is our only security for law and liberty . . . We wished at the period of the revolution, and do now wish, to derive all we possess as an inheritance from our forefathers.

You will observe, that from Magna Carta to the Declaration of Rights, it has been the uniform policy of our constitution to claim and assert our liberties, as an entailed inheritance derived to us from our forefathers, and to be transmitted to our posterity;

. . . the people of England well know, that the idea of inheritance furnishes a sure principle of conservation, and a sure principle of transmission; without at all excluding a principle of improvement . . . By a constitutional policy, working after the pattern of nature, we receive, we hold, we transmit our government and our privileges, in the same manner in which we enjoy and transmit our property and our lives. [In this French Revolution of 1789 the people of Europe] have seen the French rebel against a mild and lawful monarch, with more fury, outrage, and insult, than ever any people has been known to rise against the most illegal usurper.

. . . This was unnatural . . . Laws overturned; tribunals subverted; industry without vigour; commerce expiring; the revenue unpaid, yet the people impoverished; a church pillaged, and a state not relieved; civil and military anarchy made the constitution of the kingdom; every thing human and divine sacrificed to the idol of public credit. Were all these dreadful things necessary? Were they the inevitable results of the desperate struggle of determined patriots, compelled to wade through blood and tumult, to the quiet shore of a tranquil and prosperous liberty? No! nothing like it. The fresh ruins of France, which shock our feelings wherever we can turn our eyes, are not the devastation of civil war; they are the sad but instructive monuments of rash and ignorant counsel in time of profound peace. They are the display of inconsiderate and presumptuous [authority], because [it is] unresisted and irresistible.

Government is not made in virtue of natural rights . . . government is a contrivance of human wisdom to provide for human wants. Men have a right that these wants should be provided for by this wisdom. Among these wants is to be reckoned the want, out of civil society, of a sufficient restraint upon their passions. Society requires not only that the passions of individuals should be subjected, but that even in the mass and body, as well as in the individuals, the inclinations of men should frequently be thwarted, their will controlled, and their passions brought into subjection. This can only be done by a power out of themselves; and not, in the exercise of its function, subject to that will and to those passions which it is its office to bridle and subdue. In this sense the restraints on men, as well as their liberties, are to be reckoned among their rights.

had arrived. For example, the English poet William Wordsworth wrote, in 1809:

> Bliss was it in that dawn to be alive
> But to be young was very heaven.

The scale of the changes introduced through the Revolution elicited a sense of wonderment.

Opposition to the Revolution and Fear of 'the mob'

In other groups, however, attitudes towards the French Revolution were negative. Some regarded the events as a source of evil. The most influential of these critics was Englishman Edmund Burke, who published the widely read work *Reflections on the Revolution in France* in 1790. Burke had been a voluble supporter of the American Revolution, but regarded the decisions of the French revolutionary leaders as gross folly because they constituted too severe a break with the accumulated social practices built up over generations of experience. If society were to achieve reforms, Burke argued, change would have to evolve out of the existing social practices, and not as a result of a total breaking away from proven standards. Society involved not just a contract between governors and governed, but also between the past and the present.

Burke argued that if people became too obsessed with claiming their rights, without balancing this with the need to maintain a stable society, their passions could be inadequately controlled. If the urban masses became simply an uncontrollable 'mob' achieving their objectives through violence rather than reasoned debate, then the very fabric of society would be under threat. Most of Burke's predictions were fulfilled during the Reign of Terror, to the horror of observers in other nations.

As the ongoing turmoil of the French Revolution produced in turn a single-party dictatorship, then an unstable regime based on the separation of powers between executive and legislature, then a Consulate which was akin to an American-style presidency, and finally a military dictator who transformed himself into an emperor, thousands of influential and thoughtful Europeans heeded the wisdom of Burke. The Revolution, they observed, in smashing the intangible bonds of social obligation, custom and religion which bound a society together, had destroyed stability and released the forces of disorder. While 'all reformers rejoiced' in the words of P.A. Brown, conservatives developed a determination to resist sudden change.

MAJOR EVENTS IN THE FRENCH REVOLUTION AND THE NAPOLEONIC ERA

The Estates-General and the National Assembly, 1789–91

1789 *5 May* The convocation of the Estates-General
17 June The Third Estate declared itself the National Assembly and refused to disband
14 July Bastille Day
July-August National Guard formed to safeguard the National Assembly
4 August The assembly abolished feudal dues and declared all citizens eligible for all offices of State
26 August Declaration of the Rights of Man and the Citizen
5 October The Paris mob, including women, marched on Versailles and forced the royal family to Paris. The National Assembly also moved to Paris.

1790 *July* Civil Constitution of the clergy declared. Oath of allegiance by the clergy to the constitution enforced.

1791 *June* King Louis' attempted 'flight to Varennes' intensified republican feeling in France

The Legislative Assembly, October 1791– September 1792

1791 *October* Legislative Assembly took office. Political parties formed. The Jacobins and the Girondists proposed a republic.

1792 *10 August* The Paris mob stormed the royal palace of the Tuileries—the monarchy was 'suspended'. Assembly decreed the election of a National Convention to form a republican constitution.
20 September The Battle of Valmy. French volunteer forces defeated Prussian and Austrian pro-royalist forces.
21 September The monarchy was formally abolished. France was declared a republic with a single-chamber Legislative Assembly.

The Convention, 1792–95

1793 *January* King Louis XVI executed. War declared against Britain, Holland and Spain. The Jacobins seized power and dominated the convention through the Committee of Public Safety.
April The most severe period of the Reign of Terror began. Cult of the 'Supreme Being' established by Robespierre.

The Directory, 1795–99

1795 France governed under a new constitution consisting of the Council of Elders and the Council of Five Hundred. The executive consisted of five directors.

1796 Napoleon's brilliant victories in Italy

1799 Napoleon returned to France a national hero

The Consulate, 1799–1804

1800 Code Napoleon established

1801 Concordat with the pope

1802 Napoleon voted consul for life
Peace of Amiens signed by France, Britain, Spain and Holland

The Empire, 1804–13

1804 Napoleon crowned emperor

1805 Battle of Trafalgar (English fleet defeated the combined French and Spanish fleets)

1806 Napoleon introduced the Continental System in an attempt to force all of Europe to comply with France's policies

1808–14 French military resources consumed in the Peninsular War (Spain and Portugal fighting France whilst receiving aid from Britain)

1812 Napoleon invaded Russia in an attempt to force Russia to abide by the Continental System. Huge losses to French army.

1813 Napoleon defeated at Leipzig by combined German forces

1814 Napoleon abdicated, and was exiled to Elba Island
French monarchy restored in the person of Louis XVIII

1815 Napoleon escaped from Elba, reclaimed his authority, and exercised power for 'One Hundred Days'. His reconstituted army was defeated at Waterloo by Prussian and British forces. Napoleon was deposed and exiled to the island of St Helena in the South Atlantic Ocean.

chapter five

A Call to Revolution:
The Challenge of Socialism

The Communists lay stress on the common interests of the whole proletariat and of the collective movement. Their aim is the organisation of the proletariat into a class, the overthrow of middle-class domination, and the conquest of political power by the proletariat.

The Communists disdain to conceal their views and intentions. They declare openly that their ends can only be attained by the forcible overthrow of every obtaining order of society. Let the ruling classes tremble before a Communist revolution; the workers have nothing to lose by it but their chains. They have the world to win. Workers of every land, unite!

K. Marx and F. Engels, The Communist Manifesto,
1848

In the modern era the single greatest influence in the fostering of revolutionary attitudes and activity since 1848 has been the Marxian version of socialist theory. Karl Marx and Friedrich Engels taught that revolution was not only likely, but was, they said, inevitable. Their followers, in believing this, virtually ensured that the prediction would be fulfilled.

The practice of free-enterprise capitalism ensured that, although some people became rich, thousands or millions of others became poor. These were the exploited wage-earners, earning at best subsistence wages, and living in miserable slums. Even worse off were the unemployed.

For centuries people have sought ways of doing away with inequalities in society. Because private ownership created the division between rich and poor, one of the frequently proposed remedies has been *socialism*—the proposal that wealth should be collectively owned by society as a whole rather than by private individuals. If this was achieved, the theory ran, wealth could be equitably distributed.

Theme Questions

➤ What were the defects in nineteenth-century society that helped to make socialism an appealing alternative?

➤ What did socialism and the idea of the 'brotherhood of the proletariat' offer to disadvantaged people?

➤ How effective was socialism in winning people's loyalties from the Church and the nation?

➤ What were the features of Marxian socialist theory that increased the likelihood of revolution?

I THE EXISTING ORDER: THE CAPITALIST SYSTEM

By the mid-nineteenth century the practices and the products of **capitalism** were apparent all over the world. The theory of capitalism was that if free enterprise was permitted, individuals would exert themselves in the search for profits. The competition thus generated would hold prices down, so that everybody would benefit. Early capitalist governments were expected to adopt a policy of *laissez-faire* (let things be), meaning that there should be as few regulations as possible within the basic needs of law and order, and that the profit motive should be allowed to function as the incentive for business enterprises.

However, although this system brought prosperity to people in some countries, the wealth was usually very unevenly distributed. There was a rich investing class but also large numbers of poorly paid workers.

By the mid-nineteenth century many criticisms could be directed at the workings of capitalism. In theory all people with initiative could benefit from the free-enterprise system and ensure their own affluence, and in fact it was common in the capitalist heyday to regard any poor person as being a victim of his or her own laziness. But it was often the case that honest workers were unemployed or poverty-stricken through no fault of their own. Their livelihood was at the mercy of shifting demand,

'Over London by Rail', an engraving by Gustave Dore, 1872. Dore was an artist who drew pictures of industrial Europe. Here he depicts a dismal section of the slums of London. Trains and factories added smoke to the smog-filled air. Look at the people crowded in the narrow backyards, peering out of windows, and the sameness of all the houses. These people had journeyed to the industrial cities in search of employment, but their standard of living was steadily diminished.

production for goods, changing fashions and world-wide trade recessions.

Capitalists claimed that open competition between producers would benefit all sections of the community through the forcing down of prices. However, when a major producer reached the stage of being able to buy out his competitors, competition no longer applied; a monopoly had been created in which high prices could be demanded.

Socialist opponents of capitalism also pointed out that the application of *laissez-faire* policies greatly disadvantaged the workers. Labour was treated as just another commodity, to be 'purchased' as cheaply as possible. In the decades when *laissez-faire* prevailed, in Britain up to the 1830s for example, there were no government-imposed regulations covering

workers' wages and conditions. As a result, workers were grossly exploited through being forced to work long hours for little reward. Although the workers received only meagre wages, their skills and labour brought rich returns to investors.

Capitalist nations, as bitter rivals for markets, sources of raw materials, and fields for investment, also became competitors for empires. In imperialist wars the common people, conscripted into armed forces through the emotional appeal of nationalism, became 'cannon fodder' for the interests of their capitalist masters.

For these reasons, socialists argued that a capitalist society created inequalities, fostered severe class distinctions, and robbed millions of people of their basic rights of human dignity and personal fulfilment. Socialists claimed that

Slum conditions in an industrial city in Britain, late nineteenth century. In the rush to build living quarters for wage-earners close to factories, little thought was given to urban planning, and the residential slums were located within walking distance from the factories. The extreme pollution of the atmosphere through the combustion of fossil fuels is emphasised in this sketch. What evidence is there that the sketch pre-dates the invention of electricity?

A Call to Revolution: The Challenge of Socialism

piecemeal reforms could not remedy the evils of capitalism; what was needed was a total transformation into a socialist society in which all people could be equal.

The theory of **socialism** stressed that the major source of discontent in society was this uneven distribution of resources. Socialists argued that if the means of production were owned by society itself instead of by private capitalists, then wealth could be evenly shared and poverty eliminated. Socialism therefore advocated the replacement of private ownership with social or community control.

II REVOLUTIONARY IDEAS AND LEADERS

The idea that inequalities in society were unjustified was not new. In classical times, in the eras of Buddha and Christ, and in the medieval period, thinkers and writers had stressed that a more even distribution of wealth could promote greater human happiness. Social injustices led people to believe that a better structure of society could be planned. Many visionaries devised idealistic but apparently unattainable 'Utopian' societies (named after the ideal community governed by moral principles portrayed in Sir Thomas More's *Utopia*, published in 1516).

The Age of Reason left a legacy: a belief that humankind could find a rational solution to society's problems; that is, by planning social reforms rather than accepting conditions as they were and looking forward to happiness in the next life, a community could achieve improvements.

The process of secularisation added to this trend; if humanity's major problems were material (rather than spiritual), perhaps there was a secular remedy. The critics of the Church pointed out that it had failed to alleviate the problems of the masses, and that there was perhaps another way.

French and British Influences

Although the most influential leaders of the French Revolution were capitalist-aligned

(stressing that ownership of property was one of the basic human rights), a socialist-inclined movement emerged from the French Revolution under the leadership of François Babeuf (1760–97), who argued that all men had equal rights (a) to enjoy the goods provided by nature; (b) to be assured of fruitful employment; and (c) to receive an education; and that these objectives, involving a more equal distribution of wealth, could best be attained if the resources of production were owned by the government instead of by individuals. Babeuf's ideas did not produce much effect at the time, and he died on the guillotine in 1797, but his arguments became influential in later years.

The Revolutionary and Napoleonic periods in France further opened the way to socialism by demonstrating that an established order was not necessarily permanent. The path to change was opened up; the feudal system was destroyed, and old loyalties to feudal overlords and local districts were replaced by devotion to 'the nation'. But this also made possible a different loyalty—loyalty to a particular social class.

By the 1820s it was clear, in fact, that class conflict between the capitalists and the proletariat was likely if not inevitable. It was in this period that the word 'socialists' came into circulation to describe those who were seeking a complete transformation of the economic and moral bases of society by replacing private control of production with *social control*. Disadvantaged workers supported this theory; property-owning capitalists saw it as a deadly enemy.

In the early nineteenth century several important ideas were added to the socialist theory. Count Henri de Saint-Simon (1760–1825), a Frenchman, argued that one of the main causes of poverty was waste of resources, and that this could be overcome through government-owned industries and central planning. Saint-Simon thus foreshadowed the socialist planned economy.

Robert Owen (1771–1858), a British industrialist and employer, claimed that workers would be more productive if they enjoyed good working and living conditions, and that it was the responsibility of employers to consider the welfare of their employees. Owen thus helped pioneer the 'welfare state' strand of socialism— the theory that the employer (which would be the government in a socialist society) should assume responsibility for both the working and the living conditions of the people.

A further dimension was added in France by Louis Blanc (1811–52) and his supporters. During the months of violence in Paris in 1848, when the bourgeoisie and the proletariat were competing for political control, Blanc strongly promoted the concept that the people had a 'right to work', and that the government should compete with private enterprise by opening national workshops (government-owned factories) in which the people could obtain satisfying work under good conditions for a fair wage. The French national workshops did not fulfil Blanc's principles, and their closure precipitated the dreadful carnage of the 1848 'June Days' conflict in Paris, when the bourgeoisie and the proletariat fought one another in a virtual civil war. The bourgeoisie victory demonstrated the determination with which the capitalists would oppose socialist ideas. The 'national workshops' issue nevertheless added another strand to socialist development in the assumption that a government should create employment opportunities.

Socialism by the 1840s

By the mid-nineteenth century the socialists, through activity and debate, had established the following doctrines:

- Inequality was an unnatural denial of human rights, and prevented individuals from developing their natural abilities.
- Social classes were not ordained by God, nor should it be expected that a person should remain permanently in a fixed 'station in life'.
- The State could be the means by which wealth was more evenly distributed, and suffering diminished. A planned (government-controlled) economy could override the selfish individualism generated by the profit motive and use resources to ensure human progress.
- The employer (which would be a State-owned enterprise in a socialist society) should take responsibility for both the working and the living conditions of the people. This foreshadowed the 'welfare state' of the twentieth century.
- Workers were entitled to expect that they would be gainfully employed.
- The capitalist structure of society was vulnerable, and could be overthrown.

The major obstacle to socialist goals was the sheer power of the capitalist ruling classes. As the terrible events of the June Days had shown, the workers' courage was no match for the firepower of troops. In most Western nations the bourgeoisie controlled the means of enforcing law and order, and could suppress pro-socialist uprisings or attempted seizures of power.

III MARXIAN SOCIALISM AND THE PREDICTION OF REVOLUTION

During the nineteenth century, as the poor classes—the proletariat—expanded in numbers, belief in socialism gained so much vigour that millions came to believe that their loyalty lay, not with the nation, but with what they called an 'international brotherhood of workers' dedicated to establishing a socialist reorganisation of the world. Thus the forces of nationalism were countered by the challenge of socialism.

Much of this change in loyalty was generated by the writings of Karl Marx and Friedrich Engels, whose theories aroused a hope that society could be reformed. In examining the nature of capitalist Europe in the nineteenth century, Marx and Engels stated that the history of humanity was the history of class struggles, but that all this would be ended when the proletariat overthrew the middle-class system of ownership and set up a proletarian system of common ownership of the factors of production (land, labour and capital).

SOURCE 5.1

Marx and Engels claim that all History has been a history of class struggles, and that the proletariat is destined to win power and establish a system of social ownership, 1848

HISTORICAL CONTEXT: The year 1848 was a year of turmoil and revolutionary activity throughout Europe. Most of these uprisings and protests were nationalist and liberal in character, rather than socialist or communist. Nevertheless, many historians now regard the publication of *The Communist Manifesto* as the most important single event of 1848. Translated into scores of languages, it became the inspiration for proletarian-based, anti-capitalist movements throughout the world.

Source: **K. Marx and F. Engels,** *The Communist Manifesto*, **1848**

The movements within middle-class society, as well as in feudal and ancient society, where freeman and slave, patrician and plebeian, baron and serf, guild-master and journeyman, capitalist and working man stood and stand in constant antagonism to one another, prove that the whole history of mankind since the rise of private ownership is the history of class struggles, and that in these class struggles, carried on now openly, now under the surface, either new forms of society and of ownership, new economic systems arise or else end with the common destruction of the two classes.

The antagonistic classes are supporters of conflicting economic interests, systems of ownership and ideals of culture. The craftsman and tradesman of the towns, the burgher, fought against the feudal lord and knight for individual property, for freedom of industry and trade, for freedom to dispose of personal property and for the national State.

With the triumphal progress of the middle-class, private property fell into fewer and fewer hands. The proletarians are without property, they have no share in the wealth of their country; on the other hand, the production of capital becomes more and more a matter of common co-operation, and capital becomes a joint product. The proletariat can, accordingly, no

longer fight for individual ownership but for the socially conducted utilisation of the means of production belonging to the community and of the goods produced. The middle class has therefore created in the proletariat a social class which must have as its object to do away with the middle-class system of ownership and to set up the proletarian system of common ownership.

In this struggle of the working classes the Communists are therefore the pioneers of the movement. They are at once the philosophers and the self-sacrificing champions of the proletariat awakened into class consciousness.

The Communists lay stress on the common interests of the whole proletariat and of the collective movement. Their aim is the organisation of the proletariat into a class, the overthrow of middle-class domination, and the conquest of political power by the proletariat. They support everywhere any revolutionary movement against the existing social and political conditions.

QUESTIONS

1 On what basis, according to Marx and Engels, have classes been antagonistic to one another over the 'history of mankind'?

2 In the second paragraph Marx and Engels use the class rivalry of the feudal system to illustrate a 'cause' for which a struggle was raised. What was the 'cause' at issue?

3 The authors claim that the only way that the proletariat can improve its position in the nineteenth century (the time of publication) is to campaign for a new system of 'ownership'. What is this proposed system, and what should it achieve for the proletariat?

4 What motivation appears to be operative to encourage working-class people to support the communist movement?

Socialism was thus transformed from a vague collection of idealistic principles into a world force by the intellectual energies of these two men. Marx (1818–83) was a German Jew by birth, although his family adopted the Christian religion. Engels (1820–95) was the son of a successful German industrialist, sent to England as the Manchester agent of his father's business.

In 1848, the 'year of revolutions' (when proletarian uprisings occurred in almost all of the monarchies of Europe), Marx and Engels published *The Communist Manifesto*, a document that may not have attracted much attention at the time but whose publication must now rank as the single most important event of that year. The *Manifesto* was a statement for action. It began with these words: *'A spectre is haunting Europe—the spectre of communism'*, and concluded with the prediction that communists seek the *'forcible overthrow of every obtaining order of society'*.

The working people of the world, it was said, had *'nothing to lose but their chains'*. This was a clear call for revolution. Marx and Engels also said: *'Let the ruling classes tremble before a communist revolution'*, and tremble they did for the next 145 years.

In their manifesto Marx and Engels converted the vague expressions of optimism and idealism that had characterised early communist thought into a forceful, logical statement. Marx called it 'scientific socialism', applying scientific principles of cause and effect, interaction and result.

Socialism was depicted as a social and political system that would inevitably come about as the result of predictable forces in History. The Marxian formula rested on an interpretation of History as a series of class struggles. Any dominant ruling class, Marx predicted, will eventually be challenged by a new rising class and be overthrown. The capitalist ruling classes were therefore destined to lose their control of society.

Marx and Engels argued that the free-enterprise system of production was chaotic and socially unjust. Emphasis on the search for profit produced economic conditions that

Karl Marx (1818–83). Marx was born at Trier in the Rhineland region of Germany, into a German-Jewish family that had accepted Protestant Christianity. As a student in Bonn and Berlin he adopted socialist ideals, and in association with Friedrich Engels (1820–95) published *The Communist Manifesto* in 1848. To escape persecution he fled in 1849 to London, where he spent the remainder of his life. The first volume of his massive critique of capitalism (*Das Kapital*) was published in 1867. Marx claimed that the history of all peoples was the history of class rivalries, and that eventually the proletariat would overthrow the bourgeois system of private ownership of the factors of production. A system of social ownership (socialism) would then follow, ensuring an equitable distribution of wealth. Marx wrote: 'The philosophers have interpreted the world in different ways; the point, however, is to change it.'

fluctuated wildly between booms and depressions, with their associated problems of mass unemployment. If the evils of inequality were to be eliminated, the system of private ownership practised under capitalism would have to be replaced by the common, or social, ownership of the factors of production. The term 'socialism' was derived from this concept.

Friedrich Engels (1820–95), like Karl Marx, was born in Germany. The son of a successful textile manufacturer, he became his father's agent in Britain. Although an industrialist himself, he was appalled at the effects of the *laissez-faire* policy upon the living conditions of the workers. He published a book on this subject, and supported the Chartist movement in Britain. In 1844 he visited Marx in Paris, and the two men found they had independently arrived at almost identical opinions on the nature of social problems and the need for a communist revolution. In Marx's later years Engels assumed the role of Marx's supporter, both intellectually and financially. It has been claimed that Engels wanted to ensure that 'the world's greatest thinker should be allowed time to think'. After Marx's death in 1883, Engels edited the second and third volumes of Marx's great work, *Das Kapital*.

With public ownership of the factors of production, a **planned economy** could operate. This would eliminate depressions and uncertainties and safeguard the welfare of the people.

Such optimistic predictions were not new; they had been the basis of socialist thought for decades. Marx and Engels added an extra dimension, a formula for achieving a socialist world. They did not simply write and talk about what they hoped would occur; they explained how they were going to reach this goal.

Marx adapted from the German philosopher Friedrich Hegel (1770–1831) the theory of the 'dialectic'. Hegel argued that development or change is a result of a 'clash of opposite forces', a process from which a solution, or new situation, is produced. Struggle, or conflict, is essential to the process. But while Hegel thought in terms of conflict between cultures or races, Marx applied the dialectic principle to the conflict between opposing classes.

Marx related all his thinking on class interests and the behaviour of the leaders of social classes to material factors. He wrote that 'the mode of production of material life determines social, political and intellectual life processes in general'; that is, he claimed that it was what humankind produced and who owned it that determined the nature of society. Material factors were more important than religions or other ideologies in shaping society. Because Marx combined a materialist interpretation of historical development with the theory of the dialectic, his philosophy has been termed **dialectical materialism**.

The theory of the dialectic can be understood if you visualise a *thesis*, or starting point; an **antithesis**, or opposing force; and a *synthesis*, which is the new situation resulting from this conflict of opposites. Marx argued that a process can be observed throughout History in which a dominant class (the thesis) is challenged by a counterforce (the antithesis), producing a new dominance (the synthesis). In referring to the overthrow of the feudal system, for example, he wrote: 'The modern bourgeois society that has sprouted from the ruins of feudal society has not done away with class antagonisms. It has but established new classes, new conditions of oppression.' The rise of the bourgeoisie, Marx observed, had also ensured the growth of the proletariat, the counterforce destined to destroy capitalism by revolution.

Friedrich Engels sums up the importance of the intellectual theories of Karl Marx, 1883

HISTORICAL CONTEXT: Much of the influence achieved by Karl Marx's theories was attributable to the work of his collaborator, Friedrich Engels. German-born, Engels lived in England from 1849, ironically as a wealthy industrialist managing his father's investments in British industry. It was Engels's translations of Marx's writings that ensured the influence of Marxian philosophy in the English-speaking world. In this speech at Marx's graveside, Engels stressed the significance of Marx's perception of the role of materialist forces in History.

Source: F. Engels, quoted in M. Beer, *The Life and Teaching of Karl Marx*, George Allen & Unwin, London, 1925, p. 92

Just as Darwin discovered the law of the evolution of organic nature, so Marx discovered the evolutionary law of human history—the simple fact, hitherto hidden under ideological overgrowths, that above all things men must eat, drink, dress, and find shelter before they can give themselves to politics, science, art, religion, or anything else, and that therefore the production of the material necessaries of life and the corresponding stage of economic evolution of a people or a period provides the foundation upon which the national institutions, legal systems, art, and even religious ideas of the people in question have been built, and upon which, therefore, their explanation must be based, a procedure the reverse of that which has hitherto been adopted.

QUESTIONS

1 What relationship is postulated between politics, science, religion etc. and the 'material necessaries of life'?

2 What effect did the discovery attributed to Marx have upon political theories and political parties in later years?

The organisers of this impending revolution (the 'communists', as Marx called them) would have the task of developing the proletariat into a politically conscious class, which could then achieve the forcible overthrow of the bourgeois state. Once the capitalist-dominated society had been destroyed, however, the next cycle in the operation of dialectical materialism would be permanent, because instead of the synthesis taking the form of yet another dominance of one class over the others, a classless society would be created. The factors of production would be owned by the community, so there would be no material basis for a ruling class This, Marx said, would be true communism.

Marx added that to eradicate the evils of capitalism effectively, a short-lived dictatorship by the proletariat would be necessary. The State, in its role as a means by which one class held others in oppression, would then 'wither away'.

The Revolutionary Appeal of Marxian Socialism

As the ideas of **Marxian socialism** reached the masses, they gained hope and optimism. Marxism, in effect, said that the capitalist stage of development was essential; but even as the capitalists gathered their profits, they were ensuring their own ultimate defeat because the proletariat, which would overthrow them, was steadily growing in power. The proletariat was being told that the machines that enslaved them were, by the logic of History, undermining the capitalist system. Marxist ideas gave the socialist movement an air of certainty.

Thus was created a new faith—a secular faith with the force and effectiveness of a religion. The workers were encouraged to identify themselves with the force of the belief, and drew collective strength from it. They were encouraged to develop a new loyalty to the proletariat as a revolutionary class instead of to

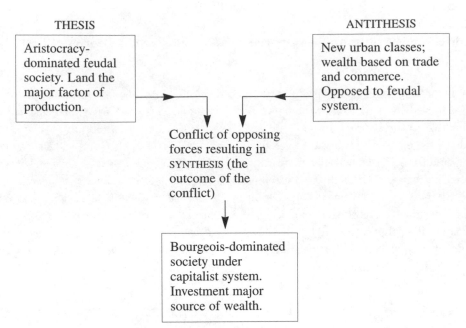

THESIS

Aristocracy-dominated feudal society. Land the major factor of production.

ANTITHESIS

New urban classes; wealth based on trade and commerce. Opposed to feudal system.

Conflict of opposing forces resulting in SYNTHESIS (the outcome of the conflict)

Bourgeois-dominated society under capitalist system. Investment major source of wealth.

The synthesis, or last stage, of the earlier cycle would become the thesis, or beginning stage, of the next cycle.

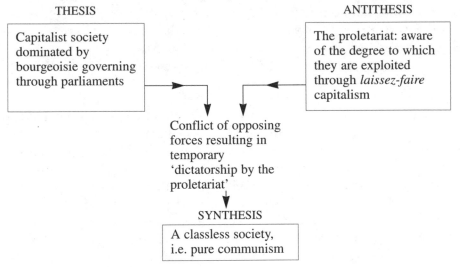

THESIS

Capitalist society dominated by bourgeoisie governing through parliaments

ANTITHESIS

The proletariat: aware of the degree to which they are exploited through *laissez-faire* capitalism

Conflict of opposing forces resulting in temporary 'dictatorship by the proletariat'

SYNTHESIS

A classless society, i.e. pure communism

DIAGRAM 5.1 The theory of dialectical materialism

The Marx-Engels theory of dialectical materialism was based on the premise that all changes in History are the result of conflicts between opposing material forces. The operation of the dialectic (conflict of opposites) can be understood with reference to a *thesis*, or starting point; the *antithesis*, or opposing force; and the *synthesis*, which is the new situation resulting from this conflict of opposites. Marx explained that a process can be observed throughout History in which a dominant class (the thesis) is challenged by a counterforce (the antithesis), to produce a new dominance (the synthesis).

In pre-industrial Europe the dominant class had been the landowning aristocracy, governing through the feudal system. The Industrial Revolution had produced an opposing force, the urban commercial class. Through the conflict of opposites, the bourgeoisie had thus emerged as the new dominant class. By the mid-nineteenth century, in the opinion of Marx and Engels, the effect of the 'conflict of opposites' was on the verge of bringing about the overthrow of this bourgeois dominance by the new force in society, the proletariat.

the nation, which only sent them off to die in imperialist wars. A world-wide revolution would come, and they would be part of the greatest movement in History.

Marx expanded upon his economic theories in his great work, *Das Kapital* (1867). He claimed that under the capitalist system the skilled workers created wealth by transforming raw materials into products, but received only a small fraction of this new wealth in their wages. The remainder (the *surplus value*) passed into the hands of greedy capitalists. In the classless society after the revolution, this wealth could be entrusted to the community and evenly distributed for the benefit of all.

Marxism thus also implied a promise of improved living standards. It said to the poor that it was not their fault that they were poor, and that greed and profiteering, which made capitalists rich and workers poor, would be eliminated in a new classless society in which everyone would find fulfilment. Conflict and hatred would disappear because the State would no longer be the means by which one class oppressed another. Humankind would create a co-operative, rational society in which everyone would be freed from the dehumanising effects of slavery to technology, and the alienation of people from their essential humanity (under the capitalist system) would be reversed.

Marxism appealed to a wide range of classes: to the proletariat, as a means of ending their misery; to anti-Christians, because it offered a secular society; and to intellectuals, because it was based on rational arguments. Most significantly, Marx's theories were convincing. His philosophies explained the process of revolution, and his economic theories justified it.

Marxism was different from earlier socialist movements because it was more than a utopian dream. It was a plan for action. Marx talked about changing the world. His ideas have changed it more effectively and more significantly than any other force in modern history. By the 1970s approximately half the world's population was living under Marxist governments. Yet, in the late 1980s there were massive rejec-

tions of Marxist principles in Eastern Europe and the USSR. It was widely claimed that Marxism as a system had failed.

What is still to be experienced, however, is how influential Marxist teachings will continue to be, even as a doctrine to be argued against. The dialectic principle—the conflict of opposites—may now be seen to operate in relation to Marxist theory itself. Marx may have been wrong—millions of words have been written to prove it—but if so, he has been more influentially 'wrong' than any other philosopher in history.

IV OTHER PROPOSED FORMS OF SOCIALISM

Not all socialist thinkers have supported Marxian theories, particularly in the form in which they emerged in the Union of Soviet Socialist Republics after 1917, and in other nations after World War II.

The **anarchist socialists** are similar to the Marxists in that they believe that a centralised system of government (the State) is an instrument of repression. Anarchism is the ideology which rejects all centralised forms of authority (*a*, without; *narkhos*, a ruler). Anarchists totally reject the concept of a central government.

The most influential anarchist spokesperson, Frenchman Pierre Proudhon (1809–65), proclaimed that 'property is theft'. The anarchists believe that State-owned factors of production are almost as unsatisfactory as private capitalism. Marx's 'dictatorship by the proletariat' would be, in their view, another tyrannical form of centralised government. True liberty of the individual and true economic equality, can only be attained, the anarchists believe, if the State itself were abolished and the working people organised into 'communes' of several hundred families, loosely linked with other communes in an association pledged to mutual aid.

Some branches of the anarchists have proposed the use of extreme violence and widespread civil disobedience to destroy the State. In recent decades many idealist socialists have

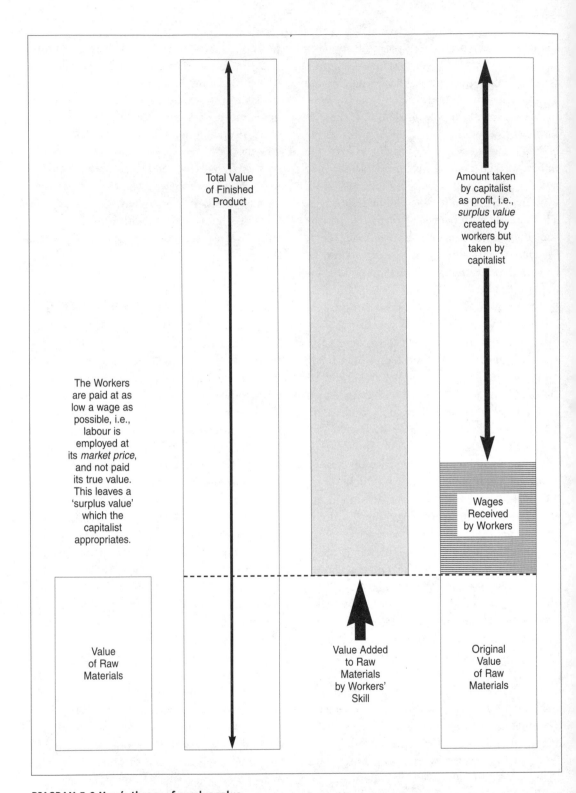

The Workers are paid at as low a wage as possible, i.e., labour is employed at its *market price*, and not paid its true value. This leaves a 'surplus value' which the capitalist appropriates.

Total Value of Finished Product

Amount taken by capitalist as profit, i.e., *surplus value* created by workers but taken by capitalist

Wages Received by Workers

Value of Raw Materials

Value Added to Raw Materials by Workers' Skill

Original Value of Raw Materials

DIAGRAM 5.2 Marx's theory of surplus value

Marx claimed that most of the value of a manufactured or processed product was added to the original raw materials by the workers' skill and labour, but only a fraction of this was passed on to the workers in wages. This 'extra value', taken by the capitalist as profit, was described by Marx as 'surplus value'.

returned to an emphasis on anarchism because they believe that the post-1917 developments in Russia have shown that Marxian socialism simply ensures a return to rule by an authoritarian state. The anarchists fly a black flag in contrast to the red flag of Marxian socialism.

The **Fabian socialists** disagree with the Marxian emphasis on seeking change through violence. While they seek an equitable distribution of wealth, and support the idea that society itself should own many of the factors of production, they believe that essential reforms are best achieved by gradual methods.

The Fabian Society, founded in 1884 in England, argued for a step-by-step and peaceful transformation of society from capitalism to socialism. The name was derived from Quintus Fabius Maximus (died 203 BC), the Roman general who applied the policy of wearing down Hannibal, the Carthaginian invader, by slow but sure strategies. The early twentieth-century Fabians wanted to achieve a great improvement in the welfare of the people without destroying the structure of political democracy. Rather, they intended to gain power through the existing institutions by forming a socialist political party and seeking votes. The plan was to attain political power through the ballot-box, and put socialist theories into practice after this had been done.

During the nineteenth century the Fabian principle of gradual change did not attract a great amount of working-class support because, in their oppressed and miserable state, the workers were eager for more rapid change. Later, as the Labo(u)r parties of Britain and Commonwealth nations (including Australia) and the Social Democratic parties of Western Europe were formed to apply Fabian principles, working-class people used their newly won voting rights to support them.

The Fabian parties' emphasis was on gradually transforming the capitalist state into a welfare state, in which the wealth of society would be extensively redistributed to the poor, not solely or necessarily as cash, but also in the form of such welfare services as free schools, free hospitals, workers' benefits and child endowments. They wanted to achieve a semi-planned economy. This involved a large degree of public ownership of the means of production, but not necessarily total nationalisation of all the factors of production. The semi-planned economy would put enough restrictions on free enterprise to prevent recessions and their accompanying distress. Government or community ownership of some of the major industries would ensure that goods would be produced to meet public need and not just for profit, and the proceeds of the successful industries would be available for distribution to the people.

Fabian socialist ideas aroused less animosity in Western societies than did Marxian socialism because Fabianism did not advocate violence and the overthrow of the constitution, nor did it preach a doctrine of world revolution. A person could be a Fabian socialist and remain loyal to his or her nation. Moreover, Fabian socialists did not propose the abolition of other political parties.

V SOCIALISM AS A FORCE OPPOSING EXISTING LOYALTIES

Socialism was in opposition to liberalism, because socialism rejected the liberal ideals of individualism and competition. In the opinion of socialists, these principles encouraged greed and accentuated inequalities in society. Socialists wanted a more co-operative society, with a system of government that put the welfare of the people before that of the property-owners. Their emphasis was less on political democracy (in which persons might be equal only on election days), and more on what they termed 'social democracy'—equality in society.

All socialists aimed to modify or destroy the capitalist system because they believed it inevitably created monopolistic practices through which the wealthy became more wealthy and the wage-earning class remained poor while being denied the fair rewards of their labour. The more extreme socialists (the

After the Franco-Prussian War (1870), the citizens of Paris were resentful of the decisions of the national government, which by that time was seated at Bordeaux. The Parisians were offended by the government's decision to allow German occupation forces into Paris, and were also opposed to the government's proposal to restore the monarchy. When the Bordeaux government troops attempted to confiscate the arms of the Parisians, they rose in revolt, proclaiming the independence of Paris under a government of its own—the Paris Commune, broadly based on communist principles. This photograph shows some of the 'communards', at a barricade on Rue St. Sebastien, armed and ready to resist the government troops sent to suppress them. In the terrible fighting that ensued, more people were killed in Paris than during the 'Terror' of the 1789–99 Revolution. Both sides committed deplorable atrocities. The suppression of the Commune supplied the world communist movement with a group of martyrs to be admired for their devotion and sacrifice.

communists) believed that the exploitation of the masses could only be stopped if the capitalist system were overthrown by force, and factories and farms were taken over by society. This was described as the social ownership of the factors of production.

Socialist teachings also rejected nationalism. Marxian socialism was in theory a form of internationalism; it proposed that proletarians of all nations should work together in a spirit of solidarity to destroy the capitalist system and the nationalist governments which supported it. Loyalty to the nation was to be superseded by loyalty to the proletariat of the world, and to the concept of ultimate co-operation.

Marxian socialism was thus an anti-nationalist force; it encouraged workers to forget that they were Germans or French or British, and to devote their faith to a new ideal and a new association. A better society would be attained through the '**world revolution**'. Fabian socialists, however, did not regard a world revolution as necessary or practicable; they planned to achieve reform within the nation and through the existing institutions of parliamentary government by bringing in extended franchise. They did not seek the destruction of the nation.

Imperialism, too, was condemned by the socialists. In their opposition to all forms and practices of inequality, they labelled empires as one of the evils of capitalism, because empires resulted in the exploitation of subject peoples. The colonial subjects of the capitalist imperial powers were regarded as part of the world-wide proletariat. The revolution would bring equality to all races and all peoples.

Similarly, the Marxists opposed religious practices, claiming that they were used to indoctrinate the working classes into obedience to the beliefs of their masters and overlords. Marx had written that religion was but 'the opiate of the masses'; a means of keeping them passive with promises of a better life after death. He claimed that religion was used to delude the people and should be eliminated in the secular society that would be set up after the proletarian-led revolution.

Effects of Socialist Teachings

Socialism in its various forms aroused fears among many different groups. People who believed in liberalism, multi-party democracy, capitalism, property ownership, nationalism and racial superiority all feared and suspected socialism. Because it was also opposed to any religion, so too did Christians, Moslems, Buddhists and Hindus.

But to millions of starving poverty-stricken, underprivileged people in countries all over the world, socialist theories (or the versions of the theories that were explained to them) aroused hopes for better standards of living and a more even sharing of wealth. If reforms could only be achieved through revolution, then as Marx said, these people had 'nothing to lose but their chains', and would be very likely to support revolutionary action.

Animosities inevitably developed between those who supported and opposed socialist theories. Animosities and suspicion produce conflict, and the source of the conflict is still with us today.

MAJOR EVENTS ASSOCIATED WITH THE GROWTH OF SOCIALIST AND COMMUNIST THEORIES AND PRACTICES 1796–1919

1796 Francois Babuef, a political agitator in Paris, advocated a communist 'republic of equals' in which all men [sic] would have an equal share in property

1820 Count Henri de Saint-Simon (in France) proposed social ownership of industries and central planning as a means of avoiding waste of resources

1821 Charles Fourier (in France) proposed the organisation of society into 'phalanxes': small, co-operative communities that would share resources and eliminate the 'evils' of competition

1824 Repeal of the Combination Acts in Britain allowed British wage-earners to form trade unions (a modifying act in 1825 prohibited strike action, and so made trade unions virtually powerless)

1834 Formation in England of the Grand National Consolidated Trades Union, led by Robert Owen, for the purpose of organising a general strike for an 8-hour day (thus demonstrating socialist priorities)

1836 A Communist League was formed in Paris

1839 Louis Blanc, in France, published *L'Organisation du travail*, which proposed 'national workshops' for the unemployed, and recognition of the 'right to work' for all. Blanc is credited with being the originator of the socialist formula: 'From each according to his ability; to each according to his need.'

1840 P.J. Proudhon published *Qu'est ce que la Propriete?*, in which he claimed that 'property is theft'. Proudhon favoured the organisation of society into communes, with no central government.

1844 Rochdale Pioneers founded a co-operative society (in Lancashire, England)—a form of socialism in which the workers co-operatively owned a business and returned any profits to the customers in lower prices and shared dividends

1845 Friedrich Engels published *The Condition of the Working Classes in England*, an attack on the capitalist system

1848 Revolts against monarchist rule broke out in Sicily, Naples, Rome, Tuscany, Venice, Berlin, Paris, Vienna; Prince Metternich was forced to resign; end of the 'Metternich system' Abolition of serfdom in Habsburg Empire King Louis Philippe of France abdicated;

France was declared a republic with universal manhood suffrage

National workshops were opened in France to provide work for all

Socialist supporters of Louis Blanc engaged in civil war in Paris (the 'June Days'), but were defeated by the National Guard; national workshops closed

Karl Marx and Friedrich Engels published *The Communist Manifesto*, the most influential of all socialist documents

1850 Taiping Rebellion in China, now regarded by Chinese communists as a genuine proletarian uprising

1861 Emancipation of serfs in Tsarist Russia

1862 Abraham Lincoln, president of the USA, proclaimed emancipation of all slaves (during the American Civil War)

Ferdinand Lasalle of Germany, founder of the German Working Men's Association, announced his 'Working Class Programme', which advocated a system of State socialism

1864 International Working Men's Association founded in London by Karl Marx. This was a federation of working-class parties aimed at the transformation of capitalist societies into socialist communities.

1867 First socialist representative, Ferdinand Bebel, elected to Reichstag of North German Confederation

1871 After the French forces of Napoleon III were defeated by invading German troops, the working classes of Paris declared the 'Paris Commune'—the first communist state. After two months the Commune was destroyed by French soldiers.

1878 Anti-socialist laws were passed in Germany, prohibiting public meetings and publications, driving the socialist movement underground

1884 Fabian Society founded in England, standing for the evolutionary or gradual attainment of socialism to create the 'welfare state'

1889 May Day (1 May)—designated by International Socialist Congress in Paris as the occasion for Labo(u)r Party and socialist political celebrations

1890 German anti-socialist law expired; Social Democratic Party adopted a Marxist programme

1893 Independent Labour Party formed at Bradford, England, under Keir Hardie

1894 Sidney and Beatrice Webb, leaders of the Fabian Society, published *The History of Trade Unionism*

1899 Labor government formed in Queensland, lasting only six days; often called 'the first labour government in the world'

1900 British Labour Party founded

1901 The Social Revolutionary Party was organised in Russia. Italian socialists used strike action to extend their political influence.

1902 Lenin published *What Is To Be Done?*, which put forward a programme for socialist revolution in Russia

1904 First Labor government formed for Commonwealth of Australia, with John Watson as prime minister

1905 'Bloody Sunday' uprising in St Petersburg, Russia. Russian workers formed first 'soviet' (workers' council). Protesting workers were fired upon by troops.

1912 After the 1911 revolution which deposed the emperor of China, the Guomindang, led by Sun Yatsen, emerged as a political party with some socialist principles among its policies

1914 Outbreak of 'The Great War' amongst the imperialist powers

1917 Revolutions in Russia resulted in overthrow of the Tsar Nicholas II, and the seizure of power by the soviets (workers' councils)

Lenin became effective ruler of Russia as 'Chief Commissar of Peoples', proclaiming socialist principles

Lenin published *Imperialism, the Highest Stage of Capitalism*, which predicted the collapse of the capitalist system

1919 Spartacists (communists) attempted a seizure of power in Berlin; crushed by anti-communist *Freikorps* (ex-servicemen)

A socialist regime, led by Bela Kun, functioned in Hungary for a few months, but was overthrown in August 1919

International Labour Organisation established

Communist Third International founded. Known as the Comintern, it aimed at the overthrow of capitalism throughout the world.

chapter six

The Bolshevik Revolution in Russia in 1917

The system has led, through the perpetual shifting of responsibility, to the annihilation of responsibility; and this in its turn has produced a revolution of irresponsibility. Some people talk as if the revolution were an evil element which had sprung from hell without any cause, a sudden visitation like the plague, as if it were not the absolutely logical and inevitable result of the particular form of bad government which has obtained in Russia during the last twenty years.

M. Baring, *What I Saw in Russia,* **Thomas Nelson, Edinburgh, 1907, p. 240**

Tsarist Russia in the nineteenth century was the most authoritarian of all the nations of Europe. The principles of feudal vassalage and absolute monarchy prevailed. In 1815 one hundred million people lived with the conviction that they owed unquestioning obedience to the tsar.

A rigid mechanism of repression prevented even the discussion of 'human rights'. Censorship and illiteracy combined to ensure that most of the subject peoples of the Russian Empire had never even known of the campaigns for liberalism and democracy that occurred in western and central Europe in the late eighteenth and early nineteenth century.

Yet by 1917 the Tsarist Empire had col-lapsed, and Russia had advanced further along the road to a radical communist organisation of society than any other nation.

Theme Questions

➤ Why did the principle of absolute monarchy prevail in Russia for so much longer than in Western Europe?

➤ What was the nature of the society, and the system of government, which was overthrown by the 1917 revolution in Russia?

➤ Was revolution the only possible course towards a change in Russian society, or could reforms have been achieved by peaceful or gradual means?

➤ When reforms were attempted by the Tsarist regime, why did they create more discontent rather than solve the problems?

I THE NATURE OF THE 'OLD ORDER'

A 'snapshot' of Russia and the territories of the Russian Empire in 1815 would have disclosed a vast community in which class distinction and rigid control were the dominant facts of life. The emperor of the **Romanoff** dynasty the **tsar**—or czar—(derived, like the German word *kaiser*, from the Latin *caesar*) ruled as an absolute

A cartoon portraying the structure of society in Tsarist Russia.

1 Describe each of the six strata, or levels, portrayed, and explain the impression the artist is seeking to convey.

2 What is the overall message the artist is trying to project?

despot from the capital, St Petersburg; the nobility were dominant in the country areas; and the vast majority of the populace endured crippling serfdom. The system of administration was thus feudal in character and **authoritarian** in spirit.

The Structure of Society and the Nature of Economic Practice

The systems of economic practice and the structure of society in pre-revolutionary Russia were so closely inter-related that changes in the one were dependent upon changes in the other.

The economy was almost wholly agricultural, commercial activity was undeveloped, and only rudimentary communications existed. There were 50 million ignorant and backward peasants, yet only (in 1825) 200 000 industrial workers. Such foreign trade as existed was almost totally foreign-sponsored; even as late as 1847 the share of export trade held by Russian firms was as low as 2 per cent. Yet even agricultural practice was unprogressive and unenterprising. Yields did not increase between 1810 and 1870. Methods of production had not changed for centuries. Socially and economically, Russia was still in the Middle Ages.

The Class System

Both the stability and the rigidity of Russian society were a product of the privileged status of the aristocracy and the institution of serfdom. At the beginning of the nineteenth century peasants comprised fifty million of the sixty million people in European Russia (that is, Russia west of the Ural Mountains). Most of the peasants were serfs, living a life of ignorance under a system of bondage akin to slavery.

Some eleven million serfs were 'private serfs', regarded by their aristocratic owners as chattels to be bought and sold with land. Another twelve million were 'State serfs', directly owned by the tsar himself and assigned to work on his estates. The peasant serfs worked for their lords or the State several days a week, but were permitted to cultivate a small area for their own use. For this, however, they were required to make a payment in cash, produce or additional hours of labour. In addition to the peasant serfs there were 'house serfs', who were in effect domestic slaves, the number of whom totalled 1.5 million in 1815.

In essence the social system in nineteenth-century Russia was no different from the most severe forms of feudalism practised in Europe eight hundred years earlier. The serfs were under the complete legal control of their owners; they could not travel or change their place of residence, and could be forced into working extra hours or making higher payments for the use of their land at the whim of their overlord. Brutal floggings and even deportation to Siberia awaited any serf bold enough to oppose the will of the master.

In addition to the State serfs, another large group of disadvantaged persons were bound into an obligation of total obedience to the tsar. Serfs were drafted into the army at the command of the emperor, and landlords could send a domestic serf into army service as punishment. To be sent into the army was to pass into another life, because the length of service was twenty-five years. A soldier's wife was, in effect, a widow. The children of the marriage were reared in a military orphanage—also to become soldiers in time. The army under Tsar Nicholas I numbered 1 500 000, and was controlled by an inhuman system of brutal punishments. Floggings were administered for even minor offences, and the rigid class structure ensured that the ordinary soldier had no career path to promotion.

To service such a vast authoritarian society, another quasi-army, the **bureaucracy**, was required for administrative purposes. These officials, or *chinovniks*, exceeded half a million in number, and were recruited from the nobility. While controlling all aspects of the administrative machinery, they used their official positions to indulge in bribery, extortion and misappropriation of funds.

The most powerful of the official organisations under the Tsarist system was the security police force. Russia was an authoritarian

'Gambling with Souls', a caricature by Gustave Dore, drawn in the mid-nineteenth century. Wealth in Tsarist Russia was often measured by the number of 'souls' (serfs) owned by the landowner. Dore here shows that he believed that, to the landowners, the serfs were simply property, akin to currency.

society in which the general populace was denied any machinery of justice or recourse to legal appeal: the people had no rights, only orders.

Although the bourgeoisie and the proletariat were active agents for change in the nations of western Europe in the early nineteenth-century, these classes were not yet prominent in Tsarist Russia. Towns were of little importance in this predominantly agricultural society, and commercial activity was on a small scale, so an entrepreneurial bourgeoisie scarcely existed. There was an intellectual middle class, but Tsarist suppression of university teaching in the fields of philosophy and politics stifled its activities and its effectiveness.

The commercial bourgeoisie, when it did emerge in the period of 1880–1900, was a conservative force, allying itself with the landowners in a bid to delay change. Thus Russia did not have a reforming bourgeoisie leading the nation towards liberalism.

Nor was there an active industrial working class capable of exerting much influence. The Industrial Revolution had scarcely touched Russia by 1850. Even by 1855 there were only 483 000 industrial workers in the whole of Russia. As a class they were as yet too small in number, and too lacking in organisation and leadership, to be of influence in society.

The common people, whether private serfs, State serfs or soldiers, were ruthlessly exploited in the interests of the privileged aristocracy and the Tsarist regime. The enslavement of the great majority of the population ensured a stagnant social situation. Enterprise and initiative were stifled; rigid conservatism enforced a resistance to change. Talent was not even discovered, let alone developed.

At a time when the Western nations were accepting the principles of majority rule and the right of the people to 'alter or abolish' governments that failed to uphold their rights, serfdom in Russia paralysed economic growth as surely as it stifled individual liberties.

The Power of the Church

Deeply ingrained in Russian society was a devotion to the Christian Church. The unquestioning acceptance by the mass of the

An English traveller in Tsarist Russia describes the devotion of the peasants to God and the tsar, 1907

HISTORICAL CONTEXT: The British observer who published this report had at the time travelled from north to south and east to west in Tsarist Russia. He claimed that on his observation the Russian peasants were bound to the tsar by an unquestioning sense of loyalty. It was apparent, he said, that any reform movement would have to convince the people that God was not all-powerful and that the tsar did not have God's blessing. Just how difficult this was likely to be was shown by this story.

Source: **M. Baring, *What I Saw in Russia*, Thomas Nelson, Edinburgh, 1907, p. 357**

A Socialist arrived in a village to convert the inhabitants to Socialism. He wanted to prove that all men were equal and that the Government authorities had no right to their authority. Consequently he thought he would begin by disproving the existence of God, because if he proved that there was no God, it would naturally follow that there should be no Emperor and no policeman. So he took a holy image, and said 'There is no God, and I will prove it immediately. I will spit upon this image and break it to bits, and if there is a God He will send fire from heaven and kill me, and if there is no God nothing will happen to me at all.' Then he took the image and spat upon it and broke it to bits, and he said to the peasants, 'You see God has not killed me.' 'No', said the peasants, 'God has not killed you, but we will,' and they killed him.

QUESTIONS

1 What did the socialist believe was a necessary step before the society could advance towards socialism reforms?

2 In what way did the peasants affirm their belief in God?

people of the authority of the tsar was based on the blessings bestowed on the monarch by the Church, in this instance, the branch of the Christian Church known as the Eastern Orthodox, or Russian Orthodox, Church. (In this context 'orthodox' means 'authentic' or 'original'.) The clergy of the Orthodox Church claimed that theirs was the true Christian Church as founded by St Paul, and that their blessing on the tsar was the source of his divine authority to govern 'Holy Russia'.

Devotion to the teachings and priesthood of the Church permeated the whole of Russian society, especially the uneducated and superstitious peasantry. This presented an enormous barrier to reform, because if the authority of the tsar was to be challenged or diminished, it was necessary to convince the common people that God was not all-powerful and that the tsar did not have God's blessing. The achievement of this alteration in attitude was going to be difficult.

II REVOLUTIONARY IDEAS AND LEADERS

Although Tsar Peter the Great (in office 1696–1725) sponsored a major effort to bring to Russian society an awareness of Western culture, he only partially succeeded. The new capital, St Petersburg, displayed Western influences, but the rest of the vast nation continued its long-established way of life. The illiteracy of the vast population also acted as a most effective form of censorship.

The awakening of Europe that followed the French Revolution brought some knowledge of the principles of liberalism to the literate classes of Russia. The Napoleonic invasion of Russia in 1812 confronted the ordinary people of Russia with the challenge of another society—albeit as an intruding enemy. In defeating and repelling Napoleon, the Russians generated a new sense of national pride. To this day the victory over Napoleon is called the 'Patriotic War' of 1812–14.

In expelling the Napoleonic forces, the Russian army marched right across Europe to Paris. The officers and men of the Tsarist forces were able to witness at first hand the progress made in western Europe. If Russia was a victorious great power, they reasoned, its social and administrative systems should not have been so inferior to those of France, the defeated power. Contact with Western principles of legal equality and social liberty fostered among the thinkers of the Russian army a feeling of discontent with the authoritarian character of the Tsarist system. They had become aware of the concept that a ruling body had a duty to respond to the 'general will' and should hold office only with 'the consent of the governed'. On their return to Russia in 1815, officers and men of the Tsarist army carried these ideas and attitudes back into the mainstream of Russian society. They objected to the authoritarianism and repression of the Tsarist regime.

After narrowly surviving a revolt which attempted to overthrow the monarchy (the 'Decembrist Revolt' of 1825), Tsar Nicholas I (1825–55) proceeded to place the subject peoples of the Russian Empire under a harsh regimen known as the 'Nicholas system', one of the most effective of all the autocrat-imposed systems of repression operating in Europe at that time. The 1848 disturbances, which forced Prince Metternich of Austria into exile and plunged the rest of Europe into turmoil, scarcely became news in Russia and did not disturb the tsar's hold on his nation. Censorship was so all-encompassing that the Russian people knew little of Europe, and Europe knew little about Russia.

The repressions of the Nicholas system were of the mind as well as of political action or dissent. Intellectuals had to endure almost complete denial of the freedom to express initiatives or propose alternative systems. Works on logic and philosophy were forbidden. Servility was demanded and expected; the police administration reached into every phase of life, controlling or inspecting all activities of society. The nobility were pressed into the service of the State as members of a ruthless bureaucracy, governing in their own interests but implementing the policies of the tsar. This was the Nicholas system: the total subordination of the largest nation in Europe to the will of one man. Russia was a 'police state'.

In all aspects of life the emphasis was on receiving and obeying instructions. Because there was no mechanism for gradual change, the only possible avenue for an alteration in conditions was the removal of the tsar. As a result, the tsar lived in constant danger of assassination.

Resistance to Western Influences

The relatively slow pace of acceptance of Western ideas in Russia was the result of a combination of two factors—repression and reluctance. The educational institutions of Tsarist Russia laboured under the restrictions of authoritarian control. The study of European constitutional principles and philosophy was forbidden.

Russian educational institutions were devoted to the inculcation of Russian values, with an emphasis upon the acceptance of autocracy and conservatism, and the exclusion of the liberal and democratic teachings of the West. University autonomy and academic freedom disappeared, and the security police saw to it that writers and journalists published only 'acceptable' statements on the nature and organisation of society. Censorship was reinforced by a denial of the right to travel outside Russia. Very few of the tsar's subjects were allowed to expose their minds to the 'corroding' influences of Western society.

Supporting this imposed conservatism was what some historians have adjudged a natural resistance to Western ideas among the leaders of Russian society. The great debating point among the intellectuals, insofar as debate was possible under the conditions of censorship and restrictions on academic freedom, was whether Russia could revitalise itself as a nation. Should the Russians adopt Western ways, or should they concentrate on their own cultural heritage? This debate led to the emergence of two opposed groups—the Westernisers and the Slavophils.

SOURCE 6.2
A French observer visiting Tsarist Russia describes the absolute power exercised by the tsar, and the closed society of the time, 1839

HISTORICAL CONTEXT: The description provided is of Russia at the time of the full operation of the 'Nicholas system', a totally repressive regime.

Source: P.N. Kohler (ed.), *Journey for Our Time: the Journals of Marquis de Custine* (1839), Arthur Barker, London, 1951, pp. 55, 58, 74, 237

One does not die, one does not breathe here except by permission or by imperial order; therefore, everything is gloomy and constrained. Silence presides over life and paralyses it. Officers, coachmen, cossacks, serfs and courtiers are all servants, of different rank, of the same master, and blindly obeying orders they do not understand.

. . . The Russian government is the discipline of the camp substituted for civil order—it is the state of siege become the normal state of society.

The Tsar speaks and everything is done; the life, the fortune of the laity and of the clergy, of the nobility and of the citizens, all depend on his supreme will. He has no opposition, and everything in him appears just—as in the Divinity—for the Russians are persuaded that the Great Prince is the executor of celestial decrees.

The more I see of Russia, the more I understand why the Emperor forbids Russians to travel, and makes access to his country difficult for foreigners.

The political system of Russia could not withstand twenty years of free communication with Western Europe.

. . . this exorbitant power is hurting itself; Russia will not submit to it forever; a spirit of revolt smoulders in the army. The nation has become eager for enlightenment. The Customs Officers cannot keep out thought; armies cannot exterminate it, ramparts cannot stop it; it goes underground; ideas are in the air; they are everywhere, and ideas change the world.

The Russian government is an absolute monarchy moderated by assassination . . . He lives, therefore, between fear and disgust.

QUESTIONS

1 What effect is the writer seeking by stating that the Tsarist government is the 'discipline of the camp'?

2 Explain the meaning of 'the Great Prince is the executor of celestial decrees'.

3 What is implied by the statement that 'the political system . . . could not withstand twenty years of free communication with Western Europe'?

4 What is predicted to overthrow this repressive regime?

5 Describe the frame of reference of the writer.

The *Westernisers* advocated the adoption of the economic organisations, liberal political institutions and cultural dynamism of the West. They favoured the freedom of the individual, in order to liberate talent from the bonds of serfdom and authoritarian control.

The Westerners were opposed by the *Slavophils* (literally, lovers of Slav culture), who argued for a continued emphasis on the virtues of the Slavic, or Russian, way of life. They believed that Russia should make its own improvements based on the best features of its own culture, seeing in the history of Holy Russia and the Orthodox Church a great source of strength capable of revitalising the nation.

III CRISES PRECEDING REVOLUTION

In the three decades after the Napoleonic Wars, Tsarist Russia had not had to test its military strength against any other great power. In the Crimean War (1853–56), Tsar Nicholas I, having become involved in a war with Turkey, found himself fighting against Britain and France as well. British and French support for Islamic Turkey against Christian Russia was based on 'balance of power' principles; they were primarily concerned with the curbing of Russian power. The Russians suffered the humiliation of defeat on their own soil.

The Emancipation of the Serfs 1861

The painful experience of defeat in the Crimean War revived debate on the need for reform in Russian society. The system of serfdom was a blight upon the nation. Tsar Nicholas I having died during the Crimean War, his successor, Alexander II (tsar 1855–81), took the momentous decision to begin a process of reform by emancipating the serfs. In the long term this bold action completely transformed Russian society and the Russian economy, effecting a transition from a feudal to an early capitalist society.

The changes were not achieved painlessly, but the situation demanded reform, and under an autocracy reform could be most effectively initiated by the autocrat himself, especially as it could be controlled from above. Such was the power of the tsar that it was assumed that any edict he issued would be met with the complete compliance of his subjects.

The emancipation of the serfs was a fundamental change to a social system that was ages old. The aristocracy, still very influential, naturally expected to have their interests considered. Alexander II, however, insisted on three principles: (a) the emancipated serfs must be assured of the use of land, and not become a landless mass; (b) the operation must be peaceful; and (c) the serfs must be guaranteed full personal freedom. The Edict of Emancipation, proclaimed in 1861, nevertheless decreed that the 'liberated' serfs would have to pay rent for their land.

When the new regulations took effect, all the private serfs, and later the tsar's serfs and the serfs on State lands, were released from bondage during the period 1861–66. About 50 million people thus received legal freedom, but the landed peasants either had to pay rent or borrow money to become landowners in their own right.

Millions of serfs, although now legally free, therefore found themselves under a crushing debt, labouring to pay their former landlord for their land either by service or labour payments, or making 'redemption payments' to the State over a period of forty-nine years. They had reason to believe that little had altered—that they had been defrauded. They had not attained private ownership of land, and still could not leave the village without police permission. Most were now simply poor wage-labourers instead of serfs. The millions of household serfs were even worse off; they were released without any form of compensation or access to land.

Discontent spread rapidly. The hard truth—that some reforms can actually increase instability in society—was brought home to Tsar Alexander II. In the first four months following the Edict of Emancipation there were over 640 instances of peasant rioting. The poorer serfs became enmeshed in debt and even more impoverished. The rural masses, trusting the tsar, came to suspect that his will had not been implemented and that they had been cheated of their rights. When it became known that the laws as enforced did have the tsar's authority, their disappointment turned to a sense of betrayal. Animosity towards Alexander II grew. The attempt to reform Russian society on the basis of a liberated peasantry had produced another round of problems.

Part of the problem was that even those peasants who did gain land (whilst still carrying the debt of the redemption payments) did not enjoy individual ownership, as did the French peasants, but held the land collectively as a village, or *mir*. The *mir* was responsible for the unpopular task of collecting the redemption payments and for decisions on the cultivation of the land. Thus the Russian peasants found themselves still required to be obedient to a **paternalistic** authority.

Living standards did not improve, and the rapid growth of population between 1870 and 1900 kept most country families at subsistence level. The landowners retained large estates, and

SOURCE 6.3
Tsar Alexander II proclaims the emancipation of the serfs, 1861

HISTORICAL CONTEXT: Tsar Alexander II, son of Nicholas I, although brought up in the Tsarist court and indoctrinated with the traditions of divine right and absolute monarchy, nevertheless became convinced that the emancipation of the serfs was necessary if Russia was to make progress. For this bold reform he was named 'the Liberator'. Despite his readiness to grant gradual reforms, he was assassinated in 1881. The emancipatory pronouncement decreed that the liberated serfs would have to pay rent for their land and acquire loans from the government to enable them to cope over the first few years. This meant that most of them were crippled with debt for decades thereafter.

Source: **Proclamation by Alexander II, Tsar of all the Russians, 3 March 1861**
We, Alexander II, by the grace of God Tsar and Autocrat of all the Russians, King of Poland, Grand Duke of Finland, etc., make known to all our faithful subjects:

. . . The peasants now bound to the soil shall, within the term fixed by the law, be vested with the full rights of free men. The landed proprietors, while they shall retain all the rights of ownership over all the lands now belonging to them, shall transfer to the peasants, in return for a rent fixed by law, the full enjoyment of their cottages, farm buildings, and gardens. Furthermore, in order to assure to the peasants their subsistence and enable them to meet their obligations toward the State, the landlords shall turn over to the peasants a quantity of arable and other land provided for in the regulations above mentioned. In return for these allotments the peasant families shall be required to pay rent to the landlords . . . Since the new organisation, owing to the unavoidable com-

plexity of the changes which it involves, cannot immediately be put into execution, a lapse of time is necessary, which cannot be less than two years . . .

In order to render the transactions between the landlords and the peasants easier, so that the latter may acquire in full proprietorship their houses and the adjacent lands and buildings, the government will grant them assistance, according to a special regulation, through loans of money or a transfer of mortgages encumbering an estate.

When the first rumours of this great reform contemplated by the government spread among the people who were scarcely prepared for it, it gave rise in some instances to misunderstandings among individuals more intent upon liberty than mindful of the duties which liberty imposes. But generally the good sense of the country has asserted itself. It has been understood that the landlords would not be deprived of rights legally acquired, except for a fit and sufficient indemnity [payment], or by a voluntary concession on their part; that it would be contrary to all equity for the peasants to accept the enjoyment of the lands conceded by the landlords without at the same time accepting equivalent charges. And now we confidently hope that the freed serfs, in the presence of the new future which is opened before them, all appreciate and recognise the considerable sacrifices which the nobility has made on their behalf . . .

QUESTIONS

1 Explain why the tsar made provision for loans from the government.
2 What is the principle of 'equity' being put forward by the tsar?
3 On what premise is the tsar arguing that the nobility has made 'sacrifices'?
4 Describe the frame of reference of the tsar as author of this proclamation.

these were looked upon covetously by the struggling peasantry, who became potential supporters of a political party that would offer them the real land possession they sought.

Attempted Reform of Local Government

Alexander II's reforms extended beyond the Edict of Emancipation. The old system of administration, based on the servility of the people to the landed aristocracy, was also destroyed. New local councils, termed *zemstva*, were established in 1864 at both district and provincial levels. Members were elected through electoral colleges on a system that favoured the nobility; nevertheless, the principle of elected representation was admitted. The great step away from total authoritarian control had thus been made.

The *zemstva* had little executive power and were concerned with local matters such as roads, schools, public health and poor relief. But they were intended to allow all classes to share in the conduct of local affairs, and were therefore significant in destroying the monopoly of administrative positions previously held by officialdom and the gentry. They grew into a potent force for liberalism, frequently contesting the actions of the Tsarist bureaucracy.

In 1870 the principle of elected representative bodies was extended to the towns, in which elected town councils called *dumas* were created, with functions similar to those of the *zemstva* in the rural districts.

The introduction of the representative bodies, restricted though their power may have been, further diminished the power of the aristocracy and eroded the centralisation of control that had hitherto operated in Russia. As strict centralisation was relaxed, so did the autonomy of local bodies increase.

Educational Reforms

The greatest achievements of the *zemstva* and *dumas* were in the field of education. It was again Tsar Alexander II who opened the way for progress by breaking down the conservative barriers that had previously dominated. In 1862 it was decreed that only schools actually opened by the clergy could be controlled by the Holy Synod (the controlling body of the Russian Orthodox Church). This meant that schools opened by the local councils were outside Church control, facilitating a great expansion in secular education. In 1856 there were 8 000 elementary schools in European Russia, but by 1880 there were 23 000, of which 18 000 were

financed by the local *zemstva* and therefore secular. In the cities the *dumas* likewise established secular schools. Secondary education was modernised, and opened to a wider section of society.

The great expansion of secular education meant that a large percentage of the Russian people were receiving an education that encouraged critical thinking, whereas the system of Church education tended to inculcate acceptance of authoritarian controls and unquestioning obedience to the absolute power of the tsar.

Effects of Reform on Intellectual Life and Economic Activity

Alexander II, in his reforming period, also relaxed censorship on publications, reestablished the autonomy of the universities, lightened the burden of service in the army, and reformed the court system. His reforms thus touched virtually every aspect of Russian society. The influence of the landowning classes was diminished, the general populace was admitted for the first time into representative bodies— the *zemstva* and *dumas*—and the first breaches in total centralised control were achieved.

The reforms generated economic repercussions. The liberation of the serfs initiated a moderate drift to the cities, producing the first signs of growth in the numbers of the industrial proletariat. When Alexander II took office in 1853, there were 1 110 kilometres of railway; on his death in 1881, there were 23 335 kilometres, much of it built specifically to promote grain export. Credit institutions and municipal and joint-stock (shareholder-owned) banks and companies were also developed in the 1860s, forming the foundations for long-delayed commercial and industrial growth.

By the 1880s, encouraged by this railway expansion and by increases in coal and iron production, the small-business and commercial classes of Russia began to expand their activities and their numbers. With a labour force available as a result of the emancipation of the serfs, only substantial capital investment was lacking, and this began to flow into Russia from Western capitalist nations, particularly from France. Along with Western investment came Western teachings about political and social freedoms.

Return to Repression

Tsar Alexander II found that, although he had begun his work with a genuine reforming zeal, he earned little gratitude from his people. As was the case with many authoritarian rulers before and since, he discovered that the granting of some reforms, however generous the concessions appeared to be, generated a demand for more. Restraints previously endured were now regarded as burdensome. Throughout Russian society there arose a demand for further reforms, including an increase in the scope of responsibilities for elected representative bodies.

In this climate of ferment some groups resorted to terrorism as a means of forcing continued change. In 1866 the first of many attempts on the life of the tsar was made, and this had the effect of inducing Alexander II to abandon his great reform effort.

All the severity of the earlier Nicholas system was now reapplied. The education system was again placed under restrictive controls, and teachers became officials acting on behalf of the government. To combat liberal ideas and Western attitudes, a massive return to classical teaching was decreed, with the exclusion of science, history and geography. The education of women was discouraged. Universities lost much of their freedom of action, travel was again restricted, censorship was imposed upon books and papers, and the newly gained powers of the *zemstva* were curtailed. Russia was again subjected to police-state rule. But the attempts on the life of Tsar Alexander continued. Finally, in 1881, he was killed by a bomb explosion in a St Petersburg street. The 'reforming Tsar' had himself become a victim of the instability produced by his attempts to liberate his people.

IV CONTENDING PROPOSALS FOR A REFORMED SOCIETY

By the 1880s there was widespread agreement among the intellectual leaders of Russian society that there was a need to overthrow the autocratic centralised rule of the tsar in the interests of a more modern, more purposeful Russian nation. But the means of reaching this goal, and the nature of the new society that was to follow, became subjects of much debate and disagreement in the period 1880–1900. As a result, many groups emerged in the Russian intellectual community, each with its theory on how progress could best be achieved for Russia.

The strands of debate were products of the broad division that had already been developed between Slavophils, who favoured the promotion of a Slavonic society, and the Westernisers. But within these broad groupings there were additional factions proposing different policies.

A major Slavophil reformist group, the *populists*, sought total freedom from the centralised control of Tsarism in its opposite—a society organised through a series of loosely linked communes. The populists (or *narodniks*—men of the people) favoured a form of peasant socialism, in which the essentially Russian nature of society could be preserved. They did not support the Marxist idea of urban-based revolution. Believing that the existing *mir*, or peasant commune, could be adapted to become an administrative force, the *narodniks* hoped to save the Russian people from both the all-powerful centralised State and the 'evils' of Western-style individualism.

The 'police state' of Tsarist Russia was further challenged by another revolutionary group known as the *nihilists*. Tsarist autocracy was so entrenched, and so apparently incapable of granting more than token reforms, that the nihilists set out to annihilate (destroy) the existing order as a necessary prelude to reform. Their name was derived from the Latin *nihil*, meaning 'nothing'. The term was introduced into Russian society by the great novelist Turgenev in his *Fathers and Sons* (1862), in which a nihilist was defined as 'a man who does not bow before any authorities, who does not accept any single principle on trust, however much respect surrounds this principle'. The doctrine of nihilism was therefore destructive rather than constructive, but attracted support as a means of expressing extreme disaffection. Many assassination attempts on the tsar and powerful members of the aristocracy were plotted by the nihilists. Their activities further increased police repression.

A 'Westerniser' group, drawn mainly from the relatively small middle class, favoured the transformation of the absolute monarchy into a constitutional monarchy, with real political power vested in an elected parliament, on the British model. Sensible as this may have appeared as an evolutionary step, stemming from the local representative principle established in the *zemstva* and *dumas*, it was seen as a Western formula for change, and was regarded with suspicion by the Slavophils. When the tsar attempted reform along this path with the calling of a national *duma* in 1906, the sense of trust necessary for its success did not emerge.

The strongest sentiment among the bulk of the Russian people was support for socialist-based proposals for reform based on the sharing of production. Supporters of socialism, however, differed in their opinions on the best way to achieve reform, and on the best form for Russia. By the 1890s several groups of socialist activists were operating in Russian society.

The *anarchist socialists* were so called because they favoured the destruction of all components of central government. Largely basing their policies on the theories of the French socialist, Proudhon, the anarchists argued that any centralised government was a form of tyranny, and that they were prepared to work towards its overthrow. But they did have an alternative: they favoured a form of socialism based on small communes in local communities, in which individual freedoms could be assured. Thus although the word 'anarchy' means 'without rule', this group did not stand for total disorder, as some of its critics alleged.

The *Socialist Revolutionary Party* was the successor to the populists of the earlier decades. It was thus of Slavophil disposition. Socialist revolutionaries favoured representative institutions, universal suffrage, the guarantee of civil and personal liberties, and a federal State allowing a large measure of local self-government. They still envisaged a peasant-based form of socialism, believing that capitalism would not develop in Russia, and that the history of Russian communal life would permit a direct leap into a rural-style socialism, omitting the capitalist stage of development that Marx and Engels held as necessary. In their imaginary ideal society, the common ownership of land and property would achieve social ownership vested in the whole nation, eliminating inequalities. The party commanded considerable support in rural areas, but lacked tight organisation. When the revolutionary opportunity came in 1917, it was no match for the well-organised Bolshevik (Marxian Socialist) Party.

It was to be the *Marxian Socialists*—the *Social Democratic Party*—that were to seize power in late 1917 and control Russia (and later the USSR) for 75 years. Because its followers based their beliefs on the teachings of the German-born Marx, this group constituted a Western strand in the reform movement.

The Marxists found their first great leader in George Plekhanov, a former populist who became a convert to Marxism and a supporter of the argument that socialism could be based only on the industrial working class. Plekhanov became, in fact, a rigidly orthodox Marxist, insisting that the whole cycle of the class struggle, as outlined by Marx, had to occur if the revolution was to succeed. Thus he argued that support should be given to the development of capitalist activities in Russia because only when capitalism had called an industrial proletariat into existence could the true socialist revolution take place.

As the Marxists were almost totally city-based, they were readily detected by the Tsarist secret police. Many were imprisoned; others chose exile in foreign countries. In

1898 the Marxists formed themselves into the Social Democratic Labour Party, and it was by this name that they were best known in the pre-revolutionary period. By 1900 the party newspaper *Iskra* (The Spark) was being produced by a rising member of the party, Vladimir Ilyich Ulyanov, known to his colleagues as Lenin. He argued that the old policy of forcing reforms through terrorism was of no value; success lay in the creation and organisation of a tightly disciplined party that could lead and educate the workers in revolutionary activity. **Trade unionism** and mass workers' organisations were of little value, said Lenin, as they left the initiative to the masses themselves, whereas strong direction was required.

Other members of the party, however, rejected this concept of 'managed' revolution. They regarded it as an indefensible manipulation of the masses, and favoured instead a broader party membership and slow, steady progress towards socialism through the expansion of representative institutions such as the *zemstva* and *dumas*.

This difference of opinion came to a head at the 1903 Congress of the Social Democratic Party, held in Brussels, over the manner of organising the party. The followers of Lenin and Plekhanov won, by a narrow margin, a vote to administer the party through a small élite of dedicated militant members. Because this group constituted the majority on this occasion, they became known as the *Bolsheviks* (majority men). The minority group, from 1903 called the *Mensheviks*, had favoured an open socialist party similar to those operating in Western nations. They felt that this would win for the movement the trust and loyalty of the masses. The Bolsheviks believed that such a party would be too easily crushed by Tsarist despotism, and that the particular situation in Russia demanded a more ruthless approach. They later 'proved' their assertions by their success.

V CRISES PRECIPITATING REVOLUTION

Economic Developments

Despite the repressive nature of the Tsarist regime, the 1880s witnessed a steady growth in overseas investment in Russia. This in turn fostered the expansion of the two classes—bourgeoisie and proletariat—that were to be influential in any revolutionary movement.

By the 1880s, encouraged by the huge increases in coal and iron production in the preceding decades and the great growth in railway construction achieved under Alexander II, the small-business and commercial classes of Russia began to expand their activities and their numbers. With a labour force available, a result of the emancipation of the serfs, only large-scale capital investment was lacking, and this began to flow into Russia from Western capitalist nations.

But Russian capitalism, while exhibiting some of the features of Western capitalism, offered also a striking contrast in its high degree of large-scale production (in other words, there were few small firms), and in its close connection with the State in planning and marketing. The State thus became the chief promoter of manufacturing industry, and it was the needs of the State, rather than the profit motive and the motivations of private enterprise, that tended to be the determining factor in the foundation of an industry. Even under Tsarist rule, therefore, Russian industry was State-dominated. Nevertheless, an inevitable consequence of the expansion of industry and commerce was a steady increase in the numbers of both the commercial and the intellectual and professional bourgeoisie.

During the reign of Alexander III (1881–94), industry continued to expand. Although the administration's repression of educational activity was aimed at crushing liberal thought, technical progress was encouraged.

Two years before his death, Alexander III made the most significant executive decision of his reign when he appointed Count Sergius

Witte as finance minister. Witte held this position from 1892 to 1903, and later became prime minister. He vigorously pursued a policy encouraging the attraction of large foreign loans, particularly from France and Germany. He also negotiated trade treaties, imposed protective tariffs to prevent Russian industries being destroyed by foreign competition, and was successful in encouraging railway development.

Witte sponsored the arrival of foreign experts as well as foreign capital, and as a result Russian technological knowledge developed. By 1900 there were 269 foreign companies operating in Russia, 162 of them Belgian, 54 French, 30 German, and 19 British. The French companies contributed the greatest amount of capital investment. The coal, iron and textile industries continued to expand. In the decade 1890–1900 Russian pig iron production increased by 190 per cent; by 1900 it was the fourth largest producer in the world. Coal production increased sixfold in the period 1880–1904.

By 1910, therefore, in at least the few key industrial cities, there existed in Russia an industrial proletariat totalling 2.25 million, albeit working under insanitary and dangerous conditions, and exploited through long hours of work and low wages. These conditions were conducive to the spreading of mass discontent, especially as both strikes and trade unions were forbidden. These workers constituted a ready audience for proposals for agitation and insurrection. It was upon this class that the Social Democratic (Bolshevik) Party was to depend for its revolutionary muscle.

The 1904–05 Russo–Japanese War and the 1905 Insurrection

Under the reign of Tsar Nicholas II, who succeeded to the imperial throne in 1894, the great empire of Russia, though torn by intellectual dissension and discontent, still lay under a tight autocratic rule that seemed impregnable. But as was the case with the Crimean War of 1853–56, external forces and involvement in foreign affairs were destined firstly to shake and finally to shatter the Tsarist regime.

By the first decade of the twentieth century discontent with the regime was being widely expressed. In 1902 the great novelist Leo Tolstoy wrote an open letter to the tsar, complaining about the intolerable oppression of the people and claiming that 'autocracy is an outgrown form of government'. While a 'good' Tsar may emerge as 'a stroke of luck', Tolstoy wrote, tsars 'may be, and have been, monsters and maniacs'.

As has often been the case in other nations, the general discontent was escalated into a revolutionary situation by the onset of a war, the Russo–Japanese War of 1904–05. The Russians and the Japanese had become embroiled in a quarrel over trading rights in northern China and Korea. Japan demanded trading concessions in a zone previously regarded as a Russian 'sphere of influence', but Russia, confident of its military supremacy, refused. Japan attacked Russia, inflicting a decisive defeat on the Russian army in the Battle of Mukden, and seizing Port Arthur, a Russian-controlled port in northern China, in February 1904. The Russian navy, having undertaken a lengthy voyage from the Baltic to the Far East, and having been denied the use of the Suez Canal by England, Japan's ally, was devastated by the guns of the Japanese navy in Tsushima Straits in May 1905. This was the first significant defeat of a European power by an Asian nation.

Russia's performance in war had again highlighted the weaknesses of the regime. The Russian soldiers and sailors lacked national spirit and were poorly led by a corrupt and incapable officer class. The humiliation of the military and naval defeats, together with the sacrifices and burdens borne by the people before and during the war, aggravated to breaking point the domestic discontent over taxation burdens, the denial of representative institutions, and the curtailment of individual civil liberties.

In 1904 a strike of workers at Baku (on the Caspian Sea) was the forerunner of a series of uprisings and anti-government demonstrations throughout the country. By January 1905 the

'Bloody Sunday', St Petersburg, 22 January 1905: an artist's impression. The soldiers are depicted firing upon the demonstrators led by Father Gapon. This incident was very influential in breaking the mystical bonds of loyalty between the tsar and his people.

capital, St Petersburg, was seething with discontent. On Sunday, 22 January, a mob of 150 000 workers and their families marched on the tsar's palace to demand a constituent assembly based on universal suffrage, an eight-hour working day, and the distribution of the land to the people.

Although the tsar was not in the palace, loyal troops assembled in the streets opened fire on the marchers, killing over one hundred. This tragic event—'Bloody Sunday' as it came to be called—marked the final cleavage between the tsar and his people. He lost forever his mystical hold over the masses, who had till then somehow retained a hope that the 'Little Father' of the people would heed their complaints and lead them to a better life.

This insurrection of 1905 did not result in a true revolution (although many historians use this term to describe it) because the established order, although shaken, was not overthrown. Nevertheless, it was the prelude to the 1917 revolutions. The long-imposed Tsarist system

of demanding total obedience had generated a violent counterforce.

The Emergence of the Soviets

Most of the working-class people of the cities in 1905 contributed to the sustained defiance of Tsarist rule by supporting a (theoretically illegal) general strike. The organisation of these workers' protests passed into the hands of a significant new form of workers' organisation— the **soviet** (or council) of workers' deputies (representatives). The soviets thus represented the proletariat as an organised force. In December 1905 the tsar's troops crushed the soviets in all the centres; 15 000 people were reported killed and 70 000 injured.

The 'October Manifesto': Promise of Reform

Although the soviets had been suppressed by military force, their emergence had the effect of forcing the tsar to make some concessions. He

Tsar Nicholas II (1863–1918) and his family—the last royal family of the Romanoff Dynasty of Russia. The tsarina, Queen Alexandra, was a German-born granddaughter of Queen Victoria of Britain. All members of this family, it is widely believed, were murdered by Bolshevik troops in 1918 when it seemed likely that they could be rescued by White Russian forces, who would have attempted to restore the tsar to power.

issued, in October 1905, the 'October Manifesto', in which he guaranteed civil liberties and promised to allow the election of a national *duma* or parliament. This was to be elected on a wide but male-only franchise, and was to have power to pass legislation. The tsar was induced to allow the peasants a large share in representation, for his advisers believed that the peasantry would act as a conservative element and thus counter the influence of the city-based soviets.

Executive power, however, was to rest in a Council of Ministers (or cabinet) appointed by the tsar; thus the form of government was different from the 'responsible government' system of Britain, in which the cabinet was answerable to the parliament.

By making these promises, the tsar divided and weakened the forces of the opposition. The bourgeoisie, suspicious of the objectives of the soviets, were satisfied that reform would go this far and no farther. The Mensheviks, who supported the policy of working towards social reform through parliamentary institutions, were also ready to allow the new system a chance to succeed. The soviets therefore lost their appeal as a revolutionary force, because the new machinery of government appeared to offer the prospect of a reformed society without the necessity of subversive action by the workers' committees.

The *Dumas*: Apparent Reform and Severe Reaction

The first national *Duma* ('place of deliberation') met in 1906. The representatives formed themselves into five major parties, ranging in sentiment from a counter-revolutionary group, the monarchists, opposing any further changes, to the extremely left-wing Bolshevik group within the Social Democratic Party, which preached the policy of armed insurrection.

SOURCE 6.4

A famous Russian novelist appeals to the tsar to abandon autocracy and allow civil liberties and democratic forms of government, 1902

HISTORICAL CONTEXT: By the first decade of the twentieth century Western teachings about liberalism and democracy had permeated Russian society, yet the Tsarist secret police still maintained a repressive regime that stifled all dissent. No move had yet been made to allow the election of a national parliament.

Source: Leo Tolstoy, 16 January 1902, reprinted in *The Times*, London, 3 January 1905

A third of Russia lies in the state of 'special control', that is, outside the law; the army of police, visible and secret, goes on continually increasing; prisons, places of exile and of penal servitude are overflowing; political prisoners, with whom working men are now classified, being added to the hundreds of thousands of ordinary criminals; the censorship of literature extends to such absurd prohibitions which it did not reach even during the worst period of the forties. Religious persecution has never been so frequent and cruel as it is now, and becomes ever more cruel and frequent . . .

The reason for all this, so terribly evident, is this: your helpers assure you that, by the arrest of all progress of life in the nation, they will thereby ensure the welfare of this people and your own peace and safety. But one can sooner arrest the flow of a river than that incessant progressive movement of mankind which is established by God . . .

As to autocracy, if it were natural to the Russian people while this people still believed that the Czar is an infallible earthly deity who alone rules the people, it is far from natural to them now, when they all know, or at least find out as soon as they get a little education, first, that a good Czar is only a 'stroke of luck', and that Czars may be, and have

been, monsters and maniacs . . .

Autocracy is an outgrown form of government which may answer to the demands of a people somewhere in Central Africa apart from the world, but not to the demands of the Russian people which is growing ever more enlightened . . .

. . . It is first of all necessary to give the people the possibility of expressing their desires and wants; then, lending ear to these desires and wants, to fulfil those of them which will answer to the demands not of one group, but of all the majority . . .

First of all, the working people would say that they wished to be delivered from those special laws which deprive them of the rights of all other citizens. Then they would say that they desired freedom to move from place to place; freedom of education; and freedom to profess the religion which corresponds to their spiritual needs; and above all, all the one hundred million people would say with one voice, that they desired freedom in the use of land, that is, the abolition of the right of landed property.

QUESTIONS

1 What is the 'act of God' identified by Tolstoy that contradicts the Tsarist view that God ordained the tsar's absolute power?

2 What argument is used against the claim that a tsar is an 'infallible deity'?

3 Why, according to Tolstoy, is autocracy no longer suitable for the 'demands of the Russian people'?

4 What basic freedoms are being denied to the Russian people, according to this letter?

5 For which political ideology does Tolstoy reveal support (as shown in the last paragraph)?

When the Duma met in May 1906, a substantial majority seeking additional reform was revealed. The tsar immediately antagonised this group by declaring a set of 'fundamental laws', by which he would retain control of the executive (the cabinet), as well as defence and foreign affairs. He further decreed that the old Imperial Council would act as an upper house. This contradicted the essence of the October Manifesto by virtually ensuring that the Duma would have so little power that it would exist only as a formality.

The Duma met the challenge to its effectiveness by criticising the tsar's administration in detail on every point of inefficiency and privilege, even finding enough common purpose to pass a vote of censure on the government. But the tsar, confident once again that the situation was under control, dissolved the body in July 1906. He had revealed his lack of trust in the parliamentary system.

The Duma had been in session for only ten weeks. In a move reminiscent of the actions of the Third Estate in Versailles in 1789, a body of 200 deputies appealed to the people of Russia to defy Tsarist rule by refusing to pay taxes or to accept army service until the Duma was reconstituted. But with no nation-wide system to organise resistance, this effort bore no fruit.

The tsar nevertheless resolved to persevere with the experiment in parliamentary rule by allowing the election of another Duma. Critics of his regime labelled this as 'window-dressing', probably intended to impress Western nations and thus encourage them to maintain their policies of investing in Russia's industrial growth. In July 1906, Nicholas II issued an appeal for the election of a more co-operative Duma. In this statement he revealed that he harboured the delusion that he was still accepted as a father figure by the people.

The second Duma (1907) was called, but it was denied effective power, and achieved no more success than had the first Duma. This time Socialist Revolutionaries and Social Democrats took a more prominent part in the elections and constituted a significant section of the assembly. The Duma was dissolved within three months, after it had severely criticised the tsar's administration. The third Duma ran its full course from 1907 to 1912, but for its election the tsar broke yet another of his earlier promises—that the electoral law could not be changed without the consent of the Duma—and altered the franchise to limit representation to landed gentry and the more wealthy city-dwellers. It was in effect a 'landowners' Duma' and therefore largely a conservative force. This helps to explain why the tsar persevered with the Dumas. Their very existence, powerless though they might have been, helped to satisfy some advocates of constitutional reform. A fourth Duma, of 1912–17, was virtually a force backing the status quo and was of little significance, having no influence on events.

The ineffectiveness of the Dumas resulted in another upsurge of unrest. The industrial proletariat was being denied any of the social reforms now becoming common in the West; hours were long, wages low, and conditions primitive. The workers were forbidden to form trade unions, and strikes were illegal. Although some start was made in 1912 on the provision of health and accident insurance for the workers, little was done about a systematic programme of welfare legislation. Like the landless peasants, the city workers were angry and discontented with the government. In the years 1912–14 strikes and uprisings appeared again on the Russian scene, even though by going on strike the workers risked either deportation without trial, or death. Their preparedness to do so showed the extremity of their desperation. An international crisis—'The Great War of 1914–18' as it was later called—became the eventual stimulus for the destruction of the 300-year-old Tsarist regime.

VI WORLD WAR I AND THE COLLAPSE OF THE TSARIST REGIME

In the July–August crisis of 1914, when the small nation of Serbia was threatened by

The tsar dissolves the first Duma for challenging his authority, but resolves to allow another, 1906

HISTORICAL CONTEXT: The first national Duma permitted by a tsar met in May 1906. Tsar Nicholas II immediately circumscribed the authority of this 'parliament' by declaring a set of 'fundamental laws' covering matters over which he was resolved to retain control. The Duma attempted to defy the emperor's authority and was dismissed.

Source: **Proclamation by Nicholas II, Tsar of all the Russians, 20 July 1906**
We summoned the representatives of the nation by our will to the work of productive legislation. A cruel disappointment has befallen our expectations. The representatives of the nation, instead of applying themselves to the work of productive legislation, have strayed into spheres beyond their competence . . . and have been making comments upon the imperfections of the fundamental laws, which can only be modified by our imperial will. In short, the representatives of the nation have undertaken really illegal acts.

In dissolving the Duma we confirm our immutable intention of maintaining this institution, and in conformity with this intention we fix 5 March 1907 as the date of the convocation of a new Duma. Faithful sons of Russia, your Tsar calls upon you as a father upon his children to unite with him for the regeneration of our holy fatherland. We believe that giants in thought and action will appear, and that, thanks to their assiduous efforts, the glory of Russia will continue to shine.

QUESTIONS

1 What is revealed by the tsar's use of the term 'strayed into spheres beyond their competence'?
2 Describe the attitude of the tsar to his subjects as revealed in this proclamation.
3 What might the tsar have been expecting when he expressed hope that 'giants in thought and action will appear'?

Austria–Hungary, and the great powers all took sides, Tsarist Russia found itself embroiled in a war it could not avoid without loss of honour, but could not afford to fight.

The tsar was emotionally committed to his role as the father of all the Slav peoples, and this created an obligation to support Serbia. The two nations' common devotion to Eastern Orthodox Christianity created another bond. Moreover, Russia had a formal alliance with France (the Franco–Russian Alliance of 1894), and this, together with the tsar's dependence on French loans, left Russia with no alternative but to order the mobilisation of its armed forces. Germany interpreted Russia's mobilisation as a threat, and declared war in August 1914 on both Russia and France.

Despite Russia's huge resources of manpower, it was an unequal struggle. Germany's highly organised army, supported by a modern industrialised nation, was superior to the army of Russian peasants in every way except sheer numbers. Meanwhile, in the southern half of the front the Russians also faced millions of Austro–Hungarian troops. The Russian soldiers were handicapped by uncertain supplies, inefficient transport support, and incompetent leadership. Morale collapsed rapidly as a series of defeats forced the army into disorganised retreat.

Conscription of men and requisition of horses from the villages and rural areas contributed to a drop in food production just when it was most needed. Starvation was common both at the fighting front and in the cities. The intangible pressures of loyalty and adherence to the established fabric of society, that normally ensure the continuing operation of a national community, started to erode away. Enormous losses of life at the front drained the nation of hope, will and, most of all, of faith in its leadership.

The Rasputin Factor

While the disasters of the war were eroding faith in the Tsarist leadership, an additional element of doubt arose from the fact that Empress Alexandra, wife of Nicholas II, was a German princess. Some rumours said that she was a German spy and agent.

From 1905, the influence at court of a debauched Orthodox 'monk', Grigori Rasputin, contributed further to the alienation of the tsar from his people. The thoughts and actions of Empress Alexandra had become dominated by the problem that her only son, Alexis, the *tsarevich*, or heir to the throne, suffered from haemophilia, a disorder of the blood that could lead to almost unstoppable bleeding, even from minor wounds or bruises. The failure of doctors and of medical science to cure the disorder made it even more remarkable when Rasputin proved on frequent occasions that he was capable of bringing relief to Alexis (possibly through hypnosis). Rasputin became an almost permanent resident in the Tsarist court and, through the impressionable Alexandra, a major influence on all aspects of policy.

In some accounts Rasputin is portrayed as the principal factor in the failure of the Tsarist regime to avoid revolution. This is too simple an outlook; it must, however, be recognised that in the last few years of the 300-year dynasty of the Romanoff family, the empress virtually ruled Russia (because of the absence of the tsar at the front), and Rasputin ruled the empress. Rumours of the debauched, dissolute and drunken life led by Rasputin swept Russia and outraged the nobility and people alike. The royal family cut itself off from the Russian people who had for centuries retained a strange, almost mystic loyalty to the tsars who oppressed them. If the influence of Rasputin caused Nicholas to close his ears to sensible advice until it was too late, then Rasputin must be regarded as one of the major causes of the uprising in 1917.

By December 1916 a desperate group of Russian nobles decided that only the murder of Rasputin could save Russia. Having lured him to a rendezvous, the assassins used poisoned cakes, poisoned wine, and then bullets, in their attempt to dispose of the monk, yet he proved almost indestructible. He was finally drowned in the River Neva. By this stage the tsar, in what was to prove his last effort to assume leadership of his nation, had left Petrograd (changed from St Petersburg in 1914 because the latter name had German associations) to go to the front.

The death of Rasputin left the control of the capital in the hands of Empress Alexandra. Morale was now so low that rumours about corruption in government were common. It was alleged that German agents and the German empress were virtually pushing Russia towards defeat and to subjugation by Germany. This loss of morale, plus the economic disorganisation, famine, corruption and the appalling carnage at the battle front (more than 2 million dead), contributed to a situation in which the national spirit—the will to act as a nation—turned almost completely to rebellion.

The First Revolution of 1917

The combined miseries of national defeat and the extreme winter of 1916–17 built up a great sense of bitterness and resentment in Petrograd. The once respected armies of the tsar had suffered over two years of humiliation. Demonstrations, strikes and protests about bread shortages increased, while the willingness of the tsar's soldiers to suppress them correspondingly declined.

The war effort, based on Russia's vast resources of manpower and launched without the necessary support of adequate economic and transport facilities, had exhausted the nation. Instead of effective leadership there was a vacuum waiting to be filled. The food supply problem reached a crisis in January 1917, and as had occurred in France in 1789, this was the breaking point. On 23 February according to the Russian calendar (or 8 March in Western

Europe), an insurrection began, initially in the form of a strike by female textile workers in Petrograd. Thousands of other workers joined the strike, paralysing the capital city.

The members of the fourth Duma, although mainly supporters of the tsar, almost reluctantly decided to take control. At the critical moment the tsar (absent at the front) ordered the dissolution of the Duma. By this action he broke the last link between himself and his people, and virtually ensured the outbreak of revolution. The Duma refused to disband and, in an action reminiscent of the Third Estate's declaration of itself as a National Assembly in Paris in 1789, reconstituted itself as a **provisional government** with Prince Lvov as premier. In thus defying the will of the tsar, the Duma had launched a revolution.

Simultaneously, a revitalised 'soviet' of soldiers, sailors and workers was formed in Petrograd. The two organisations (the soviet and the provisional government) were not, then, rivals for power, but allies in the process of effecting the most significant change in Russian history. The tsar attempted to reach Petrograd, but the railways were no longer under the control of loyalist groups. His train was halted and, faced with the evidence of his own impotence, he agreed to abdicate. His brother, Grand Duke Michael, refused the throne, and the Romanoff Dynasty came to an end.

A New Order

Immediately, the provisional government acted to proclaim some of the legal and political reforms for which Russia had been waiting for centuries—an amnesty (forgiveness) for political prisoners, freedom of expression, and free elections. A truly national revolution had occurred under conditions broadly similar to those that had prevailed during the French events of 1789 and 1848. Affinity between the rulers and the governed had eroded away simultaneously with the growth of an economic problem into a national emergency, while the intellectuals were feverishly active in favouring radical change. Russia was now a republic, but it was still embroiled in a massive war effort. German armies were still on Russian territory, millions of Russians were still in the trenches, and the prevailing mood was still anti-German. The provisional government, now chiefly representative of the liberal-minded nobility and the bourgeoisie, decided that it was necessary, for the honour of Russia, to continue the war.

The mass of the people, meanwhile, were looking for socialist-style reforms of the economy and society. The only prominent socialist in the provisional government was Alexander Kerensky, who rapidly rose to the position of Minister of War, and later prime minister. Kerensky's affiliation was to the Socialist Revolutionary Party, the group which favoured peasant-based socialism and which regarded the Social Democrats (the Bolsheviks) as a dangerous proletarian-based body. He proposed to maintain the war effort because the alternative would be a humiliating peace in which Russia would lose great areas of land, but hoped to be able to achieve at the same time a 'democratisation' of the army and a measure of land reform to satisfy the peasants. He allowed himself to believe, however, that the people would be willing to wait for the conclusion of the war before true social reform could be attempted. He was mistaken.

VII THE BOLSHEVIK PARTY AND THE SECOND REVOLUTION OF 1917

At the time the March Revolution occurred, the Marxist-aligned Social Democratic Party was not strongly represented in the Duma, membership of which had been restricted to representatives of the landowning and upper middle classes. The Menshevik section of the party, however, was a powerful influence within the Petrograd soviet, and was advocating a period of co-operation with the provisional government. This was in conformity with the Marxist prediction that capitalism would proceed to the stage of bourgeois dominance, thus creating, through urban industrial development,

The provisional government announces both the end of the old regime and the introduction of basic human rights, March 1917

HISTORICAL CONTEXT: Upon the abdication of Tsar Nicholas II on 15 March 1917, the provisional government acted immediately to proclaim the implementation of the basic human rights for which the Russian people had been waiting for decades.

Source: *Izvestia*, No. 4, Petrograd, 16 March 1917

Citizens, the Provisional Executive Committee of the Duma . . . has triumphed over the dark forces of the Old Regime to such an extent as to enable it to organise a more stable executive power. The Cabinet will be guided by the following principles:

1 *An immediate general amnesty for all political and religious offences, including terrorist acts, military revolts, agrarian offences, etcetera.*

2 *Freedom of speech and press: freedom to form labour unions and to strike. These political liberties should be extended to the army in so far as war conditions permit.*

3 *The abolition of all social, religious and national restrictions.*

4 *Immediate preparation for the calling of a Constituent Assembly, elected by universal and secret vote, which shall determine the form of government and draw up the Constitution for the country.*

5 *In place of the police, to organise a national militia with elective officers, and subject to the local self-governing body.*

6 *Elections to be carried out on the basis of universal, direct, equal, and secret suffrage.*

QUESTIONS

1 What is an 'amnesty', and what was the significance of such a proclamation?

2 If clause 2 were to take effect, what basic feature of Tsarist society would be no longer operative?

3 From what feature of this proclamation could the provisional government be credited with not seeking to retain power?

4 What expression implies that the provisional government intends to maintain the war effort against Germany?

---

an urban proletariat sufficiently large to launch the revolution.

The Influence of Lenin

The Bolshevik strand of the Social Democratic Party, although in the majority, was temporarily lacking in leadership in March 1917. Most prominent Bolsheviks were either in exile (many in Switzerland) or imprisoned in Siberia. The amnesty declared by the provisional government brought them rushing back to Petrograd to seize their opportunities.

There now stepped on to the stage of the Russian Revolution one of the most influential and inspiring leaders of the twentieth century—Vladimir Ilyich Ulyanov (1870–1924), known to his fellow Bolsheviks as Lenin. In 1887 Lenin's brother had been hanged for complicity in a plot to assassinate Tsar Alexander II, and Lenin had been dedicated to the overthrow of Tsarism ever since. Exiled to Siberia from 1896 to 1899, he thereafter lived outside Russia, except for a risky return visit at the time of the 1905–06 upheavals.

Possessed of a powerful intellect, Lenin wrote prolifically for the revolutionary journal *Iskra* (The Spark), which was widely distributed within Russia, and published the books *Imperialism, the Highest Stage of Capitalism* (1916) and *The State and Revolution* (1917), which rank in prestige second only to the works of Marx and Engels in the communist library.

Lenin was the driving force behind the Bolsheviks. He believed that a small 'workers' party', if tightly disciplined, well led, and well educated, could destroy the existing form of government and lead the workers to socialism. He thus opposed the Menshevik policy of temporarily co-operating with the bourgeoisie while waiting for the growth of the proletariat.

In thus proposing an acceleration of the Marxian formula for the stages of a successful revolution, Lenin was modifying or 'revising' Marx's teachings. He rationalised this action by claiming that the situation in Russia was not what Marx had envisaged, in that there was already a revolution in progress, and if the Bolsheviks acted resolutely they could take control.

Caught in exile in Switzerland at the time of the March Revolution, Lenin nevertheless immediately began planning to bring down the provisional government. In April 1917, after German agents had reported to their government that the injection of the personality of Lenin into the Russian revolutionary situation would probably result in Russian withdrawal from the war to Germany's advantage, Lenin was permitted to travel through Germany by sealed train.

On reaching the Finland Railway Station in Petrograd on 16 April, Lenin immediately set out to extricate Russia from what he saw as the imperialistic war with Germany. He wanted to push on with what he saw as the real war—the world-wide socialist revolution against capitalism and the bourgeois class. To the revolutionary sailors gathered to welcome him he is reported to have said that the urgent priority was to push on with the socialist world revolution.

In advocating this policy Lenin was attempting an enormous about-face. His own Bolshevik Party had been supporting the provisional government up to the point of his arrival, and the Mensheviks were adamant that too rapid an advance towards proletarian dominance could mean total failure of the long-term plan.

Lenin was a compelling debater and orator. He used his powers of persuasion and determination to inspire the various groups who wanted to push on to another revolution. The drive of his personality; the compelling logic of his arguments; the emotional strength of his oratory—these were the influences he brought

SOURCE 6.7
Lenin exhorts his possible supporters to disregard the provisional government and fight for the 'Social Revolution', April 1917

HISTORICAL CONTEXT: Lenin, leader of the Bolshevik faction of the Social Democratic (Marxist) Party, arrived at a Petrograd railway station on 16 April 1917, having been permitted by the German authorities to leave his place of exile in Switzerland and travel through Germany, Sweden and Finland on the journey to Russia. The German government (correctly as it transpired) believed that Lenin could be instrumental in effecting a withdrawal by Russia from the war. Until Lenin's arrival, the Social Democrats had been applying a policy of co-operating with the provisional government. Such was Lenin's prestige that his speech made on arrival at the Finland Station changed this policy at a stroke.

Source: **V.I. Lenin, 16 April 1917, quoted**

in E. Wilson, *To the Finland Station*, W.H. **Allen, London, 1940, p. 474**
Comrade sailors, I greet you without knowing yet whether or not you have been believing in all the promises of the Provisional government. But I am convinced that . . . they are deceiving you and the whole Russian people. The people need peace; the people need bread; the people need land. And they give you war, hunger, no bread—leave the landlords still on the land. We must fight for the social revolution, fight to the end, till the complete victory of the proletariat.
Long live the world revolution.

QUESTION
Which two Marxian predictions was Lenin attempting to implement?

to bear upon his followers in the months of April to November 1917.

Lenin was convinced that the socialist world revolution was about to burst out as a protest against the enormous sufferings imposed upon the working-class people of the world by the imperialistic greed of the capitalist powers. He expected that the German socialists would aid the coming revolution in Russia by launching their own onslaught against capitalist control, and that, because Germany was a country well advanced in capitalist development, the workers' revolution there would be an even more decisive contribution to the ultimate victory of international socialism than the Russian revolution would be.

But Germany in 1917 was still at war, still under the control of capitalist elements, and still capable of maintaining a potentially victorious war effort. The members of the provisional government decided to continue the war effort against Germany, because they believed that a peace settlement with Germany could only be achieved at the cost of staggering concessions and losses of territory. They felt that if Russia could maintain its effort against Germany until the final victory of the Allies, the goodwill of those powers would be preserved—and Russia was going to need their economic aid. It was further felt that surrender to the Germans would constitute a betrayal of the Russian people and nation, and that such an act could virtually invalidate the holding of power by the provisional government.

So Russia—disorganised, famine-stricken, shattered in morale—fought on. Kerensky, as war minister, mobilised the Russian armies for another great offensive in Galicia: the 'July Offensive'. It failed to achieve any significant gain. Thousands more Russian peasant lives were poured away as sacrifices of war, and desertions from the Russian army became a flood as the peasant soldiers simply 'voted with their feet' and returned to their villages.

By the end of July 1917, Lenin had won the Bolshevik congress to his policy of attempting a seizure of power. Emboldened by the convic-

Lenin (top) making a speech, with Trotsky (right) also making himself prominent. The combination of Lenin's political genius and Trotsky's military leadership ensured the victory of the Bolsheviks in the Civil War of 1918–22 in Russia.

tion that other socialist revolutions in other nations would not only occur but would also come to the aid of a revolution mounted in Russia, the Bolsheviks set out to overthrow the provisional government, which, by continuing the programme of war with Germany, had failed to make a significant enough departure from Tsarist policy. Its 'on paper' reforms had not been transformed into practical realities. The masses wanted change, whereas the provisional government was perpetuating the problems of the old regime, and still failing to solve them.

The Policy of 'all power to the soviets'

Lenin's plan to attain power involved using the soviets—the councils of soldiers, sailors and workers ('toilers', as he called them)—as the key instruments of change. He professed to see in these soviets true proletarian bodies that could make possible the immediate transition from the bourgeois to the proletarian revolution. But in

SOURCE 6.8

Lenin calls for 'All power to the soviets' as a means of ending the war and establishing a workers' and peasants' government, October 1917

HISTORICAL CONTEXT: By early October 1917 Lenin and his supporters became convinced that their campaign had sufficiently undermined the status of the provisional government to make a seizure of power attainable. He called for 'all power to the soviets', convinced that the people could be persuaded to regard these workers' committees as valid forces for democratic reform. Anti-war sentiment was so influential that Lenin was also able to represent the termination of the war as a step towards a 'just peace' instead of as a national humiliation.

Source: **Tract by V.I. Lenin, from** *Collected Works*, **vol. XXI, bk II, International Publishers, New York, 1932, pp. 59–60**
To the workers, peasants, and soldiers! Comrades! The party of the 'Socialist Revolutionaries', to which Kerensky belongs, appeals to you . . . to 'be patient' . . . Comrades! Look around, see what is happening in the village, what is happening in the army, and you will realise that the peasants and the soldiers cannot stand it any longer. Over the whole of Russia, like a broad river, sweeps an uprising of the peasants, from whom the land has hitherto been withheld by fraud. The peasants cannot stand it any longer. Kerensky sends troops to suppress the peasants and to defend the landowners . . .

Go, then, to the barracks, go to the Cossack units, go to the toilers and explain the truth to the people:

If power is in the hands of the Soviets, then not later than November 7 . . . a just peace will be offered to all the belligerent peoples. There will be in Russia a workers' and peasants' government; it will immediately without losing a single day, offer a just peace to all the belligerent peoples. If power is in the hands of the Soviets, the landowners' land will immediately be declared the property and heritage of the whole people. Are you willing to 'be patient' in order that Kerensky may quell with armed force the peasants who have risen for the land?

Are you willing to 'be patient' in order that the war may be dragged out longer? Whoever believes in the Kerensky government is a traitor to his brothers, the peasants and soldiers!

QUESTIONS

1. What basic appeal is Lenin using to make the people discontented with the provisional government?
2. Explain how Lenin is attempting to distract the people from the thought that the ending of the war with Germany could be seen as a surrender.
3. What 'carrot' is being offered to induce the people to support the soviets?
4. Which tactic for ensuring loyalty to 'the party' (seen also in the French Revolution) is being introduced here by Lenin?
5. Sum up the possible motives of Lenin in making this proclamation.

April 1917 the Bolsheviks were only weakly represented in the soviets that had sprung up in most of the towns and cities of Russia. In the months of May, June and July, they worked with stealth and dedication to achieve a stronger position, and it is in this Bolshevik drive to seize control of the soviets that justification can be found for Lenin's insistence on organising a dedicated professional élite of conspiratorial revolutionaries. The Bolshevik Party was organised; its rivals were not.

The problems besetting the Kerensky-led provisional government were so vast, and the failure of its military effort in the July Offensive was so demoralising, that widespread discontent and despair again swept through the ranks of the soldiers, sailors and workers. In the midst of the chaos and indecision one party was promising the people what they wanted to hear—one party was offering action while the others were telling the people to wait. This was the Bolshevik Party.

The simplicity of the Bolshevik slogan 'Peace, Bread, Land' was its major appeal. It promised the people—workers, peasants and soldiers alike—their basic desires. While the liberal, middle-class and moderate socialist leaders of the provisional government advocated restraint and steady progress towards social improvement, the Bolshevik slogan cut right to the heart of the people's discontent and bitterness, expressing the proletariat's accumulated resentment against the old order.

Genuinely believing in democracy and in the right of free speech, Kerensky tolerated Lenin's criticism and opposition for some time, but was soon forced into a policy of crushing the Bolshevik Party. A series of uprisings in Petrograd led Kerensky to place the blame on the Bolsheviks, and in July Lenin was forced into exile in nearby Finland. Yet this episode did not weaken the Bolsheviks, because they now stood as the only party with a positive policy different from that of the provisional government.

The confused situation was further complicated in September 1917 by an attempted counter-revolution led by General Kornilov. Conservative and military elements supported his attempt to seize power because they sensed that the provisional government would soon succumb to socialist policies.

The military drive failed, partly because Bolshevik agitators had successfully won over many of Kornilov's soldiers, and partly because the Petrograd soviet had organised the city masses into an effective resistance. The significance of the Kornilov march on Petrograd was that it revealed the weakness of the provisional government; it showed that the soviet was the political entity with the greatest standing amongst the 'toilers' and ordinary citizens. The 'Kornilov incident' also showed that the weary and desperate masses were prepared to follow decisive leadership from their own people. They were not prepared to allow the former privileged classes to return to power.

By late September the Bolsheviks had gained control of both the Petrograd and Moscow soviets. Lenin decided that the critical moment had come: in October he launched his campaign against what he called 'indecisive parliamentarianism' and promoted the slogan 'all power to the soviets', calling for a rejection of the provisional government.

Equal in influence to Lenin in these days of action was the leadership supplied by Leon Trotsky (1879–1940), a brilliant orator, thinker and organising genius. Until 1917, Trotsky, although a Social Democrat, had been loyal to the Menshevik rather than to the Bolshevik plan of action. Now, as president of the Petrograd soviet, he became the key figure in three months of exciting political manoeuvring and jostling for power. He placed all his energy and genius at the service of the Bolshevik Party.

The November Revolution

With an All-Russian Congress of Soviets called for 7 November 1917, the critical moment had arrived. It was apparent that the Bolsheviks would not command a majority, so Lenin made the decision to force a seizure of power. He told the Bolshevik Central Committee: 'We must not wait! We may lose everything. The government is tottering, we must deal it the death blow.' Lenin and Trotsky organised a 'military revolutionary committee' to plan an uprising.

On 7 November the precise and carefully orchestrated seizure of power took place, with Trotsky the central figure in its execution. The 'Red Guards'—bodies of workers grouped on military lines—and the soldiers and sailors loyal to the Petrograd soviet seized key control points in the city and drove the members of the provisional government from their official buildings. By the end of the day the Second All-Russian Congress of Soviets voted approval of the coup and declared that the soviets would immediately assume the functions of government. The next day the Second Congress appointed a Council of People's Commissars as a cabinet to carry out the functions of government. Lenin was appointed chairman (in effect premier), Trotsky Commissar for Foreign Affairs, and Josef Stalin, recently released from exile in Siberia, Commissar of Nationalities. This seizure of power is still known to Russians as the 'October Revolution', as it occurred on 26 October in the Russian calendar.

The Bolsheviks now controlled Petrograd. It was to take another four years of dispute and conflict before they controlled all of the former Tsarist Empire from the Polish border to the Pacific Ocean.

VIII CAUSES AND OUTCOMES OF THE BOLSHEVIK REVOLUTION

Why did the Bolsheviks Succeed?
Although the Bolsheviks played little part in the March Revolution that deposed the tsar, by November they were in control of the two major cities, and four years later, of all the territory of the former Tsarist Empire. The search for an explanation of the success of the Bolshevik Party involves a review of the key factors that created the revolutionary opportunity.

Lenin and Trotsky were able to seize power because of four major conditions: firstly, the anarchy and disorder prevailing after the collapse of a government administrative structure brought about by the crisis of a war; secondly, the widespread misery and discontent of the people; thirdly, the long-standing influence of a revolutionary intelligentsia offering new ideas on organising society; and finally, because the Bolsheviks had formed a tightly organised conspiratorial élite determined to guide the revolution and not wait for it to occur.

Of these factors, only the last named was of Lenin's making. It is not possible to state categorically that it was the decisive factor. It is significant to observe that the communist regimes established in Europe after World War II were also dependent for their foundation on the destruction of the existing administration through the extremities of defeat in war. Evidence of this can be seen in the events in the nations of Poland, Yugoslavia, Czechoslovakia and Hungary in the years following 1945.

Nevertheless, this war-related factor raises another question: why did the extremity of war cause the Tsarist regime to collapse instead of bonding the people even more closely to the tsar through patriotic fervour? Other administrations survived the extremity of war; perhaps the Tsarist regime also might have done so had it not become an autocracy almost completely sealed off from the people, dominated by an alien empress and a corrupt and debauched monk.

In preventing the Duma from effecting gradual change and controlled reform, the tsar held his nation in such a vice-like grip of bureaucratic control that change could only come through violence. When the sense of disgust and despair in the nation at large reached breaking point in March 1917, there was no deeply seated sense of faith in the processes of parliamentary government; the ineffectiveness of the Dumas had ensured that.

Subsequently the provisional government also misread the mood of the people. The Western nations, learning of the March Revolution, confidently expected the nation to settle down under a Western-style parliamentary form of government. But this was really only wishful thinking. That the provisional government did not have the support of the masses was obvious to observers in Russia itself; but can reasons be found for its unpopularity?

The revolutionary urge was not satisfied by the provisional government's cautious approach to change. The people wanted an end to the war; they wanted to be fed; and the peasants wanted land. The provisional government, in deciding to sustain the war effort against Germany, misread the mood of the nation, in whose eyes it seemed to be continuing the tsar's war. So the people turned their loyalty and their hopes to the soviets, and found that, within the soviets, one party, the Bolsheviks, was offering a decisive policy of 'Peace, Bread, Land'.

Lenin had identified the basic war-weary attitude of the people, and their desire for further and immediate social reforms. Additionally,

Lenin was prepared to depart from pure Marxist teachings in seeking and developing the support of the peasantry. While he believed that the proletariat was the only true revolutionary party, and that it could be led by a trained revolutionary élite, he also felt that without peasant support the revolution could not succeed in Russia. He cultivated the concept of the collaboration between the city workers and the peasants, symbolised in the hammer and sickle emblem, and he promised the peasants land ownership. It was Kerensky's great mistake to give priority to winning the war ahead of the reform of land tenure, when the great interests of the peasants (the army was really millions of peasants in uniform) was in owning their own land. Thus only the Bolsheviks planned a revolution combining the support of the proletariat, the ex-soldiers and the peasantry.

Was There a True Proletariat?

Much debate has developed on the question of whether or not a sufficiently large industrial proletariat had developed in Russia to justify the Revolution being termed 'proletarian'. The question is not wholly relevant because, while the March Revolution was truly a national uprising against a bankrupt regime, the October Revolution was a seizure of power in the capital by a small, determined group which was relying on the appeal of its policies to consolidate its position after it had taken over.

The Bolshevik Revolution was thus not dependent on a large industrial proletariat having grown within the capitalist system, on the pattern predicted by Marx. It was more dependent on dissatisfied ex-soldiers and sailors, and an intellectual organisational élite. Both of these groups worked through the soviets, particularly the soviets of Petrograd and Moscow, and these soviets were true proletarian councils.

Lenin was advocating 'the dictatorship of the proletariat', so he needed a proletariat. Russia by 1914 had still not reached the stage of industrialisation of Western countries. In proportion to its size, its railway network was only one-twelfth that of Germany or Great Britain; its coal output was only one-fifteenth that of Germany and only one-thirtieth that of Great Britain. Its comparative industrial lag was clearly shown by its need to import vast quantities of guns, shells, rifles and ammunition to mount its war effort. Thus the proportion of its population actively involved in manufacturing industries in 1914 was still very low; industrial workers constituted less than two per cent of the population—there were about 2.5 million urban workers in a population of 170 million. It is, however, relevant to note that the potential influence of this class was greater than its numbers might suggest because it was concentrated in the key cities of Moscow and Petrograd.

In contrast to the Bolsheviks' plan, the Mensheviks claimed the proletarian class was too immature to lead the revolution, and that bourgeois-guided capitalism should be allowed to develop before a socialist revolution was attempted. This theory was largely invalidated by the peculiar nature of the industrial development thus far achieved in Russia; for it had been the needs and the demands of the Tsarist regime, and not a true spirit of free enterprise, that had promoted industrial expansion in Russia.

Lenin argued that because capitalism in Russia had developed in this way, the Russian bourgeoisie was not sufficiently anti-Tsarist to be permitted to lead the first stage of revolution; the proletariat had to advance almost immediately to a seizure of power. This is why he had confidence in the effectiveness of the proletariat, for all its comparative lack of numbers, to achieve a revolution if the Bolsheviks offered a policy that also appealed to the peasants, and provided such a revolution in Russia would quickly receive support from proletarian revolutions in more advanced capitalist countries like Germany. Lenin refused to offer support to the provisional government and demanded 'all power to the soviets'.

Why did the first Communist Revolution occur in Russia?

At the time of the Russian Revolution parliamentary reform in Western nations had advanced to the stage where workers' political parties could hold some hope of gaining socialist objectives through parliamentary means. Their militant revolutionary zeal had therefore been blunted. They looked to legislation rather than to violence as a means of achieving reform.

Moreover, secular education systems and **jingoistic** propaganda had fostered a considerable degree of nationalism amongst the workers in the West. They had developed an emotional loyalty to the interests of the nation that prevented them from viewing revolution as an attractive policy; revolution implied the weakening of the nation and was therefore an act of treason.

Only in Russia did there exist a strong socialist party, the Bolsheviks, prepared to put aside national grandeur for the class revolution. Ruthless in planning and daring in execution, the Bolsheviks, impelled by the drive and determination of Lenin, alone believed in the possibility of pushing straight on to the social revolution (the changes to society) that the political revolution of March 1917 had not yet produced. And it was precisely because they were prepared to go on to this further stage of change that they gained support at the expense of the Mensheviks, whose policy of allowing the bourgeois–capitalist stage of development to proceed was unexciting and unimaginative.

In the revolutionary showdown in Russia three critical factors co-existed: the collapse of the former administrative structure, brought about by colossal war damage and the associated breakdown of both national morale and any sense of loyalty to the old order; the presence of a conspiratorial revolutionary party ready to seize power rather than wait to earn it through democratic processes; and the leadership of two brilliant and ruthless men, Trotsky and Lenin. Lenin's effectiveness as a political leader was enhanced by the talents of his wife, Nadezhda Krupskaya (1869–1939), who displayed remarkable organisational skills in the early years of the Revolution, and later served as Vice-Commissar for Education in the post-Revolutionary Soviet regime.

MAJOR EVENTS AFFECTING THE TSARIST REGIME IN RUSSIA 1682–1917

1682–1725 Reign of Peter the Great (who sponsored Westernisation in Russia)

1762–96 Reign of Catherine the Great

1812 Napoleon invaded Russia: reached Moscow French army driven out of Russia

1814 Russian army reached Paris, contributing to overthrow of Napoleon

1825 'Decembrist' uprising against autocratic nature of Tsarist rule; severely repressed

1825–55 Reign of Nicholas I, characterised by extreme censorship and repression under the 'Nicholas system'

1848 Revolutions in most nations of Western Europe (demanding liberal forms of government). These had almost no effect in Russia because of the censorship system.

1853–56 Crimean War. The Russians suffered the humiliation of not achieving victory on their own soil against the combined British-French-Piedmontese supporters of Turkey.

1855–81 Reign of Alexander II

1861 Emancipation of the serfs by Alexander II (followed by peasant insurrections)

1864 Establishment of the *zemstva* (local governing bodies)

1881 Alexander II assassinated in St Petersburg

1891 Reign of Alexander III

1894–1917 Reign of Nicholas II

1903 Russian Social Democratic (Marxist) Party formed; later split into Bolshevik and Menshevik factions

1904–05 Russo–Japanese War

1905 *January* 'Bloody Sunday': an insurrection put down with severe loss of life
Soviets (workers' committees) formed

1906 First Duma (ostensibly a national parliament) formed

1907 Second Duma formed and dissolved

1907–12 Third Duma

1914 Russia became embroiled in a war against Austria-Hungary and Germany

1917 Tsar Nicholas II forced to abdicate in 'First Revolution'
Provisional government formed
Lenin returned from exile
Bolsheviks seized power in 'Second Revolution' on the policy of 'all power to the Soviets'
New decrees issued on ownership of land and the factors of production

The Consolidation of the Communist Political and Cultural Revolution in Russia and the USSR

It has been Russia's lot to see most clearly, and experience most keenly and painfully the sharpest of sharp turning-points in history as it swings round from imperialism towards the communist revolution. In the space of a few days we destroyed one of the oldest, most powerful barbarous and brutal of monarchies. In the space of a few months we passed through a number of stages of collaboration with the bourgeoisie and of shaking off petty bourgeois illusions, for which other countries have required decades. In the course of a few weeks, having overthrown the bourgeoisie, we crushed its open resistance in civil war. We passed in a victorious triumphal march of Bolshevism from one end of a vast country to the other. We raised the lowest strata of the working people oppressed by tsarism and the bourgeoisie to liberty and independent life. We established and consolidated a Soviet Republic, a new type of state, which is infinitely superior to, and more democratic than, the best of the bourgeois parliamentary republics. We established the dictatorship of the proletariat supported by the poor peasantry, and began a broadly conceived system of socialist reforms. We awakened the faith of the millions upon millions of workers of all countries in their own strength and kindled the fires of enthusiasm in them. Everywhere we issued the call for a world workers' revolution. We flung a challenge to the imperialist plunderers of all countries.

V.I. Lenin, 'The Chief Task of Our Day', 11 March 1918, quoted in V.I. Lenin, *Against Imperialist War*, Progress Publishers, Moscow, 1966, pp. 324–5

The term 'revolution', as has been established in Chapter 2, can be used to describe an act by which a regime is overthrown and replaced by another significantly different in character, and also to the more prolonged process by which a society is redefined and reconstructed under a new ideology. This latter process involves the establishment of new institutions and new societal practices, a re-education of the people (to accept and support the new regime), and usually a new set of concepts (new terminology) to communicate new key priorities.

Humankind's search for a better life, and for ways to counter injustice, has given rise to many different ideologies. Of these, none has been taken up by so many people, in so many nations, and with such fervour, as socialism and its extreme form, communism.

Belief in socialism is based on the rational argument that wealth can be fairly and evenly distributed. Instead of there being a wealthy few and a huge proportion of miserably poor, everybody in society could therefore enjoy a reasonable standard of living. Poverty would be eliminated.

As an ideology, socialism is the opposite of capitalism. Capitalism extols the advantages of the individual search for profit and the benefits of competition. Socialism, by contrast, advocates co-operation, sharing and compassion for others. It is, on paper, a more noble, more humane, more sensible system, but it appears to have failed in recent decades in many nations because of the basic competitiveness of human nature.

The seizure of power in November 1917 by the Bolshevik branch of the Russian Social Democratic Party opened the opportunity for the building of a socialist (and eventually a communist) State. This is what the Bolshevik leader, V.I. Lenin, claimed to be attempting in 1918 (see quotation above). The Bolsheviks exercised power in Russia for seventy-four years (1917–91), and in most of the eastern European nations from 1945 till 1990. It is important for the current generation to examine what was achieved in these periods.

The recent collapse of the communist regimes of eastern Europe does not necessarily mean that no social reforms were achieved in the decades of socialist/communist rule. Many advocates of socialism, moreover, would claim that the failures were not due to defects in the ideology of socialism, but to its misapplication and betrayal. It must also be remembered that the world's largest nation—China—is still operating a version of communist governance.

Karl Marx had predicted that when bourgeois control of society was overthrown, a socialist society would emerge, in which the defects of capitalism would be gradually eliminated. Finally a true communist society would evolve; there would be no scarcities, and no person would be denied his or her full share of human fulfilment. The attainment of this type of society would be the true outcome and purpose of the socialist revolution.

For three-quarters of the twentieth century the Communists held power in Russia with the avowed purpose of bringing about such a revolution in society. When we focus upon this era, several key questions arise.

Theme Questions

➤ Did the Bolsheviks (or the 'Soviets', as they were later widely known) profess and apply a systematic plan for a reformed society?

➤ Did the Bolsheviks make a new society, or did the long-established features of Tsarist society reappear in the form of a new bureaucracy?

➤ Did the Bolshevik seizure of power affect peoples and governments in other nations?

➤ Did the economy and society of the Union of Soviet Socialist Republics (USSR) attain some of the characteristics of the 'higher phase' of communist society (see Source 7.1) as predicted by Marx?

I THE COUNTER-REVOLUTION AND THE BOLSHEVIK VICTORY IN THE CIVIL WAR: 1918–21

The Bolsheviks emerged from the Second Revolution of 1917 as the dominant power in the two key cities of Petrograd and Moscow, but they still had to bring the vast areas of the former Tsarist Empire under their control. Lacking the military resources to resist Germany at the time, the Bolshevik leaders, Lenin and his Commissar for War, Leon Trotsky, 'bought time' by arranging for the cessation of the war against Germany. This fulfilled one of Lenin's promises—the attainment of 'peace'.

The Treaty of Brest–Litovsk 1918

'Peace' it may have been, but it was gained at an enormous price. By the Treaty of Brest–Litovsk, signed in March 1918, Russia

Karl Marx predicts that after the full development of capitalism, bourgeois power can be overthrown and a socialist society established, 1875

HISTORICAL CONTEXT: Karl Marx, writing in 1875, stresses that in his opinion the capitalist-sponsored development of productive resources by the bourgeoisie is a necessary prelude to the ultimate overthrow of the bourgeoisie class and its replacement by a socialist society in which wealth is shared evenly.

Source: **K. Marx, writing in *A Critique of the Gotha Programme*, 1875, quoted in R. Freedman (ed.), *Marx on Economics*, Penguin, Harmondsworth, 1962, p. 240–1**

In the higher phase of communist society, after the enslaving subordination of individuals under division of labour . . . has vanished; after the productive forces have also increased with the all-round development of the individual, and all the springs of co-operative wealth flow more abundantly—only then can the narrow horizon of bourgeois power be fully left behind and society inscribe on its banners 'from each according to his ability, to each according to his needs'.

QUESTIONS

1 What is implied by 'subordination of individuals under division of labour'?

2 Why is 'bourgeois power' described as having a 'narrow horizon'?

3 The last sentence states the great motto of the socialist communist movement. Paraphrase its meaning.

4 Were the ideals expressed in this motto ever attained in a communist society? If not, what may have been 'proved' about human nature?

5 Some critics of communist theory claim that in practice the allegedly desirable maxim became 'from each according to his mediocrity, to each according to his greed'. What view of human nature is revealed in this version of the motto?

---

surrendered to Germany all the territories bordering the Baltic Sea, together with Poland and parts of Belorussia. In addition, Russia recognised the independence of Ukraine and Finland, which, by this treaty, were supposed to be established as new nations under German sponsorship.

The severity of the German terms shocked the nations of the West. Russia had surrendered over one-third of its agricultural land, 54 per cent of its industrial enterprises, 75 per cent of its coal mines, 73 per cent of its iron ore supplies, and 85 per cent of its sugar production. In addition, Russia was also expected to pay huge reparations (repair) bills.

Lenin and Trotsky claimed that this massive surrender of territory and resources was justified because it achieved the main objective—the cessation of the fighting. They expected that the provisions of the treaty would soon be inopera-

tive, because they believed that the proletarian revolution to overthrow bourgeois control (as predicted by Marx and Engels) was about to occur in Germany, and that the kaiser's government would be overthrown within months. The Bolsheviks expected that the world revolution of the proletariat would then occur, and all imperialist treaties would be cancelled.

A socialist uprising of the expected type (known as the Spartacist Uprising) was attempted in Germany in January 1919, after the general war armistice. It was suppressed by the *Freikorps* (volunteer corps), who were predominantly ex-soldiers intent on protecting property ownership.

The Treaty of Brest–Litovsk was in time rendered invalid, not by a world proletarian revolution, but by the German acceptance of an armistice on the Western front in November 1918. Nevertheless, the harshness of its terms

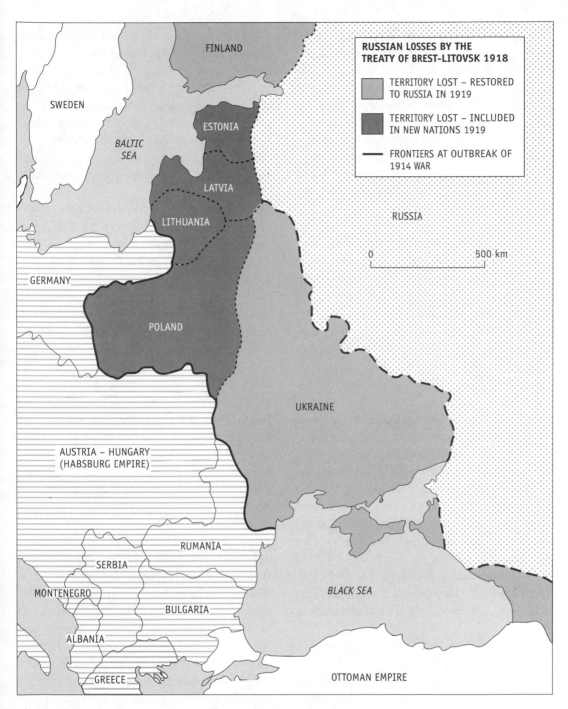

MAP 7.1 Russian losses by the Treaty of Brest–Litovsk 1918

When the Bolsheviks gained power in Russia in November 1917, they promised to end the war with Germany. With the Russian army demoralised and German troops occupying vast areas of Russia, the Bolshevik representative, Trotsky, was in no position to demand terms. By the treaty, signed in March 1918, Russia renounced control over Finland, Estonia, Latvia, Lithuania and Russian Poland. Ukraine, which had been set up by Germany as a separate nation, was recognised as such by the new Soviet government. All provisions of the treaty, however, were annulled by the general armistice of 11 November 1918, which marked the final capitulation of Germany. On 13 November 1918 the Bolshevik government of Revolutionary Russia declared the Brest-Litovsk treaty inoperative.

The Consolidation of the Communist Political and Cultural Revolution in Russia and the USSR left a bitter suspicion among the Russians of the motives and policies of capitalist nations. Similarly, the Russian withdrawal from the war aroused deep animosities among the Western powers. Russia's separate treaty allowed the Germans to concentrate their whole army on the Western front, and the heavy casualties inflicted upon the Allied armies in France in 1918 were attributed by Western public opinion to 'Bolshevik treachery'. These mutual suspicions were to prevail for many decades.

The Civil War between the Forces of Revolution and Counter-revolution

Even after the Treaty of Brest–Litovsk had eliminated—albeit at great cost—the problem of German soldiers on Russian soil, Lenin and his followers had to deal with another problem. Thousands of Russians and other nationalities who had previously been subjects of the tsar refused to acknowledge the authority of the Bolshevik government.

Before the Bolsheviks assumed power in November 1917, they had strongly advocated the election of a Constituent Assembly. Shortly before the November coup, the provisional government had arranged for such an election (in November). Lenin decided to let it proceed. But the election results were disappointing to the Bolsheviks. Their rivals, the Socialist Revolutionaries, won majorities in most rural areas, commanding over half the total vote. The Bolsheviks, still regarded as an urban party, were represented by only one-quarter of the assembly.

Lenin moved quickly to cancel this apparent disadvantage, using Red Army soldiers (a red flag being the symbol of communism) to close the assembly the very day it opened in January 1918. The delegates were dispersed and harassed into flight. In justification of this naked exercise of power, Lenin restated his argument that the soviets (the workers' councils), being organs of proletarian revolution, were a higher form of democratic principle than the assembly, which was a manifestation of the now discredited bourgeois stage of the revolution.

Some historians claim that the Bolshevik attainment of power in November 1917 was less a seizure of power than the filling of a vacuum in power. The real Bolshevik seizure of power came with this forceful dismissal of the Constituent Assembly. In an act of unprincipled self-interest, the Bolsheviks betrayed the democratic aspirations of the anti-Tsarist revolution and set Russia on the path to a one-party dictatorship.

The Forces of Counter-revolution

Four years of civil war followed the dismissal of the assembly. It was not until 1921 that the Red Army led by Leon Trotsky attained control over most of what had been the Tsarist Empire. Many groups in Russian society opposed the Bolsheviks (renamed the Communist Party in March 1918). These counter-revolutionary forces were of mixed origins. Members of the non-Bolshevik left wing, particularly the rural-based Socialist Revolutionaries, had been alienated from Lenin by his high-handed actions. **Right-wing** elements—property-owners and supporters of the deposed tsar—formed an army from remnants of the Tsarist forces, and became known as the White Russians. Their objective was to defeat the Red Army and depose the Bolshevik government.

The Western Allies, anxious in early 1918 to reopen an eastern front against Germany if possible, encouraged the White Russians. A small British force was landed at Murmansk in north Russia, and Japan (one of the Allied powers) put forces into Vladivostok (at the eastern end of the trans-Siberian railway). French and American troops were also landed in Russian ports to protect capitalist investments. For a time it was assumed in the West that a large-scale Allied effort would be made to support the White Russians, but the armistice with Germany in November 1918 removed the need for intervention, and the forces were withdrawn. Official Soviet publications later labelled these incidents as 'the imperialist military intervention', and they were cited as evidence of the basic antagonism of the capitalist nations towards the ideology of communism.

This photograph, taken in Red Square, Moscow, shows Vladimir Ilyich Lenin (1870–1924), the intellectual leader of the Bolshevik faction of the Social Democratic Party. He was forced to live in exile from Russia during the periods 1899–1905 and 1907–17. He returned from Switzerland in 1917, and became the driving force behind the Second Russian Revolution (November 1917). He became head of the new government, the Council of People's Commissars. He died on 21 January 1924, and the city of Petrograd was renamed Leningrad in his honour five days later.

1 What 'image' of himself is Lenin appearing to strive for?

2 What is the significance of the dress and posture of his companions?

3 What overall effect is the photographer seeking?

The victory of the Red Army in the Civil War can be attributed to a number of factors: the Communists (Bolsheviks) projected a passionate revolutionary zeal, and were brilliantly led by Leon Trotsky as Commissar for War; the peasants were promised ownership of the land; the Communists gained great propaganda advantage from their claim that they were defending Russia against foreign capitalist invasion; and opponents of the Communists were disunited, being from opposite ends of the political spectrum.

The White Russians were themselves ruthless, arousing fears among the common people of a return to Tsarist dictatorship. Moreover, the Whites had not been able to form a united command, and peasants generally supported the Reds because it was assumed that the White factions would restore landlord control of rural areas. The Red Army was also able to lay greater claim on the patriotism of the Russians because the Whites had received foreign aid. Finally, in the midst of the excitement and anticipation of a reformed society promised by the very occurrence of 'a revolution', the forces of counter-revolution could easily be made to appear as the obstacle to progress.

'War Communism'

During the Civil War Lenin enforced a policy known as 'War Communism', by which the Communist government requisitioned supplies and conscripted soldiers in an all-out effort to achieve victory. This policy provoked resentment. In 1921 unrest in Petrograd resulted in a strike involving the industrial workers and the sailors at the nearby naval base of Kronstadt, who had been among the earliest supporters of the Bolsheviks in 1917. The sailors and workers held socialist views, but they opposed the iron control exercised by the Communist Party over the soviets. Declaring the strikers to be agents of the White Russians, Lenin used military force to crush the opposition. A news item in *The Times* (London, 19 March 1921) reported that the Kronstadt naval base had fallen to an attack by Soviet troops, numbering 60 000 men, led by Trotsky himself.

The ruthless suppression of the Kronstadt uprising indicated that the Communists would tolerate no dissension, even among their own supporters. Any likelihood that organisations similar to trade unions could be established in Soviet Russia was eliminated. Lenin insisted upon dictatorial power for the Communist Party.

In their drive for victory in the Civil War, the Communists adopted a policy of terror similar to that applied by the Committee of Public Safety during the French Revolution. In a period of extremity, with survival at stake, an enemy of the prevailing political party can all too readily be labelled as a traitor. The *Cheka*, a secret intelligence department, was formed to locate and imprison opponents of the Communist government. This further contributed to the creation of a one-party State.

Communist Party control was further consolidated at the Tenth Party Congress of 1921, when it was decreed the 'fractionalism' of the party was prohibited. Individuals were permitted (if they dared) to criticise party policies as individuals, but if any party member attempted to enlist the support of another individual, he would then be regarded as being guilty of forming or creating a 'fraction', sometimes referred to as a 'faction', and could be expelled. A monolithic dictatorial party thus was established. Simultaneously, members of the Social Revolutionaries, Mensheviks and other political parties were exiled or arrested. By 1922 the one-party State had been established.

The Union of Soviet Socialist Republics (USSR)

In 1923 the surviving parts of what had been the Tsarist Empire were merged into the USSR—the Union of Soviet Socialist Republics. This name is in itself a piece of historical evidence, the four words implying the following:

• as there are several republics in a union, the name signalled the establishment of a federal constitution rather than a unitary State;
• as 'soviet' means 'committee', specifically a workers' committee, the system of government was clearly allocating these committees an important place;
• as the term 'socialist' was featured, the federation was obviously committed to the principle of the social ownership of the means of production, distribution and exchange;
• as the constituent units of the union were republics, the previously reigning royal family must have been deposed.

Much of the character of the 'Soviet State' thus established had already been formulated in the four years of civil war. The government (in effect, the party) had appropriated property and assets. Peasants had assumed they now owned the land, and workers had taken control of the factories. A Supreme Council for the National Economy (the *Vesenkha*) had been established, creating the basis for a totally planned economy. The railways and all merchant vessels had been nationalised. In the cause of maximising the war effort, all rural production had been appropriated for 'the cause', and unco-operative peasants had been severely punished. An all-pervasive apparatus of control had been established, supported by all the emotional coercion associated with 'defending the revolution' and 'countering treason'. Events such as the Kronstadt mutiny had been used to validate the establishment of the repressive procedures of a new totalitarian State. Many historians regard these results of the Civil War as the standards which prevailed for the next seventy years.

II THE NEW REGIME: BUILDING A SOCIALIST-COMMUNIST STATE

The Bolsheviks used the word 'socialist' in the nation's name (USSR), but called themselves 'communists'. They did this because they believed that, although they would apply socialist principles in their reconstruction of society, it might take many decades to eliminate all 'bourgeois' (capitalist) practices. Only then could the pure communist society be attained. Persons

working for this eventual goal could, however, regard themselves as communists.

The Redistribution of Land Ownership

The Bolshevik promise of land for the peasants was quickly implemented—on paper—by the Land Decree of the Council of People's Commissars, issued on 8 November 1917. This decree abolished, without compensation, all private ownership of large holdings of land. The possessions of the former imperial royal family, and of the Church and the monasteries, were to be taken over by the State. The expectation was that the use of the land would be available equally to all peasant peoples. The

---

SOURCE 7.2

The newly empowered Bolshevik rulers of Russia issue the Land Decree of the Council of People's Commissars, 8 November 1917

HISTORICAL CONTEXT: This decree was an attempt by the Bolsheviks to fulfil part of the promise of 'Peace, Bread, Land' they had used to support their claim to the right to govern. The decree abolished without compensation all private ownership of large holdings of land. The decree was important to the Bolsheviks' attempt to establish their credentials with the peasant class, who had hitherto regarded them as primarily an urban-based interest group. The decree aroused fears in the landowning classes of all other nations, and thus contributed to the categorisation of the Bolsheviks as a threat. Such fears later helped the rise to power of the Fascist and Nazi parties as anti-communist forces.

Source: **Land Decree of the Council of People's Commissars, Petrograd, 8 November 1917**

1 *The right of private ownership of land is abolished forever. Land cannot be sold, bought, leased, mortgaged, or alienated in any manner whatsoever. All lands—state . . . monastery, church . . . private, communal, peasant, and any other lands pass to the nation without indemnifi-*

cation and are turned over for the use of those who will till them. Persons who have suffered from the loss of property will be entitled to public aid only during the time necessary for their readjustment to the changed conditions of existence.

2 *All the underground resources, such as ores, petroleum, coal, salt, etcetera, as well as forests and waters which have national importance, are transferred for the exclusive use of the state.*

3 *Holdings under intensive agriculture—orchards, gardens, plantations, nurseries, etcetera—are not to be divided, but turned into model farms and handed over to the state or the community, depending upon size and importance. Small private estates, city and village land in fruit or market gardens, are to be left in possession of their present owners, but the size of these holdings and the amount of tax to be paid on them shall be determined by law.*

QUESTIONS

1 What is meant by the statement that all lands 'pass to the nation . . . without indemnification'?

2 What was the ideological justification for this action?

---

actual proclamation contained many key principles of socialist ideology, in particular, one stating that the factors of production should be transferred from private ownership to community or 'social' ownership.

Source 7.2

The 'New Economic Policy'

During the Civil War Lenin had enforced an economic policy known as 'War Communism', by which the Communist government claimed complete authority over supplies and manpower in order to achieve victory. Such sacrifices were perhaps recognised as necessary during the conflict, but were resented once the fighting ceased.

At the end of the Civil War, Lenin faced the problem of convincing the Russian people that socialism was going to be a great improvement on the previous system, under which the prole-tariat had been exploited by the operation of market forces. The Civil War had caused a devastating famine, and many thousands had died from starvation. Production had ground to a halt. There was a drastic need to get the economy active again. Lenin therefore advocated what he called the 'New Economic Policy' (NEP): a proposal to discontinue War Communism and allow a large degree of private enterprise to re-emerge as a way to boost productivity.

Lenin's NEP was not as great a departure from communist teachings as it might appear. Marx's prediction had been that the communist revolution would occur *after* the capitalist system had lifted a nation's productivity to a suitably high level. Although an industrial revolution had begun in Tsarist Russia, the nation as a whole was still basically a peasant community at the time of the Bolshevik takeover. The NEP,

---

SOURCE 7.3

Lenin attempts to explain why the New Economic Policy (NEP) involves the reintroduction of some features of capitalist practice, 1921

HISTORICAL CONTEXT: After the three years of war with Germany and Austria–Hungary (1914–17), and the four years of civil war (1918–21), the economy of Russia was stagnant. Marx's predictions for a proletarian takeover of the State and the economy had depended on a preceding 'capitalist phase', in which wealth would be created (see Source 7.1). Lenin's policy of the NEP was an attempt to revive the economy of Russia by introducing a 'lost phase' into the stages of development by which a socialist, and eventually a communist, society could evolve. Lenin took pains, however, to reassure his followers that this capitalist phase would be strictly controlled.

Source: **V.I. Lenin, in a speech delivered to a meeting of Communist Party officials in the Moscow region, 9 April 1921**
We do not shut our eyes to the fact that a free market entails some development of capitalism, and we say: This capitalism will be under the control and surveillance of the state. We need have no fear of it because the workers' state has taken possession of the factories and railways. It will help to stimulate the economic exchange of peasant produce for the manufactures of neighbouring craftsmen, who will satisfy some, if not all, of the peasants' requirements in manufactured goods. The peasant economy will improve, and that is something we need to do desperately. Let small industry grow to some extent and let state capitalism develop—the Soviet power need have no fear of that. We must face the facts squarely and call a spade a spade, but we must also control and determine the limits of this development.

QUESTIONS

1 What reassurance is Lenin offering when he refers to 'the workers' state'?

2 What is contradictory in his expression 'state capitalism'?

3 Sum up the overall intention of this declaration. What is Lenin wanting to achieve?

by reviving private enterprise, was a means of ensuring that the 'lost phase' of industrial capitalism was reintroduced into the stages of development that would result in a communist society. Lenin justified the NEP with what his critics called 'double-speak'—arguing for the revival of some capitalist practices but calling the move 'state capitalism' because it would be under the 'surveillance of the state'.

The NEP discontinued direct State seizure of all farm produce, and instead placed a tax on part of the farmers' surpluses. The peasants were thus encouraged to produce above the minimum amount because they were permitted to keep for themselves their surplus foodstuffs, and to sell them on an open market. From 1925 the **kulaks**, or wealthier peasants, were allowed to hire agricultural labour. The result was a great upsurge of private retail trading: in 1922–23 private traders controlled about 75 per cent of the retail trade of the USSR.

Under the NEP, private enterprise was also permitted in small secondary industrial enterprises. According to the census of 1923, 88 per cent of industrial enterprises belonged to individuals. This figure is however, misleading, because these private enterprises were almost all small-scale operations; they employed only 12.5 per cent of the workers employed in industry, and accounted for only 5 per cent of gross production. The State continued to control all the larger industries, as well as services such as transport, credit and banking.

In the 1920s therefore, while the NEP was operative, the USSR presented the strange picture of what was officially a socialist command economy in which the State virtually monopolised the secondary and service industries, but in which agriculture was controlled by something like 25 million independent small producers. In terms of what had prevailed in Tsarist society, these changes in the economy constituted a revolution of substantial proportions.

The Consolidation of the One-party State

By 1922 the Communist Party had outlawed 'fractions' within its membership, and eliminated all other political parties. Despite the apparent liberalisation of some aspects of economic policy under the NEP, Lenin and Trotsky were still totally committed to the ultimate creation of a purely communist State.

The Bolshevik party organs, the newspaper *Pravda* (Truth) and the journal *Isvestia* (News), were established as the official news channels, and other papers were suppressed. The banks were nationalised, church property was confiscated, and religious education abolished. The trade unions, being proletarian organisations, were recognised, but fell under Communist control, and eventually ceased to fulfil any function.

Under the one-party structure, the only elections held were those which decided who was to represent the Communist Party in the district and central soviets. There was no multi-party elected parliament. Thus, one of the principles of democracy—that the people should possess the means of changing the government—was lost. Marxian socialism, which as an ideology claimed to be 'democratic' in the sense that the welfare of the mass of the people was of paramount importance, had, in practice, produced a totalitarian State.

III THE PROSPECTS OF 'WORLD REVOLUTION'

Marx had predicted that the ruling classes of the capitalist world would tremble at the prospect of a communist revolution. The proletarians, he said, had nothing to lose but their chains, and had a world to win.

The Bolshevik takeover in Russia in 1917 brought about the 'trembling' that Marx predicted. The capitalist classes in Western Europe and other industrialised nations watched the events in Soviet Russia with extreme suspicion. In 1918 public opinion in the Western powers blamed 'Bolshevik treachery' for the withdrawal of Russia from the war and the consequent increase in the military burdens of the Allied forces in France. After the war, it became evident to the West that the Communists saw their success as only the first stage of a **world revolution**. The supporters of multi-party democracy and capitalist free enterprise regarded this prospect with fear and trepidation.

On the other hand, socialists in all nations looked to the Communists in the USSR for support. The Soviet example appeared to indicate that the socialist ideology could be put into practice, and that it would work.

Other Attempts at Revolution

The success of the Bolsheviks, in a relatively under-industrialised nation, had at first led Marxists to expect similar communist uprisings in the more highly industrialised nations, as Marx had predicted. But by the end of 1919 only two attempted communist takeovers, both unsuccessful, had offered any sign of further revolution. In Germany a radical communist group called themselves the 'Spartacists', a name derived from Spartacus, a slave who led a revolt against Rome in 73 BC. They regarded themselves as slaves of capitalism, rising in revolt. In January 1919 they attempted to seize power in Berlin, but were crushed by pro-capitalist forces. Similarly, a Soviet republic in Hungary, led by Bela Kun, was proclaimed in March 1919, but was overthrown by August.

Thus, in practical terms, spontaneous revolutions failed to eventuate. The Soviet Communists, therefore, needed to encourage revolutions in other nations, and an organisation known as the Third Communist International, or **Comintern**, was formed in 1919 for this purpose. (There had been a First and a Second Communist International, established in 1864 and 1889 respectively.)

The Russian Revolution helped raise the political expectations of the working classes of the world. When the emotional patriotism of the war years was replaced by more rational thought, the wage-earners of the capitalist nations quickly realised that the grandiose wartime promises (which held up hopes of 'a land fit for heroes to live in' and a 'better world') were not being fulfilled. Many wage-earners still lived in squalor, with little hope of achieving better conditions. When the lean times of the 1920s were succeeded by the even more dispiriting hardships of the Great Depression, many thousands of the world-wide proletariat looked hopefully towards the socialist-communist remedy of redistribution of wealth.

Wide prominence was given in the English-speaking world to the statements issued in support of the communist organisation of society by an English Anglican clergyman, Dean Hewlett Johnson. Johnson visited the USSR in 1938, and in 1939 published a book, *The Socialist Sixth of the World*, in which he praised the social reforms applied there. His support aided the widely held impression that the proletarians of the world could be helped by communist practices.

Reactions against the Threat of Communism

Fear of communist revolution in turn promoted a reaction. Property-owners, businessmen, landowning peasantry and Church leaders in Western capitalist nations all opposed communism. When it appeared that the more liberal political parties in Italy and Germany were not ruthless enough to stem the growth of Marxian socialist thoughts and practices, public opinion in these nations swung towards the Fascist and Nazi parties, whose main appeal was their determination to resist communism. In pursuing this objective, these parties established cruel one-party **totalitarian** regimes just as destructive to basic human rights as the one-party dictatorship in the USSR.

The opponents of communism did not lack convincing evidence of the threat posed by this ideology. The Comintern was specifically pledged to the cause of world revolution, and was clearly involved in interference in the internal affairs of foreign countries and their colonies.

Naturally, the established governments of capitalist powers were reluctant to award official recognition to the USSR. Many, particularly France, were additionally resentful towards the

SOURCE 7.4

A clergyman from England expresses support for the social reforms being achieved in the USSR, 1938

Hewlett Johnson, a clergyman of the Church of England, holding the office of Dean of Canterbury, visited the USSR in 1938, and published a book, *The Socialist Sixth of the World*, which attracted world-wide attention because of its praise for the economic and social reforms applied in the USSR.

Source: **H. Johnson, *The Socialist Sixth of the World*, Victor Gollancz, London, 1939, pp. 15–16**

The experiment which is being worked out on a sixth of the earth's surface is founded on a new organisation of economic life, based on clearly defined principles which are thoroughly understood and gladly accepted.

Our system lacks moral basis. It is only justified on the grounds that no alternative exists. It gives rise, when Christian men and women accept it and acquiesce in it, to that fatal divergence between principles and practice of Christian people, which is so damning to religion, and which found its sternest critic in Christ Himself. The gap between Sunday, with its sermons on brotherhood, co-operation, seeking of others' good, and Monday, with its competitive rivalries, its veiled warfares [sic], its concentration upon acquisition, its determination to build up one's own security, becomes so wide that many of the better men and women of today remain outside the Churches altogether.

Slumps and booms, unemployment and misemployment, the dole and the multi-millionaire, the scales weighted for financiers and against the workers, frustrate society and produce strains and stresses whose logical conclusion is war.

In opposition to this view of the organisation of economic life is that of the Soviet Union, where co-operation replaces competitive chaos and a Plan succeeds the riot of disorder. The emphasis is different. The community rather than the self-seeking individual stands in the centre of the picture. The welfare of the whole and of each individual within it

replaces, as the ruling factor, the welfare of a select class or classes. The elimination of the profit-seeking motive makes room for the higher motive of service. The rational organisation of production and distribution of wealth welcomes science as an ally and transfers the emphasis from scarcity to abundance.

A new attitude towards human life is the natural counterpart of the new economic morality. Individuals, all individuals, become ends as well as means. The development of the human potentialities of each individual receives fullest opportunity and encouragement, and leads to a new humanism. The mass of the people are inspired to play a creative role in life, and culture receives a fresh stimulation. The cultural heritage of the past is treasured and reverenced and becomes the spring board for the future. Provided that no war intervenes to wreck the growth, the removal of economic shortage, and the substitution of plan for chaos, promise to open up new avenues of freedom, liberty, and creative personality.

QUESTIONS

1 What hypocrisy does Dean Johnson identify between Christian teachings and capitalist practice?

2 What does Johnson see as the logical outcome of the competitive practices of capitalism?

3 What, according to Johnson, stands at 'the centre' of the Soviet system?

4 A 'higher motive' than profit is identified in the Soviet system. What is it?

5 How might individuals benefit from the Soviet system, as envisaged by Johnson?

6 Which of the apparent virtues of the Soviet system, as described, was already (by 1939) being cancelled out?

7 Describe the frame of reference of the author, and identify his motives in making these statements.

USSR because the Communist government had simply refused to repay huge debts built up by the Tsarist regime.

The suspicions held concerning the activities of the Comintern were heightened by events in the British Empire and Britain. Anti-capitalist Comintern propaganda in some of the British colonies resulted in a strongly worded protest from the British Conservative government in May 1923. In early 1924, however, the new Labour government in Britain, in an attempt to be more co-operative with the Soviet government of USSR, officially recognised the new nation. But before this spirit of recognition could become established, a scandal developed in Britain that again damaged the relationship. During the election campaign of October 1924 it was alleged that Zinoviev, the president of the Comintern, had given instructions to his agents in Britain to support the Labour Party. Annoyed at this apparent interference in their domestic affairs, the British voters resoundingly rejected the Labour Party. Suspicions of the Comintern were reawakened, not only in Britain, but in all nations of the capitalist world.

Official acceptance of the USSR by other nations was therefore only slowly achieved. In addition to Britain, nine other nations, including France and Italy, recognised the USSR in 1924. Japan did not do so until 1925, and the USA delayed until 1933. The USSR was not admitted to the League of Nations until 1934, by which date both Japan and Germany had resigned.

Suspicions of the motives of the USSR remained, with the capitalist powers emotionally and diplomatically estranged from the USSR right up till the outbreak of World War II.

In the immediate post-war period (1945–49) the number of communist States was greatly expanded as a result of Soviet sponsorship of one-party governments in the east European nations. The capitalist nations' suspicions were thus revived. Two opposing and apparently irreconcilable forces, each convinced of its moral superiority, faced each other with hostility. This 'two-world' rivalry was then greatly accentuated in what became known as the '**Cold War**', and the enduring animosity was evident in the vast expenditure on armaments within the opposing military alliances of the North Atlantic Treaty Organisation (NATO) and the Warsaw Pact over the period 1949 to 1992.

Josef Stalin (1879–1953) (right), with Lenin. Stalin began training as an Orthodox Christian priest, but was expelled from the seminary. He became a loyal worker for the Bolshevik cause, founding the newspaper *Pravda* (Truth) in 1911. In the Lenin administration he was Commissar for Nationalities, and from 1922 General Secretary of the Communist Party, a post he made the most powerful in the nation. On the death of Lenin in 1924, he outmanoeuvred Trotsky to become the undisputed dictator of the USSR.

IV THE CULTURAL AND ECONOMIC REVOLUTION: 'SOCIALISM IN ONE COUNTRY'

In 1924 Lenin died, and after a period of group leadership, the struggle for authority narrowed to a contest between Leon Trotsky, the brilliant leader of the Red Army during the Civil War and one of the original revolutionaries, and Josef Stalin, the General Secretary of the Communist Party. Stalin emerged as virtual dictator of Russia in 1928. Trotsky was expelled, and was murdered in Mexico in 1940 by a Stalinist agent.

The struggle involved both a clash of personalities and a disagreement on policy. The demonstrative, energetic Trotsky favoured 'world revolution' (or 'permanent' revolution) on the Marxist model. He argued that the USSR should push on with the task of encouraging other proletarian masses to overthrow their capitalist masters. Stalin, less flamboyant in temperament, was also more cautious in policy; he believed that the USSR was industrially too weak to attempt the task envisaged by Trotsky, and that if it so acted, the capitalist nations would crush Russia and destroy communism forever. Because the USSR was the first and only base for the eventual attainment of world communism, argued Stalin, the major priority should be to consolidate the Marxian socialist system within the USSR and make the country strong enough to resist any invasion.

The policy that Stalin advocated and pursued came to be called 'socialism in one country'. This was a contradiction of the Marxist principle that proletarians of the world should forsake their loyalty to the nation and work for the interests of the working classes everywhere. Through this policy Stalin reignited Russian patriotism, and his appeal to the people was as much a nationalist urge to make Russia great as a plea to build a communist society. That the USSR survived the Nazi invasion of 1941 and smashed the German army was ultimate proof of the success of the plan.

The Secularisation of the State

A major feature of the cultural revolution in Russia and the other Soviet republics was the **secularisation** of society. In Tsarist Russia the Orthodox Christian Church (and, in some regions, the Roman Catholic Church) had been the binding force of society. All authority, from the tsar down, had been based upon and validated by the Church's teachings. In most of the southern republics of the USSR, the Islamic faith fulfilled the same purpose.

Under the Communist Party rule, the Churches were 'nationalised' and in effect closed down. Under Stalin, all public professions of faith in anything other than the ideology of Marxist-Leninist socialism were prohibited. Offenders risked disappearing into the vast prison system. All wisdom and all power now flowed from Leninist–Stalinist teachings. Statues and memorials to Lenin appeared in virtually every town and on every major construction project. A new deity had been created.

Political Control in a Totalitarian State

There were remarkable similarities between the totalitarian State erected by Stalin and the **fascist** regimes of Mussolini and Hitler, despite the fact that the latter both rose to power as bitter opponents of communism. Just as Hitler purged from the Nazi Party many of the 'brownshirt' henchmen who had supported him in his early years, so too did Stalin conduct an even greater purge in Russia. Two of the most prominent former party leaders, Zinoviev and Kamenev, were accused of plotting to assassinate Stalin and to restore capitalism, and were tried and executed. Over 400 generals and almost half the officer class of the army probably met their deaths; thousands, perhaps over one million officers, were executed, and hundreds of thousands were sent to concentration camps. The NKVD, a secret police force similar to Hitler's Gestapo, reached into all strata of Soviet society, including government and party officials. Through terror and control, Stalin completely muzzled dissent and enforced total obedience.

Similarly, just as Hitler kept the Reichstag intact as a 'parliament' but ignored it, and used mass plebiscites to attain the appearance of approval, Stalin promulgated a 'democratic' constitution in 1936, right in the midst of the purges. It seems that he wanted to pose as the saviour of the people's liberties in contrast to the 'traitors' who had tried to subvert the

Revolution. All citizens over eighteen were authorised to vote by secret ballot for two houses of the Supreme Soviet (a council).

The constitution also guaranteed most liberties for individuals—freedom of speech, conscience and association—and stated that every citizen had the right to work, to holidays with pay, and to social services. On paper it seemed that something approaching an ideal society was being attained in the USSR.

But the realities of Soviet politics were quite different; there was only one candidate to vote for in each constituency, and voting against him was a hazard to life and liberty. Real power lay not with the elected soviets, but with the Communist Party; and within the party Stalin's will was absolute. The USSR became a police State under a personal dictatorship.

Details of the total extent and nature of the police-State administration in the USSR are still to be revealed, and the full truth may never be known. In December 1973 the Russian Nobel Prize-winning author, Alexander Solzhenitsyn, published a description of the State terror practised in the USSR. He stressed that the power of the Soviet secret police had reached into every workplace, every factory, every school, every army unit and every family on a scale far worse than had ever been the case under Tsarist rule.

It has now been estimated that under the Stalinist regime (1924–53), the party's administration was responsible for the deaths of perhaps 26 million people. Millions of peasants died during the great famine of 1931–33, which was exacerbated by Stalin's policies for the collectivisation of farmland and by his refusal to acknowledge the devastating effects of the 1932–33 drought or to provide relief for its victims. Others lost their lives in the great purge of 1936–38, by which Stalin eliminated all opposition in the party, and through 'administrative murder' in labour camps.

The Five Year Plans and the Command Economy

Once he consolidated his power, Stalin set out to transform the USSR from a semi-feudal economy, with relatively small-scale secondary industries, into a great industrial State. This was essential if it was to survive in a world of powerful and hostile capitalist States. Stalin's method was to enforce economic change by State control through the 'Five Year Plan' scheme—an extreme example of a command economy, that is, one in which all the key economic decisions are made by central control rather than by market forces.

By 1928 the NEP had brought about most of the desired results, and total production had reached and surpassed the 1914 levels. It was now possible for Stalin to declare an end to the NEP and to launch a policy to reorganise the economy on Marxist principles. Private ownership of most of the factors of production was ended, and the first Five Year Plan (1928–32) was launched, with an emphasis on industrial growth, technical and scientific education, and the attainment of self-sufficiency in relation to the capitalist world. A second Five Year Plan (1933–37) followed, and the third (1938–42) was interrupted by the German invasion of 1941.

Iron and steel factories, dams and power stations, canals and railway lines were all built under State supervision—on a scale private enterprise had never attempted in Russia. In all three Five Year plans, the developments were directed by the State Planning Commission of the USSR, or GOSPLAN.

Despite many failures and setbacks, the Five Year plans were successful in attaining what must be seen as something close to an economic miracle. In a little over ten years, the USSR expanded its productive capacity to become one of the great industrial nations of the world. In 1928 heavy industry accounted for 40 per cent of industrial production; by 1940 it had grown to 61 per cent. Steel production by 1940 was four times greater than it had been in 1913. Stalin explained the purposes of the Five Year plans in a statement he released at the launching of the third Five Year Plan, in 1938.

SOURCE 7.5
Stalin explains the purpose of the Five Year plans, and claims success, 1938

HISTORICAL CONTEXT: By 1938 the second Five Year Plan for the transformation of the Soviet Union had been fulfilled. These Five Year plans were directed by the State Planning Committee of the USSR (GOSPLAN). The emphasis on industrialisation had been accompanied by huge costs in human suffering associated with the collectivisation policies applied to agriculture (see Source 7.4). It was important for Stalin to prove that the Five Year plans were succeeding.

Source: **J. Stalin, 1938, published in J. Stalin, *Problems of Leninism*, Foreign Languages Publishing House, Moscow, 1949, pp. 12–14**

The fundamental task of the Five Year Plan was to convert the USSR from an agrarian and weak country, dependent upon the caprices of the capitalist countries, into an industrial and powerful country, fully self-reliant and independent of the caprices of world capitalism.

The fundamental task of the Five Year Plan was, in converting the USSR into an industrial country, fully to eliminate the capitalist elements, to widen the front of Socialist forms of economy, and to create the economic base for the abolition of classes in the USSR for the construction of Socialist society . . .

The fundamental task of the Five Year Plan was to transfer small and scattered agriculture to the lines of large-scale collective farming, so as to ensure the economic base for Socialism in the rural districts and thus to eliminate the possibility of the restoration of capitalism in the USSR.

Finally, the task of the Five Year Plan was to create in the country all the necessary technical and economic prerequisites for increasing to the utmost the defensive capacity of the country, to enable it to organise determined resistance to any and every attempt at military intervention from outside . . .

What are the results of the Five Year Plan in four years in the sphere of industry? Have we achieved victory in this sphere?

We did not have an iron and steel industry, the foundation for the industrialisation of the country. Now we have this industry.

We did not have an automobile industry. Now we have one.

We did not have a machine-tool industry. Now we have one.

We did not have a big and up-to-date chemical industry. Now we have one.

We did not have a real and big industry for the production of modern agricultural machinery. Now we have one . . .

And we have not only created these new great industries, but have created them on a scale and in dimensions that eclipse the scale and dimensions of European industry . . .

And as a result of all this our country has been converted from an agrarian into an industrial country; for the proportion of industrial output, as compared with agricultural output, has risen from 48 per cent of the total in the beginning of the Five Year Plan (1928) to 70 per cent at the end of the fourth year of the Five Year Plan period (1932).

QUESTIONS

1 Why would Stalin have described the USSR (before the Five Year plans) as having been 'dependent on the caprices of the capitalist countries'?

2 What was the connection between 'large-scale collective farming' and the proposed elimination of 'the possibility of the restoration of capitalism'?

3 What feature of socialist–communist thought would have contributed to Stalin's reference to the USSR's 'defensive capacity'?

4 What might have been achieved by Stalin's technique of posing a series of questions and answering them himself?

5 Describe Stalin's frame of reference, and analyse his purpose.

The Collectivisation Policy

As Stalin prepared for the great uplift in industrial production expected from the Five Year plans, he realised that he would need to be assured of increased supplies of farm products, both to feed the greatly expanded urban population and to generate exports as a means of purchasing machinery. Accordingly, at the end of 1929, he launched a massive 'collectivisation' policy, designed to end private enterprise on the farms. The peasants resisted bitterly and strenuously, often deliberately slaughtering stock and destroying crops to ensure that they did not fall into the hands of the government. Many peasants were brutally treated, imprisoned or even executed for defiance of government regulations.

In the course of a few years virtually every Russian peasant was forced to join a collective farm (*kolkhoz*) and to surrender his or her livestock and other assets except for a 'private plot' of about 0.4 of a hectare. The *kolkhoz* itself was a very large production unit, comprising about six thousand hectares and perhaps four hundred peasant families.

It was expected that these large collective farms would become efficient producers of foodstuffs. Their size was meant to make possible a high degree of mechanisation, and their chief function was to deliver to the State at low cost the food supplies and raw materials for industrial expansion. But because the collectivisation campaign was resisted by the peasants, there were in fact periods of acute distress and famine in the 1930s. Low productivity in agriculture remains a serious and recurring problem in Russia to this day, even though the Communist system collapsed in 1991.

Work on a collective farm established in the USSR. Stalin's collectivisation policy forced thousands of peasants to abandon their small holdings. These large collective farms were expected to become efficient producers of foodstuffs. Their size was meant to make possible a high degree of mechanisation after the process of reorganisation, and their chief function was to deliver to the State at low cost the food supplies and raw materials for industrial expansion. Millions of peasants were brutally ill-treated, imprisoned or executed for defying the regulations establishing the collective farms.

SOURCE 7.6:

An American eye-witness reports on the coercive tactics of the Soviet government in the policy of collectivisation, 1938

HISTORICAL CONTEXT: Josef Stalin believed that his ambitious industrialisation programme could only be achieved if it was supported by increased food production. Accordingly, he enforced a policy of collectivisation of agriculture. Long-practised primitive subsistence agriculture was to be superseded by mechanised methods, using tractors and mechanical harvesters. Many of the peasants of Russia and the Ukraine resisted the policy. Stalin retaliated by branding the dissidents as *kulaks* (thus labelling them as bourgeois or capitalist-aligned), and decreed their liquidation as a class. Millions of these dissidents were imprisoned or deported to slave camps; millions more died.

Source: **E. Lyons, *Assignment in Utopia*, George Harrap, New York, 1938, pp. 279–80**

It was ordained that the . . . grain growing regions . . . must be completely collectivised . . . and that 'kulak farmers' . . . be wholly eliminated.

The strategy of the campaign was plain enough. Obliteration of the allegedly kulak elements was not only an end in itself, but a means for stampeding the rest of the population into submission to collectivisation . . . The palpable objective was to scare the poor and middling peasants themselves into merging their land, livestock, and implements. Indeed, the only sure way to prove that they were not kulaks was to apply and be accepted as collective members. The fearful kulak doom was a weapon for terrorising the rest of the peasantry . . .

The true measure of the terror, therefore, is not alone in the millions who were despoiled and deported from their native soil, but the sixty million peasants who rushed madly for the shelter of hastily

organised kolkhozes (collective farms).

Hell broke loose in seventy thousand Russian villages. The pent-up jealousies of a generation, the sadistic instincts of self-important little officials, the inflamed zeal of local communists, were unleashed and whipped into fury. The haphazard persecutions of the preceding months were systematised and legalised and invested with a high crusading fervour . . . Though no one knew precisely what a kulak was, there was no dearth of them, anywhere. Sometimes mass meetings of the village poor, under the steamrollers of local or visiting officials, confirmed the choice of victims . . . As many as 15 or 20% of the peasants were 'liquidated' in some villages.

At the moment it was distinctly 'unfriendly' on a correspondent's part to describe these events in detail. Those who wished to remain in the good graces of the Kremlin regime had to limit themselves to the spurious formulas used by the press and the statistical boasts about collectivisation victories: to reduce a major human catastrophe to meaningless impersonal percentages. For a few correspondents it provided a useful opportunity to demonstrate their 'friendship' and 'loyalty' for the Soviet regime by explaining away ugly facts, wrapping them in the cellophane of Marxist verbiage, slurring over them with cynical allusions to broken eggs for Soviet omelettes. Others were curbed by the censorship, and grateful enough on occasion for this convenient alibi for silence.

QUESTIONS

1 Explain the likely consequences of being labelled a 'kulak'.

2 Which group was, apparently, driving the persecution described here?

3 Why did little information of this process reach the Western world at the time?

A tractor is introduced to the rural workers on a Soviet collective farm, *circa* 1934. One of the reasons Stalin offered for the collectivisation policy was that collective farms would make possible the utilisation of agricultural machinery, which in turn would boost production. Notice that the introduction of this tractor is being accompanied by much banner-waving promotion and speeches, to convince the peasants of the advantages that the tractor will bring.

Stalin concentrated on industrial development and (later) defence resources production, with the objective of developing the USSR's capacity to survive attack. Because of this emphasis, the USSR was later able to repulse the Nazi invasion of 1941–45. To ensure a concentration on **capital goods** and defence equipment, Stalin curtailed the production of consumer goods. He made the USSR strong, but did not greatly increase the standard of living of the people.

The 'New Tsar'

Historians have continued to debate whether or not the Stalinist regime constituted a genuine cultural revolution. Although Stalin was ostensibly leading the forces of a 'revolution', he permitted and indeed facilitated the re-emergence of most of the features of the Tsarist regime.

Instead of the initiative for social change and decision-making emerging from the masses (which had been the intention of the revolutionaries of 1917), all legislation and all executive control was exercised by Stalin. A centralised **bureaucracy** was re-established with extensive privileges, and a new autocrat ruled from the capital city. The 'revolution' had not succeeded in eliminating the distinctions of class. The State owned the resources of the nation, and a new ideology was applied to justify the uses to which those resources were being applied. Other than this, the Russian people appeared to have merely exchanged Tsar Nicholas II for dictator Stalin.

A convincing counter-argument can also be raised, to the effect that the Stalinist regime in the USSR did indeed implement a revolution. Under Stalinist rule there were no longer any

THE OLD MAN OF THE STEPPES.

"WE'VE REACHED THE FIFTH MILESTONE, LITTLE BROTHER, BUT THE BURDEN ISN'T ANY EASIER YET."

[The first Five Year Plan of Soviet Russia under the directorship of STALIN has failed to realise expectations.]

'The Old Man of the Steppes': a British cartoonist's interpretation of the Soviet Five Year plans. The 'ordinary Russian' is portrayed as bearing the burden of Stalin's administration.

1 What is the symbolism of the hammer and sickle, held in this position, in Stalin's hands?

2 Which proletarian class is represented by the hammer?

3 Which other group, regarded by the Communist Party of Russia as essential supporters of communism, is represented by the sickle?

4 What is the cartoonist's purpose in showing a whip?

5 Study the expressions on the two faces and explain what the cartoonist might be suggesting in each instance.

6 What message is the cartoonist conveying by his sketch of the landscape and the road?

7 What is the cartoonist implying in his caption?

8 This cartoon was published in *Punch*, London, on 11 January 1933, for a magazine with a predominantly capitalist reading public. How does this affect your interpretation of the cartoon as historical evidence?

classes living off the ownership of property. After the elimination of the kulaks, all 'citizens' were working for the State on 'wage labour'. Moreover, a transformed society was evident in the form of a completely new range of institutions: collective and State farms; economic planning agencies forcing industrial development; and a controlled communication system deciding what the people should receive as information. Institutions such as the secret police and the centralised bureaucracy were indeed similar to those of the Tsarist regime, but the other institutions were so radically different from those of Tsarist society that a 'revolution' could be claimed.

Further support of this claim can be found in the practice of a new form of communication, through which the aims and objectives of social control were expressed in a new terminology—or 'revolutionary' vocabulary. Conformity to this new discourse was obligatory. Even music and literature were 'directed', under instructions that all 'bourgeois' elements (regarded as vestiges of the 'corrupt' capitalist society) should be purged out.

The altered status of women constituted another component of the transformation of society. All careers and occupations were opened to women, and this was welcomed and indeed admired by women's rights organisations around the world. Only civil marriages were recognised, divorce was made easily attainable, and abortion was legalised. The 'down side' of the fortunes of women in Soviet society were that they were subject to mobilisation in the State-directed occupations, and, because of the consumer-goods deprivation, became 'prisoners of the queues', spending hours each week attempting to obtain the basic necessities for their families.

V THE GREAT PATRIOTIC WAR: 1941–45

In 1941 Hitler unleashed the might of the German army in a massive invasion of the USSR. The world held its breath at the scale of this invasion, expecting the Soviet regime to collapse. Yet the USSR absorbed the power of Nazi Germany's onslaught, and eventually repulsed the invaders. At a colossal cost in human lives (some 20 million dead), the USSR defeated Hitler. Despite the contributions to the anti-Nazi cause by Britain, the USA and their allies, it was principally the effort of the USSR that ensured Hitler's defeat.

Throughout the nations of the former USSR today, the memorials to this great victory all refer to the 'Great Patriotic War'—a telling reminder that when survival was at stake, an emotional appeal was made to **patriotism** and to the defence of 'Mother Russia', and not to the ideology of socialism.

Yet, the military victory of the USSR over Germany could not have been won without the industrial base achieved through Stalin's Five Year plans. In twenty years this hitherto relatively backward nation had produced the tanks, guns, aeroplanes and support structures that made it possible for the Soviet military leaders to outfight and outgeneral the professional army of Germany with its long tradition of military discipline and military science. The command economy met the challenge that Stalin had foreseen.

VI THE POST-STALIN REACTION

After Stalin's death in 1953, a period of 'collective rule' followed, with Nikita Khrushchev emerging, by 1956, as the dominant figure, holding the key position of General Secretary of the Communist Party. At the 20th Party Congress in February 1956, Khrushchev astounded the party members by vigorously denouncing the policies and personality of Stalin. This introduced a period of what was called 'de-Stalinisation', during which many of the claims made by Stalin about plots against him were debunked, and many of his policies reversed.

Khrushchev further consolidated his position by also acquiring the position of Chairman of the Council of Ministers (in effect, prime

The Five Year plans were intended to bring about the rapid industrialisation of Russia. This photograph, taken in the Ural Mountains region in 1931, shows a group of construction workers assembling a mineral excavator designed to service a new iron and steel factory.

minister) in 1958. He next set out to de-centralise control of industries, and to increase production of consumer goods for the comfort of the ordinary Russian citizen. He also hoped to offer the people more leisure time through a shorter working week.

Khrushchev was dismissed from office by his colleagues in 1964. Leonid Brezhnev then became Secretary of the Communist Party, and Aleksei Kosygin took office as Chairman of the Council of Ministers. Many of Khrushchev's reforms were dismantled by his successors.

The Modern Command Economy in the USSR

Right up till the collapse of the USSR in 1991, the Soviet economy was still officially desig-nated as 'socialist' rather than 'communist'—the term reserved for the 'ultimate society' towards which the USSR was theoretically making progress. Under the Soviet regime all natural resources, including land, had been declared State property, and the whole Soviet economy was administered by a vast conglom-eration of planning and administrative bureau-cracies, most of which carried out directives handed down from above. The most powerful planning agency was in fact the Communist Party itself, or its dominant leaders. The econ-omy was thus responsive to 'command' from central controlling agencies.

Nevertheless, in housing and retail trading there was a surprising degree of private owner-ship. By the 1980s almost all rural housing and about 26 per cent of urban housing was privately owned (the rest was State-owned or held by co-operatives). In addition to the wages the peasants earned on the *kolkhoz*, they were permitted to farm a private plot and could freely sell the produce from it on the *kolkhoz* 'market' at unregulated prices according to demand. By 1980 the trading in these markets accounted for about 4 per cent of total retail trade.

In meeting and repelling the invasion by Nazi Germany, and in maintaining a high level of armament readiness during the post-war Cold War period, the command economy of the USSR had proved to be an effective means by which a totalitarian State could mobilise the resources of the nation for rapid industrialisation. However, once the forced modernisation had been achieved, the excessive degree of centralisation and bureaucratic control inhibited the efficient operations necessary to sustain an expansion in the economy.

For this reason the Soviet government began experimenting in the 1960s with means of loosening centralised control and of introducing incentives for production. Called the 'Libermann system' after its advocate, Professor Yevsea Libermann of Kharkhov University, who had criticised the command system, the new arrangement gave factory managers some responsibility for planning their own production in relation to projected consumer demand, and an opportunity to earn profits and distribute them to the workers as bonuses in reward for efficient work.

Sponsored by the new dual leadership team of Brezhnev and Kosygin, the reforms were reported in the Western press as allowing managers of productive enterprises to retain from their profits 'more funds for the development of production, improvement of technology, material incentives for workers, and better living and working conditions'(*The Australian*, Sydney, 29 September 1965).

Before the introduction of this system, each factory manager simply carried out the directives from above, and was responsible for production, not sales. The Brezhnev–Kosygin reforms were intended to give incentives for managers to be concerned about the quality and market appeal of their produce, and carried the implied admission that Marx was wrong when he forecast that eventually people would work without the profit motive.

The reforms, however, did not significantly alter the command economy, or shift it in nature towards a market economy, because the government continued to fix prices and control the allocation of resources—functions that, in a market economy, are free to respond to the pressures of supply and demand. It was not until the collapse of the Communist regime in 1991 that the full operation of market forces was permitted in the republics of the former USSR, with some unfortunate results.

Was the Stalinist Regime a Betrayal of the Revolution?

Many followers of Marxist teachings claim that what happened in Russia and the USSR over the period 1917 to 1991 cannot be regarded as a failure of Marxist principles. Rather, they see the events as a betrayal of the true purposes of a people's revolution and as a perversion of Marxism.

They claim that free-enterprise capitalism had been displaced by State capitalism, and that the true purpose of Marxism—the equitable redistribution of wealth in a society controlled by the proletariat—did not occur. What happened was that a new élite—the Communist Party officials—replaced the old Tsarist-sponsored élite, and that class distinctions were reinforced rather than eliminated. Thus while a 'revolution' (in the sense of a total displacement of the former ruling class) may have occurred, it was not a true revolution according to the Marxist formula. Once power was seized by the Bolshevik leaders, they never permitted the establishment of a true 'government by the proletariat'.

Supporters of the Russian Revolution replied to this argument—right up until the collapse of the regime in 1991—that it was not fair to label the Revolution as a failure, because it was never completed. The Russian Communist leaders claimed for decades that their society was in the 'socialist' stage of development (as the very name, Union of Soviet Socialist Republics, demonstrated) and was moving towards the communist condition of the 'classless society'. The 22nd Party Congress, meeting in October 1961, claimed, for example, that the foundations of a classless communist society would be achieved in Russia by 1980. This attitude was maintained right through to the 1990s. Even on literally the eve of his downfall in 1991, the last General Secretary of the Communist Party of the USSR, Mikhail Gorbachev, claimed that he was restructuring the Communist Party in order to fulfil the aims of the Revolution.

MAJOR EVENTS IN THE HISTORY OF SOVIET RUSSIA AND THE USSR 1917–45

1917 Seizure of power by the soviets (workers' councils), and the Bolshevik Party. Vladimir Lenin became chief commissar; Leon Trotsky became premier.

1918 *March* Treaty of Brest-Litovsk with Germany
December Soviet government annulled Treaty of Brest-Litovsk after Germany agreed to an armistice on the Western front

1919 Comintern (Communist Third International) formed, to work for the overthrow of capitalism throughout the world

1921 The 'New Economic Policy' in Russia allowed a partial return to capitalism

1922 A great relief operation was launched by the USA and European nations to relieve severe famine in Russia

1923 The Union of Soviet Socialist Republics (USSR) was established

1924 Lenin died. Josef Stalin emerged later as his successor as General Secretary of the Central Committee of the Communist Party.

1928 The first Five Year Plan was launched

1929 Leon Trotsky was forced out of USSR as a 'deviationist'

1931–33 The great famine

1934 The League of Nations admitted USSR as a member

1935 Purges of the Communist Party; prominent leaders, including Grigori Zinoviev, convicted of treason

1936 Germany and Japan signed Anti-Comintern (anti-communist) Pact; later joined by Italy

1939 Germany and USSR signed a non-aggression pact (sometimes called the Molotov-Ribbentrop pact) which appeared to cancel the Anti-Comintern Pact
Germany invaded Poland, and Britain and France declared war on Germany
USSR occupied eastern Poland
USSR invaded Finland
USSR was expelled from the League of Nations

1941 Germany repudiated the 1939 non-aggression pact and invaded the USSR, advancing to within 100 kilometres of Moscow
Britain and Allies undertook to aid the USSR

1943 Russian counter-offensive led to the capture of a German army at Stalingrad

1945 Russian troops reached Berlin after having repulsed the German invasion
Nazi regime in Germany terminated

---

chapter eight

The Collapse of Communism in Europe: Another Revolution?

*For everything there is a season, and a time for
every matter under heaven:
a time to be born, and a time to die;
a time to plant, and a time to pluck up what is
planted;
a time to kill, and a time to heal;
a time to break down, and a time to build up;
a time to weep, and a time to laugh;
a time to mourn, and a time to dance; . . .
a time to seek, and a time to lose;
a time to keep, and a time to cast away;
a time to rend, and a time to sew;
a time to keep silence, and a time to speak;
a time to love, and a time to hate;
a time for war, and a time for peace.
What gain has the worker from his toil?*

Ecclesiastes 3: 1–4, 6–9

On 'Victory in Europe' (VE) Day (8 May
1945), a cease-fire was achieved in the European sphere of conflict in World War II. Within
three years pro-communist, one-party States
had been established in all the eastern European
nations adjacent to the USSR.

The leaders of the Western nations were
outraged by this development because at the

Yalta Conference of the 'Big Three' powers in
February 1945, Stalin, on behalf of the USSR,
had committed himself to the so-called 'Declaration on Liberated Europe'. This promised
that the liberated nations would be able to 'create democratic institutions of their own choice'.

Mutual suspicions between the Western
capitalist world and the communist bloc quickly
escalated into open hostility. Winston Churchill
warned that the Communists had erected an
'iron curtain' around their empire. Each 'side'
embarked on a massive re-armament programme to prepare for the possibility of war. So
was launched the so-called 'Cold War', which
was to prevail for forty-five years from 1946 till
1991. When the communist regimes of eastern
Europe collapsed in the years 1989–91, the
astonishing series of events were described
as 'another revolution', or sometimes as a
'counter-revolution'.

Theme Questions

➢ To what extent did the USSR create a
'Soviet Empire'?
➢ What factors generated the 'counter-
revolution' against communism?

I THE CONSOLIDATION OF COMMUNIST REGIMES IN EASTERN EUROPE

Historians may sit in judgement on events such as the Soviet domination of Eastern Europe in the post-1945 era, but in the real world emotions must be considered along with 'facts'. The Soviet Union's post-war foreign policy must be evaluated in the context of the fears and triumphs of the Soviet peoples.

Twice in thirty years the citizens of Russia and later the USSR had fought against massive land invasions by Germans, Austrians, Hungarians, Italians and Rumanians coming from the west. On the second of these occasions the Soviets suspected that the Nazi invasion was essentially an assault on their socialist society by the capitalist powers.

In every republic that was a part of the USSR until its dissolution in 1991, war memorials commemorating the victory over the fascist forces of Nazi Germany and Mussolini's Italy abound—flowers are placed on them daily in memory of the 23 million Soviet war dead. One of the memorials near Moscow memorably states: 'no one is forgotten; nothing is forgotten'.

The Soviet determination to build a pro-communist 'buffer zone' in eastern Europe after 1945 should be evaluated with this understandably defensive obsession in mind. Because the leaders of the USSR harboured the suspicion that the capitalist West would continue to plot the downfall of the communist regimes, the wartime alliance quickly changed into the condition of permanent suspicion known as the Cold War.

Tension between the two ideologically opposed groups came close to breaking point in 1948. Germany had been divided into four occupation zones (British, French, American and Soviet) after the defeat of the Nazi regime. The city of Berlin was likewise divided into four segments, but was surrounded by the territory of the Soviet zone. The British, French and American sectors of the city constituted West Berlin.

On 24 June 1948 Stalin closed all land communication routes to Berlin in an attempt to absorb it into the Soviet zone. The Western powers were in a quandary: they could abandon West Berlin and sacrifice their declared principles (as had occurred at Munich in 1938); force land access with troops and risk a world war; or attempt to supply 2 250 000 West Berliners with all goods, including coal and food, by air. The last course involved the use of air transport on a scale never before envisaged. In eleven months American, French and British pilots flew 277 728 flights to deliver 2 243 000 tonnes of supplies into Berlin. The Soviet bluff was countered, and a new sense of solidarity had been fostered between the German people and their former enemies.

The hostility between the capitalist and communist powers led to the withdrawal of the USSR from the Allied Control Commission on Germany (set up in 1945 to co-ordinate the Allied occupation). The British, French and Americans then agreed to merge their three zones economically (by 1948), and proceeded to permit free elections for a new government for the merged zones. Thus the Federal Republic of Germany (later referred to as West Germany) emerged, under a democratic constitution, by August 1949.

A new capitalist-aligned nation in central Europe had thus been created. In sponsoring this development the three Western powers had broken a clause in the Yalta Agreement (the great powers had agreed to divide Germany into four zones of occupation and ensure its disarmament before allowing a reunification of the nation). Britain, France and the USA had now created a reunified Germany excluding the Soviet zone, but claimed they were justified in this action because of the USSR's earlier betrayal of the principles expressed in the Declaration on Liberated Europe (that is, in the USSR's installation of communist one-party regimes in all the east European nations).

In October 1949 the Soviets responded to the establishment of the pro-capitalist West Germany by converting their occupation zone into the German Democratic Republic (East Germany) and installing a communist government. (The republic was 'democratic' in the

SOURCE 8.1
Winston Churchill signals the descent of the Iron Curtain, 1946

HISTORICAL CONTEXT: By 1946 the alliance of the 'Big Three' which had defeated Nazi Germany—Britain, the USSR and the USA—was splitting apart. The common purpose that had held them together was no longer operative. The USA and Britain were capitalist democracies, while the USSR was a group of socialist republics, to all appearances establishing a satellite empire in eastern Europe, thus threatening a world-wide expansion of communist regimes.

Source: **W.S. Churchill, in a speech at Fulton, Missouri, USA, 5 March 1946**

A shadow has fallen upon the scenes so lately lighted by the Allied victory. Nobody knows what Soviet Russia and its Communist international organisation intends to do in the immediate future, or what are the limits, if any, to their expansive and proselytizing tendencies . . . We understand the Russian need to be secure on her western frontiers by the removal of all possibility of German aggression. We welcome Russia to her rightful place among the leading nations of the world. We welcome her flag upon the seas. Above all, we welcome constant, frequent and growing contacts between the Russian people and our own people on both sides of the Atlantic. It is my duty, however, for I am sure you would wish me to state the facts as I see them, to place before you certain facts about the present position in Europe.

From Stettin in the Baltic to Trieste in the Adriatic, an iron curtain has descended across the Continent. Behind that line lie all the capitals of the ancient states of central and eastern Europe. Warsaw, Berlin, Prague, Vienna, Budapest, Belgrade, Bucharest, and Sofia—all these famous cities and the populations around them lie in what I must call the Soviet sphere, and all are subject in one form or another, not only to Soviet influence, but to a very high and, in many cases, increasing measure of con-trol from Moscow . . . The Communist Parties, which were very small in all these eastern states of Europe, have been raised to pre-eminence and power far beyond their numbers and are seeking everywhere to obtain totalitarian control. Police governments are prevailing in nearly every case, and so far, except in Czechoslovakia, there is no true democracy . . .

I have felt bound to portray the shadow which, alike in the west and in the east, falls upon the world . . .

From what I have seen of our Russian friends and Allies during the war, I am convinced that there is nothing they admire so much as strength, and there is nothing for which they have less respect than for weakness, especially military weakness. For that reason the old doctrine of a balance of power is unsound. We cannot afford, if we can help it, to work on narrow margins, offering temptations to a trial of strength. If the Western democracies stand together in strict adherence to the principles of the United Nations Charter, their influence for furthering those principles will be immense and no one is likely to molest them. If, however, they become divided or falter in their duty and if these all important years are allowed to slip away, then indeed catastrophe may overwhelm us all.

QUESTIONS

1 What is Churchill hinting at when he used the term 'Communist international organisation'?

2 What accusation is Churchill making in his observation that 'the Communist Parties . . . have been raised to pre-eminence and power far beyond their numbers'?

3 What is Churchill trying to achieve by his call to avoid 'temptations to a trial of strength'?

4 What is Churchill's frame of reference, and what effect on public opinion is he seeking?

economic sense of assuring equal standards of living for the inhabitants, but not in the political sense of permitting the free function of numerous political parties.) Eventually, both East Germany and East Berlin were cut off from the rest of Germany by border fences and the notorious Berlin Wall. This prevented the full reunification of Germany, and further intensified what were termed East–West tensions.

NATO and the Warsaw Pact

The Americans were alarmed at how close to a shooting war the two sides had come in the 1948 Berlin quarrel. The problem of keeping the peace was intensified by the fact that the so-called 'Big Five' great powers—Britain, Nationalist China, France, the USA and the USSR—all possessed the power of veto in the United Nations Security Council. The promise of this procedure had been needed to persuade the great powers to join the UN, but in the late 1940s the frequent use of the veto by the USSR had rendered the Security Council useless as a peace enforcement agency.

The United States therefore turned to an alternative means of attaining collective security. It formed a new military alliance.

Belgium, Britain, France, Luxembourg and the Netherlands had already formed the Brussels Treaty Organisation. In April 1949 these five powers, under US leadership, were joined by Canada, Denmark, Iceland, Norway, Portugal and the USA in the North Atlantic Treaty Organisation (NATO)—an 'automatic response' defence alliance. If one member of the alliance was attacked, all the others would come to its aid. Greece and Turkey were added to NATO in 1952, and West Germany in 1955.

The creation of NATO formalised the Cold War as a grim confrontation and sparked off a renewed arms race that greatly increased the risk of war. The rearming of West Germany by the West, and its admission to NATO in 1955, provoked the Soviets into forming a counter-alliance under the Warsaw Pact (1955). This encompassed all the eastern European communist States except Yugoslavia. The pact included a statement that an attack on any one member would be regarded as an attack on all, and made provisions for a unified military command.

Thus two armed camps had again emerged in Europe (although it would be reasonably correct to say that the Warsaw Pact simply formalised a situation that already existed). In the eyes of the critics of Soviet imperialism, the nations who had joined the Warsaw Pact were simply subject nations within the Soviet Empire. An impartial observer might conclude that two rival empires now faced each other in mutual hostility.

Enforcing the Revolution: the 'Soviet Empire'

Although the theory of Marxian socialism claimed that the mass of the people would be well provided for under socialism and its eventual successor, communism, when the socialist-communist governments in eastern Europe did take over, the people in those nations soon showed their discontent. Protest demonstrations were staged, claiming the right to express individual opinion and freedom of choice. The State apparatus in the communist nations quickly became geared to the task of enforcing obedience. The people were required to be obedient to their State Communist Party; additionally the smaller communist States were required to be obedient to the USSR.

Even before the formation of the Warsaw Pact in 1955, events in the Soviet sphere demonstrated the determination of the rulers of the USSR to keep their satellite States under control. In East Berlin in 1953, a citizens' protest against the authoritarian Communist government was suppressed, at first by the *Volkspolezei* (the East German Republic's police force), and then by Soviet tanks. This emphasised the fact that although East Germany was officially a separate republic, it was really part of a Soviet-controlled empire.

After 1955 the Warsaw Pact ensured that Soviet troops were permanently stationed in all the member nations. It should be noted that British and American troops were similarly

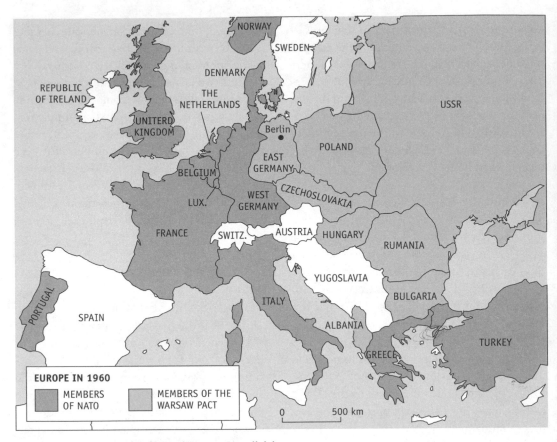

MAP 8.1 Europe in 1960: NATO and Warsaw Pact divisions

The North Atlantic Treaty Organisation, founded in 1949, had expanded by 1954 to include all the western European nations except Austria, Eire, Sweden, Switzerland and Spain. NATO also included the USA, Canada, Iceland and, in eastern Europe, Greece and Turkey. By 1960 communist administrations controlled all eastern European nations except Finland and Greece, although Communist Yugoslavia decided not to align itself with the Soviet bloc. All these communist countries except Yugoslavia became members of the Warsaw Pact Organisation, founded in 1955, in order to create a counterforce to NATO.

stationed in West Germany. The difference, however, lay in the way in which the USSR enforced membership of the Warsaw Pact.

In both Hungary in 1956 and Czechoslovakia in 1968, Soviet forces were used to crush mildly reformist governments that had attempted to modify the communist system. Many lives were lost in the demonstrations of the determination of the leaders of the USSR to maintain the unity of the Soviet Empire.

The Brezhnev Doctrine

The Czechoslovakian incident resulted in the formalisation of the principle of obedience within the Soviet Empire. Speaking in 1968 at the Polish Communist Party Congress (and thereby warning the Poles), Leonid Brezhnev, the Soviet leader at the time, proclaimed what became known as the Brezhnev Doctrine when he stated that any threat to the 'cause of socialism' in any country was to be 'a matter of concern for all socialist countries'. Brezhnev thus assumed, on behalf of the USSR, the right to intervene in the affairs of what he called other 'socialist' (that is, Marxian socialist) countries.

'Exporting the Revolution': the Wider Soviet Empire

To Western eyes, the USSR was actively attempting to 'export' the socialist revolution to other parts of the world. By Marxist theory this was thoroughly justified as part of the long-term plan to liberate the proletariat of the world from capitalist exploitation.

The Soviet-sponsored pro-communist regime established by Fidel Castro in Cuba in 1959 was quickly labelled in the West as an out-post of the Soviet Empire, particularly after Castro permitted the location in Cuba of Soviet-made ballistic missiles. Americans saw the missiles as a direct threat to their security. This led to the 1962 Cuban crisis, in which the rivalry between the USA and the USSR almost resulted in a war. Later, Cuba became in effect an agent of Soviet imperialism by supplying troops to support pro-communist insurgencies in the African nations of Mozambique and Angola, created from the former Portuguese colonies of the same names.

North Korea in the 1950s, and North Vietnam in the 1960s, were also regarded in the West as surrogate States acting in the interests of Soviet imperialism. During both the Korean War (1950–53) and the Vietnam War (1963–75) the capitalist world was convinced that the pro-communist forces were receiving Soviet aid. In the West it was believed that determined resistance to these communist regimes was necessary as a means of forestalling Soviet ambitions.

II THE EMERGENCE OF A COUNTER-REVOLUTION: 'SOLIDARITY' IN POLAND

Until 1980 the permanence of the one-party communist regimes in the Eastern Bloc appeared to be unquestioned. The Soviet-imposed Brezhnev Doctrine had enforced the policy that none of these States could leave the 'team'. Massive military resources under Warsaw Pact command stood ready to punish any transgressor. This had been done in Hungary in 1956, and Czechoslovakia in 1968.

In the original Communist revolution in Russia in October 1917, the campaign slogan had been 'all power to the workers'. The leaders of the Bolsheviks (the Communist Party) had

---

SOURCE 8.2
Leonid Brezhnev proclaims the Brezhnev Doctrine, demanding obedience from satellite communist states, 1968

HISTORICAL CONTEXT: After communist-aligned regimes had been established on the western borders of the USSR (see Map 8.1), the Soviet leaders were determined to ensure that these regimes followed communist poli-cies. In Hungary in 1956 and Czechoslovakia in 1968, Soviet troops intervened in the inter-nal affairs of these nations to ensure that there was no 'liberalisation' of policies.

The Brezhnev Doctrine thus stated a demand for rigid obedience to direction from Moscow. It was a denial of the principle of self-determination.

Source: **Leonid Brezhnev, in a speech at the Polish Communist Party Congress, 13 November 1968**

When the internal and external forces hostile to socialism seek to turn back the development of any socialist country to restore the capitalist order, when a threat emerges to the cause of socialism in that coun-try, a threat to the security of the Socialist Com-monwealth as a whole, this is no longer a matter only for the people of the country in question, but it is also a common problem, which is a matter of con-cern for all socialist countries.

QUESTIONS
1 What is implied by Brezhnev's use of the term 'Socialist Commonwealth'?
2 What arguments could be advanced to support the validity of this concept?
3 What principle of revolution is being denied by this 'Doctrine' (see Source 3.3)?

claimed that their victory was part of the world-wide revolution predicted by Marx, in which the proletariat (the wage-earning classes) would seize power, distribute wealth evenly, and develop first a socialist, and ultimately a communist, society. Class distinctions would disappear, and poverty would be eliminated.

Through a supreme irony, it was a newly emergent proletarian workers' organisation that challenged and eventually overthrew the communist regime in Poland. Discontentment with work conditions and petty bureaucratic regulations in the port city of Gdansk (Danzig in pre-war times) led to the formation, in August 1980, of a trade union. The members called themselves *Solidarnose* (Solidarity), and called upon other wage-earners to join. A 37-year-old electrician, Lech Walesa, assumed leadership.

The Solidarity members right from the beginning proclaimed their loyalty to the Roman Catholic Church. It had been a visit to Poland by the Polish-born Pope John Paul II, who had proclaimed that Christianity and communism were incompatible, which had triggered the creation of Solidarity.

Dissatisfied with the hardships of life under communism, the members of Solidarity demanded a relaxation of censorship of both press and radio (including the broadcast of religious services), an increase in food supplies, and a reduction in the working week. In August 1980 they won the legal right to strike, and extracted concessions from the Polish Communist Party that ended the government's press monopoly. Solidarity was the first independent trade union to emerge in a communist bloc country, and by 1981, with a membership of 9.5 million, it was challenging the Communist government to respond to more of the people's demands.

In December 1981 the leader of the Polish Communist Party, General Jaruzelski, placed Poland under military law, arrested most of Solidarity's leaders, banned all trade unions and abolished the right to strike.

For nineteen months Jaruzelski attempted to govern Poland under martial law, but was finally forced by the pressure of public opinion to lift the repressions in July 1983. In 1989 Jaruzelski bowed to the inevitable and also lifted the ban on Solidarity. He further declared that open elections would be held in 1989 for the Senate (the upper house) and for 35 per cent of the seats in the Sejm (the lower house). The remaining 65 per cent of seats were reserved for the Communist Party.

In a sensational result, Solidarity won all but three of the seats in the 100-member Senate, and all of the seats it had been permitted to contest in the Sejm. Its power in the upper house ensured that Solidarity could exercise a veto over parliament, and it soon became clear that the Communist Party could not govern the country.

The significance of these events in Poland was enormous. For the first time since Stalin had imposed one-party communist regimes in eastern Europe after World War II, elections permitting the participation of another political party had been held. As a result, an anti-communist opposition party had been able to enter parliament. By August 1989 a Solidarity nominee, Tadeusz Mazowiecki, had taken office as prime minister of a coalition government—the first non-communist prime minister in Eastern Europe since 1947. The word 'socialist' was dropped from the name of the nation, which was now simply called the Republic of Poland.

The victory of Solidarity in Poland marked the beginning of the end for what had been viewed as the Soviet Empire. In 1990 the rejection of both communism and of Poland's forced association with the USSR were announced to the world by the declaration by the Polish government that the nation was leaving the Warsaw Pact. Three months later, in December, Jaruzelski was displaced as president by Lech Walesa, the man whom he had once placed under house arrest. Walesa was the first democratically elected president of post-war Poland.

Poland then set a pattern that other nations in Eastern Europe were quick to follow. The new government encouraged a free-market economy, with freedom of expression, free enterprise and multiple political parties. A prototype 'counter-revolution'—reversing the expansion of communism which had prevailed since 1945—was on display.

III THE END OF THE COLD WAR: 1989–90

The momentum of the counter-revolution was further increased in 1989–90 by the great reduction in the East–West Cold War animosities that had prevailed for forty-four years. This easing of tensions came as a surprise, for the preceding decade had been notable for high levels of animosity between the two ideologically opposed groups. When the Republican candidate, Ronald Reagan, assumed the office of president of the USA in January 1981, a new intensity had been injected into the existing Cold War suspicions. The Americans and the rest of the Western world were at the time outraged by the Soviet invasion of its neighbouring nation, Afghanistan, in the previous year.

The practices of the USSR, Reagan claimed, were based on 'tests of will'. He said that the Soviets sent out challenges in various forms to the democratic capitalist world, and if these challenges were not rebuffed, it would be assumed that the West was weakening in resolve. Accordingly, the Reagan administration set out to convince the Soviets that any expansionist aggression, whether by the USSR itself or by its satellite States, would be countered. It was apparent that another round of war-threatening East–West challenges was imminent.

The Significance of the Administration of Mikhail Gorbachev in the USSR

The nature of the leadership of the Soviet Union was a crucial factor influencing Cold War tensions. Between 1982 and 1985 there were three leadership changes. In November 1982 Leonid Brezhnev, who had been leader for eighteen years, died in office. Two short-lived administrations followed. Then, in April 1985 Mikhail Gorbachev, at the age of fifty-four a comparatively young man, assumed the key office of General Secretary of the Communist Party, to which he later added the position of president.

Gorbachev totally altered the Cold War atmosphere by developing a policy of *glasnost* (openness), inviting free expression of opinion, including comments challenging domestic and foreign policy. Many dissidents were released from detention. At the same time Gorbachev promised *perestroika,* the restructuring of the political and economic systems of the Soviet state. He also said that a 'new image of socialism' would be created through *demokratizatsiya* (democratisation of the system of government).

Gorbachev's apparent willingness to introduce and discuss ways to reduce Cold War tensions was welcomed in the West. But ill-feeling lived on. The Americans believed that the Soviet invasion of Afghanistan had shown that the Soviets could not be trusted.

This same suspicion operated to cast doubt on Gorbachev's motives. It was thought that he was reverting to the old trick of appearing to be co-operative, in order to lull the West into a false sense of safety. The fact that the Warsaw Pact—the communist military alliance—had been renewed in April 1985 for twenty years, was cited in the West as the true indication of Soviet policy.

Despite their residual suspicions, representatives of the USA and the USSR began talks in 1985, seeking agreement on ways of cutting down on their huge stockpiles of missiles and nuclear weapons. This apparently simple matter was hampered by the fact that whatever the words used, the superpowers remained suspicious of each other. Generations of indoctrination had ingrained the belief that each system—capitalist and communist—was dedicated to the overthrow of the other. Gorbachev still had to convince the West that he really wanted to end the Cold War.

The Retreat from Animosity

Despite the failure of the leaders to reach specific agreement, subsequent events quickly

SOURCE 8.3
Mikhail Gorbachev attempts a major adjustment to the Communist Revolution—*perestroika* in the USSR, 1987

HISTORICAL CONTEXT: Mikhail Gorbachev became the key figure in the government of the USSR in 1985. To revitalise communist society he launched a policy of 'reform from within', by means of *perestroika* (restructuring) and *glasnost* (open expression of criticism).

Source: **M. Gorbachev, *Perestroika: New Thinking for our Country and the World*, Collins, London, 1985, pp. 34–5**

Perestroika means overcoming the stagnation process, breaking down the braking mechanism, creating a dependable and effective mechanism for the acceleration of social and economic progress and giving it greater dynamism.

Perestroika means mass initiative. It is the comprehensive development of democracy, socialist self-government, encouragement of initiative and creative endeavour, improved order and discipline, more glasnost, criticism and self-criticism in all spheres of our society. It is utmost respect for the individual and consideration for personal dignity.

Perestroika is the all-round intensification of the Soviet economy, the revival and development of the principles of democratic centralism in running the national economy, the universal introduction of economic methods, the renunciation of management by injunction and by administrative methods, and the overall encouragement of innovation and socialist enterprise.

Perestroika means a resolute shift to scientific methods, an ability to provide a solid scientific basis for every new initiative. It means the combination of the achievements of the scientific and technological revolution with a planned economy.

Perestroika means priority development of the social sphere aimed at ever better satisfaction of the Soviet people's requirements for good living and working conditions, for good rest and recreation, education and health care. It means unceasing concern for cultural and spiritual wealth, for the culture of every individual and society as a whole.

Perestroika means the elimination from society of the distortions of socialist ethics, the consistent implementation of the principles of social justice. It means the unity of words and deeds, rights and duties. It is the elevation of honest, highly-qualified labour, the overcoming of levelling tendencies in pay and consumerism.

QUESTIONS

1 What does Gorbachev see as the most effective means of revitalising communist society?

2 What method of directing production is scheduled to be 'renounced'?

3 In which statement does Gorbachev make provision for rewards for initiative and enterprise simultaneously with the rejection of the concept of 'total equality' under socialism?

4 What attitude, evident throughout this statement, signals that Gorbachev's proposed reforms would constitute a 'fine-tuning' of communism rather than a revolution?

---

contributed to a wind-down of Cold War tensions. In the sphere of domestic policy, Gorbachev demonstrated his commitment to *perestroika* by opening the door to capitalist practice. In newspaper reports in November 1986 it was stated that the Soviet government, for the first time since the 1917 Bolshevik Revolution, had clearly defined the 'ground rules' for individual enterprise, in an 'open recognition of the failure of the existing communist regime to provide the necessary goods and services to satisfy the population' (*The Australian*, Sydney, 21 November 1985).

In the next two years Gorbachev acted quickly and decisively to dismantle the long-standing Soviet armament policy based on the

'Roll Over, Play Dead', a cartoon by Vines in the Brisbane *Courier-Mail*, 27 December 1989. Despite all Mikhail Gorbachev's efforts to reduce tension between the USSR and the West, the suspicion remained in the West that it was all a ploy. For decades Western diplomats had believed that if the USSR seemed to be sealing down its aggressive tendencies, it would simply be a trick to lull the West into a false sense of security. In this cartoon Gorbachev is portrayed as telling the 'big bad Russian bear' to pretend he is no longer a threat. (Mac Vines)

premise that the Western nations were a military threat. He announced huge reductions in the Soviet armed forces, and withdrew all Soviet contingents from the Warsaw Pact command.

In the opinion of Western leaders, however, the USSR still needed to prove that it was no longer expansionist and aggressive. The greatest obstacle to a Western willingness to trust the USSR was the fact that since 1980 the Soviets had been involved in a military invasion of Afghanistan. This had drawn enormous condemnation from the West. In May 1988 Gorbachev ordered the beginning of a phased withdrawal of Soviet troops from Afghanistan. The war had lasted over eight years, and had caused 15 000 deaths. Gorbachev admitted that the Soviet invasion had been 'a sin'. His foreign minister, Eduard Shevardnaze, went further, and was later quoted (*Time Australia*, Melbourne, 31 December 1990) as saying that in invading Afghanistan, the USSR had 'set itself against all of humanity, and had ignored human

values'. In its withdrawal from Afghanistan, the USSR had repudiated the Brezhnev Doctrine, and had created a new opportunity for a reduction in East–West tensions.

In December 1988 the 'thaw' continued at a startling pace. Addressing the UN General Assembly, Gorbachev promised further reductions in armaments and repudiated the Marxist theory of the inevitability of conflict between capitalist and communist forces. He was reported as stating that he 'rejected that wars and social and political clashes should be accepted as workings of immutable law' (*The Courier-Mail*, Brisbane, 16 December 1988).

During 1989 hundreds of headlines proclaimed the Cold War to be over. Gorbachev had signalled that the Brezhnev Doctrine was dead, and that he did not intend to use military force to hold the nations of eastern Europe under communist rule. By July 1990 the North Atlantic Treaty Organisation (NATO), specifically formed in 1949 to 'fence in' communism, declared that the USSR was no longer the identified adversary.

By November 1990 the oft-proclaimed burial of the Cold War was celebrated yet again in two significant events. The 'Conventional Forces in Europe' treaty committed twenty-two nations, including the USSR, to a massive 'scrapyard' campaign in which 100 000 items of military equipment, guns, tanks and aeroplanes would be destroyed and the arms race cancelled. In the same week thirty-four nations signed the 'Charter of Paris for a New Europe', affirming that every individual has the right to 'freedom of thought, conscience and religion or belief, freedom of expression, freedom of association and peaceful assembly'. As the USSR and its former satellites all accepted this charter, it was widely observed that perhaps the demise of one-party authoritarian communism had indeed arrived.

At the same meeting the six members of the Warsaw Pact agreed to dissolve their military alliance by the beginning of 1992, thus eliminating the rival military force to NATO.

IV THE POLITICAL REVOLUTION IN EASTERN EUROPE: 1989–91

With the elimination of the tensions of the Cold War, and the repudiation of the Brezhnev Doctrine which had kept the Eastern European States subordinate to the dictates of Moscow, the communist regimes in those nations now came under challenge from their own people. In August 1989 the Solidarity Party (the outgrowth of the trade union of the same name) formed in Poland the first non-communist government in Eastern Europe since the 1940s. Most of the Communist governments in the other satellite States likewise collapsed in the ensuing months.

During 1990 the thaw proceeded apace. In all of the communist nations of eastern Europe

Czechs demonstrate for democratic freedoms in Wenceslas Square, Prague, in 1989. In all the Eastern European States, where one-party communist regimes had been in power for over forty years, mass demonstrations campaigned for multi-party democracy and the freedom of choice.

During the massed street protests against the Communist government of the German Democratic Republic (East Germany) in 1988–89, the people often chanted 'We are the people'—a challenge to the bureaucrats to acknowledge that they should be fulfilling the wishes of the people. Shortly afterwards, this slogan was altered to '*Wir Sind ein Volk*' (We are one people), thus expressing a desire for a reunified Germany.

THE WALL COMES TUMBLING DOWN

From staff reporters in East and West Berlin

THE Berlin Wall – the most enduring symbol of the Cold War and communist repression – is being washed away by the dramatic tide of Eastern bloc reform that is changing the course of 20th century history.

In a desperate gamble to maintain communist rule, the East German leader, Mr Krenz, yesterday threw open his country's frontiers.

As the world watched the Iron Curtain crumble, Mr Krenz's move – on the eve of Remembrance Day – triggered alarm in Bonn and among East German reformists.

Unnerved by the sea of East German refugees, the Bonn Government – which has expressed ideological support for reunification even in the face of apprehension from its European Community partners – yesterday sought urgent talks with Mr Krenz.

At the same time, a spokesman for the newly legalised East German Opposition group New Forum warned

INSIDE

● US opens bases for shelter; Stay home, Bonn advises refugees – Page 11
● The night the wall lost its meaning; Events leading to a new dawn – Page 12
● Nato offer to be 'midwife of change'; Arms take back seat – Page 13
● Editorial – Page 22
● In search of the next German phoenix – Focus 1

land is a good member of the Warsaw Pact ... governments change, but international obligations remain."

East and West Berlin were last night glowing with joy as jubilant East Germans danced on top of a Wall that had crushed their hopes for nearly 30 years.

"What joy, what joy. This is the best thing that happened in 300 years," shouted one West Berliner greeting hundreds fleeing from the East.

"I just can't believe this," said Angelika Wachs, 34, the first East German to cross

'The Wall Comes Tumbling Down'. The dramatic newspaper headline of 11 November 1989 showed the importance placed on this event. The Berlin Wall, which had divided West Berlin from East Berlin for twenty-eight years, was demolished. The newspaper report read: 'The Berlin Wall—the most enduring symbol of the Cold War and communist repression—is being washed away by the dramatic tide of Eastern Bloc reform that is changing the course of 20th century history.' A separate report was headed: 'It's like a dream, I can't believe it.'

the political authority of the Communist Party virtually disappeared as the people demanded multi-party political systems and market economies.

In Poland, Hungary, the German Democratic Republic (East Germany), Czechoslovakia, Bulgaria and Rumania, the rapid emergence of anti-communist political forces destroyed the Communists' monopoly of power. So sweeping was this development, and so momentous were the results, that 1989 will be regarded in History as an epoch-making year, ranking perhaps with 1789, 1848 and 1917 in this regard.

The major catalyst for this change was the influence of Gorbachev as General Secretary of the Communist Party of the USSR and president of the USSR. Through 1988 and 1989 Gorbachev gave frequent signals that he no longer wished to assert Russian control over the so-called satellite States of Eastern Europe. He wanted to reduce the USSR's huge commitment to military expenditure so that the productive forces of society could be better directed to consumer goods. His policies of

glasnost and democratisation clearly implied the surrender of imperial power.

It was significant that the rapid changes in Eastern Europe were achieved by 'people power'. In all of the East European States huge gatherings of citizens crowded the streets and public squares shouting slogans. They endured pain, hardship and loss of life in confrontations with the police forces of the hardline regimes.

The results of 'people power' followed in a classic 'domino effect': one regime toppling quickly after another. It took nine months for the demonstrators in Hungary to depose the one-party government; nine weeks for the same effect in East Germany; nine days in Czechoslovakia; five days in Romania. Moreover, the protests in one nation helped those in others. When, for example, the authorities in Hungary opened the borders with West Germany, hundreds of thousands of East Germans used that route to escape into West Germany. It was estimated that by October 1989, 200 000 citizens of the so-called German Democratic Republic had 'voted with their feet' to seek a better life in the capitalist West. This exodus caused a massive decline in production levels in East Germany.

The Wall Comes Down: *'Wir Sind ein Volk'*

The most newsworthy event of 1989 was the demolition of the Berlin Wall. Erected in 1961 to seal off communist East Berlin from the capitalist West, the Berlin Wall was a universally recognised symbol of Cold War animosities. President John Kennedy had used it, in June 1963, to dramatise the contrast between the values placed on human freedom by the two world systems of capitalism and communism.

Earlier in the same year, protests against the authoritarian regime had broken out in several East German cities. Since the Communist government claimed to act on behalf of the people, and the people thought otherwise, the latter began to shout, in huge demonstrations, *'Wir Sind das Volk'* (We are the people). Within a few weeks, beginning in Leipzig, this slogan was altered to *'Wir Sind ein Volk'* (We are one people), a call for the reunion of East and West Germany.

Events moved with bewildering pace. The East German government attempted to reform itself by a change of leadership, but failed to stem the tide of dissent. The Berlin Wall was demolished in November 1989, allowing East German citizens free access to West Berlin and West Germany, where, by the terms of the constitution, they could claim citizenship. In March 1990 free multi-party elections were held in East Germany, resulting in the defeat of the Communist Party and the victory of the Christian Democrats. The stage was now set for a dramatic reunification of the German nation, divided since 1945.

In the post-mortems regarding the end of the German Democratic Republic (East Germany), even its former leaders declared that the communist regime had ceased to be democratic in spirit, and had used socialism as a 'baton'—a means of coercion.

Of all the momentous events of 1989–91, the reunification of Germany within the capitalist system and as a united nation within NATO was perhaps the most astonishing. A few years earlier this would have been regarded as impossible.

SOURCE 8.4

An ex-premier of East Germany admits that the 'German Democratic Republic' was misnamed, 1990

HISTORICAL CONTEXT: Lothar de Maiziere, the outgoing prime minister of East Germany, was reported as making the following statement just before the reunification of the 'two Germanies' in 1990, after forty-five years of separation.

Source: **The Age, Melbourne, 4 October 1990**

'The country called itself democratic without being it,' Mr de Maiziere said. 'The Wall and barbed wire were a shocking abuse of power. It began with good intentions, but by the end, socialism had deteriorated into a baton. The regime could not tolerate criticism.'

It was a 'farewell without tears', he said. 'What was a dream for most of us has now come true. We're part of a past that will be difficult for many of us to leave behind. What matters is not what we were yesterday, but what we will be tomorrow.'

QUESTIONS

1 Explain what the speaker intended by his use of the metaphor 'socialism had deteriorated into a baton'.

2 If, as de Maiziere said, the country 'called itself democratic without being it', what had been missing in the political system of the 'German Democratic Republic'?

Soviet president Mikhail Gorbechev (left) and US president George Bush at a meeting in London in July 1991. The ability of these two leaders to maintain a cordial working relationship was a key factor in the termination of Cold War animosities, which in turn (perhaps unexpectedly) brought about the collapse of the Union of Soviet Socialist Republics in the Third Russian Revolution.

V THE THIRD RUSSIAN REVOLUTION: 1985–91

Historians have for seventy-four years written about what they call the First and Second Russian revolutions. These both occurred in 1917. In February 1917 the First Revolution overthrew the tsar; in October 1917 the Bolsheviks (the Communist Party) seized power in the Second Revolution, and held it for seventy-four years. The momentous events of 1985–91, by which the Communist control of the USSR was severely modified, then, in 1991, ended, must be regarded as a Third Revolution.

The 'Old Regime'

In the matter of the Third Russian Revolution, the 'old regime' open to challenge and possible overthrow was the 74-year-old Communist regime. Back in 1917, this had been the 'new order'.

It was an irony of History that the Russian Bolshevik Party, which set up the first Marxist government in Europe, was a branch of what had been called the Social Democratic Party, in these words laying claim to be an advocate of a form of democracy. The Bolshevik view of democracy, however, was conditioned by the word 'social'. What its followers were claiming was that the concept of 'equality' meant more than equality once every few years at an election; rather, it should mean equality every day in a share of the wealth of the community.

The plan for the Bolshevik Revolution (or the Second Russian Revolution) was that the working class would stage a revolution in order to take power from the dominant forces—the monarchy, aristocracy and bourgeoisie. A new government, which Marx called 'the dictatorship of [by] the proletariat', would then take over, to ensure the elimination of bourgeois capitalist practice and to achieve a redistribution of the ownership of the factors of production.

The newly organised society would be termed 'socialist' because the administration would be for the benefit of society as a whole rather than for the selfish interests of a few individuals.

After the Bolsheviks had attained government in Russia from November 1917 and in the Union of Soviet Socialist Republics (USSR) from 1923, they claimed that they were embarking on a social and cultural revolution to create a purely classless society. This, they said, would be a communist society.

As a version of democracy, however, the Marxian Socialist formula as applied by the Bolsheviks, was discredited by a major contradiction—the grand design was to be fulfilled under a one-party dictatorship. The reasoning to support such an arrangement was that because the Bolshevik, or Communist, Party was the only organisation dedicated to the elimination of inequalities in society, it should be assured of continuity of office.

'Elections' were held in the USSR, but they were solely to decide which candidates represented the people within the Communist Party. No other political parties were permitted to exist. Thus, one of the major criteria of Western democracy—that it should be possible for the will of the people to be exercised through elections to bring about a change of government—did not operate.

The rule of the Communist Party in the USSR produced another characteristic sometimes operative in one-party regimes professing to be democratic. This was the formation of a secret police organisation, ostensibly created to defend the revolution against counter-revolutionary forces. The Soviet version functioned under a variety of names, but was best known to the outside world as the KGB, a set of initials derived from the Russian words for a State Security Committee. A similar organisation operated during the French Revolution under the name of the Committee of Public Safety. From 1793 to 1795 in France this committee used its powers to conduct the infamous Reign of Terror—persecuting and executing many persons accused of obstructing the cause of the revolution. The French Committee of Public Safety, together with the KGB in the USSR and similar organisations in other one-party dictatorships, all violated the basic principles of democratic process: freedom of expression, freedom of association, and freedom to dissent from the policies of the government in power and to work for its displacement.

The supposed communist regimes, moreover, failed to create a classless society. A new privileged class emerged, that of the party officials, who enjoyed the use of special consumer-goods shops, together with homes, cars and facilities superior to those of the general populace. The party's bureaucrats were openly acknowledged as the all-pervading force of government. Their authority and influence were encapsulated in two memorable Russian terms: the party functionaries who controlled the 'apparatus' or workings of the system were known as the *apparatchiks*, while the more powerful officials, who in effect 'named' those in authority, were called the *nomenklatura*. This was perhaps the supreme example in modern times of government by a bureaucracy.

Challenges to the Existing Order

Mikhail Gorbachev's policies of *glasnost*, *perestroika*, and *demokratizatsiya* had, by 1989, permitted vigorous debate within the USSR on the nature of Soviet society and government. The new democratically elected Congress of Peoples' Deputies, which met for the first time in May 1989, included many non-Communists. Some were former dissidents, ready and willing to speak out against the Communist Party's domination of power.

In all the preceding seventy-three years of the Bolshevik State, real power had lain with the office of the General Secretary of the Communist Party. Perhaps sensing that the party's power would be eroded, Gorbachev sought another power-base. In May 1989 he was elected President of the Congress of Peoples' Deputies, and in March 1990 he was appointed executive president of the USSR, with greater powers than any of his predecessors. This was still not a president elected directly by the people, but nevertheless an office closer to that formula than any before in the USSR. Because the president's source of power was from the Congress of Peoples' Deputies rather than the Communist Party, this development effectively ended the party's monopoly of power. But its members were still entrenched in all positions of authority.

Long-established principles of Marxian socialism were abandoned. In February 1990 the party, under Gorbachev's urging, declared that it now accepted the principle of ownership of private property, 'including ownership of the means of production', stating that this 'did not contradict the modern stage in the country's economic development' (*The Courier-Mail*, Brisbane, 14 February 1990). The party also passed a resolution allowing the functioning of other political movements, officially terminating the one-party State. Then in July 1991, again speaking on behalf of the party, Gorbachev declared the class struggle—the central plank of Marxist doctrine—a dead issue. The Communist Party was to be the party of all social groups, embracing a policy of social democracy rather than class-based doctrinaire socialism. Tolerance of the free-enterprise market economy and of diverse religious practices was proclaimed. All these attempts to reform the Communist Party from within were, however, but preludes to its imminent overthrow.

Another result of the *glasnost* policy was the break-up of the Soviet Union on ethnic grounds. At the time of Gorbachev's accession to power, the Union of Soviet Socialist Republics comprised fifteen republics. Three of them—Lithuania, Latvia and Estonia—had been independent nations from 1919 till 1940. Because they all faced the Baltic Sea, they were called the Baltic States. In 1940 they had been annexed to the USSR.

With the freedom of expression made possible by *glasnost*, the citizens of the Baltic States began to demand their release from the USSR. In March 1990 Lithuania declared its independence. Gorbachev resisted the claim, and demonstrations for independence were repressed by Soviet troops. Latvia and Estonia nevertheless gave notice that they too sought independence.

Many people in other republics within the USSR followed suit. Of the total population of the USSR, only about 52 per cent was of the Russian racial group, and many of the non-Russian ethnic groups began to put forward claims to self-determination. Citizens in Georgia and Azerbaijan, for example, claimed the right to secede. But in both of these republics and in the Baltic States, sentiment was not unanimous. Large numbers of people, ethnic Russians among others, opposed the claims to independence, wishing to remain within the USSR. Street rallies, marches and demonstrations for and against secession were staged in many parts of the USSR, and great turmoil and loss of life ensued. Gorbachev tried to persuade the republics of the USSR to stay together, for their common good and economic welfare.

The push for independence, however, reached an unexpected climax through events in Russia itself. Russia—officially the Russian Soviet Federated Republic—was on paper only one of fifteen republics, but with a population of 147 million and a land area constituting 75 percent of the total union, it was the massive core around which the USSR had been built.

In May 1990 a vigorous Communist Party official, Boris Yeltsin, was elected president (chairman) of the Russian (RSFR) parliament. Proclaiming a commitment to reform at a faster pace than that being provided for the USSR as a whole by Gorbachev, Yeltsin publicly resigned from the Communist Party in July 1990. So too did the popular mayors of the two major Russian cities of Moscow and Leningrad. These events gave the Russian republic a group of charismatic leaders, all demanding reform.

Yeltsin, in particular, became the symbol of the push for change. He accused Gorbachev of being too slow to reform, too much under the influence of old-guard communists resisting change. Seizing the mood of the moment, Yeltsin declared that Russia was claiming its sovereignty, and in November 1990 he began introducing a free-enterprise economic system. To further consolidate and validate his power, he persuaded the Russian people to agree to a direct election of a president. The election was held in June 1991, and Yeltsin defeated five other candidates. This was of enormous significance. It was the first time that the people of Russia had elected their own president, and it was a president who had already repudiated the Communist Party. Yeltsin's moral authority now outranked that of Gorbachev, who was a president appointed by a Congress, but not one elected by the vote of the people.

The Attempted Coup d'État, August 1991

From March 1990 to August 1991 the world watched the gradual disintegration of the Union of Soviet Socialist Republics. There were many members of the old guard, that is, Communist Party officials, determined to prevent this.

Gorbachev decided (as part of his *perestroika*) to set up a system whereby the various republics could have a greater degree of self-government, yet remain in the union. By August 1991 he had ready for signing a new 'Union Treaty' to establish this arrangement. But such a treaty would have vastly decreased the power of the party officials and the military hierarchy. All their positions of power and associated privileges were at risk. This crisis situation brought on an attempted military **coup d'état.**

On 19 August 1991, one day before the scheduled signing of the proposed Union Treaty, the Soviet news agency, Tass, announced that Vice-President Gennady Yanayev had taken over as head of state. It was stated that Gorbachev, holidaying in the Crimea, was too ill to continue in office. A State committee of eight hardline Communists took over, imposed censorship of the press, and declared a state of emergency. The army was called out of barracks, and tanks were ordered into the streets. Demonstrations were banned.

For three days the world held its breath as it seemed that a new military dictatorship might be established in the USSR. The Cold War rivalries could have been reactivated and the enormous progress in arms reductions lost. A new era of great-power tension seemed to be on hand.

However, a new era had indeed come to pass—an era when people power was dominant, and in which ordinary citizens could persuade soldiers to change sides. Thousands of people took to the streets in Moscow, Leningrad and other cities to defy the leaders of the group seeking power. They appealed to the soldiers not to use force against their own citizens. Yeltsin, as president of the Russian Federation, spoke to large rallies of protesters. Despite his earlier criticisms of Gorbachev's slowness to reform, Yeltsin now declared his total support for the constitutional validity of Gorbachev's position and demanded his reinstatement.

In the turmoil three Yeltsin supporters lost their lives, becoming instant martyrs to the cause of freedom. Faced with resistance both within the USSR and from abroad, the leaders of the coup lost their nerve and fled Moscow. By 21 August Gorbachev had returned to Moscow and had reclaimed his status as president. Still holding the position of General Secretary of the Communist Party, Gorbachev astounded the Soviet peoples and the rest of the world by proclaiming that the Communist Party could still reform itself and play a part in rebuilding the USSR.

Gorbachev's continued public support for the party was an act of political suicide. Events had overtaken and discredited the party beyond salvation. Yeltsin had already declared he had taken control of all armed forces on Russian territory. He had suspended *Pravda* (the official Communist Party newspaper), and had signed a decree terminating the work of the Communist Party within the Russian Republic. In a hugely effective gesture symbolising a total severance with the communist past, Yeltsin publicly supported the re-emergence of the white, blue and red striped pre-Revolutionary Russian flag. The red flag with the hammer and sickle emblem, the very emotional focus of the Bolshevik Revolution, was discarded.

Two days earlier the general public of Moscow had shown their contempt for the KGB by tearing down the huge statue of its founder, Felix Dzerzhinsky. This was a tangible signal for the sudden and apparently total dissolution of the party. Yeltsin ordered the seizure of all party and KGB archives in Russian territory. On 28 August the Soviet parliament suspended the Communist Party altogether.

Thus the Third Russian Revolution—the total overthrow of the Communist Party which had effected the Second Revolution of 1917—was achieved. In November 1991, on the seventy-fourth anniversary of the Bolshevik Revolution, for the first time there were no official celebrations. The demise of the once all-powerful party seemed to be complete.

However, there were many who were doubtful that the party was really finished. The Communist Party, at its height, encompassed some 18 million functionaries within the total Soviet population of 286 million. Its members controlled all political, administrative, judicial, cultural and police functions. Could all these millions of ex-party members think in different terms? Could they join in the building of a new reformed society?

The Dissolution of the Union of Soviet Socialist Republics

In the hectic days of the August 1991 crisis, the Baltic States acted swiftly to consolidate their independence. Yeltsin, as president of the Russian Republic, recognised them as independent nations, and Gorbachev virtually had no choice but to follow. By September 1991, Lithuania, Latvia and Estonia had all been admitted to the United Nations Organisation as independent nations.

This left twelve republics in what had been the USSR. Several of the republics declared their intention to become independent. Even

Boris Yeltsin acknowledging the zeal of thousands of supporters in Moscow, August 1991. At the time of the attempted overthrow of Mikhail Gorbachev as president of the USSR by communist hardliners, it was Yeltsin, president of the Russian Republic (one of fifteen republics in the USSR), who rallied mass support to prevent the coup. Yeltsin stressed that Gorbachev was the constitutionally appointed president of the USSR. Ironically, it was Yeltsin's later action in withdrawing the Russian Federation from the USSR that precipitated the collapse of the USSR.

'People power' opposing the military forces. In subverting the attempted coup in August 1991, the ordinary people of Russia played a key part. In this photograph Moscow citizens are shown clambering over an armoured personnel carrier to show their disapproval of the coup, and to persuade the soldiers not to support the attempt by their generals to seize power.

Russia, with its 147 million people, had, through Yeltsin, declared its own sovereignty. Without Russia there could be no USSR.

After only a few days of emotional commitment to independence in August 1991, the leaders of the republics quickly realised that they needed one another. Economic interdependence in the supply and distribution of oil, gas, electricity and raw materials, which had developed over seventy years, was inescapable.

There was much debate. In November 1991 the leaders of Ukraine expressed support for a proposed new economic union. But in a vote of the people held on 1 December 1991, the Ukranians opted for full independence as a sovereign nation. This decision, by the second largest republic, with a population of 53 million, meant there could not be an effective union. The remaining choice was an association of independent nations, agreeing to co-operate in matters of trade, defence and perhaps foreign policy.

The three Slav republics—Russia, Ukraine and Belorussia—agreed on 8 December 1991 to form a Commonwealth of Independent States (CIS). To symbolise the break from Soviet control, the headquarters of this new association was established at Minsk, a city in Belorussia, instead of in Moscow. On 13 December eight more of the former Soviet republics joined the CIS, making a total of eleven members. On 31 December the red flag with the hammer and sickle was lowered from the Kremlin masthead, and replaced by the three-colour flag of the Russian Republic. Mikhail Gorbachev had become a president without a country: the USSR had been dissolved.

An Evaluation of the Communist Regimes

Despite the almost triumphant cries in the Western media that capitalism had prevailed over communism, a more balanced judgement is

The removal of the massive statue of the founder of the KGB, August 1991. When the people of Moscow and Leningrad rejected the attempted coup against Mikhail Gorbachev, they also, finally, rejected the Communist Party. Perhaps the most striking image in this process was the demolition of the statue of Felix Dzerzhinsky, the founder of the KGB (the State security service). This defiant act, right outside the headquarters of the KGB, showed the total rejection of the Communist Party by the people, and their defiance of its authority.

required. In the seventy-four years of Communist rule in the USSR, some amazing achievements were recorded. In World War II the Soviets turned back the Nazi invasion, despite the great productive capacity of capitalist Germany. Although the Soviets received much help from the USA and Britain, their own designers, engineers and factory workers made enormous contributions to the war capacity of the nation.

Of even greater significance was the human war effort of the Soviet soldiers. Hitler had assumed that the communist system would not be able to command the loyalty of the Russian and Ukrainian peoples, and that the Nazis could 'kick the house down'. Instead, the Soviet troops exhibited great courage and endurance. Commentators have stressed, however, that the war effort was termed the Great Patriotic War of 1941–45—a war for nationalist motives, not overtly one for the communist system.

Despite the terrible sufferings and injustices caused by Stalin's collectivisation policies and the associated famines, the USSR also eventually evolved a productive system that fed 286 million people adequately, led the USA for a time in space technology, produced some of the most sophisticated aeroplanes in the world, and entered all fields of modern industrial production, albeit at somewhat lower levels of expertise than its Japanese and European competitors.

On the debit side, the Leninist–Stalinist system terrorised its own peoples, enslaved and indeed executed millions of dissenters, and deprived three generations of people of their most basic human rights.

In the move towards free-enterprise economies, the people of the former socialist societies faced many years of difficulties. Unemployment was previously unknown. (In a well-worn but largely accurate joke about the

Soviet system it was said that the workers pretended to work, and their bureaucratic bosses pretended to pay them.)

By the early 1990s, however, it was apparent that the drastic shortage of consumer goods in the communist regimes could be blamed on the system. Western examples of the range of choice in food, clothing, furniture, electronic equipment and vehicles constantly provoked the people into expressions of discontent. They craved higher levels of consumer satisfaction. In the long term, the communist regimes collapsed because their people rejected Marxist ideology for a consumer-goods ideology.

Our legacy in the 1990s is therefore an apparent world-wide acceptance of the free-enterprise capitalist system as the proven most successful means, despite its faults, of ensuring freedom, democracy and rising standards of living. Another legacy is the possibility that the liberal-democratic capitalist states, who desire

to trade with one another, will have much less incentive for war than the former status-seeking authoritarian powers, which reached for imperial possessions as a means to greater power. The 1993 acceptance by the world's major powers of the GATT (General Agreement on Tariffs and Trade) principle of free trade may well prove to be one of the most effective war-prevention measures of all time.

It is our responsibility, however, to remind ourselves that capitalism is founded on a conception of human beings as individualistic, aggressive, acquisitive and competitive. On the other hand, socialism is based on the perception of humankind as being co-operative, community-minded, unselfish and collectivist. It is difficult to imagine that such an ideal has been lost forever. The reappearance of support for socialist principles is almost predictable, particularly as contemporary capitalism is producing grave inequalities between the 'haves' and the 'have nots'.

THE AUSTRALIAN

NUMBER 8400   MONDAY AUGUST 26 1991   60 CENTS*

GORBACHEV QUITS PARTY, TELLS CENTRAL COMMITTEE TO DISBAND

DEATH OF COMMUNISM

Yeltsin moves quickly to fill political void

By our world cable service and NICOLAS ROTHWELL in London

COMMUNISM lies in tatters today after President Gorbachev resigned yesterday as head of the Communist Party and called for the disbanding of the Central Committee that has ruled the Soviet Union with an iron fist for 74 years.

In the face of mass demonstrations across the Union's 5 republics, Mr Gorbachev appeared on Soviet television yesterday to tell his 280 million citizens he was bowing to the pro-democracy forces harnessed by the President of the Russian Federation, Mr Boris Yeltsin, to defeat last week's attempted coup.

The demise of the party federally and its rapid disintegration within the republics opens the way for the establishment of democratic institutions that would permit the republics to follow the Kremlin's former East European satellites in joining the democratic nations.

But Mr Gorbachev's personal future is unclear. Although he has quit the post of general-secretary, he remains President. He has tripped all control over the armed forces and KGB from the party and passed control of all party property to the Supreme Soviet. He has disbanded the engine of Soviet policy-making, the Central Committee, and ordered the Presidential Council to resign.

Inside: 6-Page Special

a new interim Presidential Council headed by Yeltsin loyalist and Prime Minister, Mr Ivan Silayev, and including radical free-market economist Mr Grigory Yavlinsky and the reform-minded former deputy mayor of Moscow, Mr Yuri Luzhkov.

● MR Gorbachev stepped up the purge of the armed forces hierarchy, appointing General Yevgeny Shaposhnikov to replace the shadowy General Mikhail Moiseyev as Defence Minister. The President's military adviser and

This is the text of President Gorbachev's statement announcing his resignation as general secretary of the Soviet Communist Party:

❝ THE Secretariat, the Politburo of the Soviet Communist Party Central Committee did not speak out against the coup d'etat, the Central Committee did not take a firm stand condemning and resisting it, did not launch the communists into the struggle against the violation of constitutional legality. Members of the party leadership were among the conspirators, a series of committees and party press organs supported criminal acts against the State. This put millions of Many party members refused to co-operate with the conspirators, condemned the coup d'etat and fought it. No one has the moral right to level accusations lightly against all communists and as President, I consider I have an obligation to defend them as citizens from groundless accusations. In this situation, the Central Committee of the Soviet Communist Party must take the difficult, but honest, decision to disband itself. Communist parties in the republics and local party organisations will decide their futures for themselves.

I consider that it is no longer possible for me to fulfil my functions as general secretary of the Central Committee of the Soviet Communist Party and I divest myself of my corresponding full powers.

I believe that communists who support democracy, constitutional legality and the policy of restructuring society will commit themselves to creating a party on new foundations, capable, with all progressive forces, of engaging itself actively in the pursuit of authentic democratic reforms in the interest of the workers. ❞

Gorbachev tells Central Committee to disband

From Page 1

"I do not consider it possible to continue to carry out the functions of the general-secretary."

Stripped of assets — the jobs, money, cars, country homes, apartments and special food shops — that allowed it to buy loyalty with favours and privilege, Mr Gorbachev has effectively crippled the party.

But he has held out the hope that a new political formation could still be forged from the ashes of the old communist machine. "I believe that democratic-minded communists loyal to constitutional legality, to the course of renewing society, will call for the setting up of a party on a new foundation that is capable, along with all progressive forces, of actively joining the continuation of radical democratic transformation in the interests of the working people."

Mr Gorbachev's announcement marked the passing of an historic epoch and the inexorable rise of the Russian republic and the radical reformers around Mr Yeltsin.

in future be controlled by their Russian counterparts.

This is a stunning inversion of turns of authority, with the Soviet State now subject to the Russian — a move that may alarm the other republics.

Mr Silayev has transferred two of the most powerful all-union ministries — economic planning and natural resources — to Russian control "indefinitely".

Little remains of the communist apparatus in the wake of Mr Gorbachev's declaration. Mr Yeltsin had already suspended the Russian Communist Party's activities while a judicial inquiry examines its role in the coup.

International recognition

Icons of the system continue to tumble in the Dzerzhinsky statue before the Lubianka toppled on Friday, was added during the weekend the figure of Sverdlov, first Soviet premier and the man who signed

dependence, the second-largest and most prosperous republic, the Ukraine, declared its own independence, subject only to popular referendum in December. The other three republics that have already rejected membership in the Soviet Union — Armenia, Georgia and Moldavia — are also taking steps to declare their independence and to take revenge on communism.

Moldavia, which will now almost certainly join neighbouring Romania immediately, outlawed the Communist Party yesterday and ordered the seizure of all its assets.

And Lithuania, always the leader in its journey towards republican independence, says it will start guarding its Western borders today and issuing its own visas.

Other Baltic States are believed to have similar plans and international recognition of the Baltics' independence seems only a few days away.

Germany and Belgium are calling on the European Community to recognise Latvia, Lithuania and Estonia, while

G-7 talks to decide aid plan

By BRYAN BOSWELL in Washington and agencies

A JUBILANT White House ordered last night a new approach to economic aid for Moscow.

The first details are expected to come from a meeting of officials of the Group of Seven leading industrialised nations called in London this week.

President Bush did a turnaround on economic aid in less than 12 hours yesterday.

He said early in the day that he had seen "no sign of reform" from President Gorbachev. Then he did an about-face when confirmation was received from US ambassador Mr Richard Strauss that the Soviet leader was quitting as general-secretary of the Communist Party and calling on the Central Committee to disband.

The White House and officials of the G-7 would meet in London on Thursday. Al-

The 'Death of Communism'. This was the memorable headline in *The Australian*, Sydney, 26 August 1991, announcing the disbandment of the Communist Party in the USSR.

The Collapse of Communism in Europe: Another Revolution?

chapter nine

European Imperialism in China and the First Chinese Revolution

China is a sleeping giant. Let her sleep, for when she awakes she will astonish the world.
Attributed to Napoleon Bonaparte, 1815

In the centuries during which complex city civilisations developed in Mesopotamia, Egypt and Europe, equally advanced civilisations were flourishing in Asia. In the country we now call China (which Europeans for many years called Cathay), ruling dynasties (royal families) provided order and stability for almost 5 000 years.

When European explorers began to penetrate China from the thirteenth century AD onwards, the Chinese Empire was longer established than any European society. The Chinese called their country *Zhong guo*, meaning 'middle kingdom' or 'central states'. Convinced of their superiority in cultural achievements, the Chinese regarded the 'lesser' peoples who lived beyond the **Middle Kingdom** as 'barbarians'. Nevertheless, the Europeans came to China in increasing numbers, demanding the right to trade and the right to conduct missions for Christianity.

In a series of bitter experiences the Chinese discovered that they lacked the technology to resist the demands of the European powers. After they had suffered many military defeats and humiliations over the period 1830–1910,

the Chinese people, acting on the conviction that their ruling dynasty could no longer resist the foreign intrusions, staged a revolution and proclaimed a republic. In destroying the system that had prevailed in the past, they carried hopes for a future in which the Chinese people could be independent of foreign domination, and free to devise their own system of government.

Theme Questions

➤ When the Chinese people deposed the Manchu Dynasty, was there a measure of agreement on what was to take its place?
➤ Did the first revolution in modern China, which ended government by an emperor and introduced a republic, alter the nature of Chinese society?

I THE OLD ORDER AND EUROPEAN IMPERIAL INTRUSIONS

The Portuguese, Dutch, Spanish, British, French, and later the Americans and Russians, all came to China seeking trade, profit and, in some cases, converts to Christianity. The Chinese regarded them with hostility; the Europeans in turn were both suspicious of and fascinated by the Chinese.

The 'Old Order': Traditional Chinese Society

The most difficult 'mental leap' for the Europeans was to understand that the Chinese regarded their own civilisation as the most advanced in the world, and could not conceive of any means by which it could be improved upon. In fact, the Chinese regarded their civilisation as the only 'normal' one, and could not imagine that any other civilisation could claim validity. Persistent Chinese refusals to trade with Europeans as equals eventually generated antagonism from the European leaders.

The traditional Chinese way of life was possibly the longest established on Earth. It was bound together by a uniformly accepted code of life based predominantly on the teachings of Confucius (*circa* 551–479 BC) and his disciples. This body of precepts and codes for behaviour was labelled 'The Teaching of the Learned'. Confucianism was supplemented and supported by the teachings of Daoism, another Chinese-originated philosophy.

Neither of these Chinese sources of wisdom was a religion in the Western sense. Neither emphasised life after death, or indeed any notion of a redeemer or saviour. It is recorded that Confucius, on being asked to teach about death, replied: 'As we have not yet learned to know life, how can we know death?' The combined effect of Confucianism and Daoism was to inculcate an acceptance of a specified way of life. ('*Dao*' means 'the eternal way'.) All Chinese youth were taught a code of conduct based on five virtues (loyalty; integrity, or 'wholeness'; righteousness; altruism; humanity) and on key relationships in society. Centuries of thought and education had been devoted to the identification of an ideal society and how it might be attained.

From these teachings, and their inculcation over hundreds of generations, there had emerged a very stable society. Family loyalties and relationships were the cohesive force of this society. Ancestors were revered, and family duties and responsibilities were established as the most important feature in life. Families cared for their own sick and aged members, ensuring that nothing similar to the welfare funding burdens of modern Western governments even emerged. In China, dynasties might come and go, but the stability of the family unit ensured continuity of lifestyle. The kingdom was in effect a huge family; and just as families conformed to long-established codes of behaviour, so too did the whole kingdom. From as early as AD 175 common laws for the whole kingdom were promulgated and given permanence by their inscription on stone pillars and tablets.

Chinese society was totally immersed in Confucian principles through the long-established practice of appointing civil servants by means of a formal examination system. To succeed in this selection process, the young aspirant to the bureaucracy had to commit to memory vast portions of the Teaching of the Learned. As a result its precepts were deeply internalised in the minds and consciences of the ruling élite, and passed from generation to generation without question.

Chinese society thus established the principle of a 'rule of wisdom'. As early as 135 BC, Wu Ti (the martial emperor) set up the equivalent of a university by appointing Five Erudites (learned men: the 'professors' of the time) to guide the work of scholars. Scholars were awarded the highest status in the community, well above that of soldiers.

Having invented a distinctive form of writing, and paper as a medium, the Chinese were able to install a common means of communication throughout the entire kingdom, even though spoken dialects varied so much that many groups could not understand one another in conversation. By the eighth century AD, the Chinese had invented block printing, making possible the production of multiple copies of printed statements. Until the nineteenth century, the Chinese civilisation produced and distributed books on a scale greater than that of any other civilisation. The printed page was respected, and skill in calligraphy honoured as a major achievement. Shared familiarity with literature was thus a major influence in the attainment of a unified society.

Chinese society would not have been stable, however, had the Chinese people not developed highly efficient forms of government and a successful division of labour. From as early as the first and second centuries of the Western Christian calendar, the emperor had established monopolies of iron and salt, ensuring that, in effect, central government funds existed for the construction of canals and roads, and the maintenance of the Great Wall as a defence system. A comparison can be drawn with the French monarchy, which collapsed in 1792 primarily because it could not raise sufficient funds from its taxation system.

Successful food production, essential for the most populous kingdom on Earth, was ensured by efficient irrigation techniques, together with a system of land ownership that established an aristocracy dedicated to stability, and a peasant class that was honoured and respected. The first two of these factors were additional products of the successful centralisation of power in the hands of the emperor.

Despite their revered position as holders of a '**mandate from heaven**' (akin to the European concept of 'divine right'), the dynastic rulers—from intuition or wisdom—successfully delegated authority to local aristocrats and their civil servants. Although the central government required services from the people as labourers on roads, defence works and canals, the people were otherwise under the direction of local authorities. This greatly diminished the pressure for insurrections against the central authority of the emperor. Many rebellions did occur, but as we shall see no true revolution overthrew the Chinese system of government for *circa* 3 600 years (that is, until AD 1911). In sum, the centuries of conditioning meant that this vast society was virtually of one mind in regarding the Westerners as intruding barbarians.

European Reaction to Chinese Culture

The Chinese insistence that they were the superior civilisation, and the Europeans were the barbarians, was, for Europeans, a shock and a surprise. The first British royal mission to China was led by Lord George Macartney, in 1792. He was a Lord of the Realm and a former governor of Grenada. His ship was a man-of-war with sixty-six guns, accompanied by two other vessels, with a retinue of almost 100 scientists, artists, language teachers and observers. Despite the fact that he was representing King George III, and Britain as a major world power, Macartney was expected to 'kowtow' (that is, prostrate himself full-length on the ground) to the Chinese emperor. In the event, Macartney only agreed to bow on one knee, but the expectation shocked the British.

Further shocks ensued from the Chinese insistence that they did not have 'the slightest need' for European products. Several incidents in which visiting Europeans were summarily executed for offences against Chinese law—even for what in European eyes were accidents—increased the sense of alienation between Europeans and Chinese. This resulted in the European nations later demanding residential zones in Chinese ports, where European laws would apply.

The intruding European powers proceeded to use their military and industrial superiority to establish control over the Chinese people—either by direct annexation or through the consolidation of 'spheres of influence'—but they did not necessarily succeed in convincing the Chinese of the superiority of the European religion or way of life.

The Chinese did not concede that the Europeans could teach them anything valuable. Chinese thinking was just as 'Sino' or China-centred as the European thinking was Eurocentric—the Chinese believed that China was the centre of the world, that the emperor ruled through a 'mandate of heaven', and that the Celestial (Heavenly) Court of their rulers was undoubtedly superior in wisdom and enlightenment to any group of administrators in 'barbarian' nations from the outer world.

So confident were the Chinese in the superiority of their societies that early attempts by

Chapter 4

SOURCE 9.1

A Chinese emperor informs the King of England that China does not need any foreign manufactures, but will allow trade as a 'mark of favour', 1793

HISTORICAL CONTEXT: In 1793 a British mission, led by Lord George Macartney, visited Beijing (Peking) in an attempt to open up trade relations with China. The British brought many gifts and samples of manufactured goods. They were astonished that the Chinese regarded these as 'tribute payments' from an inferior state to the 'Celestial (Heavenly) Kingdom'. The Chinese emperor, Qianlong, insisted that China did not need any European goods, but would permit the British to buy goods they needed from China. The following are excerpts from the message sent back to King George III.

Source: H.F. MacNair, *Modern Chinese History: Selected Readings*, Shanghai, Commercial Press Ltd, 1923, pp. 2–9 passim

You, O king, from afar have yearned after the blessing of our civilisation and in your eagerness to come into touch with our converting influence have sent an embassy across the sea . . . I have already taken note of your respectful spirit of submission and have treated your mission with extreme favour . . . honouring you with the bestowal of valuable presents. Thus has my indulgence been manifested

. . . Our Celestial Empire possesses all things in prolific abundance and lacks no product within its own borders. There was, therefore, no need to import the manufactures of outside barbarians in exchange for our own produce.

The Celestial Court has pacified and possessed the territory within the four seas. Its sole aim is to do its utmost to achieve good government and to manage political affairs, attaching no value to strange jewels and precious objects.

As a matter of fact, the virtue and prestige of the Celestial Dynasty having spread far and wide, the kings of the myriad nations come by land and sea with all sorts of precious things. Consequently there is nothing we lack, as your principal envoy and others have themselves observed. We have never set much store on strange or ingenious objects, nor do we

need any more of your country's manufactures.

But as the tea, silk, and porcelain which the Celestial Empire produces are absolute necessities to European nations and to yourselves, we have permitted, as a signal mark of favour, that foreign hongs [Chinese business associations] should be established at Canton so that your wants may be supplied and your country thus participate in our beneficence . . . the Throne's principle is to treat strangers from afar with indulgence and exercise a pacifying control over barbarian tribes the world over.

If you allow your barbarian merchants to proceed to Chekiang and Tientsin with the object of landing and trading there the ordinances of my Celestial Empire are strict in the extreme . . . and your merchants will assuredly never be permitted to land or to reside there but will be subject to instant expulsion . . . Do not say that you were not warned in due time! Tremblingly obey and show no negligence. A special mandate!

QUESTIONS

1 What is the Chinese emperor implying by stating that the British are seeking the 'converting influence' of the Chinese civilisation?

2 What effect on the British is the emperor seeking by stating that they have shown a 'respectful spirit of submission'?

3 What is the meaning of 'Celestial Empire', and what concept of the monarchy is conveyed by the use of this expression?

4 How might the British react to being called 'outside barbarians'?

5 What attitude of mind (that eventually weakened China's position as a world power) is conveyed by the assertion that the Chinese 'have never set much store on . . . ingenious objects'?

6 What reason is given for allowing, 'as a signal mark of favour', trade with Britain to begin?

7 What is the meaning of 'a special mandate'?

Europeans to penetrate east Asia were rejected. When the concessions to allow European trade were finally given, they were in the spirit of an extreme favour, rather than from any necessity on the part of the Chinese.

The Opium Wars 1839–42 and 1856–60

Confident that they could issue commands to 'foreign devils', the Chinese permitted trade in the early nineteenth century at only one port, Guangzhou (Canton). The Europeans nevertheless persevered in their efforts to gain wider access to Chinese markets.

Although Chinese goods such as tea, silk and porcelain were in great demand in Europe, the Chinese were reluctant to buy European goods in exchange. This created an imbalance in trade, and a 'run' on European stocks of silver and gold, used to pay for Chinese goods. In an attempt to remedy this imbalance, the British East India Company brought in supplies of opium from India. Prohibited by an imperial decree, opium was nevertheless greatly desired by many Chinese as a relaxant. The British trade was in flagrant defiance of Chinese laws. In the sixteen years from 1818 to 1833 the share of opium in the total British imports into China jumped from 17 per cent to 50 per cent.

In the 1830s the imperial Chinese government appointed a special commissioner to control trade at Guangzhou. His intention was to encourage legitimate trade, but to suppress and eradicate the traffic in opium. Large quantities of British-owned opium were seized and destroyed. British ships were ordered to leave the port after a squabble between British sailors and Chinese residents had resulted in a death. Chinese war junks were assembled to enforce the rulings, but the British brought up two armed frigates and, without waiting for negotiations, destroyed the junks. Thus began, in 1839, what was later called the First Opium War.

The Chinese had no idea of their relative weakness in naval and military power. Centuries of peace and isolation had reduced the effectiveness of the Chinese military forces, who ranked low in status in Chinese society. By 1842 British superiority in naval armaments and firepower had ensured that the Chinese suffered a series of humiliating defeats. British naval vessels carried the war into several other ports, ranging far up the Yangzi River. British forces occupied Shanghai and attacked the great river city of Nanjing (Nanking).

The Chinese now paid dearly for their attempt to impose their own laws within their own territory. Moral principles were subordinated to the British belief that they had the right to force their own access to a huge market in order to promote British commerce. The Treaty of Nanking (1842) ceded the island of Hong Kong to the British as a base, and opened another five ports (so-called 'treaty ports') to trade. Soon afterwards, the French, Portuguese and Americans were granted similar trading concessions.

In a Second Opium War (1856–60), the Europeans imposed further indignities upon the Chinese. This time the French participated in the military actions. In a complete display of contempt for Chinese authority, the Anglo–French forces occupied Guangzhou, captured the viceroy (the emperor's representative), and deported him as a prisoner to India. They occupied Tianjin (Tientsin) in the north, and invaded Beijing (Peking) itself. There, to display the totality of Western power, they destroyed the magnificent Summer Palace of the Manchu Dynasty. In Chinese eyes, this action confirmed the 'foreign devils' as barbarians.

By the Treaty of Tientsin (1858) and the Treaty of Peking (1860), another eleven treaty ports were opened to the West, as was the right to take ships up the full navigable length of the Yangzi. Many thousands of Chinese had died attempting to exclude the 'foreign devils', and this would not be forgotten.

The Chinese were grossly humiliated by these European and American intrusions. Exposed by their relative military weakness in contrast with the industrially powerful European nations, the Chinese had been forced to agree to treaties that stressed their inferiority.

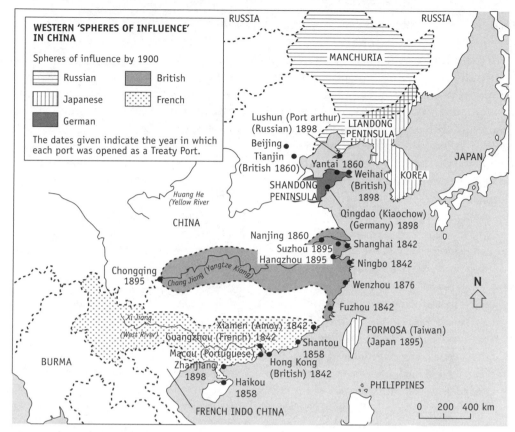

MAP 9.1 Western 'spheres of influence' in China

Western military superiority enabled the imperialist powers to coerce the Chinese into opening their ports and markets to European traders and bankers. As a result of Britain's victory in the Opium War of 1839–42 and the Treaty of Nanking (Nanjing), five ports were opened to European residence and trade, and the island of Hong Kong became British territory. Trading privileges and 'extra-territorial' rights were also acquired by citizens of France, Belgium, Russia and the USA.

Additional concessions were given to the imperialist powers by the Treaty of Tientsin (Tianjin) in 1858, and the Treaty of Peking (Beijing) in 1860. In 1887 Macao, which was the longest-established port for European trading activities, was formally ceded to Portugal. All these enforced conditions were blows to Chinese pride. In the 1890s Japan further humiliated the Chinese by defeating China in war and annexing the island of Taiwan, which the Japanese named Formosa.

By the 1890s the intruding powers, now including Germany, had established the 'spheres of influence' (regions in which the particular power exercised trading and banking dominance) shown on this map. Although China had not been formally divided up into annexed colonies, as had Africa, the interests of the Chinese people had been subordinated to the commercial interests of numerous foreign powers.

This 'loss of face'—enormously painful to a civilisation that had considered itself the most advanced in the world—left a bitter memory. Burning resentment of this humiliation, and a determination to reverse the position, became a driving force in Chinese society for the next hundred years. The legacy of the early years of European involvement in China was that both groups, Chinese and European, regarded each other with mutual suspicion.

Extra-territorial Rights

The British had acted in contempt of the Chinese people through their acts of plunder and destruction during the Opium Wars. Particularly callous components of the European-imposed **unequal treaties** that followed were the British demands for compensation for destroyed opium and for the payment of 'ransoms' for cities not attacked (the British made several Chinese cities pay huge amounts for the 'privilege' of not having been plundered). In their input into the treaty terms, the French added a clause which ensured further long-term resentment—the right to promote Christianity. In Chinese eyes, this was a claim to impose an alien religion upon a proud civilisation.

Equally significant was the enforcement by the Europeans (and later the Americans) of **'extra-territorial' rights** ('extra' here means 'outside'). The intruding powers demanded the right to claim areas of land in the treaty ports in which their people would be 'outside' Chinese law and customs. The British and French, for example, each claimed a 'concession' in a city such as Shanghai, and in this concession only British (or French) laws would apply. This privilege became of great importance in persuading European nationals to leave their homelands to serve trading companies in the East.

Under this principle of extra-territoriality, the European powers set up miniature imperial enclaves, the very existence of which was a continual humiliation to the Chinese sense of independence. At Shanghai, the most prominent example, an international settlement functioned as a sovereign city–state, where Chinese laws did not apply, and the Chinese were treated as an inferior race without human rights. An infamous notice on a park within this enclave is alleged to have stated: 'Chinese and dogs are not allowed'. Shanghai developed into a showcase Europeanised city, sometimes called 'the Paris of the East'. It became the financial capital of China. To this day 'The Bund'—the major riverside thoroughfare of Shanghai—still displays the impressive commercial buildings erected by the Western occupiers, who conducted business in the city until 1949.

'Spheres of Influence'

The military helplessness of China allowed the intruding powers to stake out defined areas of control in mainland China. These were known as 'spheres of influence', that is, zones in which a particular power claimed predominance in trading rights.

The weakness of the Manchu Dynasty was further highlighted in the 1890s, when Japan provoked a war with China (1894–95) over trading rights in Korea. The Japanese destroyed the remnants of the Chinese navy. The terms of the ensuing Treaty of Shimonoseki (1895) were disastrous for China. The Chinese had to pay a huge indemnity to Japan, and were forced to borrow from European powers to do so. They further had to recognise the 'independence' of Korea (which in effect became a Japanese protectorate), and cede to Japan all of Taiwan and the Pescadores Islands. Japan also demanded and received the same rights of access to Chinese mainland ports that European powers had already gained. The total powerlessness of the Manchu regime was now revealed.

Thus, by 1900 large sections of China had been marked off as spheres of influence for the intruding powers, including Japan. Britain claimed dominance in central China, from Shanghai on the coast to Chongqing 1 600 kilometres up the Yangtzi River. France asserted its rights in the south, Germany staked out the Shandong Peninsula, and Russian and Japanese claims overlapped (with resultant tensions) in Manchuria. But the areas were not formally annexed, and did not become actual colonies. This was because the intruding foreign powers did not want to assume full responsibilities for governing millions of Chinese people if they could gain commercial advantages through alternative arrangements.

Another key influence was the USA's 'Open Door' policy, which insisted that all trading nations should have access to Chinese markets, and that China should not be dismembered. Britain supported the US policy.

II CRISES LEADING TO THE EROSION OF THE POWER OF THE MANCHU (QING) DYNASTY

The Manchu, or Qing, Dynasty, assumed control over China *circa* AD 1644, and ruled until 1912—almost 270 years. The Manchus came from the north, from Manchuria, and were regarded by the Chinese as foreigners. Their administration of China was in some ways similar to the 200-year British *raj* (rule) over most of India. In displacing the Ming Dynasty, the Manchus stressed the legitimacy of their power. They called their first reign *Shunzhi*, meaning 'obedience to rule', which indicated that they were claiming the mandate of heaven. Then they named their dynasty *Qing*, meaning 'pure' or 'clear', again attempting to show up, by contrast, the alleged corruption of the displaced Ming Dynasty.

Throughout their regime the emperors of the Qing Dynasty were troubled by challenges to their authority. They adopted Chinese ways and endorsed traditional Chinese practices and Confucian values, but were regarded by the people as alien rulers. When the Chinese civilisation was forced, through its military weaknesses, to yield so many humiliating concessions to the West, doubts grew about the authority of the Qing. From these doubts, challenges emerged.

The Taiping Rebellion

The most extensive of the rebellions against the Qing Dynasty was that of a religious sect, the *Taiping*. For fourteen years (1850–64) this group defied the dynasty, at one stage ruling over almost all of central China. They established their capital in Nanjing (Nanking), the second city of the empire.

The rebel regime named itself *Taiping Tianguo* (great peace: kingdom of heaven). It was the only movement of nineteenth-century China that showed reliance on Western influences in that it was vaguely based on Protestant Christian teachings. Its founder, Hong Xiuquan, claimed that, in a vision, he had been identified as a younger brother of Jesus Christ. He proclaimed five other 'princes of heaven', who eventually caused the collapse of the regime by quarrelling among themselves. Leaders of modern-day Communist China acknowledge the Taiping Rebellion as a prelude to their regime, not for its Christian associations, but because of its anti-Western policy and its programmes for land reform and for the redistribution of wealth to ensure the elimination of inequality.

The Taiping movement attracted a great deal of support from the peasantry, particularly in southern China, and grew so powerful that at one stage its forces threatened Beijing itself. Some Westerners, especially missionaries, had at first been supportive of what appeared to be a Christian revolutionary force promising social reforms. But when the eccentricities of Hong's version of Christianity became apparent, and it

Cixi (1834–1908), Dowager Empress of China. For many decades Cixi was the dominant force in China, acting as regent during the terms as emperor of her son and her nephew, the latter whom she imprisoned. Cixi resisted all attempts to introduce modernisation programmes to China. It is widely believed that, a day before her own death in 1908, she ordered the murder of the imprisoned emperor, Guangxu.

SOURCE 9.2

The leaders of the Taiping Rebellion proclaim a belief that God intends that there should be no inequality anywhere, *circa* 1855

HISTORICAL CONTEXT: The Taiping Rebellion of the mid-nineteenth century posed a serious challenge to the authority of the Manchu Dynasty. Using a mixture of Christian teachings and the basic principles of socialism, the Taipings gathered a huge following. By the 1860s they controlled most of central China, and threatened to depose the emperor. The Western powers, however, supported the Manchus, mainly to ensure the continuance of the established trading arrangements. By 1866 the rebellion had been suppressed, with enormous loss of lives.

Leaders of present-day Communist China recognise the Taipings as precursors of their own regime, principally because the Taiping policy encompassed proposals for land reform and the equitable redistribution of wealth.

Source: **Lo Erh Kong, *Taiping t'ien kuo Shin kang*, Shanghai, 1938**

The following is an extract from a Taiping proclamation: *The land of the world must be tilled in common by the people of the world. When we have an insufficiency here, the people must be moved there, and vice versa, so that plenty in one place may relieve famine in another. All the world must enjoy the happiness given by God the Heavenly Father, and land, food, clothing and money must be held and used in common, so that there is no inequality anywhere, and nobody lacks food or warmth. For the world is the family of God the Heavenly Father; if men do not hold things in private, but pass them to the Sovereign Lord, then the Lord will use them and everybody everywhere will be equal. This is the edict of salvation especially enjoined by God the Heavenly Father on the True Lord of T'ai ping.*

QUESTIONS

1 Why would this policy attract a large following to the Taipings?
2 Which influential classes of traditional Chinese society would oppose these teachings, and why?

also became clear the Taiping leaders aimed at removing all foreign influence from China, the Western powers provided military support for the existing government. The Europeans did not want the newly won trading arrangements in the treaty ports disrupted or threatened.

The Taiping Rebellion was suppressed with enormous loss of life (estimated at 20 million lives: as huge a human catastrophe as World War I). Nevertheless, its temporary success demonstrated the declining prestige of the Manchus and heralded the revolution that eventually deposed them in 1912.

Resistance to Reform

The Manchu emperor and his advisers were caught in a dilemma. They were determined to adhere to traditional Chinese practices because these held the kingdom together. But in their refusal to recognise the likely advantages of adopting some of the practices of the West, they failed to revitalise Chinese society or to build up a sense of national unity that might have generated a modernisation effort. The Manchus were doubly handicapped by their lack of popular appeal as virtual intruders from Manchuria; they were not accepted by the great mass of the Chinese as a focus for a sense of national unity. Their many defeats robbed them of prestige—the people came to believe that the Manchus had lost the mandate of heaven which was the basis of their right to govern.

Further resistance to any means of rejecting the Europeans came from the numerous wealthy and influential Chinese merchant families of the coastal cities. Having become rich from their involvement with Western commerce, they did not want to disrupt the existing arrangements, and had themselves become Westernised. They had alienated themselves from the mass of the Chinese people and did not wish to provide national leadership.

After the humiliation of the defeat at the hands of Japan in 1895, an intellectual movement within China called for a 'self-strengthening' campaign. The young emperor, Guangxu, had just assumed effective governing rights from his aunt, the Empress Cixi (known as the dowager empress). Influenced by the teachings of some of the reformist-minded intellectuals, Guangxu attempted to embark on a modernisation programme.

Between June and September 1898, Guangxu issued a comprehensive series of edicts for reform, which earned for this event the label 'The Hundred Days' Reforms'. He announced reforms in the education system and the civil service, and planned to introduce a constitutional form of government in the hope of building a restrengthened China that could stand up to the West. Alarmed by these radical proposals, Empress Cixi plotted with the senior Qing bureaucrats to resume power. She placed Guangxu under house arrest and had his advisers executed. The projected reforms were annulled. Conservative reaction had prevailed in China, serving only to delay for a time the overthrow of the dynasty.

The Boxer Rebellion

The European intrusions into China over the period 1840–1900 steadily built up Chinese resentment. Particular anger was directed towards the work of the Christian missionaries. From among the uneducated and superstitious peasantry there emerged a secret society dedicated to driving out the 'foreign devils'. Its name, translated, was 'The Righteous Harmony of Fists'. The Europeans called them 'the Boxers'.

The enmity of the Boxers was focused on what they called 'the primary hairy ones' (the missionaries) and the 'secondary foreign devils' (Chinese who had converted to Christianity).

They also attacked officials of the Qing Dynasty who permitted the missionaries to operate in their districts.

The Boxers were at first regarded by the bureaucrats of the dynasty as a threat to the normal functioning of society, and their actions thus officially constituted a 'rebellion'. The Empress Cixi, however, saw in the fanaticism of the Boxers a likely means of repelling the Westerners. She secretly encouraged their attacks on Western persons and possessions. The Boxers committed many horrific slaughters of Western missionaries and Chinese converts to Christianity.

The Boxer-led crisis reached a peak when their forces attacked and besieged the European legations in Beijing in 1900. Many Western lives, including those of women and children, were lost in the carnage. In August 1900 a foreign expeditionary force of 20 000, made up of troops from Japan, Russia, Britain, France, Germany and the USA, fought its way inland from Tianjin and relieved the siege.

Animosities between Westerners and Chinese reached a peak with the terrible events of the Boxer Uprising. Western newspapers condemned the violation of embassy sanctuary as a complete denial of civilised standards. On the other hand, when the European soldiers arrived at Beijing, seeking revenge, they killed and plundered in an equally disgraceful exhibition of extreme vindictiveness.

Another round of humiliating impositions upon China followed. The empress had to assume the official attitude that the Boxers were in rebellion, and ordered the leaders to be executed. A huge indemnity was levied for the damages to foreign life and property. If the Qing Dynasty had remained in power, and this indemnity been enforced, it would have taken the Chinese until 1940 to have paid it in full.

The officials of the Qing Dynasty, propped up by the Western powers, survived until 1912, but they carried the shame of persistent humiliation. Through their refusal to implement systematic reforms of Chinese society they kept China weak in the face of the Western challenge, allowed the Middle Kingdom to become a pawn to European imperialism, and virtually ensured their own eventual overthrow through revolution.

III THE TRADITIONAL CHINESE JUSTIFICATION FOR REBELLION

Traditional Chinese society was largely based on the philosophy of Confucius (551–479 BC), who had taught that the cohesion of society depended upon the acceptance of strict rules of conduct and a reverence for past generations. Chinese society therefore had a long history of continuity of attitude and values, but this did not mean that the authority to govern had been handed down from generation to generation without interruptions. In many instances one dynasty had been succeeded by another as a result of a successful rebellion.

The Chinese attitude to rebellion was related to the theory that a just emperor ruled through the mandate of heaven—the Oriental version of what was called in Europe the divine right of kings. But the concept of the 'mandate' was different from the European idea in that, in Chinese eyes, the mandate, or authority to govern, could clearly be withdrawn. If an emperor failed to rule well, it was believed that natural disasters such as earthquakes and famines could be interpreted as signs from heaven that the mandate was being suspended. In such circumstances, rebellion could be justified. If however, the emperor successfully withstood the rebellion, it could be said that the mandate continued, because his authority had been proven.

Numerous instances of attempted rebellions can be found in the detailed chronicles of Chinese society. Some were peasant rebellions, and others were led by warlords acting in defiance of the emperor. **Sinologists** (students of China) claim, however, that the only successful rebellions have been those in which the peasants and the scholars have acted in co-operation. The peasants, it is said, must give their consent to being governed, because they are so numerous that no government can operate without their basic acceptance of the administration. The co-operation of the scholar class, by virtue of their education and their key role in the civil service, is also essential to the workings of government. Thus, although peasant rebellions were quite numerous in traditional China, they succeeded, it is said, only when the literate scholar class also supported the uprising and gave it intellectual validity as a reallocation of the mandate of heaven.

The Taiping Rebellion, for example, although backed by large-scale peasant support, alienated the Confucian scholar class because of its pseudo-Christian content. It therefore did not conform to the formula for a transfer of the mandate of heaven.

A successful revolution—so runs the theory—therefore required both the support of the peasant masses and an intellectual justification. We shall see how, between 1911 and 1949, one revolutionary group (the *Guomindang*, or Nationalists) at first appeared likely to combine these characteristics but failed. Later (by 1949), a second revolutionary group, the Chinese Communist Party, succeeded, because it combined these two essential elements.

IV THE NATIONALIST REVOLUTION: 1911–37

The Fall of the Dynasty

After the shame of the suppression of the Boxer Rebellion, the Qing Dynasty, somewhat belatedly, began to attempt some constitutional reforms. The dowager empress, for decades an immovable obstruction to reform, agreed in 1905 to send a commission overseas to study forms of government. This commission recommended the formation of a type of parliament, together with provincial assemblies. Such a move would have constituted a break in thousands of years of Chinese governmental practice.

In 1907 an edict from the palace promised the calling of a parliament in nine years. A preliminary step was to be the election of provincial assemblies in 1909. These were to be gatherings

The removal of the queue. When the Chinese republic was declared in 1912, the Revolution brought a radical change in the appearance of Chinese—the removal of the 'pigtail' or queue, which all Chinese had been required to wear as a sign of their subservience to the Manchu Dynasty. The revolutionaries regarded the removal of the queue as a symbol of their liberation.

of upper gentry, and were to have no executive power. The death of both the dowager empress and the imprisoned emperor, Guangxu, on consecutive days in November 1908, however, brought a temporary halt to all proposals. The new emperor, Puyi, was an infant of two and one-half years, and his father was appointed regent. The regent resumed the slow reform process, but his advisory cabinet was so stacked with officials of Manchu descent that the Chinese officials in the lower ranks of the bureaucracy suspected that its main purpose was to protect the dynasty.

Slowly the wheels of reform appeared to turn. In 1910 a National Assembly was called together, half of it elected and half appointed by the regent. The assembly was not given the right to legislate, and the members were ordered back to their homes, winning only a promise that they would be given legislative powers in 1913. By this action the Manchu regent antagonised even the upper gentry class upon whom his predecessors had relied for basic support.

Dissent was rapidly building up in China. By 1910 many intellectual Chinese had travelled overseas and absorbed Western principles of liberalism and democracy—concepts unknown in traditional China. The Manchus' promises of constitutional reform merely served to indicate that they were ready to surrender power: the dynasty appeared to be losing its hold on the mandate of heaven.

Radical Chinese now openly advocated the overthrow of the Manchu Dynasty and sought support from freethinking Chinese working in foreign countries. Anti-Manchu secret societies flourished. The Manchu Dynasty was ripe for overthrow, and it needed only a special incident to topple the regime.

On 10 October 1911, in protest against the ease with which foreign nations were dominating Chinese trade and railway construction, a mutiny broke out among the troops in the city of Wuhan, on the Yangzi River, in central China. The mutineers declared their rejection of Manchu control, and proclaimed the province of Hubei to be independent of the central government. Their action sparked off a rapid nation-wide defiance of Beijing's authority. The primary aim of these revolutionaries, as expressed in their own slogans, was 'to avenge the national disgrace and to restore the Chinese'.

The revolution spread quickly to many other provinces, with the army rising in mutiny, killing numerous Manchu officials. Panic-stricken, the regent quickly granted the National Assembly's earlier request for a constitution, and persuaded a 'strong man' general, Yuan Shikai, to emerge from retirement to save the dynasty. By the end of the year, fourteen provinces of China had broken from Manchu rule. A provisional republican government had been set up in the central city of Nanjing, with the revolutionary leader, Sun Yatsen, proclaimed as president on 26 December 1911.

In 1912 Yuan, still acting at this stage on behalf of the Manchus, negotiated an agreement with the republicans. On 12 February 1912 the boy emperor was forced to abdicate, declaring that the new constitution would be republican in character. Yuan was appointed president, and was given the authority to organise another provisional government. Sun Yatsen stood down as president in the hope that a unified China could be achieved. Political parties were formed, and elections were held in December 1912.

The Guomindang and Sun Yatsen: Ideals supporting Revolution

The major political party that emerged was the Guomindang (*Guo* 'nation', *min* 'people', *dang* 'party'), internationally known as the Nationalist Party. Its leader was Sun Yatsen.

In many ways Sun was an unlikely candidate to lead a Chinese nationalist revolution, because he had spent much of his adult life outside China. Born near Macao in southern China, he was taken to Hawaii at the age of twelve by a wealthy brother. He then received a Western education, mastering English. He was baptised a

Sun Yatsen (1866–1925), the original leader of the Guomindang, with his wife, Soong Qingling, whose sister, Mayling, married Jiang Kaishek, Sun's successor as leader of the Guomindang. After Jiang purged the communists out of the Guomindang in 1927, Soong Qingling switched her loyalty to the Communist Party, and later served (from 1950 to 1981) as a vice-president of the People's Republic of China.

Christian at eighteen, and acquired medical qualifications after study at medical colleges in Guangzhou and Hong Kong.

By his mid-twenties Sun had become totally absorbed in political activity. He formed the Reform China Society, and began agitation to overthrow the Manchu (Qing) Dynasty, which he regarded as the great obstacle to reform and change. He encouraged a poorly planned uprising in Guangzhou in 1895, but it was easily suppressed, and many of his followers were arrested and executed. Sun fled to Hong Kong and then Japan.

From his overseas base, Sun continued to work and plan for the overthrow of the dynasty and the modernisation of China. He concentrated on obtaining the support of educated Chinese, professional men, traders and merchants. He returned to China in 1911, and was elected leader of the Guomindang. Although Sun agreed, in February 1912, to surrender the presidency to Yuan Shikai, he nevertheless hoped and expected that the Guomindang could effectively govern China through gaining a majority in the emerging parliament.

A quarrel between the Guomindang (GMD) and Yuan developed very rapidly. In 1913 Yuan concluded a financial deal with the Western powers. The GMD opposed this continuation of dependence upon foreign nations. Yuan then outlawed the GMD (November 1913), and disbanded the parliament. His term of office was extended to ten years, and he attempted to have himself declared emperor in January 1916. This sparked off waves of protests and acts of defiance in most of the provinces. So complete was this rejection of the concept of a restoration that Yuan cancelled the monarchy in March 1916. China escaped from the prospect of a return to the past when Yuan suddenly died in June 1916—the 'mandate of heaven' was not for him.

It was now apparent that a genuine revolution had been effected. For approximately 3 000 years the people of Cathay (China) had been unified under the rule of an emperor. No other civilisation on Earth had held together under one regime and one set of institutions such a large population occupying such a large territory over so long a time span as had the succeeding dynasties of China.

By contrast, Yuan's death precipitated thirty-three years of disunity in China. In the months before his death, many provinces had already declared their independence from Beijing. Sun, who had fled into exile in Japan in 1913, now returned to China. He resumed the office and status of 'president' in the south. North China, however, fell under the control of warlords, each of whom carved out his own area of dominance. There then followed ten years of civil war and confusion. The dream of democracy had been blown away.

The 'Twenty-one Demands' by Japan

From 1914 to 1918 the great powers were involved in the terrible battles of 'The Great War' (World War I). Chinese national identity was enhanced by the fact that China contributed to the Allied cause by providing 96 000 men for service in labour battalions in France. Meanwhile, Japan, allied to Britain since 1902, had been a major supporter of the victorious Allied powers, providing naval escorts for ANZAC troop convoys in the Indian Ocean and naval services in the Pacific. As a reward, Japan had been promised that, after the war, it would be able to take over the former German concessions (trading stations) in the Shandong Peninsula. The Japanese regarded this as an opportunity to establish economic dominance over China.

In January 1915 the Japanese placed a comprehensive series of demands on China for a wide range of commercial concessions. These became known as the 'Twenty-one Demands'. Had they been conceded, China would have been reduced to a condition of vassalage. Both the USA and Britain protested. In China itself nation-wide anti-Japanese rallies and a boycott of Japanese goods marked an upsurge of nationalist emotion that resulted in a rise in support for the Guomindang.

The 'May 4 Movement' in China

Because of their contribution to the war effort, the Chinese expected favourable treatment at the Versailles Conference—called to settle all claims and debts at the conclusion of World War I. They asked for the withdrawal of all foreign troops from Chinese soil, the restoration to Chinese administration of all foreign concessions and settlements, together with the termination of the spheres of influence. It became apparent, however, that the Japanese would not be prevented from taking over the former German concessions, and that the other powers would keep their concessions as well. The Chinese were being denied the principle of 'self-determination' that was being granted to other nations at Versailles.

When the news of this arrangement reached China on 4 May 1919, a spontaneous demonstration against Japanese and other foreign influences in China was launched by students in Beijing. This patriotic impulse, which became known as the 'May 4 Movement', rapidly spread to other cities of China, leaving an enduring legacy of national expression. To this day, the fourth of May is commemorated as the significant date for national demonstrations. The GMD further benefited from the May 4 Movement, as it emerged as the clear leader of nationalist sentiment. Nevertheless, warlords still dominated Beijing and northern China, and the attainment of national unity appeared to be a distant dream.

Policies of the Guomindang: a Formula for a Reformed Society

By 1919 it was obvious that, if the Guomindang (or Nationalist) Party was to secure the following of the whole nation, it would need to proclaim clear and attractive policies. Sun Yatsen therefore proclaimed the 'Three People's Principles' for the building of a new Chinese society. These were:

(a) The People's Nationalism: the liberation of China from foreign domination and exploitation, and the attainment of a national identity;

(b) The People's Government: the establishment of a form of democratic government based on the will of the people;

(c) The People's Livelihood: a version of socialist and welfare-state provisions promising an equal distribution of wealth and acceptable living conditions for all.

From 1920 till 1949 these 'Three People's Principles' were noble intentions, never fulfilled. Nevertheless, they were effective in gaining the GMD support both within China and from overseas.

The success of the Bolshevik Revolution in Russia in 1917 served to link the Russian and

Chinese revolutionaries in a sense of common purpose. Sun Yatsen was not a Marxian socialist of the Bolshevik type, but his notion of the 'People's Livelihood' incorporated many socialist principles. Accordingly, most of the Chinese revolutionaries with socialist or communist ideals were, at first, supportive of the GMD.

Many of the young radical leaders of the May 4 Movement now looked to Marxism as a means of achieving political stability and of alleviating the poverty of the Chinese people. They wanted the classless society, with equal distribution of wealth, that Marxism promised. The Communist International (Comintern), based in Soviet Russia, was dedicated to helping oppressed peoples shake off 'capitalist domination'. It seemed logical, therefore, for the Chinese to seek Russian help.

By 1922 Sun Yatsen was ready to accept contributions from the Russian communists, and encouraged the leading Chinese communists to join him as members of the GMD. In September 1923 Mikhail Borodin, a prominent Soviet leader, arrived in Guangzhou to help Sun reorganise and revitalise the GMD. Russian financial and technical aid followed.

Sun taught his followers that the process of building a Chinese nation would have to pass through three stages:

(a) a stage of military conquest, restoring order and bringing the country under one authority. (This was what Jiang Kaishek later attempted in his Northern Expedition.);

(b) a re-education or **'political tutelage'** (tuition) stage, during which the people would be educated to prepare themselves for the responsibilities of democratic procedures;

(c) a final stage of elective parliamentary government.

Sun had written that it would take a long time before the Chinese people could make good use of democratic liberties, and that the unification of the nation was the all-important prelude. For this to be achieved, the people would have to sacrifice their liberty in the meantime.

Jiang Kaishek (1887–1975), widely known as Chiang Kai Shek, succeeded Sun Yatsen as leader of the Guomindang. As military commander of the Guomindang forces, he attempted, in the Northern Expedition of 1926–28, to unify China by conquest. He was President of the Republic of China from 1928 until his death in 1975, but from 1949 (after the victory of the Communist Party on mainland China) he and the Guomindang ruled only on the island of Taiwan.

Sun Yatsen died in 1925, his dream of a unified modern China unfulfilled. His successor, Jiang Kaishek, a young general who had visited Russia in 1923 to study Red Army practices, declared, in 1926, the launching of the Northern Expedition. His aim was to defeat the warlords in the north and unify China under the one leadership.

Many of the supporters of the Guomindang gradually became uneasy about the meaning of the so-called period of 'political tutelage' and the consequent delay in the attainment of

SOURCE 9.3

Sun Yatsen explains that the Chinese people must be reunified, and the nation must become strong again, before individual liberties can be attained, 1924

HISTORICAL CONTEXT: As part of the phase he called 'political tutelage', Sun Yatsen proposed that the Chinese people would have to be led gradually to an understanding of personal liberties. In the meantime, he argued, it was more important to re-establish the strength of the nation, so that it was not oppressed by foreign powers. To achieve this, personal liberties would have to be put 'on hold'.

Source: **Sun Yatsen,** *The Three Principles of the People,* **1924**

If we speak of liberty to the average man . . . he surely will not understand us. The reason why the Chinese really have attached no importance whatever to liberty is because that word is but a recent importation into China. It is understood now only by young people and by those who have studied abroad . . . But even those do not know exactly what is really meant by liberty.

The Chinese do not know anything about liberty . . . We have too much liberty, no cohesion, no power of resistance; we are 'loose sand'. Because we have become 'loose sand', we have been invaded by

foreign imperialism and oppressed by an economic and commercial war on the part of the Powers . . .

The liberty of the individual must not be too great, but that of the nation must be unrestricted. When the nation will have freedom of action, China will become a strong nation. In order to attain this end, all must sacrifice their liberty.

QUESTIONS

1 In what way does the first paragraph help you to understand how difficult it has been in modern times to build up a commitment in China to 'liberty' and 'democracy'?

2 What is Sun Yatsen aiming to achieve by using the metaphor of 'loose sand'?

3 What condition is Sun seeking in his assertion that the liberty of the nation must be 'unrestricted' while the 'liberty of the individual must not be too great'?

4 Which European political ideology of the 1920s and 1930s was similarly stressing the subordination of the individual to the interests of the State?

---

democracy. Under Jiang Kaishek's leadership, the GMD began to look more and more like one-party domination and a military dictatorship, with many features of government practice similar to the Italian Fascist regime in the same period.

The Expulsion of the Communists from the GMD

Much of Jiang's support came from businessmen (the Chinese bourgeoisie) and landowners. These groups became suspicious of the intentions of the communist sympathisers within the GMD, who were promising the Chinese workers that eventually all wealth would be redistributed, and that all peasants would eventually share land ownership.

In 1927 Jiang, himself now wary of the likely takeover of the GMD by the communist element, decided to strike first. In a ruthless and bloody purge in Shanghai, he had many of the communists put to death, and expelled their followers from the GMD. Borodin and other Soviet advisers were evicted from China. A bitter and permanent rift between the Nationalists (the remaining element in the GMD) and the CCP (Chinese Communist Party) dated from this incident.

The GMD, having expelled the major social reformers from its ranks, had now become a conservative party supported by landlords, industrialists, bankers and foreign interests fearful of losing trading profits and privileges. The militarist groups within the GMD had established supremacy over the civilian elements. In terms of the expected social revolution, progress was now practically halted. The Three People's Principles proclaimed by Sun had not been established. Most of the efforts of the GMD had been directed towards subduing the warlords and imposing an administrative unity upon the nation. The rupture with the communists had made this task even more difficult, and perhaps impossible.

Achievement and Reversal: the Japanese Invasion

The Northern Expedition was partly successful. By October 1928 Jiang claimed to be the head (chairman) of a true national government. Much of northern China had been brought under GMD administration, but often through deals with warlords which left the latter in control of large areas. The claim that a unified nation had been achieved was largely illusory.

On the other hand, the GMD almost achieved the liberation of China from treaty inequalities imposed by foreign powers. In July 1928 the government announced that all unequal treaties would be cancelled, and in 1929 stated that all extra-territorial rights would cease on 1 January 1930.

By 1930, to external appearances anyway, the unification of China was almost fulfilled. (Unknown to most of the Western world, the communists were building new bases in the interior.) The opportunity existed for the GMD to create a new modernised China. All this was to be lost through the results of Japanese military action.

Firmly established in Manchuria by old treaty rights, the Japanese regularly encroached upon other Chinese territories to preserve their own interests. In 1931 the Japanese military forces stationed in Manchuria provoked a quarrel with the Chinese governing authorities and seized the whole of Manchuria. A new nation, Manchukuo (which means 'Manchu nation'), was proclaimed in 1932. Although officially an independent country, it was merely a Japanese **puppet state**. In 1934 the Japanese placed the deposed Chinese emperor, Puyi, on the throne of the so-called Empire of Manchukuo. The Manchu Dynasty had returned to its homeland.

During the military action involving the establishment of Manchukuo, the Japanese had attacked Shanghai, in China proper. For this, and the seizure of Manchukuo, Japan was reprimanded by the League of Nations. To show its contempt for the League, Japan resigned its membership in 1933.

In 1937 the Japanese launched a full-scale invasion of China, which ended any chance the GMD had of establishing administrative unity. Within a year the Japanese occupied most of northern and east China, and almost all the key ports. The GMD lost its jurisdiction over all the main industrial centres together with the revenue they generated. Most of the fertile agricultural land similarly passed under Japanese control. The GMD had to retreat from its capital city and major base, Nanjing, and establish a new capital 1 600 kilometres up the Yangzi at Chongqing. Similarly, the communists were landlocked in remote provinces by the Japanese occupation of the coastal zones. The reunification of China was now dependent upon the ultimate defeat and expulsion of the Japanese, which would not be achieved until 1945.

Map 9.2

The GMD's Portrayal of National Unity and Democracy

In an attempt to build up a national spirit to counter the appeal of communism, Jiang proclaimed, in 1933, the launching of what he called the 'New Life' movement. The movement promoted a return to the principles of Confucianism, and used parades, uniforms and slogans to foster loyalty to the nation and obedience to the party. It was very similar in style and emphasis to the fascist movements of the same era in Italy and Germany. The GMD even fostered a blueshirts brigade with functions similar to those of the brownshirts of Nazi Germany, together with a secret police force to coerce the populace into obedience.

The New Life movement largely 'backfired'. Instead of winning the people's support, it

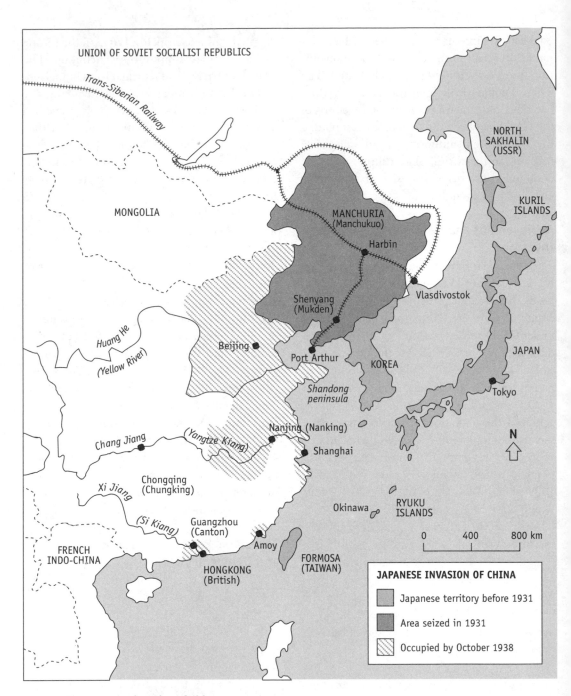

MAP 9.2 The Japanese invasion of China

Units of the Japanese army, having the advantage of military bases within the region, seized control of Manchuria in September 1931, without a declaration of war. In March 1932 the region was renamed Manchukuo, and proclaimed a separate nation, by the Japanese. To the rest of the world it was obviously a Japanese puppet state. In July 1937 the Japanese attacked Beijing (Peking) and bombed other Chinese cities, including Shanghai. By December 1937 a vast area north of the Yangzi (Yangtse) River was under Japanese control. By October 1938 the Japanese had also captured Amoy and Guangzhou (Canton). In 1940 they set up a puppet government in Nanjing (Nanking). Jiang Kaishek (Chiang Kai Shek) and his Guomindang (Nationalist Party) government withdrew to Chongqing (Chungking), in central China, and used it as their capital city until the end of World War II.

generated suspicions of a party dictatorship. Jiang justified his policy by reference to Sun's predictions regarding 'political tutelage'. The unification of the country by military strength had taken ten years (and was not really complete anyway), so the period needed for 'political tutelage' was deliberately left vague. Using Sun's theory, Jiang argued that the GMD was the only legitimate party able to undertake the task. In this way he justified the operation of what was really a one-party military dictatorship, whilst representing to the West that he was creating a multi-party parliamentary democracy.

The emperor had been overthrown twenty-five years earlier, but true national unity under a stable administration had still not been attained. The mandate of heaven had not yet passed to a successor.

MAJOR EVENTS IN THE EUROPEAN INTRUSIONS INTO CHINA AND THE FIRST CHINESE REVOLUTION

1792 First British mission to China

1839–42 First Opium War ended with the Treaty of Nanking, by which the British obtained Hong Kong, and five treaty ports were opened for European trade

1850–64 The Taiping Rebellion challenged the authority of the Manchu (Qing) Dynasty

1856–60 Second Opium War, ended with the Treaty of Tientsin and Treaty of Peking, by which eleven more treaty ports were opened to European and American trade

1894–95 Sino-Japanese (China v. Japan) War. China was defeated, and was forced to cede Taiwan and the Pescadores Islands to Japan.

1898 Emperor Guangxu launched a major reform programme. He was deposed by Dowager Empress Cixi.

1900 The Boxer Rebellion attempted to drive foreigners out of China. The rebellion was suppressed by an Allied expeditionary force.

1911 Rebellion in Wuhan challenged the authority of the Manchu Dynasty

1912 The emperor abdicated; China was declared a republic. Yuan Shikai was installed as president. Sun Yatsen became leader of the Guomindang.

1915 Japan placed 'Twenty-one Demands' on China

1916 Yuan Shikai died, after unsuccessfully attempting to have himself declared emperor

1916 Sun Yatsen returned to China and assumed the title of 'president', but warlords dominated north China

1919 'May 4 Movement' claimed national status for China

1925 Sun Yatsen died. Jiang Kaishek assumed leadership of Guomindang.

1926 Jiang launched the Northern Expedition in an attempt to reunify China

1927 Jiang Kaishek purged the communists from the GMD. This began the long civil war between the GMD and the Chinese Communist Party.

1931 Japan seized Manchuria and renamed it Manchukuo

1934–35 The Long March, from Jiangxi to Shaanxi, by the Communist forces

1937 Japan invaded China

1945–49 Civil war between the GMD and the Chinese Communist Party

---

chapter ten

The Communist Revolution of Chinese Society

The east is red from the rising sun,
In China appears Mao Zedong.
He is our guide,
He leads us onward to build a new China.
The Communist Party is like the sun.
Wherever it rises there is light.
Where the Party goes
The people are liberated.
Extract from the 1960s Chinese film, *The East is Red*

For thirty-seven years from the abdication of the last emperor of the Qing Dynasty (1912) until 1949, China was fragmented and disunited. Although the Guomindang (the Chinese Nationalist Party) appeared to have unified China through military conquest in its Great Northern Expedition of 1926–30, there were large areas of China it did not control. In the north, several warlords governed their own regions, just like the feudal barons of old. In south-central China the Chinese Communist Party (CCP) proclaimed the Chinese Soviet Republic in the province of Jiangxi in 1931. By 1949 the Communist Party controlled all China, and the surviving members of the GMD had retreated to the island of Taiwan.

Theme Questions

➤ Why did the Guomindang fail to achieve a cultural revolution in China, while its successor in power, the Communist Party, succeeded?

➤ What conditions, circumstances and events contributed to the success of the Chinese Communist Party?

➤ Did the Communist regime fulfil its promise to create a new society in which class distinctions were to be eliminated?

➤ Did some features of traditional Chinese society survive in Communist China?

I THE CIVIL WAR AND THE COMMUNIST VICTORY

Guomindang versus the Chinese Communist Party

In the early 1920s Chinese socialists and communists served as members of the Guomindang under Sun Yatsen's leadership. They believed that the third of Sun Yatsen's Three People's Principles—the principle of the People's Livelihood—was consistent with their socialist beliefs.

In 1927 Jiang Kaishek ruthlessly purged the communists from the Guomindang.

Henceforth the GMD represented the investing classes and the landlords, and became a conservative, rather than a reformist, party.

The opposing forces in China were now identified. The GMD, or Nationalist Party, was supported by bankers, merchants, industrialists and foreign commercial organisations fearful of losing trading profits and privileges. The GMD was also supported by the Western capitalist powers, because it appeared to be a pro-capitalist government working towards the establishment of parliamentary democracy in China. The Chinese Communist Party, by contrast, was offering social reform, land ownership (in a communal sense) for the peasants, and the redistribution of wealth.

The Establishment of the CCP

When the main communist and trade union leaders were purged from the GMD in April 1927, the surviving communists formed a separate organisation, the Chinese Communist Party (CCP). On 1 August 1927, a group of communists within what had been the Nationalist Army (the GMD army) led a military uprising in Nanchang, in Jiangxi province. This group then founded the 'Red Army'—later called the People's Liberation Army—to further advance the communist cause. This date is still commemorated as the birthday of the PLA.

Retreating into mountain country, and supported by peasant groups who regarded them as the true inheritors of the revolutionary effort that had overthrown the Manchus, the Communist soldiers waged guerrilla warfare against the Nationalist troops. A slogan, widely used among the Red Army, explained their tactics:

The enemy advances, we retreat;

The enemy camps, we harass:

The enemy tires, we attack;

The enemy retreats, we pursue.

The Long March

To consolidate their recently achieved supremacy, the GMD made a big effort to crush the Communist Party. In several rural districts the CCP had established soviets (that is,

local governments based on workers' committees). These had to be disbanded if the GMD was to be an effective national government.

By October 1934 the main Communist forces were encircled in Jiangxi. In desperate retreat, the Red Army marched and fought their way through incredibly difficult terrain, over 13 000 kilometres, to gain safety by linking up with their colleagues in the remote north-western province of Shaanxi in 1935. Of the 120 000 who set out, only about 30 000 reached Shaanxi. This feat of endurance, which took over twelve months, became immortalised among the Communist deeds of heroism as the 'Long March'. Key figures in this momentous journey—Zhu De, Zhou Enlai and Mao Zedong—emerged from this ordeal with the authority and prestige that later enabled them to lead the Chinese nation for many decades.

Map 10.1

Mao Zedong (1893–1976), photographed during the period of the Long March. Mao's vigorous and inspiring leadership was critical in the success of the Communist Party in the prolonged retreat and rebuilding process.

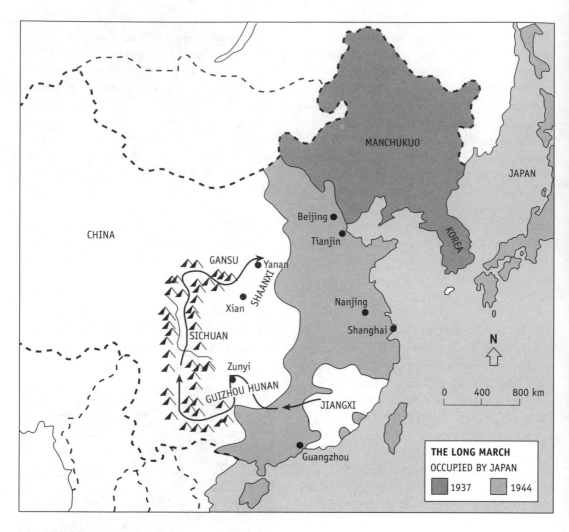

MAP 10.1 The Long March

The Long March proved the total determination of the Chinese Communists to build a new society, and became the most acclaimed achievement amongst their deeds of heroism.

In 1934, surrounded by Guomindang forces in Jiangxi, the Chinese Communist army broke out to the west in an attempt to journey through the remote mountain country and join up with their colleagues in distant Shaanxi. Over 100 000 Communist supporters set out on the march, but only about 30 000 finally reached Shaanxi over twelve months later. About 7 000 of these were members of the original group. During the march, at the city of Zunyi in Guizhou Province, Mao Zedong was elected leader. In December 1936, after having struggled through the difficult terrain of Szechwan Province, Mao established a capital city at Yanan in Shaanxi.

Jiang Kaishek's attempt to destroy and demoralise the Communists had the reverse effect. Their dedication to their cause, and their journey through thousands of villages, won them an enormous following among the Chinese peasants.

During the prolonged war against the Japanese invaders (1937–45), both the GMD and the Communist Party sent troops to fight the Japanese. To the outside world, which knew little about the Communist enclaves in remote regions of China, it was the GMD that appeared to be providing the main resistance to the Japanese. Jiang Kaishek received a great deal of aid from the USA and Britain, and was recognised as one of the 'Big Four' Allied leaders.

During the war, however, the American advisers sent to China came to the conclusion that Jiang—who had withdrawn his capital to Chongqing, deep in the interior—was avoiding the task of fighting the Japanese. More recent historical judgements have confirmed this. It seems that Jiang's main objective was to wait for an Allied victory over Japan in the hope that his forces would survive the war and then use their superiority (based on Allied-supplied equipment and planes) to establish total domination over the Communists.

The Renewed Civil War

When Japan surrendered in August 1945, and subsequently withdrew all its troops from China, the Communists under Mao Zedong resumed their struggle with the GMD. The Communist Party had won a considerable following among the peasants. They had maintained a more consistent resistance to the Japanese than had the GMD, and had applied their policies of land reform. After the Japanese surrender, the GMD, with their superiority in equipment, moved troops by air into zones evacuated by the Japanese, and were thus able to reoccupy the key cities and ports of the east coast which had been their power-base in the 1930s. But the Communists meanwhile consolidated their hold on the rural areas of northern China.

The renewed Civil War raged from 1946 till 1949. While at first the GMD troops held a strong advantage, the CCP steadily increased its following. The Communists acquired modern equipment and greater manpower when many individual soldiers, and sometimes complete

units, deserted from the GMD to join them.

By 1948 the Nationalist armies were falling apart and their administrative arm, the Guomindang, was rent with dissension. By the end of that year the remaining supporters of the GMD, having lost all their holdings on the mainland, re-established the 'Republic of China' on the island of Taiwan under the protection of the US navy. Their administration of Taiwan has continued to the present day.

In October 1949 Mao Zedong proclaimed the People's Republic of China. In a speech on that occasion he stressed that the distinguishing feature of the Communist Revolution was that the nation had at last 'stood up' against foreign intrusion. The Communists, however, were promising more than this. They were planning an economic and cultural revolution: a transformation of the nature of Chinese society.

II WHY DID THE GUOMINDANG FAIL WHILE THE CCP SUCCEEDED?

The failure of the GMD and the success of the Communist Party were two sides of the one coin. As one organisation lost its effectiveness, the other expanded its influence.

The Failure of the Guomindang

To the people and leaders of the capitalist West, the failure of Jiang Kaishek and the GMD came as a substantial shock. At the beginning of the Civil War, Jiang appeared to hold every advantage: he controlled the sea ports and the lines of supply, he held a vast superiority in manpower, and he was receiving American arms and equipment. Yet within four years he was forced to find refuge on Taiwan. Many Chinese would account for this simply by explaining that the Guomindang, through its corruption and mismanagement, had surrendered the mandate of heaven.

Other factors, of course, contributed to the GMD failure. Although the GMD leaders had proclaimed their intention to prepare the people for democratic forms of government and

Mao Zedong (1893–1976) is shown here in the act of proclaiming the People's Republic of China in Tienanmen Square on 1 October 1949. In his speech he claimed that the Chinese people had at last 'stood up'.

Western interests, it was 'nationalist' in name but not in spirit. The help it received from the USA eventually became a hindrance, because it identified the GMD with Western interests and allowed the Communists to portray Jiang as a tool of Western imperialism.

Accusations of corruption further diminished the reputation of the GMD. Jiang's enemies, and later even his sometime supporters, accused him of allowing the 'Four Great Families' (wealthy and influential families related to Jiang by marriage) to amass great influence through government-backed monopolies. This spirit of nepotism and corruption spread right through the GMD; its officials lined their own pockets and showed little concern for the problems of the peasants and the poor. In 1948, with the Communists poised for success, the GMD antagonised even its city-based supporters by a ruthlessly enforced policy of taking possession of all gold, silver and American dollars in exchange for a new paper currency. The rumour was that the wealth thus acquired would be directed to the post-war needs of the Four Great Families.

Jiang's reluctance to combat the invading Japanese in the period 1937–45 further lowered his prestige. He had appeared more eager to fight the Communists than repel the invaders. Many Guomindang officials openly collaborated with the Japanese for their own advantage. It was the Communists in the northern provinces who put up the most effective resistance to the Japanese invasion.

In the vast interior of China, the peasantry mistrusted the GMD. They believed that Mao and the Communists would bring them the land reforms and the stable society they desired. In the Civil War the Nationalist soldiers, despite their initial numerical advantage and superior equipment, soon fell victims to the better led and more enthusiastic Communist troops, most of whom were recruited from the rural areas.

eventually to introduce parliamentary institutions, they tended to talk about democracy on one hand, but move towards one-party rule on the other. The communists, accepted till 1927 as co-workers in the task of establishing a modern republic, were in that year purged out of the GMD with a brutality and ruthlessness that clearly indicated that any future coalition was virtually an impossibility.

In the judgement of many overseas observers, and the bulk of the Chinese themselves, the GMD had betrayed the original objectives of Sun Yatsen's proposed revolution. It was not Jiang Kaishek, but the Communists, led by Mao Zedong, who had worked for equality, and had awakened the masses of the people, thus attempting to fulfil one of Sun's objectives.

Relying for support mainly on east-coast merchants and capitalists, the Guomindang failed to win the loyalty of the masses. Led by converts to Christianity, and identified with

By constantly distrusting the ordinary people and steadily concentrating power in the hands of a few privileged followers, Jiang had

Mao Zedong proclaims the establishment of the People's Republic of China, 1949

HISTORICAL CONTEXT: After long years of civil war (1945–49), the People's Liberation Army of the Chinese Communist Party won control of all the major ports and cities of China, driving the remnants of the Guomindang from the mainland to Taiwan. On 1 October 1949, at the Gate of Heavenly Peace in the Manchu Dynasty's Forbidden City, Mao Zedong claimed that the Chinese people had unified themselves and had formed the People's Republic of China.

Source: **Mao Zedong, in a speech in Beijing, 1 October 1949**

Our work will be written down in the history of mankind, and it will clearly demonstrate the fact that the Chinese, who comprise one quarter of humanity, have from now on stood up . . . We have united ourselves and defeated both our foreign and domestic oppressors by means of the People's War of Liberation and the People's Great Revolution, and we announce the establishment of the People's Republic of China. Our nation will from now on enter the large family of peace loving and freedom loving nations of the world. It will work bravely and industriously to create its own civilisation and happiness and will, at the same time, promote world peace and freedom. Our nation will never again be an insulted nation. We have stood up.

QUESTIONS

1 Why did Mao refer to China as having been 'an insulted nation'?

2 What did Mao mean by claiming that China had 'stood up'?

3 What were the two main 'audiences' for Mao's speech, and what two messages was he sending out?

virtually become a military dictator. The GMD secret police treated any citizens suspected of Communist sympathies with great brutality. This terrorised the general populace. By the middle of 1949 Jiang had alienated almost every section of the community—businessmen and fervent nationalists (who had earlier supported him), intellectuals and peasants. Large sections of his army deserted and surrendered their equipment to Mao. Support for the GMD faded away.

The Success of the Communists

Mao's success can be explained in what are reputed to be Mao's own words: 'power grows out of the barrel of a gun'. By 1949 Mao had the larger number of soldiers and guns. But in reality it had been Jiang who had placed his hopes for victory in military strength. Mao succeeded because he had also won the people's hearts, either as the less unacceptable of two alternatives, or in the positive sense, as a means of achieving a reformed society.

Through all the years of retreat, hardship, and consolidation, Mao and his supporters had consistently and stoically advocated a revolution 'from within' China. Although Marxism was of Western origins, and the Russian Revolution had already occurred as a precedent, China was ripe for a peasant communist revolution even without outside influences. The wealthy landlords had for centuries waxed rich on the labour and poverty of the peasants. The Communists were determined and patient; they took a 'long view' on the inevitability of the peasant revolution, tracing its origins back to the Taiping Rebellion of the 1850s. Because they were working for a 'people's republic', they claimed to be the true heirs of the 1911 revolution which overthrew the Manchu Dynasty. They thus more successfully aroused a Chinese nationalist spirit than the 'nationalists' themselves.

In contrast to the affluence of the Guomindang officials, the Communist Party leaders wore simple clothes, ate simple food, and shared the same accommodation as their followers. Superficially at least, no taint of privilege or corruption marred their administration. By word of mouth, the Communists gained a nation-wide reputation for dealing fairly with the common people.

In addition to their reputation for fair dealing, the Communists provided practical examples of their policies. In the 'Soviet' Republic of Jiangxi (southern China) proclaimed in 1931, they confiscated all land and redistributed it to the peasants in proportion to the size of the family, and promised low taxes and expanded education facilities. When this Jiangxi Communist republic was invaded by superior nationalist forces in 1934, the Communists escaped annihilation in the legendary and heroic Long March. The Long March established the heroism of the Communists, verified their determination, and gave their movement the aura of inevitability that later established them as just claimants to the mandate of heaven.

Map 10.1

During the humiliating years of the Japanese invasion and occupation, the Communists added to their growing stature through their unrelenting and extremely effective resistance efforts. These offered a strong contrast to the vacillating campaigns of Jiang Kaishek, who spent more time planning how he could crush the Communists than resisting the Japanese.

Such was the nation-wide belief that the Guomindang was a corrupt organisation serving only the interests of the privileged classes (the landowners and the urban bourgeoisie), that the bulk of the people swung their support to the Communists. They acknowledged the need, as proclaimed by Mao, for one class (the proletariat) to use armed revolution to destroy the power of the other (privileged) classes.

Moreover, the Communist formula for re-unifying and reforming China was more directly in accord with Chinese tradition than the vague GMD promises of republican democracy some time in the future. No Chinese word for 'democracy' existed—authority to rule stemmed from the 'rightness' or 'virtue

to rule' of the holder of the mandate of heaven, rather than from the Western concept of the 'general will'. The GMD's commitment to Western-style democracy appeared to be a recognition of the need to reorganise China on Western lines, and this offended many proud Chinese.

In addition, most intellectual Chinese came to regard Jiang's talk about democracy as a fraudulent device to hide a blatantly profiteering dictatorship. In contrast the Communist Party leadership appeared purposeful and resolute; its followers were loyal and dedicated. Mao in effect claimed the mandate of heaven by right of achievement in the Chinese tradition. He set out to build a new Middle Kingdom, and his references to China 'standing up' emphasised this.

III THE COMMUNIST SOCIAL REVOLUTION

Under the CCP, China was again reunified for the first time in almost forty years, or, if it is accepted that the Manchu control of the vast nation had been lost in the 1850s, for the first time in almost one hundred years.

The Communists, under Mao's leadership, set out to build a new Chinese society. Society was to be organised for the benefit of all, not for the exploitation of the people through capitalist ownership of the factors of production. Seeking to ensure an equal distribution of wealth, they promised the peasants a share in the ownership of the land. The nation was to be unified under a common purpose.

Mao expressed his basic intentions to unify China and create a 'new world' in a poem:
Great plans are being made;
A bridge will fly to join the north and south,
A deep chasm become a thoroughfare
. . . the mountain goddess, if she still is there,
Will be startled to find her world so changed.

The true 'communist revolution' was, in Mao's eyes, not simply the seizure of power, but the reformation of society. The Communists

Soldiers of the People's Liberation Army. The victory of the Chinese Communist Party over the Guomindang was based on the dedication and determination of the People's Liberation Army. The soldiers, mostly recruited from the peasantry, believed in their cause, and won the support of the masses. The Guomindang, meanwhile, lost support because of corruption within their ranks and their lack of appeal amongst the poverty-stricken masses.

claimed that they would bring about a comprehensive reform of Chinese society, something that the GMD had promised but had never fulfilled.

Land Reforms

The first obligation of the CCP was to keep faith with the millions of supporters from the peasantry, who were expecting a share in land ownership. In 1950 an Agrarian Law was introduced, with the purpose of releasing agriculture from feudal shackles—thus paving the way for industrialisation. Over the next three years almost all the privately owned land was appropriated for collectivisation, and untold thousands (perhaps as many as one million) former landholders were condemned as 'enemies of the people' and put to death. The destruction of

this privileged ruling class, which had held the peasants in a serf-like status for over 2 000 years, was indeed a revolution. Just as Stalin had done before him by his categorisation of dissenters as kulaks and his brutal consignment of people thus branded to imprisonment or liquidation, under Mao's regime to be labelled a 'land-owner', or even a supporter of the previously influential class, was to risk condemnation. Mao attained nation-wide obedience through terror.

Chapter 7

Simultaneously, great efforts were made to convince the people that the new regime was dedicated to the task of bringing joy, happiness and fulfilment to the long-suffering people. Songs were promulgated which likened the Communist regime to the sun, bringing 'light' to the people, and promising happiness as a

p. 190

The Communist Revolution of Chinese Society

relief to the preceding years of misery, as well as liberation from the 'triple tyranny' of foreign exploitation, feudal forms of control, and a corrupt bureaucracy.

A Communist Economy

Under Communist Party rule the State assumed full responsibility for the allocation of resources to production, the regulation of labour, and the marketing of goods. China was to become a socialist **planned economy**. Nevertheless the immediate task was the reconstruction of an economy shattered by thirty years of civil war and invasion.

While large private land-holdings and large-scale capitalist enterprises were 'eliminated', smaller-scale capitalists were asked to participate in the task of reactivating the economy. This policy initiated a short-lived phase similar in purpose to the NEP (New Economic Policy) sponsored in Russia by Lenin in the 1920s.

From 1953 to 1958 the policy of the Five Year plans was introduced, with the emphasis on phasing out privately-owned farms and industries and the building of a socialist economy. In an official address on 5 July 1955, the chairman of the State Planning Commission explained the necessary phases of development, stressing the need for what he called 'socialist industrialisation', backed up by efficient food production by agricultural co-operatives.

SOURCE 10.2

The people of the newly formed People's Republic of China remember the sufferings of the past and look to a bright future, *circa* 1965

HISTORICAL CONTEXT: In the first two decades of the People's Republic, the new government expended great effort in convincing the younger generation that they were beneficiaries of an enlightened regime. The words of this song, from a film titled *The East is Red*, stress that a liberation had occurred. Even in the 1990s Chinese tourist guides still referred to 1949 as the 'year of liberation'.

Source: **Extracts from the film *The East is Red*, produced in China in the 1960s**

In the new and revived China of today
everyone is happy and all the land is beautiful,
But in our happiness we cannot forget
the bitter misery that went before
and the Long March that led at last to liberation.
In that China of the past
the earth was gloomy and the sky was dark.
Our people carried brutal burdens of misfortune and
*   misery,*
were weighed down with chains,
held back by fetters,
crushed under the triple tyranny
of foreign exploitation, feudalism and corrupt

bureaucracy.

As day follows night there comes, in time,
an end to darkness.
The gunfire of revolution echoes across the land,
and angry shouts of students in Beijing,
clamouring against the partnership of foreign interests
and corrupt government,
heralds a new day for the Chinese people.
Out of this tumult the Communist Party of China
*   is born.*

QUESTIONS

1 What is the significance of the use of the terms 'liberated' and 'liberation'?
2 Explain the meaning of 'triple tyranny'.
3 What was the 'foreign exploitation' referred to in this song?
4 What was the nature of the 'feudalism' referred to, and who by inference is being blamed for its effects?
5 What was the 'corrupt bureaucracy' and 'corrupt government' here mentioned?
6 How do you interpret the song as historical evidence?

This historic photograph, taken on Josef Stalin's seventieth birthday, 21 December 1949, shows four leaders of communist nations. From left, they are: Mao Zedong of Communist China; Marshall Bulganin (Soviet defence minister); Josef Stalin of the USSR; Walter Ulbricht of East Germany; and Nikita Khrushchev, who was effectively leader of the USSR (after Stalin's death) from 1955 till 1964. The photograph shows how quickly Mao Zedong was acknowledged as the leader of a communist nation with equal status to the USSR, as it was taken only two months after his declaration of the Republic of China.

In the application of the policy of self-reliance, the long-established practice by which foreign interests controlled large proportions of Chinese trade and business activities was to be ended. Almost all foreigners were forced to leave China. Thus the Communists succeeded in re-establishing Chinese control of China—one of the major aims of the Chinese nationalist movement.

Mao nevertheless at first acknowledged that the Chinese needed advice and guidance from foreign experts if they were to catch up with more modernised nations. The natural source for such help seemed to be the fellow communist neighbour, the USSR. In theory the two nations were 'brother' communities linked in the cause of seeking a world proletarian revolution. Accordingly, Russian advisers and technicians arrived in China in 1949, and in 1950 the Sino–Soviet Treaty of Friendship was concluded, providing for economic aid to China and a spirit of close co-operation in international policy.

Later, in the 1960s, the two nations quarrelled, bringing on the 'Sino-Soviet split'. Mao then insisted that China should concentrate on attaining growth from its own resources, spurning alien economic practices and declining to seek foreign aid. The concept of self-reliance extended down to the communes (agricultural units of approximately one hundred villages), which were meant to be self-sustaining. The Chinese economy thus became much more decentralised than the Soviet economy. The Chinese central planning agencies expected the sub-divisions to assume greater roles in decision-making than did their Soviet counterparts.

Sect. V

The 'Great Leap Forward'

In 1958, to accelerate the growth in productive capacity, Mao called upon his people to participate in what was called the 'Great Leap Forward'. Declaring that they were now about to enter the fully socialist phase of development, the Maoists launched simultaneously a programme for socialist education and a campaign to eliminate the private sector of the economy. Both workers and peasants were manipulated into communes, which were meant to become the basic production unit of a new socialist society. It was believed that, through mass organisation and the inspiration of revolutionary zeal among the people, production could be boosted dramatically.

Most small-scale industrial projects and many of the attempts at lifting agricultural output launched under the Great Leap did not succeed. Many thousands of metal-smelting plants, for example, proved to be total failures, and the effort expended on them resulted in a neglect of crop production. To satisfy members of the party hierarchy, local officials frequently falsified production figures to make it appear that quotas had been met, whereas the failures in the food harvests, coupled with severe setbacks caused by floods and drought, caused what has been described as one of the greatest famines in history. Between 1959 and 1962, over 10 million people (some sources say 30 million) died.

By 1960 many of the objectives of the Great Leap Forward had been modified, and some private enterprises were permitted to survive. Examples were small agricultural plots and small-scale enterprise in marketing and light industry. Nevertheless, a basic disapproval of private-sector activity prevailed. Mao showed his policy preferences when he criticised Marshall Tito for allowing a regrowth of private enterprise in Communist Yugoslavia.

The Chinese Communist Party administration did succeed, overall, in stimulating the growth of the Chinese economy, which by the early 1960s, was expanding, in terms of gross production, at a rate of about 3 per cent per annum. Heavy industries were established, and Chinese technology produced nuclear weapons by 1964. Given the potential for expansion, however, this was not an impressive rate. The reason lay in the Maoist emphasis on the inculcation of a socialist way of life and the socialist system of production rather than on sheer volume of production for its own sake.

The 'New Socialist Man': an Ideological Revolution

Despite the emphasis on increased production, Mao Zedong stressed that the objective was not simply the attainment of higher standards of living for the Chinese people. He wanted to build a new society around what he called 'the new socialist (or communist) man'. He was seeking a moral and spiritual revolution in which the individual was expected to devote himself to the 'collective life of the Party'. This had priority over economic reform.

There was to be a revolution, too, for Chinese women. They were released from the traditional Confucian duty to obey their fathers, husbands, and sons. Communist Party rules now made it possible for women to leave their husbands. Many new jobs, previously male preserves, were opened up to women.

Mao criticised the Soviet Union for placing the creation of wealth ahead of communist ideology. Economic policy purely aimed at raising standards of living was regarded by Mao as a betrayal of communist dogma, because such reforms were deemed to be but one part of the total reconstruction of society.

Indoctrination in communist ideology was relentless and all-encompassing. Almost all men and women dressed in identical uniforms and were subjected to a stifling conformity. The emphasis was on maintaining revolutionary purity. No opportunities existed for the expression of dissent. In this emphasis on the attainment of communist ideals, Mao insisted that the people pay homage to some of the key personalities in the history of the movement. After the 1949 victory, the citizens of Beijng found new objects for adulation: the city was decorated, at prominent points, by four gigantic poster pictures of Mao Zedong, Marx, Engels and Stalin.

IV CHINESE INVOLVEMENT IN THE KOREAN WAR

In 1950, the year after the CCP's proclamation of the People's Republic of China, a war broke out in the neighbouring peninsula of Korea. Communist China's participation in this war was to have extremely significant repercussions for the Chinese Revolution, and for the perception of Communist China held by people in other nations.

In the distant past, Korea had been a tribute state of China, but was occupied by the Japanese after the Sino-Japanese War of 1894–95, and then annexed by Japan in 1910. Japan controlled the peninsula from 1910 till 1945.

At the end of World War II, Russian troops occupied northern Korea, and American troops southern Korea, as a means of disarming the Japanese troops. These Allied occupation procedures resulted in the emergence of rival governments north and south of the thirty-eighth parallel of latitude. Each claimed to be the legitimate government of the whole of Korea.

The government of North Korea was Russian-sponsored and communist-aligned, and although the government of South Korea was correspondingly American-sponsored, to Western eyes it appeared to be more legitimate as it was based on a parliamentary republic, proclaimed on 15 August 1948. The UN General Assembly recognised this government as the authentic government of all Korea. The USA withdrew its military forces by June 1949, and appeared to have adopted the policy that the settlement of the Korean question had become a matter for UN jurisdiction.

On 25 June 1950 the news services of the Western world carried a report that North Korean forces had invaded South Korea. In the communist world, a different version of events was issued; it was claimed that Southern forces began the fighting. Such discrepancies were to become common in reports on this war, and other **Cold War** disputes, for the next forty years.

In the West the dispute was immediately

SOURCE 10.3

Mao Zedong teaches his people that they should subordinate their individual interests to the cause of the revolution, 1967

HISTORICAL CONTEXT: Mao believed that it might take several decades to eliminate all bourgeois and capitalist values from Chinese society. He sought to convince the people that their true destiny lay in serving the communal cause.

Source: Quotations from Chairman Mao Zedong, Foreign Languages Press, Beijing, 1967, p. 268

A Communist should have largeness of mind and he should be staunch and active, looking upon the interests of the revolution as his very life and subordinating his personal interests to those of the revolution; always and everywhere he should adhere to principle and wage a tireless struggle against all incorrect ideas and actions, so as to consolidate the collective life of the Party and strengthen the ties between the Party and the masses; he should be more concerned about the Party and the masses than about any individual, and more concerned about others than about himself. Only thus can he be considered a Communist.

QUESTIONS

1 What might Mao be hinting at when he refers to 'incorrect ideas and actions'?

2 Why might millions of Chinese be receptive to the message in this statement?

3 To what extent can the sentiments expressed in this extract be equated with democracy?

---

interpreted as being of greater significance than a local war. Because the North Koreans were equipped with Russian armaments and apparently backed by Russian advisers, the invasion was regarded in the West as an attempt to spread world communism under the guise of Asian nationalism, using the armed forces of a puppet state instead of those of a great power.

Korea lay between Japan, which the USA was trying to rebuild as a parliamentary democracy, and China, which had only just been 'liberated from imperialism' (or 'oppressed under communism', depending on the political viewpoint). In the far north of Korea the USSR and Korea shared a common frontier.

The Korean crisis thus emerged as a major test of several key policies: could the USSR 'get away' with the expansion of communism?; would the newly formed United Nations be effective in meeting this crisis? The UN, on paper anyway, had a policy of applying '**collective security**' to combat aggression. The USA, moreover, had proclaimed its intention to 'contain' communism to its existing domains. Could these two policies be successfully applied? Would the Korean crisis aid or obstruct the proposed social revolution in Communist China?

Acting in response to a UN Security Council resolution, sixteen member nations, including Britain, Australia and New Zealand, supplied troops for the collective security operation. The bulk of the manpower and resources were supplied by the USA. The North Korean forces were driven back into North Korea.

The Entry of Chinese Forces

Once the UN forces, commanded by the American general, Douglas MacArthur, drove beyond the thirty-eighth parallel deep into North Korea, they had themselves become aggressors and were acting on dubious moral grounds. In justification of this action, MacArthur claimed that he was fulfilling the UN resolution authorising his forces to take action to ensure conditions of stability in Korea. As the UN forces advanced, the North Kore-ans increasingly received help in the form of both men and materials from Communist China.

By November 1950 the UN forces had almost reached the Yalu River, the border with China. Although the Western forces regarded themselves as agents of liberation, and servants of the world peace-keeping organisation, they were not so regarded by the Chinese and most other Asian peoples. Because the Americans were fighting on Asian soil thousands of kilometres from their home, they were easily portrayed as imperialist invaders. They had crossed the thirty-eighth parallel; who could be sure that they would not cross the Chinese border? Rumours abounded that MacArthur intended to utilise the Nationalist Chinese army from Taiwan in a joint American–Guomindang invasion aimed at countering the People's Revolution in China.

Suddenly, catching the UN forces by surprise, one million Chinese soldiers entered the war in aid of the North Koreans. According to the Beijing government, they were volunteers, helping their neighbouring nation. By this ruse, the Chinese government pretended that they were not officially involved. Such a massive intervention swung the balance back in favour of the North Koreans. Within a few months the UN forces had been driven right back to the original frontier and beyond it, in a desperately fought retreat, into South Korea.

The success of the campaign to drive the UN forces back into the South was of great international significance. The Communist Chinese, even more than previously, could claim to be the saviours of Asia from US imperialism. They had 'liberated' North Korea, and demonstrated that their soldiers could defeat highly mechanised American forces just as convincingly as they had routed the Guomindang. They gained in world status as a result, even though a UN resolution of 1 February 1951 branded the People's Republic of China an aggressor.

Eventually an armistice was concluded in 1953, with Korea again divided along a line very close to the division that had stood when

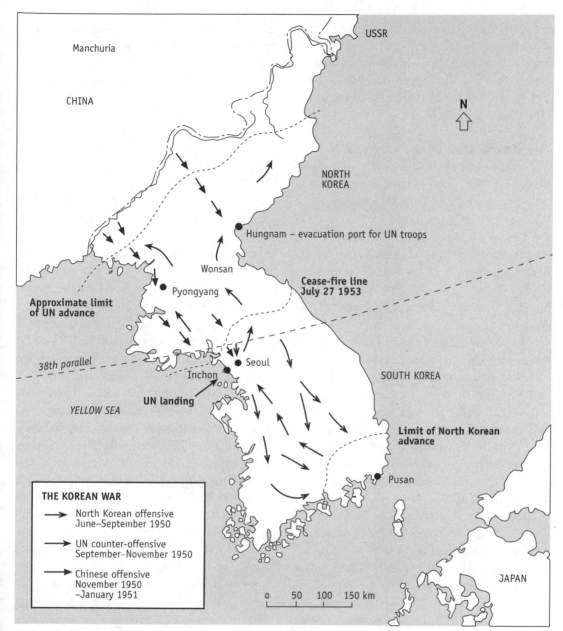

Map legend:

THE KOREAN WAR

→ North Korean offensive
June–September 1950

→ UN counter-offensive
September–November 1950

→ Chinese offensive
November 1950
–January 1951

Map labels: Manchuria, CHINA, USSR, NORTH KOREA, Hungnam – evacuation port for UN troops, Wonsan, Cease-fire line July 27 1953, Pyongyang, Approximate limit of UN advance, 38th parallel, Inchon, UN landing, Seoul, SOUTH KOREA, YELLOW SEA, Limit of North Korean advance, Pusan, JAPAN, N

Scale: 0 50 100 150 km

MAP 10.2 The Korean War

During the Korean War a multi-nation army under the United Nations Organisation flag enforced a series of UN resolutions. When forces of the communist-aligned North Korean government invaded South Korea in June 1950, their
rapid advance was not halted until UN forces bolstered the South Korean army in the extreme south-east, near
Pusan. The UN counter-offensive, staged by forces of the USA and fifteen other members of the UN (including Australia), reconquered all of South Korea.

The UN forces then advanced into North Korea for the avowed purpose of destroying North Korea's capacity to
renew an offensive. This provoked the entry of Chinese forces (officially 'volunteers'), and this conflict between the
Chinese and the UN forces was used by China's opponents (chiefly the USA and the Guomindang government of Taiwan) to prevent the admission of the People's Republic of China to the UN for twenty years. The cease-fire was
finally achieved in 1953. The line of demarcation was very close to the 38th parallel, the original (1945) frontier
between North Korea and South Korea.

the war began. To this day, however, the border is still heavily fortified by both nations, and US troops are stationed in South Korea to deter the North from resuming aggression. North Korea and South Korea have been admitted to the UN as separate nations.

The Significance of the Korean War

The involvement of the Chinese Communists in the Korean War produced significant effects on the perception of the Chinese Revolution. Some of the peoples of Asia admired the willingness of the Chinese to aid a neighbouring society in resisting capitalist forces. The opposite sentiment, however, emerged in the capitalist investing classes of South and South-East Asia, and in the populations of the parliamentary democracies of Australia, New Zealand and the USA. These people interpreted the Chinese action as proof of the menace of communist expansionism.

It was claimed at the time that the UN action in Korea was of immeasurable importance in setting the principle that aggression by an expansionist power would be countered. Had the UN failed, it would have been discredited as had the League of Nations in the 1930s.

Later events, however, showed that the Korean action had not set a strong precedent. When other acts of aggression occurred, UN action could be stopped by the use of the veto by any one of the great powers (the USSR had mysteriously not used its power of veto to halt the UN action in Korea). In the case of the Vietnam War (1965–73), no UN action was ever authorised, because agreement was never reached as to whether or not it was a civil war.

Some suspicion also remained, among **Third World nations**, that the UN had moved quickly to counter what had been labelled communist aggression, but might not act so promptly in different circumstances. It was widely claimed among some Asian nations that the Korean episode had revealed that the UN was but a tool of US policy, and it lost status accordingly. A case could be made that the official UN policies varied, in relation to varying American aims. At first the declared objective of the 'police action' in Korea was to preserve the integrity of South Korea. Then it was changed to include invasion of the North—a clear-cut example, claimed the critics, of the UN being used as an instrument of American **imperialism**.

The US government, however, showed a strong commitment to internationalist principles when President Truman dismissed MacArthur from his command on 11 April 1951. MacArthur had insisted that he should be permitted to counter the Communist Chinese offensive by bombing China, imposing a naval blockade on its ports and bringing the Guomindang army to Korea. There is little doubt that such actions would have embittered Asian-American relations and possibly triggered off a third world war. Truman's action demonstrated that the civilian government of the USA could enforce a policy of global responsibility despite the priorities of its famous generals.

The curbing of MacArthur left open the chance that—perhaps decades in the future—good relations could be re-established between China and the USA. Eventually this proved to be the case.

The mystery as to why the USSR was not present in the Security Council to prevent the action by use of the veto has never been satisfactorily answered. One theory is that it was a device to make it appear that North Korea was acting on its own in a genuine nationalist impulse to reunify the nation. Another argument is that the USSR deliberately stepped aside as a means of discovering if the members of the UN possessed the collective will to meet an aggressive act.

All the theories about the Soviet plan to test the West are, however, called into question by the fact that the USSR was still very weak from the dreadful sacrifices made in the war with Nazi Germany, and did not yet possess the atomic bomb or ballistic missiles. Any move towards war would have been to the Soviets' great and lasting disadvantage. Another possible motive behind the Soviet policy was a desire to involve Communist China in a conflict with the West as a means of drawing it irrevocably into the anti–West power bloc. The real reasons for the outbreak of the Korean War remain a matter for continuing investigation.

V THE EFFECT OF THE REVOLUTION ON CHINA'S FOREIGN RELATIONS

The success of the Communist Party in winning control of China in 1949 generated an enormous emotional reaction in Western countries. At that time Soviet-sponsored communist governments had just taken over in all the States of eastern Europe. In the capitalist nations there was widespread fear of a communist **world revolution**. When the world's largest nation, China, fell under Communist control, the very worst fears seemed to be coming true. In the USA the success of the Chinese Communists sparked off a campaign to attribute blame. Bungled policies and betrayal of Western capitalist interests, it was reasoned, must surely be the reasons why the West 'lost China'. It seemed that it was not possible to believe that the CCP had won the Civil War simply because the majority of the Chinese people supported them. In the decades that followed, the Western nations' suspicions of Communist China reached a peak. The earlier fear of a 'Yellow Peril' was now replaced by the fear of a 'Red Tide'. This was linked to the 'domino theory', by which it was believed that if one nation fell under communist domination, its neighbouring countries would also 'fall', one by one, like a line of dominoes.

When the huge Communist Chinese military contingent joined the war on the side of North Korea, they were fighting against a UN-sponsored, multi-nation army that was aiding South Korea. The USA, Britain, Australia and New Zealand, together with several other nations, had contributed forces to that army. Because of the events of the Korean War, fear of the 'Red Tide' reached hysterical levels in Australia.

By 1954, meanwhile, the nationalist movement in French Indo-China had forced the French to withdraw after military defeat. By 1956 war had broken out in Vietnam between opposing groups. One group, based in the north, wanted a unified nation with an economy organised on communist principles. The USA began to pour aid into Vietnam to help the pro-capitalist group based in Saigon in the south.

The Vietnam War escalated into a prolonged conflict that lasted seventeen years. Australian troops again became involved. For all of that time the domino theory continued to dominate Western thinking: it was feared that Communist China was actively encouraging the communist forces in Vietnam, and another nation would 'fall' to communism. Whether or not a socialist-oriented economic system was the preference of the majority of the Vietnamese people did not seem to be of concern to the leaders of the pro-capitalist (and ostensibly democratic) Western powers.

All these events, and the continuing dominance of the mainland Asian political scene by Communist China, left an enduring legacy of suspicion. China could be seen to be growing into one of the world's superpowers. The fanatical devotion of its leaders to their version of an ideologically 'pure' communism made China, in many Westerners' eyes, a nation to be feared. Because China has remained an authoritarian State, even into the 1990s, such concerns survive today.

International Recognition of Communist China

In the early years after the proclamation of the People's Republic of China in 1949, Mao Zedong's administration was not at first officially 'recognised' as the legitimate government of China by many Western nations. For over twenty years the USA and many of its allies maintained that Jiang Kaishek and the remnants of the Guomindang on the island of Taiwan were the rightful rulers of China and the legitimate representatives of China in the UN.

It quickly became a matter of conscience

among the members of the UN that it could scarcely claim to be an internationalist organisation if the world's most populous nation (containing roughly one-fourth of the world's population) was unrepresented. Communist China's involvement in the Korean War, however, in which it had fought against a UN-sponsored army, gravely delayed the possibility of China's admission.

Until the 1970s the USA, by use of the veto in the Security Council and by drumming up a two-thirds majority in the General Assembly, was able to block moves to admit China. Growing Afro-Asian voting power, however, made the event inevitable. In 1971 the USA and a group of supporters (including Australia) attempted to sponsor a compromise, by which the seat labelled 'China' (in both the General Assembly and the Security Council) would pass to Communist China, but Taiwan could be granted recognition and admission as a separate nation. Mao rejected this proposition, claiming that Taiwan was part of China, and refused to accept UN representation unless the Taiwan representatives were expelled. On 26 October 1971 the General Assembly voted 76–35 to allocate the Chinese representation to the People's Republic of China instead of the 'Republic of China' (Taiwan).

Foreign Policy Objectives of Communist China

The CCP's major foreign policy objective was the restoration of China's integrity through its complete liberation from foreign intervention and control. The Communists sought to win back what they regarded as China's rightful position as a major world power and the dominant influence in Asia. This would make amends for the many decades when China was subjected to the humiliation of both Western dominance and subordination to the wills of the imperialist powers.

For over two hundred years the national interests of China, reflected in foreign policy objectives of the Chinese people, have been as follows:

(a) to protect the national territory from foreign annexation or intrusion;
(b) to regain what had been lost through foreign intervention;
(c) to repel from its borders any threatening or hostile military presence, be it Russian, Japanese, American or any other power; and
(d) to regain for China the status of a world power commensurate with the greatness of its civilisation.

The inability of the Manchu Dynasty and the Guomindang regime to attain any of these objectives was one of the major reasons for their fall from favour. Mao's regime, however, enjoyed greater success in the pursuit of these objectives. The Chinese Communist Party clearly established stable government over all mainland China, and thus rendered impossible any further intrusion. In 1950 Chinese troops reoccupied Tibet, which even the GMD claimed to be part of China, and they intervened in the Korean War of 1950–53 when it appeared likely that the US military presence would be extended up to, and even beyond, the Chinese frontier.

The CCP'S policy regarding Taiwan and Hong Kong was consistent with these national policies. Although Taiwan had been governed by Japan for over fifty years, it has always been regarded by the Chinese as part of China, and the Communists have insisted that it must eventually be reunited with the mainland. They still refuse to recognise Taiwan as a separate nation. Similarly, the CCP have insisted that Hong Kong—obtained by the British in 1842—has always remained Chinese, and must be reunited with China. This will occur in 1997.

Ideological and National Interests in Foreign Policy

An additional factor in Mao Zedong's foreign policy objectives—one that was to affect the way Australians and other Western-aligned nations viewed China—was his commitment to world communism. Mao firmly believed in the ideological superiority of communism, and claimed for China the role of leadership in the drive for world revolution to displace capitalism.

Thus, to Mao, the export of communist thought and teachings, and the active encouragement of anti-imperialist movements in developing countries, were additional objectives in Chinese foreign policy. These two focal points—China's national interest, and the advancement of world communism—have resulted in some contradictions in the foreign policy of the People's Republic of China.

These contradictions emerged in the relationships between China and the USSR. Although, in theory, they were 'brother' communities linked in the cause of world communism, they ended up quarrelling over several matters. In the first few years after the CCP came to power, relations with the USSR were very cordial. Mao was invited to Moscow to be acknowledged as a great communist leader, and Russian advisers and technicians arrived in China to aid in its rebuilding. In 1950 the Sino–Soviet Treaty of Friendship was concluded.

The Sino–Soviet Split

Very rapidly, however, the two giants of the communist world disagreed on several policy matters. The full details of the manoeuvres preceding the outbreak of the Korean War may never be known, but it is fairly obvious that the communist powers did not act together on this matter, and that this worsened relations between the USSR and China. There is strong evidence to suggest that North Korea attacked South Korea without having informed China, and that the USSR, which must have known of the plan, may have deliberately allowed the Korean War to develop in order to embroil Communist China in an anti-West war which would distract it from direct rivalry with the USSR and commit it to an involvement in the Cold War.

When the UN forces led by MacArthur almost reached the Korea-Chinese border, the Chinese intervened, committing one million troops. This occurred in 1950, just one year after the end of the exhausting Civil War. The

Sect. IV

SOURCE 10.4

Mao Zedong affirms his belief that the world revolution of the proletariat is inevitable, but that each revolutionary society must first mount its own struggle, 1967

HISTORICAL CONTEXT: By the mid-1960s Mao Zedong was disillusioned with the leadership of Soviet Russia. The Chinese Communists had not received the help from the USSR that they had expected. This convinced Mao all the more that a true communist revolution had to be self-sufficient in the first instance, and then could 'drive on' to help other communities achieve their communist revolution. He believed that because the USSR was failing in this duty, Communist China would have to assume such a responsibility.

Source: Quotations from Chairman Mao Zedong, Foreign Languages Press, Beijing, 1967, pp. 24, 177

In the fight for complete liberation the oppressed people rely first of all on their own struggle and then, and only then, on international assistance. The people who have triumphed in their own revolution should help those still struggling for liberation. This is our internationalist duty.

The socialist system will eventually replace the capitalist system; this is an objective law independent of man's will. However much the reactionaries try to hold back the wheel of history, sooner or later revolution will take place and will inevitably triumph.

QUESTIONS

1 What is the significance of the repeated use of the word 'struggle'?

2 Explain the origin of Mao's statement that the victory of the socialist system 'is an objective law independent of man's will'.

CCP doubtless would have preferred to have concentrated on their domestic reforms instead of fighting another war, but it was clear that unless one of the two major powers had aided North Korea, world communism would have received a severe setback.

The Chinese were resentful that they, rather than the USSR, had to bear this burden. Moreover, the USSR, by relying on China to take the critical action, had virtually abandoned its claim to hegemony in east Asia. The Chinese sense of pride and cultural superiority, based on centuries of achievement, now emerged to complicate their relationship with the Soviet leadership.

Suspicions grew in the minds of the Chinese that if they accepted too much direction from the USSR, they would become a gigantic satellite State with inferior status. When the Russian leader, Nikita Khrushchev, in 1956, denounced the policies of the earlier Stalin regime, the Chinese were offended, not because they held particularly fond memories of Stalin, but because they were treated as 'junior' in rank through not being informed in advance of this major change in communist policy. The Sino–Soviet 'split' really dates from this incident.

Within a few weeks of Khrushchev's speech, the Chinese were stressing with renewed vigour that the Russians had corrupted communism and were too soft in their relationship with the capitalist world. Relations worsened when, in 1960, the USSR withdrew all its technical advisers from China and refused to help China develop its own nuclear weapons. These actions were interpreted by China as deliberate moves to hinder its industrial progress and keep it in an inferior position. With characteristic determination the Chinese applied great effort to produce their own nuclear weapons, and succeeded in detonating an atomic bomb by 1964 and a hydrogen bomb in 1967.

The tensions between Communist China and the USSR reached their greatest intensity in the border skirmishes and fighting on the frontiers of Russia and Manchuria in the late 1960s. The Chinese claimed, quite correctly, that large areas in the north-west and in Siberia beyond the Amur and Ussuri rivers had been part of China until the late nineteenth century, when the Manchu Dynasty was forced, by Tsarist Russian threats, to cede these areas to Russia. The USSR thus remained in possession of territories which, in Chinese eyes, were seized by 'imperialist aggression', and should be returned. Disputes over these areas resulted in Russia and China massing their forces in rivalry on opposite sides of the borders and threatening each other with nuclear warfare. Many lives were lost.

Rivalry for Leadership of the Communist World

Disputes over territory, however, soon came to be exceeded in importance by the deep and bitter rivalry between the USSR and China for leadership of the communist world. Both sides denounced each other as traitors to the original teachings of Marx and Lenin.

Mao and his followers accused the Russians of being **revisionist** (that is, of 'revising' and corrupting Marxist–Leninist teachings), of taking the capitalist road, and of attempting to reduce other communist nations to subordinates. Zhou Enlai said of the Russian leaders that 'what they mean by the road to internationalism is the road to reducing China to a colony of Soviet revisionist social imperialism'. Mao Zedong, claimed the Chinese, was the true leader of the world communist movement.

The Chinese also accused the Russians of weakness in backing down in such issues as the confrontation with the USA during the Cuban missile crisis in 1962, and of failing to support people's revolutionary wars in various parts of the globe. Leonid Brezhnev, Khrushchev's successor as leader of the USSR, was heavily criticised for betraying the long-term cause of world revolution through accepting the principle of 'peaceful co-existence' with the West.

Tensions between Communist China and the USSR were further aggravated by their competing foreign policies. The 1971 war between

India and Pakistan which resulted in the emergence of Bangladesh was a striking example: China supported Pakistan and opposed the secession of Bangladesh, while the USSR provided India's major support. The successful establishment of Bangladesh as an independent nation in 1972 was a blow to Chinese pride, and was a source of renewed Sino–Soviet bitterness.

VI THE GREAT PROLETARIAN CULTURAL REVOLUTION: 1965–69

After the leaders of the CCP had settled into their role as undisputed rulers of China, they set out to achieve 'the world so changed' as predicted by Mao Zedong. One of the most obvious aspects of this revolution of society was the dispossession of the landlords and the reallocation of land ownership to the people. It is estimated that about one million former landowners lost their lives in this massive upheaval. The land thus released was reallocated into people's communes.

A typical commune contained about 30 000 people. The land was communally owned, and the work and production of food and crops was centrally organised. The communes proved to be an outstanding success, as they were the means whereby the nation of 1.2 billion people successfully fed itself.

By the 1960s the Communist leaders were beginning to disagree about the pace and nature of the reforms. Whilst Mao insisted that the ideological transformation to a pure communist society was the main objective, other Communist leaders were impatient, wanting faster progress towards industrialisation.

In 1959 Mao was displaced from (or gave up) his position as head of state, and was replaced by Liu Shaoqi. Mao remained Chairman of the Party Central Committee, and retained enormous influence. Liu Shaoqi and his supporters believed that planned technological advance was important to China, and claimed that this would require help from outside nations, together with strict control of the people by the party officials.

Young Chinese communists shown studying Mao's teachings under a picture portraying him as the 'Great Helmsman'. During the Great Proletarian Cultural Revolution (1965–69), Mao attempted to galvanise the youth of China, organised in the form of 'Red Guards', to challenge the power of the established bureaucrats as a means of keeping active the socialist reform process.

Mao saw this policy as a dangerous move towards the creation of a new privileged class and bureaucratic control of the people. He believed that the great mass of the Chinese people needed to be constantly challenged and led. If allowed to lapse into routine, they would surrender initiative to the officials in authority, and the pace of the Revolution would lag.

Mao formed the opinion that the true revolution had not yet been achieved. He reminded the youth of China that a revolution was not something 'refined', but an act of violence, an insurrection by which one class overthrows another. Using his great prestige, Mao now launched what he called the '**Great Proletarian Cultural Revolution**'. It was to be a renewed upsurge of emotional commitment by the common people. The targets were to be the 'four olds'—old customs, old habits, old culture and old thinking—and this was to be achieved

Source 10.5 Part (a)

through rigorous criticism of, and challenge to, the party bureaucracy.

Mao wanted to shake the party bureaucracy out of its lethargy, and prevent officials from taking 'the capitalist road' back to the old practices. The major target of the attack was none other than the titular 'head of state', Liu Shaoqi.

He and several other key figures accused of being '**capitalist roaders**' were forced out of office.

The words 'proletarian' and 'cultural' were particularly revealing of Mao's purposes. 'Proletarian' was a reference to the mass of the ordinary people. Mao believed that they could

SOURCE 10.5

Mao Zedong emphasises that a revolution is an act of violence, and that the masses offer an inexhaustible source of revolutionary zeal which can be used against the 'old routine', 1967

HISTORICAL CONTEXT: In Extract (a) Mao stresses the need to use violence to achieve revolutionary goals, and made use of this principle to validate the violent dismissal of thousands of entrenched bureaucrats (hitherto 'servants of the revolution') during the Great Proletarian Cultural Revolution.

In Extract (b) Mao explains the policy he used to generate the fanatical zeal that was targeted against the 'four olds'.

Source: *Quotations from Chairman Mao Zedong*, **Foreign Languages Press, Beijing, 1967, p.11, 121–2**

(a) . . . *a revolution is not the same thing as inviting people to dinner, or writing an essay, or painting a picture, or doing fancy needlework; it cannot be anything so refined, so calm and gentle, or so mild, kind, courteous, restrained or magnanimous. A revolution is an uprising, an act of violence whereby one class overthrows another. A rural revolution is a revolution by which the peasantry overthrows the authority of the feudal landlord class. If the peasants do not use the maximum of their strength, they can never overthrow the authority of their landlords which has been deeply rooted for thousands of years.*

To put it bluntly, it was necessary to bring about a brief reign of terror in every rural area; otherwise one could never suppress the activities of the counter-revolutionaries in the countryside or overthrow the authority of the gentry. To right a wrong it is necessary to exceed the proper limits, and the wrong cannot be righted without the proper limits being exceeded.

(b) *The masses have a potentially inexhaustible enthusiasm for socialism. Those who can only follow the old routine in a revolutionary period are utterly incapable of seeing this enthusiasm . . . Haven't we come across enough persons of this type? Those who simply follow the old routine invariably underestimate the people's enthusiasm. Let something new appear and they always disapprove and rush to oppose it. Afterwards, they have to admit defeat and do a little self-criticism. But the next time something new appears, they go through the same process all over again . . . Such people are always passive, always fail to move forward at the critical moment.*

QUESTIONS

1 Why might Mao Zedong have devoted so many expressions to explaining what a revolution is not?

2 By implication, a successful revolution will exhibit features opposite to those listed. What are these opposite features?

3 What vital role does Mao propose for the peasant class in the attainment of the revolution?

4 Who were the 'counter-revolutionaries' to whom Mao makes reference in Extract (a)?

5 What quality is Mao seeking to nurture in the young people by his statement in Extract (b)?

6 What supposed obstacle to a successful revolution in Chinese society is Mao trying to highlight?

provide the real driving force for change. Mao stressed that any hierarchy of officials which threatened to restrict the creative energy of the people had to be combated by the sheer 'people power' of the masses.

By naming the movement a 'cultural' revolution, Mao was indicating that he was dissatisfied with the slow pace at which the Chinese people were forsaking their old ways. He was also conscious of the need to indoctrinate the young people, born since the 'year of liberation' (1949), with the principles of the revolution which had rescued them from the defects of traditional Chinese society, from the imperialist foreigners, and from the corruption of the Guomindang.

To whip up a nation-wide emotional fervour, Mao organised thousands of young enthusiasts into 'Red Guard' organisations to campaign against any remnants of bourgeois practices or 'revisionist' beliefs (impure versions of communist thought). Young people were released from schools and universities in order to attend mass rallies which swamped them in colour, movement and sound. They were encouraged to reject all 'objects of pleasure' as undesirable capitalist diversions, and were taught to criticise and attack their parents for following the capitalist road. All old routines were to be abandoned.

Eight 'bad' categories were declared. They were: renegades, spies, landlords, rich peasants, counter-revolutionaries, rightists, bad elements and capitalist roaders. If an older person could be labelled with any one of these derogatory terms, they could be mercilessly persecuted. To this 'list of eight' there was added the so-called 'stinking ninth'—the intellectuals. It was significant that in the campaign to change the nature of society, the intellectual class—the source of traditional Confucian teaching—had to be eliminated as an influence.

In the frenzy of the Cultural Revolution many officials were forced out of office after being accused of trying to preserve control through a bureaucracy of 'Old Guards' whose main priority was to perpetuate class divisions in Chinese society, or who were accused of taking the capitalist road. Many academics, teachers and intellectuals were also persecuted and driven out of their positions. The Red Guards were equipped, not with guns, but with *The Little Red Book* of quotations from the works of Chairman Mao. They were taught the slogan: '*The thoughts of Mao Zedong must rule and transform the spirit, until the power of the spirit transforms matter.*'

The Cultural Revolution was an attempt at an ideological conversion of a nation. The objective was the creation of a new 'egalitarian' society thoroughly purged of pre-Revolutionary standards and dedicated to a new pitch of revolutionary ardour. 'Maoism' was promoted as a political, economic and social doctrine that was almost a new religion.

School children sang a song which virtually elevated Mao to the status of a 'sun god':

Sailors at sea need the helmsman
All things need the sun to grow
Crops need rain and dew,
to make revolution we need Mao Zedong thought
　　Dearest Chairman Mao
You are the red sun of our hearts
Thousands of red hearts beating
Thousands of happy faces look to the red sun
With all our hearts we wish you eternal life.

Chinese society was for several years convulsed by the Cultural Revolution. A huge number (a suggested figure is 400 000) of victims of the engulfing wave of persecution died during the turmoil. Eventually, in 1968, Mao was persuaded to acknowledge that the young people had gone too far in their campaign of criticism, and military units were ordered to force them back into their schools and universities. Simultaneously, the party leaders decided that the urban youth were not sufficiently aware of the true nature of Communist reforms in the rural areas, so millions of them were sent to remote regions of China to labour on the farms. This also defused the emotional intensity previously encouraged.

In political terms, the extremely radical elements of the party (that is, those who most supported Mao's call for a renewed drive towards pure socialism) gained increased control for a time. A more moderate group, who looked to the premier, Zhou Enlai, for guidance, retained several key positions. This ultimately resulted in a power crisis when Mao died in 1976.

Mao Zedong, despite being widely criticised for causing such an upheaval, retained the prestigious position of chairman, and appeared to be convinced that his Cultural Revolution had revived the revolutionary ardour of his people. All dissent had been totally suppressed. Even senior officials who had dared to criticise the excesses of the campaign had been labelled as 'rightists' or 'counter-revolutionaries,' and deposed or imprisoned. As was the case in several modern revolutions, a totalitarian regime had been established while lip-service was being given to the avowed aim of establishing an egalitarian State.

VII THE EFFECT OF THE CULTURAL REVOLUTION ON CHINA'S FOREIGN RELATIONS

The foreign policies of Communist China in the period 1949–69 were based on a mixture of ideological and national interests. Despite the fact that the slogan on the Gate of Heavenly Peace in Beijing (at which Mao Zedong had proclaimed the People's Republic of China in 1949) stated 'Long Live the Unity of the Peoples of the World', these policies did not necessarily aid the advancement of international communism.

As time passed after the excesses of the Cultural Revolution, it became apparent that the power struggle that had ensued from that upheaval had resulted in the consolidation of a 'moderate' element in the Chinese leadership, led by Premier Zhou Enlai, who was more willing to negotiate with the West than some of the hardliners who had previously influenced policy. This moderate group applied a less suspicious and more self-confident foreign policy, which enabled China to be cordial with the West without appearing to be weak. After 1969, China sought new policy initiatives, and demonstrated an increased willingness to contribute, as a great power, to the reduction of the international tensions that might lead to a world war.

The 'thaw' was first revealed in April 1971, in a sporting event. Fifteen table-tennis players and three journalists, the first American delegation to set foot in the Chinese capital since Mao Zedong wrested control of the mainland from Jiang Kaishek twenty-two years before, were welcomed to China by Zhou Enlai. Within a few months, this so-called 'ping-pong diplomacy' had flowered into a new condition of receptiveness that led to visits to China by both the American secretary of state and president.

The Effects of the Revolution upon Relations with the USA

It was in China's relationship with the USA that the tug-of-war effect between national and ideological interests could be most clearly discerned. From 1946 until 1972, the USA was the major obstacle to China's foreign policy objectives. As the leading capitalist power, America opposed the spread of communism in every manner possible; as the major Western supplier of military personnel and equipment, it ringed China with potentially hostile military bases and alliances. Most significantly, it sponsored and protected the remnants of the Guomindang regime in Taiwan, which throughout the 1950s and 1960s persistently claimed that it intended to regain power in China through an armed invasion. To Chinese eyes, this American sponsorship was a provocative and totally unwarranted interference in a purely Chinese affair.

Even when the USA became heavily involved in fighting against the communist-aligned Viet Minh forces in Vietnam (1960–73), the Chinese, whilst aiding the North Vietnamese with equipment and ideological support, sent no troops. If support for the cause of world revolution had been the most important factor, the Chinese would have sent military aid, as they had done in Korea. But in the Vietnam War episode, the Chinese primarily acted in their national interests. Had China intervened with direct military assistance to North Vietnam, the US military presence would have been drawn into China, the resources of the nation would have been drained by war expenditure, and the possibility of a rapprochement with the USA would have been lost.

The 'ping-pong' diplomacy of 1971 led to a re-establishment of working relationships between China and the USA. Marking a shift in US policy, Dr Henry Kissinger, who was National Security Adviser and later Secretary of State for Foreign Affairs under President Nixon (in office from 1969 to 1974), set out to achieve a reduction in international tensions. His proposal was that the great powers should recognise one another's national interests, and acknowledge the existence of the opposing ideologies, without indulging in campaigns to impose these beliefs upon others.

Kissinger wanted to defuse the 'bi-polar' situation in international affairs, in which two major power blocs—the capitalist powers led by the USA, and the communist giants of the USSR and China—confronted each other in enmity. He wanted to achieve what he called a less rigid 'multi-polarity' in international relationships (that is, a situation involving several rather than two focal points of loyalty). This would decrease the likelihood of the existing two power blocs reaching a situation of immovable opposition.

Kissinger held the opinion that if the USA broke away from the 'saviour role' adopted by the earlier presidents Truman and Kennedy, which necessitated huge expenses on armaments and ceaseless tension caused by the likelihood of war, the American leaders could negotiate with their counterparts for greater co-operation. In effect, Kissinger was planning to achieve a new version of the 'balance of power' principle—by giving the communist nations less cause to feel threatened, and by increasing the inter-dependence of the great powers through trade relationships and agreements on arms control.

Accordingly, despite many American misgivings, Kissinger set out to attain a rapprochement between the USA and China without antagonising the USSR. In a spectacular series of diplomatic achievements, Kissinger and Nixon succeeded not only in winding down the Vietnam War but in opening up diplomatic relations with the hitherto 'closed world' of China and in developing better relations with the USSR. These events were hailed as the first stages of a new era of detente (or reduced tensions) among the great powers.

The rapprochement with China was a difficult undertaking, because a legacy of ill-feeling and suspicion existed between China and the USA. Chinese soldiers had fought against American forces serving under the UN flag in the Korean War, and the US government had for years refused to recognise Mao's regime as the legitimate government of China, claiming that Jiang Kaishek and his Guomindang administration on Taiwan was the true government. Until 1971, the USA had also blocked attempts to admit China to the United Nations.

President Richard Nixon of the USA, who held office from 1969 till 1974, is shown here (left) during his visit to Communist China in 1972. As president of the leading capitalist power, Nixon had hitherto been regarded by the Communists as the arch-enemy. This 1972 visit was the beginning of a rapprochement between the two nations.

In February 1972 Richard Nixon, the American president, hitherto regarded by the Chinese Communists as the leader of the capitalist imperialist arch-enemy, was welcomed to Beijing by Chairman Mao and Premier Zhou Enlai. Semi-formal diplomatic relations were secured between the two nations, and trade connections established.

As a result of this new willingness to negotiate, China attained the acceptance it sought as a world power, was admitted to the UN (in October 1971), and by acting through normal diplomatic channels, greatly contributed to the Kissinger–Nixon objective of developing multi-polar rather than bi-polar alignments in international relations.

The Significance of the Nixon Doctrine to US-Asian Relations

A critical factor in the reduction of tension between the Western capitalist world (including Australia) and Asian nations was the proclamation of the Nixon Doctrine. President Nixon explained this in his second inaugural address in January 1973, in which he declared that the time had passed when America could make every other nation's conflict its own, or make every other nation's future its responsibility. He called upon all nations to determine their own future, and, in effect assume responsibility for their own defence.

This commitment, together with Nixon's decisions to withdraw the US forces from Vietnam and reduce the rate at which the USA claimed the right to direct Asian affairs, increased the likelihood of co-operation between the USA and China despite Mao Zedong's earlier insistence that China should not associate itself in any way with capitalist nations. To show his own conversion in the matter, Mao agreed to meet Nixon personally and be photographed with him.

VIII THE END OF THE MAO ERA

The year 1976 marked an end of an era for the Chinese community. Three of the greatest figures in the Chinese Communist Party leadership died within twelve months. First, Zhou Enlai, foreign minister and premier, and leader of the moderates, died aged 78; then Zhu De, the most prominent military leader of the days of the struggle with the Guomindang, died aged 89; and then Chairman Mao Zedong himself died, aged 82 (in September 1976).

It quickly became apparent that a struggle for the leadership would occur. The new premier, Hua Guofeng, had held his position only for the few months that had elapsed since the death of Zhou Enlai, and was not one of the 'Old Guard' from the days of the Long March. Nevertheless, he was promptly appointed chairman of the CCP (the key position in China), apparently because Mao had decreed his succession.

One month later, it was announced that Mao's widow, Jiang Qing, and her three closest political allies, who together constituted a group labelled the 'Gang of Four', had been placed under arrest. This was the radical group who had gained great influence during the Cultural Revolution, having persistently hounded those members of the party accused of being 'capitalist roaders'.

For several years the radicals within the CCP had waged an incessant campaign against the moderate policies formulated by Zhou Enlai. The overthrow and imprisonment of the radicals marked a victory for the moderate elements; a victory which was highlighted by the quick restoration to responsibility of the deposed vice premier, Deng Xiaoping, one of those who had been accused of being 'capitalist roaders'. With the death of Mao and the removal from power of his widow, the scene was now set for a substantial change in the policies applied in the name of the Chinese Revolution.

MAJOR EVENTS IN THE COMMUNIST REVOLUTION OF CHINESE SOCIETY

1949 The GMD forces were defeated

Mao Zedong proclaimed the People's Republic of China

1950 Widespread agrarian land reforms were begun

The Sino-Soviet Pact of Friendship and Alliance was signed

The Korean War broke out: Chinese troops ('volunteers') help North Korea against the UN army

1953–58 Five Year Plan introduced, to modernise Chinese industry

1960–63 The quarrel between China and the USSR, known as the Sino-Soviet split

1964 China exploded its first atomic bomb

1965 The Great Proletarian Cultural Revolution was launched

1971 China was admitted to the United Nations Organisation

1972 President Nixon of the USA flew to Beijing to reopen relationships between the USA and China

1976 Zhou Enlai and Mao Zedong died

Hua Guofeng became premier and chairman

'Gang of Four' were imprisoned

Deng Xiaoping was reinstated as vice premier

1978 Treaty of Peace and Friendship with Japan

chapter eleven

The Continuing Revolution in China in the Post-Mao Years

We are trying to compress the Renaissance, the Reformation, and the Industrial Revolution into a single decade.

Ying Roucheng, a prominent Chinese actor, quoted in *Time*, Melbourne, 23 September 1985

In Mao Zedong's years of power he had kept China largely isolated from the West, and had stressed the purity of socialist life, with an emphasis on communal effort rather than individualism.

After Mao's death, it soon became clear that the new leadership was establishing a different set of priorities. They began to encourage expanded contacts with the West, rapid modernisation and individual enterprise—but they claimed to be doing all this within a socialist system. World-wide, they became known as the '**Pragmatists**', that is, people who wanted practical results with a decreased emphasis on ideology.

Theme Questions

➤ What have been the effects on the Chinese people of the repudiation of Mao Zedong's teachings?

➤ Has the modernisation policy changed the nature of Chinese society?

➤ What has resulted from the contradiction in policies—encouraging individualism but denying democracy?

I THE FOUR MODERNISATIONS POLICY: A COUNTER-REVOLUTION?

Idealists versus Pragmatists

During 1976–77, Mao's nominated successor, Hua Guofeng, broke the political power of the previously influential Gang of Four, which included Mao's widow, Jiang Qing. This group had been the major influence in demanding the hardline communist policies applied at the height of the Great Proletarian Cultural Revolution. Within a few months the moderate leader, Deng Xiaoping, had been reappointed to the party's Central Committee and to all the posts from which he had been removed in 1976 on the accusation that he was a 'capitalist roader'. The events signalled a major change in the course of the revolution.

The overthrow of the Gang of Four and the return of Deng Xiaoping highlighted a major difference of opinion among the surviving Chinese Communist leaders. Many, the so-called radicals, or idealists, still favoured a hardline communist policy. They were not as hardline as the deposed Gang of Four, but nevertheless believed that Mao's teachings decreed a continuation of a policy in which the purity of socialist life, with an emphasis on communal effort rather than individualism, was the main objective. They also favoured self-reliance rather than dependence on foreign nations, and therefore disapproved of trade with other nations.

The other group, the so-called moderates, supported a policy of reform. The moderates wanted faster development of industrial facilities, together with greater availability of consumer goods, and believed that market forces should be allowed to function as an incentive to production. These ideas were mildly capitalist in emphasis and as such marked a departure from socialist ideals. The policies of the moderates were often called 'pragmatic', and their supporters were called 'pragmatists' (defined as 'people who estimate the worth of a proposal solely by its practical bearing upon human interests').

The pragmatists emphasised results rather than the means of getting results; the attainment of certain goals was more important than the purity of an ideology. Their leader, Deng Xiaoping, for example, is reported to have stated that 'it doesn't matter if a cat is black or white, as long as it catches mice it's a good cat'.

The Revolution Betrayed? The 'Four Modernisations' Policy

Supporters of Marxist–Leninist teachings all over the world watched the swing to pragmatism in China in 1976–78 with considerable suspicion. In their eyes, the Revolution in the USSR had been a failure—a classless society had not been established because a new class, the bureaucrats, had gained control and had diverted the Revolution away from pure communism. By contrast, Mao's emphasis on trusting the masses and constantly challenging the officials had seemed likely to keep China on the road to an egalitarian society and true communism. When the radical Maoists were overthrown by the Pragmatists in 1976, it became obvious that the Chinese Revolution was also being diverted

away from pure communism and that, in effect, a counter-revolution was being launched from within the Communist Party.

After the overthrow and imprisonment of the Gang of Four, the Pragmatists consolidated their control in China, launching a major campaign of liberalisation. In 1977 their policy—of seeking modernisation and increased cooperation with the West—was given the typical Chinese blessing of a number code. The new premier and party chairman, Hua Guofeng, announced the 'Four Modernisations': in agriculture, industry, defence and science/technology. In radio broadcasts, newspapers and articles, and at rallies and meetings, the new emphasis was hammered home.

Experts and specialists were again to be respected, education was to be given high priority, and material incentives were restored. The policy also implied an inevitable strengthening of relationships with capitalist powers, which could provide the investment, products and expertise China needed to achieve these goals. Foreign technology and technical imports were actively sought.

This new policy generated a flurry of foreign investment in China. China arranged to import $29 billion worth of production equipment from Japan and the West. By mid-1979 announcements of intended Western participation in such ventures as billion-dollar steel mills, massive mining projects or vast irrigation schemes were being made almost every week.

Although Hua Guofeng had launched the Four Modernisations policy, and had broken the power of the Gang of Four, he had not won the full support of the Pragmatists. Shortly after he attained power in 1976, he made the rash statement that the Chinese people should 'obey whatever Mao had said, and ensure the continuation of whatever he had decided'. This resulted in his being ridiculed as a believer in the 'two whatevers'. In a period when change was being called for, Hua's position was one of blind devotion to Mao's teachings, and thus he had left himself no room for manoeuvre. By 1978 his authority had largely eroded.

Deng Xiaoping (1904–) became the effective leader of Communist China soon after the death of Mao Zedong. A veteran of the Long March, he was accorded great prestige because of his great experience in various roles. From *circa* 1980, Deng promoted a policy of modernisation for China on 'pragmatic' principles. His reputation was heavily tarnished by his sanctioning of the use of armed forces against pro-democracy demonstrators in Tienanmen Square, Beijing, in June 1989, and the later imprisonment of dissidents merely for disagreeing with the Communist Party's policies.

Deng Xiaoping, by contrast, argued for accelerated modernisation and reform, with a more energetic pursuit of the Four Modernisations. Deng realised that if China was to avoid economic stagnation, it had to move towards a market economy and participate in trade with other nations. This meant that the economy had to be released from centralised control, and personal incentives reintroduced. The key principles were *gaige* (reform) and *kaifang* (opening up)—both alien concepts in the world of Mao Zedong's teaching. Deng had seized control of both the party and the nation to promote another phase of the Chinese Revolution.

By the end of 1978, although he assumed no post higher than vice premier, this diminutive and elderly survivor of the Long March had become the 'paramount leader' of China. Because he carried the aura of long-term membership of the Communist Party, he rapidly gained the status of the 'new emperor' (although this term was never actually used). To consolidate his control, Deng ensured the ascendancy of his influence by having his proteges appointed to key government positions.

The new constitution forbade the development of 'personality cults', implicitly condemning Mao for having developed such a cult, and stressed the need for collective leadership. Ironically, such was the level of authority—undefined but almost limitless—concentrated in the hands of Deng Xiaoping in his role as 'paramount leader' that in effect another era of personal rule was being established.

The Pragmatists' emphasis on modernisation through the adoption of some Western practices led to several strange anomalies. Although much was said about 'democracy', it was always a reference to democracy within socialism, not multi-party democracy, with a genuine choice among policies, as in the West.

The Process of de-Maoisation

The new emphasis on practical performance rather than ideological purity was a drastic shift away from Mao's priorities. The new policies of introducing incentives for workers and stressing academic scholarship instead of class consciousness in the schools and universities were contradictions of his teachings. During the Cultural Revolution Mao had persecuted China's intellectuals in order to preserve 'revolutionary purity'.

The movement towards closer relations with capitalist powers was another departure from Maoism. Mao had preached the concepts of self-reliance and independence from foreign influence. He feared that contacts with the West would lead to 'revisionism' (a tampering with Marxist principles). Now, under the Four Modernisations policy, exactly what Mao had forbidden was actually being encouraged by the new leadership.

The people of China, however, had for decades been inculcated with a blind devotion to the thoughts of Mao Zedong. Too sudden a change was not possible. Thus, at first, the policies of economic development, scientific research and education based on enquiry were all promoted in Mao's name, despite his declared opposition to these developments during the Cultural Revolution.

After this initial phase, the Pragmatists gradually introduced, and then accelerated, a process of 'de-Maoisation'. To further justify the new policies, the post-Mao leadership began to portray the former chairman as an ordinary mortal, capable of making mistakes, instead of the infallible fount of wisdom he was once held to be. By 1978 tributes to Mao were muted. Even quotations from Mao's writings, which at one stage were always printed in the *People's Daily* in bold type and were regarded as beyond contradiction, fell under question and attack.

The downgrading of Mao's writings was accompanied by the rapid disappearance of the thousands of portraits of Mao that once adorned public places and official buildings. By 1986 there was scarcely a Mao portrait to be seen in China, apart from the large picture at the head of Tienanmen Square at the spot where Mao had declared the foundation of the People's Republic of China in October 1949.

The excesses of Mao's Cultural Revolution were by mid-1986 being roundly criticised in the official English-language Beijing newspaper, *China Daily*, although the blame was carefully directed away from Mao personally. Such statements could only appear in *China Daily* with official approval. Their appearance signalled a rejection of Maoist policies.

II THE 'FIFTH MODERNISATION' AND THE BEIJING MASSACRE OF 1989

As has frequently occurred in authoritarian regimes, once freedoms of one sort were granted, demand for other freedoms followed. The Four Modernisations policy promoted initiatives in commerce and trade, together with

---

SOURCE 11.1
'Official neglect' demonstrates the effectiveness of de-Maoisation policies, 1978

HISTORICAL CONTEXT: In Mao Zedong's lifetime virtually every utterance he made was regarded as 'holy writ', and regarded as of great importance. Two years after his death, however, the process by which his status was being downgraded was well advanced.

Source: **Time, Melbourne, 25 September 1978**
The second anniversary of the Chairman's death two weekends ago was virtually a non-event throughout his former domain. There were no rituals commemorating his long dynasty; only five small wreaths graced a monument in front of his final resting place in Peking (Beijing) . . . The absence of pomp and circumstance on this occasion came as no

surprise to informed Chinese. For months the Peking (Beijing) People's Daily, *the country's leading newspaper, has been gingerly dimming the radiance of the 'Great Teacher' by allusion and innuendo . . . In June the* People's Daily *went one step further and declared that Mao 'never regarded his theories as final or as absolute truth'.*

QUESTIONS
1 Although the June statement in the *People's Daily* was designed to diminish the authority of Mao Zedong's theories, it simultaneously was a confession. What was this?
2 What does the nature of the remark tell observers about the Chinese attitude to the source of authority?

what seemed to be a new atmosphere of intellectual freedom. For almost twenty years no one in China had been free to speak out against the party line, although this itself had sometimes changed. In late 1978, however, many Chinese began to voice their own opinions about human rights and freedom of expression.

In any move towards a democratic society the greatest handicap of the Chinese people was the lack of a democratic heritage. In the centuries of bondage under the dynastic emperors and the Confucian tradition, the people were instructed to revere their elders and be totally obedient to the emperor. The perception of feudal vassalage was entrenched through centuries of practice.

SOURCE 11.2

The official Chinese English-language newspaper condemns the excesses of the Cultural Revolution of twenty years earlier, 1986

HISTORICAL CONTEXT: By 1986, ten years after the death of Mao Zedong, and nine years after the expulsion of the Gang of Four from the party, criticisms of the errors committed under the policies of the Great Proletarian Cultural Revolution were frequent occurrences. This report, however, was particularly significant because it was published in the English-language newspaper. This indicated that the Chinese authorities were prepared to proclaim the event 'a tragedy' and 'a disaster' even in their communications with the outside world.

Source: **China Daily, Beijing, 21 August 1986**

The newspaper China Youth News *ran a lengthy commentary on August 18, the 20th anniversary of the birth of the Red Guard movement during the 'cultural revolution', analysing the lesson of the historical tragedy. We must ask 'What should we do to remove the soil of such a tragedy?'*

The bitter truth is that, in 1966, youthful faith, desire and passion led the nation to disaster, the commentary said.

Young people were blind to their leaders' political floundering. They were deceived by such conspirators as Lin Biao and the Gang of Four. They were too young to know better, it said.

But all facts show that, although Marxist quotations filled their daily propaganda, their minds were still largely occupied by ideas handed down from Chinese feudalism of more than two millenia, the article said. The 'cultural revolution,' it said, was a catastrophe for democracy and a revival of past feudalist ideologies. The emergence of the Red Guard movement itself showed a lack of democratic sense in society, it declared.

Under such circumstances, fear of a 'comeback of capitalism' was unnecessarily exaggerated. At the same time, democracy, freedom and humanism were denounced as an unwanted part of Western civilisation. As a result, it said, individual thinking, a sense of democracy and the free development of man were seldom mentioned.

An over-centralised economic and political structure devoid of strong supervision helped cripple social democracy, it said.

QUESTIONS

1 Since the purpose of the article was to discredit Mao's Cultural Revolution, why did the author refer to 'ideas handed down from Chinese feudalism'?

2 Given that the article was published after Deng Xiaoping's Four Modernisations policy was well advanced, what is the purpose of the reference to fears of capitalism being 'exaggerated'?

3 As the article stated that 'individual thinking' was seldom mentioned during the Cultural Revolution, and that social democracy was largely 'crippled', what policy was the writer supporting?

4 What does the answer to Question 3 tell you about the differences in official Chinese policy between 1986 and late 1989?

Within the Chinese language the concept of 'democracy' did not exist—no ideograph (symbol) was available to represent such an idea. To promote or foster the concept of mass participation in the processes of government, young Chinese had to generate a means of expressing such ideals.

By 1978 the most popular way of publicising proposals for the introduction of democracy was the placing of posters on a park wall in Beijing. This became known as 'Democracy Wall'. These posters stressed the need to break the power of the entrenched bureaucracy and to grant socialist democratic rights to the citizens of China.

At first the Communist Party officials tolerated the posters. A new slogan, however, gave the so-called 'democracy movement' greater impetus than the party was prepared to tolerate. In December 1978 a young dissident, Wei Jingsheng, gained national attention with a poster calling for a 'Fifth Modernisation'—democratic rights for the people.

The effectiveness of the slogan, and the zeal with which it was taken up by young people, created a direct challenge to Deng Xiaoping and his senior ministers. Deng had declared that the Four Modernisations constituted a sufficient basis for the transformation of China. Wei Jingsheng's posters proclaimed that, unless they were accompanied by the Fifth Modernisation, the Four Modernisations would be merely another promise. He and his supporters demanded the holding of power by the labouring classes

Posters on the 'Democracy Wall' in Beijing, in 1979. These posters—hitherto banned in Communist China—were a means by which the citizens of Beijing could criticise existing Communist Party policies and propose democratic reforms. After the Tienanmen Massacre of June 1989, the ban on their display was reimposed.

The Continuing Revolution in China in the Post-Mao Years

themselves, instead of by party officials. The party was accused of exercising totalitarian control over the people.

Wei Jingsheng's posters and other publications, together with the support he generated, was too destabilising a use of 'freedom of expression' for Deng to tolerate. While he had at first permitted the Democracy Wall to operate as a contribution to the de-Maoisation process, Deng now believed that it had become a means of challenging the Communist Party itself (and his authority). And so the use of the wall for this purpose was suppressed.

Many of the protesters were arrested. They were accused not only of undermining the State and the party, but of doing so with the aid of foreigners—the well-established formula which authoritarian revolutionary regimes from the French Republic's Committee of Public Safety to the USSR's KGB have used to suppress dissenters. In a demonstration of just how remote from democratic processes the party really was, in March 1979 Wei Jingsheng was convicted of anti-government activities and imprisoned for fifteen years. His 'crime' was that of dissent.

Demands for Democracy

The desire for democratic freedoms could not be suppressed for long. By mid-1986 some signs of government toleration of 'talk' about democracy emerged. A statement in the *China Daily*, an English-language newspaper published in Beijing, with, of course, Chinese government (and therefore Communist Party) approval, stressed the desirability of developing 'democratic ideas' under 'socialist democracy'.

It soon became evident, however, that such talk was mere 'window-dressing', and that the government did not intend to tolerate any form of democracy other than their own very limited version. In late 1986 the students of Beijing reclaimed their right to express democratic policies on posters, even though posters were officially forbidden. Each new batch of posters was removed overnight by authorities, then defiantly replaced the next day by the students.

In December 1986 a huge demonstration of 30 000 students paraded in Shanghai with banners proclaiming 'Give Us Democracy' and 'Long Live Freedom'.

The party countered such demonstrations by describing them as disruptions to stability and unity. The *People's Daily*, on 1 January 1987, condemned the recent events as moves towards 'bourgeois liberalisation'. The success of China's reform within the Revolution lay, it claimed, with 'Four Cardinal Principles': (a) obedience to the leadership of the CCP; (b) Marxist–Leninist–Mao Zedong thought; (c) the socialist road (in economic management); and (d) the people's 'democratic dictatorship' (in political management). Such a blatant misuse of the term 'democracy' as a means of validating one-party rule further enraged the student body.

Hardline Communist Party members were angered by the students' insistence on further moves towards democracy. They claimed that the purity of the Revolution, won through years of suffering and combat, was not appreciated by young people. A new clampdown on expressions of dissent was introduced. Troublemakers were arrested and given long prison sentences for 'counter-revolutionary activities'. Party leaders denounced the pernicious influence of Western ideas and declared the need to concentrate on two tasks: (a) combatting bourgeois liberalisation; and (b) increasing production and practising economy. Despite the political repression, the modernisation policies, including the expansion of contact with the West, were maintained.

In the peak years of the Four Modernisations policy (1986–89), the bulk of the Chinese people were clearly abandoning the austerity of the Maoist era and developing much more materialistic attitudes. It was said that what was being sought in Chinese society were the 'Three Highs' and the 'Eight Bigs'. The 'Three Highs' were (somewhat light-heartedly) said to be what a man needed if he hoped to win a wife—a high salary, a high (that is, advanced) education and a height of at least five feet six inches (1.677

SOURCE 11.3

The official Chinese English-language newspaper specifically encourages the linkage between economic reform and the development of 'socialist democracy', 1986

HISTORICAL CONTEXT: As the Four Modernisations policy took effect, the Chinese government was prepared to pay lip-service to what they called 'socialist democracy'. By this expression, however, the authorities meant so-called 'democratic' policies within the party, not the tolerance of dissenting policies from outside the party.

Source: *China Daily*, Beijing, 18 August 1986

More and more people have come to realise that successful and thorough economic reform must be accompanied by political reform, which stresses socialist democracy among other things.

In this ancient land, feudalism prevailed for so long that even today it still affects people's thinking. Our ancestors left us with a great deal of cultural wealth, but a dearth of democratic ideas. While trying to improve socialist democracy, many still hold that so long as 'good officials' can protect the people, democracy has been realised.

The Party's 12th National Congress and the Constitution have all affirmed that a high level of democracy and a high level of civilisation are the two

great goals that must be realised in the course of socialist modernisation. In the school of the Communist Youth League, democracy is a required course for young people.

The League can train young people . . . to be democratic in many other ways. So, if some of them assume leading posts in the future, they can avoid becoming bureaucrats and refrain from the feudal idea of being 'good officials' over the rank and file. Instead, they will expect to become proletarian statesmen embodying the fundamental wishes of the people.

QUESTIONS

1 What does the writer mean when he says that their ancestors left 'a great deal of cultural wealth, but a dearth of democratic ideas'?

2 What is intended by the writer in placing the words 'good officials' in quotation marks?

3 Why might the writer describe the situation whereby 'good officials' directed the rank and file as a 'feudal idea'?

4 What is the meaning intended by the expression 'proletarian statesmen'?

---

metres). The 'Eight Bigs' were the rewards of the materialistic society—a refrigerator, a colour television, a stereo, a camera, a washing machine, an electric fan, a suite of furniture and a motor cycle. Official pronouncements praised entrepreneurs who were making profits from new businesses founded under the new policies. Deng proclaimed that 'getting rich' was respectable.

The Tienanmen Square Massacre 1989: an Insurrection within a Revolutionary Movement

In April 1989 the students of Beijing used the occasion of a funeral of a liberal-minded official as an opportunity to protest against the repressive

regime. The students called for the end of corruption and nepotism, greater opportunities to express opinions, and genuine democratic decision-making processes. They produced another batch of pro-democracy wall posters in defiance of the ban.

To display their determination to insist on a new era of individual rights, the students began mass 'sit-ins', in Tienanmen Square in the heart of Beijing, and outside the Zhongnanhai Compound—the residential area where all the top party officials lived.

By mid-May 1989 the students' campaign had reached a stage of total defiance of the party. They were demanding the resignations of Deng Xiaoping and the new hardline premier, Li

An Australian journal reports on 'Communism with a capitalist face', 1983

HISTORICAL CONTEXT: Six years after the launch of the Four Modernisations policy, many Chinese peasants had found new levels of prosperity.

Source: **The Bulletin**, Sydney, 26 July 1983
Communism with a capitalist face
By Jonathan Mirsky

Zhang Yutian, a peasant near Canton, owns three houses: one for himself, one for his wife and daughter and a third to rent. He owns a small van and is troubled by the demands of his hired labourers. 'They want too much money.'

Hired labour used to be one of the hallmarks, in communist parlance, of the bad old society.

After listening to Zhang's success story and examining his Japanese TV, two-speaker cassette player and binoculars, a local official said: 'He's very go ahead, don't you think?'

A few years ago, such materialism could have earned this farmer a stretch breaking rocks on the western frontier. Maoist austerity is out of vogue today. 'Getting rich' is respectable.

There are tens of thousands of rich peasants in China. The Press describes in detail how they make their particular piles—snake farming, rearing ducks, cultivating rare medicinal plants—and how they splash their money about.

Bicycles, jeans and digital watches no longer rate

a mention. The private car is the newest rage and the party has decreed that there is no ideological objection to owning one.

From Guandong in the south to western Sichuan and beyond the mountains in Tibet, customers throng the 'free markets' in which the government neither sets the prices nor controls—except in the broadest sense—what may be sold.

Private markets furnish the food and goods that the official network cannot supply. Peasants are exhorted from the highest levels to fill this need.

Before Mao died in 1976, free markets were treated as a threat to the communes. Now, in most of China, the once-hallowed communes are condemned as one of Mao's 'tragic errors'.

They have given way to co-operatives, small groups and even families who agree to individual production targets with the State and are allowed to retain any surplus for private sale.

It is the right to the surplus which has unlocked the entrepreneurial energies of China's farmers whose incomes have soared in the past three years.

QUESTIONS

1 What label is given to the now discredited communes, and what is the significance of the plural meaning within it?

2 What has supposedly unleashed the 'entrepreneurial energies' of the Chinese farmers?

Peng. A meeting was held between the student leaders and the government officials, but it achieved nothing and exacerbated the animosities between them. Many of the students in the square began a hunger strike. Within days the square was a mass of garbage and litter. The students' actions constituted a defiance of the party's authority right on the doorstep of the Great Hall of the People—the grandiose building that supposedly represented the opportunity of the common people to participate in the processes of government.

On 20 May 1989, the State Council

declared martial law. Although the people attributed this action to the premier, Li Peng, the decision was that of the 'paramount ruler', Deng Xiaoping. Posters depicting Li Peng as a Nazi (and in some cases a pig) were displayed, arousing extreme anger among the leadership. The students added another insult in the form of the ceremonial smashing of little bottles. 'Xiaoping' means 'little bottle', and these actions were a direct defiance of the authority of the 'new emperor'. These insults brought the confrontation to a fever pitch, virtually ensuring that a crackdown would be ordered.

The 'Goddess of Democracy' statue erected by Chinese students in Tienanmen Square, Beijing, China, in May 1989. The students were expressing dissent from the style of government practised by the Chinese Communist Party. The statue symbolised their demand for multi-party democratic practices and free elections. On 4 June 1989, the government used military force to crush the demonstration. Many lives were lost, and the 'Goddess' statue was destroyed.

The Continuing Revolution in China in the Post-Mao Years

Meanwhile, the citizens of Beijing joined the student protest, in many instances blocking the streets to stop convoys of soldiers from reaching Tienanmen Square. In this moment of crisis the students further alienated themselves from the Communist Party leadership by using a Western quotation—'give me liberty or give me death' (from the American revolutionary, Patrick Henry), and a Western-influenced symbol—the 'Goddess of Democracy' (based on the Statue of Liberty), as the means of gaining world-wide attention through television. These actions totally alienated the students from a leadership whose total political education had been focused on the need of the Chinese people to liberate themselves from Western influences. The students and citizens had reached a condition of total defiance of the government and the party, which could not now back down without 'losing face'.

By early June the situation had reached an impasse. The government apparently tried to use unarmed soldiers to clear the square, but the people prevented this action by erecting barricades. A few deaths occurred, of both soldiers and students. This led to the official condemnation of the protest as a 'counter-revolutionary rebellion'. On the night of 3–4 June 1989 the impasse was broken by the forceful entry into the square of tanks and soldiers. A terrible massacre occurred. It is still not clear how many lives were lost: deaths probably numbered somewhere between 2 000 and 3 000, mostly in the streets adjacent to the square, and including soldiers as well as citizens. Similar massacres occurred in other cities. The People's Liberation Army had been used to suppress its own people.

The world was aghast at the Tienanmen Square massacre. Protests flowed in from all directions. On 9 June 1989 the Chinese leaders appeared on television to praise the work of the People's Liberation Army in suppressing 'counter-revolutionaries attempting to overthrow the CCP', and for terminating the condition of *luan* (chaos) that had threatened to destroy Chinese society.

Deng revived the bogey of predatory capitalism to justify the one-party State. He told the assembled leaders that the 'dregs of society' had been attempting to 'establish a bourgeois republic entirely dependent on the West'. Deng displayed both the typical Chinese distaste for disorder and the traditional insistence that the 'old and wise' should rule. Significantly, too, he had reintroduced the concept of loyalty to Maoist teachings as a source of legitimate power.

The limits in Chinese governmental practice were confirmed: the Four Modernisations were to be maintained; the 'Fifth Modernisation' was banned. Within this policy there lay an unresolved contradiction. If a modern nation was to be developed through incentive systems, enterprise zones (regions in which Western-style capitalist investment was encouraged) and co-operative ventures with Western nations, then the skill and practice of participatory decision-making needed to be fostered in Chinese society. The policy of repression acted as a counterforce to this development

Despite condemnations from all over the world for their repression of the pro-democracy supporters, the Chinese leadership took steps to confirm their commitment to communist one-party rule. They claimed that the party's 'dictatorial function' was needed to counter hostile bourgeois international forces attempting to subvert the socialist system. To stress the continuity of the Revolution, the new party general secretary, Jiang Zemin, praised the 'tremendous achievements' of the first-generation collective leadership headed by the late chairman, Mao Zedong, and the second generation headed by Deng Xiaoping. He further claimed that the CCP would continue to 'lead the whole party and the people unswervingly along the path explored by the old revolutionary proletariat leaders' (*New China News Agency*, Beijing, 1 July 1991).

Many Western nations lodged complaints to the Chinese government about its violations of human rights through its imprisonment of pro-democracy dissidents purely because of their

Thousands of students gathered in Tienanmen Square in Beijing in May 1989, refusing to disperse until the government granted more democratic rights to its citizens. When soldiers were despatched to the square to remove the students, more than one million citizens blocked the streets. On 3–4 June 1989, the students were dispersed by military force. The Chinese 'paramount leader', Deng Xiaoping, commended the action of the troops in suppressing what he called 'counter-revolutionary' forces.

political opinions. When the British prime minister, John Major, visited Beijing in September 1991 and questioned the human rights record of the Chinese government, the Chinese premier, Li Peng, countered Major's queries with a History

lesson. He claimed that he had received a letter from a Chinese historian, who, he said, 'reminded me not to forget the history of China being humiliated and bullied by foreigners in the past 100 years. In those more than 100 years,

SOURCE 11.5
The students of Beijing proclaim the objectives of the pro-democracy movement, 1989

HISTORICAL CONTEXT: The Pragmatists had seized power in Communist China after the death of Mao Zedong in 1976. Although they proposed policies of modernisation, and permitted token discussion about 'democracy', they did not intend to allow any reduction in the authority of the Communist Party. When groups of students and citizens organised huge demonstrations, culminating in a mass gathering in Tienanmin Square in May 1989, the government eventually used military force to crush the demonstration, labelling it a 'counter-revolutionary rebellion'. The following proclamation expresses most of the objectives for which the demonstration was mounted.

Source: **R. Wanding, 'Reflections on the Historical Character of the Democracy Movement', in Mok Chiu Yu and J.F. Harrison (eds), *Voices from Tienanmen Square: Beijing Spring and the Democracy Movement*, Black Rose Books, Montreal, 1990, pp. 47–53 passim**

This is a confrontation between masses of students and thousands of armed policemen and soldiers; but it is also a confrontation between the citizens of Beijing and the government, a political challenge and power struggle by people from all levels of society against the party . . .

Not simply a student movement, it is a great Democracy Movement led by the students and joined by all levels of society.

. . . The party finds it impossible to restore its control over the situation and the confidence of the people. The people are not opposed to the CCP's

rule, but it has performed so badly that it has lost the sympathy, support and understanding of the people. The party has suppressed democracy. Although it has many extraordinary members, they cannot change its fundamentally flawed political basis, nor its anti-democratic character. I repeat, people are not moving against socialism, but a socialist system led by a party that has performed badly. It has not created greater wealth and democracy, but has placed the burden of inflation on the people in a perpetual exploitation of them.

. . . the long-term goal of the movement is to reform, peacefully, the Communist Party's monolithic socio-political structure, and to replace it with a diversified democratic, cultural, national framework . . . Do the Chinese like and accept totalitarianism and monolithic dictatorship? The current democratic wave denies that. However, if they are disliked by the people, why does the Communist Party force us to accept them? Why does the party think that only it can represent the people, that only it can consolidate the benefits of development?

. . . The legal rights to demonstrate and to strike must prevail over the accusation that we are creating 'turmoil'. The legal right to freedom of speech must overcome their irrational accusation that we are behaving unconstitutionally and going against CCP leadership. Only if we can counteract these accusations can our Movement continue, and the legality of our actions be recognised.

. . . If the party cannot be opposed, then at times it will be dominated by destructive elements like the Gang of Four, who are the party for a time. Further, unopposed, the party can initiate random campaigns, directed against anybody, hurting people, party and country at random, without any

understanding of what is being done.

. . . The coercive unity of China, achieved in 1949, should give way to the popular franchise and people's committees. The intellectuals should inspire the people, demanding the return of power to the people.

Opposition, hesitation, pessimism, or new authoritarianism are futile. Only the great power of democracy, and a people's organisation created by it, can stabilise China and further stimulate its population. The present and the future belong to the people!

QUESTIONS

1 Why might the author have stressed that the protest involves 'all levels of society'?

2 The author stresses that the movement is not opposed to socialism, but to a party administration that has failed to implement socialism. What does he claim the party has failed to do?

3 The leaders of the movement had been accused by the government of creating 'turmoil'. How does the author rebut this accusation?

4 The author makes the point that unless the party can be 'opposed', the party itself can be taken over by extreme elements. What historical reference does he make to illustrate this possibility, and what validity would his example carry?

5 Whilst conceding the value of the unification of China by the CCP in 1949, the author claims that something else should have ensued. What was the unfulfilled phase?

those foreign powers totally disregarded the human rights of the Chinese people'.

Deng Xiaoping and his close colleagues regarded the Chinese Revolution of 1949 as the event which closed the door on over a century of Chinese disunity, disorder and humiliation dating from the Opium War of 1842. In their opinion, such unity and stability were won only after great struggle, and were not to be given up to satisfy the demands of 'misguided youth' who had no understanding of the sacrifices and suffering involved in the achievement of the People's Republic.

The Chinese ideograph for chaos (*luan*) has for centuries been a term of condemnation. The huge scale of the Tienanmen demonstration, and the refusal of the young student leaders to compromise, or contemplate gradual steps to reform, awakened the revulsion of chaos based in centuries of Confucian tradition.

III FOREIGN INVESTMENT IN A COMMUNIST ECONOMY

A major feature of the modernisation policy was the 'Open Door' policy, by which Communist China expressed its eagerness for foreign technology, expertise and investment funds. In January 1979 an agreement was signed with the USA for scientific, cultural and technological co-operation. Similar links were made with other nations. By early 1985 the Chinese claimed that they had attracted US $8 000 million in foreign investment.

This was a total reversal of Mao's policy of self-reliance, and an apparent contradiction of communist principles. Deng argued that the policy of having an 'Open Door' for capitalist investment from overseas was essential to the development of socialist productive forces. He nevertheless stressed that, although the modernisation programme would be facilitated by communicating with the capitalist societies, the Chinese would have to be particularly selective, rejecting what he called 'the pernicious things in the capitalist culture', and resisting 'the corrosive influences' of capitalism and 'bourgeois culture', which could corrupt the youth of China. If these precautions were taken, he argued, the Open Door policy could not endanger socialism, since public ownership of the factors of production remained the basis of China's economy.

In 1992 a major new development was

announced. Foreign investors were invited to develop manufacturing ventures for the sale of goods in the Chinese market itself. Previously the foreign investors were offered location concessions and access to cheap labour, provided the products were exported to earn other currencies. The Chinese people had increased their spending on consumer goods by 470 per cent between 1978 and 1990, creating a substantial domestic market of consumers with spending ability. Foreign investment could be attracted by the sheer scale of the Chinese market—1.2 billion consumers, with 50 million of them earning incomes sufficient to allow significant consumer spending.

IV ASSESSING THE CHINESE REVOLUTIONS

It is possible to identify three revolutions in modern Chinese history. The first ended the Manchu Dynasty, the second deposed the Guo-mindang and established the Maoist regime, while the third dismantled most of the work of Mao Zedong under a 'pragmatist' ethos.

The abdication of power by the Qing (or Manchu) Dynasty in 1912 appeared to bring to an end the system of rule by an emperor and his supporting bureaucracy that had prevailed for over 2 000 years. An attempt was made to establish a system of presidential rule, and the best qualified candidate for that position, Sun Yatsen, achieved a high level of respect and prestige for a time. His political party, the Guomindang (the party of the nation, or the Nationalist Party), produced a set of policies that appeared to promise the people a social revolution (including a vaguely defined socialist-style provision for a comfortable livelihood for all). Among the party's promises was a commitment to the 'People's Government', that is, the establishment of a form of democracy.

It could be claimed that although the GMD was in effective control of large parts of China

---

SOURCE 11.6
The leaders of Communist China proclaim the welcoming of investment in China by Western powers and Taiwan, 1992

HISTORICAL CONTEXT: By 1992 the Open Door policy by which foreign investment was welcomed in China (contrary to the policies of Mao Zedong) was in full operation. This announcement was particularly significant because it included an invitation for investment from Taiwan (the remaining stronghold of the Guomindang), which the CCP officially regards as an integral part of China, destined for reunification with mainland China.

Source: The South China Morning Post, quoted in *The Australian,* Sydney, 16 May 1992

China is planning the most significant expansion of its open door policy since its senior leader, Mr Deng, ended the country's isolation in 1979.

Beijing is to look for Hong Kong, Taiwan and Western business partners in commerce, foreign trade, banking, insurance, real estate, shipping and civil aviation sectors it has previously refused to expand. Present foreign investment focuses on industry, infrastructure and tourism.

In a bid to promote China's united-front policy towards Taiwan, Mr Li, the Minister for Foreign Economic Relations, said areas temporarily closed to Western companies might be opened to Taiwanese investors. 'It is subject to negotiation if Taiwan compatriots want to invest in areas not open to foreign capital, or do things (in business) that foreign companies cannot do,' he said.

QUESTIONS
1 What significant (if small) surrender of Chinese sovereignty is implied by the new investment policies?
2 Explain the significance of the term 'Taiwan compatriots'.

for over twenty years (*circa* 1920–49), it did not achieve a social revolution because it never won the combined loyalties of both the peasant and scholar classes. Although the GMD received substantial help from the USA, it could not impose its will upon the people of China. In 1927 its leader, Jiang Kaishek, purged all communists from the party. From that date the fate of the GMD was sealed, because that event ensured that its leaders—whoever they might be—could not unify the nation. Moreover, Jiang Kaishek and his main supporters were too Westernised, and too dependent on Western principles and Western aid, to win nation-wide support. Invoking the ancient Chinese principle of government authority, it could realistically be said that Jiang and the GMD had failed to win the mandate of heaven.

The Chinese Communist Party, meanwhile, succeeded in winning the loyalty of the great mass of the people. In overcoming enormous hardships during the years of the Long March and the Japanese invasion (1937–45), the Communist leaders survived to witness both the withdrawal of the Japanese and the defeat of the GMD. In the meantime they had earned a reputation for having the welfare of the people at heart. With their promises of a new social order, characterised by the ending of poverty and the equal distribution of wealth, they appeared to be true revolutionaries.

The Communist Party proclaimed their year of total victory (1949) as the year of liberation from both the oppression of the people under the centuries-old feudal system of landlord domination and from the exploitation of China by foreign powers. In effect, they mounted a double claim to power: through the traditional Chinese mandate of heaven (the justified right to govern) and through the Marxist theory of History by which the victory of the proletariat over the bourgeoisie was regarded as part of inevitable historical processes.

Once established in authority, Mao Zedong totally dismantled any concept of collective leadership through his personal domination of all his colleagues. So total was this personal dominance, regardless of which official position he held, 'Chairman Mao' virtually re-established the authority of the emperor—an authority that could not be passed on until his death even though other persons at times held office as head of state.

Mao's Great Proletarian Cultural Revolution was possibly the most convulsive attempt in history to change a culture. The young people were encouraged to 'struggle against' and challenge all authority figures (except Mao himself and his immediate supporters) in order to displace the existing bureaucracy. The 'olds'—traditional standards—were all to be swept away. Although it generated enormous upheavals, this cataclysmic event failed in the long term to change the character of Chinese society.

Once Mao had passed on, and his immediate hardline support group (the Gang of Four) had been imprisoned, a third major phase of the Chinese Revolution evolved. Another 'emperor figure' emerged—Deng Xiaoping, a Communist Party veteran carrying the aura of a survivor of the Long March. As was the case with Mao, everybody deferred to Deng, regardless of whether or not he held an official post. His authority was encapsulated in the unofficial title of 'paramount leader'. Like Mao, Deng also held power right into his years of senility, again demonstrating the Chinese custom of awarding and respecting authority until its surrender at death.

Whilst functioning as a nominally communist society, China under Deng modified Marxist–Maoist principles beyond recognisable parameters, reintroducing elements of free-enterprise capitalism and inviting foreign investment. In the eyes of fervent supporters of communist principles, the Deng-led modernisation policies could well be regarded as a counter-revolution. The Maoist communes were dismantled; the peasants were encouraged to farm their own plots and sell their surpluses for profit. 'Getting rich' was encouraged. The government still claimed to be 'communist' on the grounds that all the major factors of production remained under State ownership, and that the

CCP remained (in theory) the people's preferred instrument of government.

That the style of government was as much traditional Chinese as new-era communist was demonstrated for all the world to see in the 1989 Tienanmin Square repression of the democratic movement, and the subsequent ongoing harassment and imprisonment of dissidents solely for their expression of opposition to government policies. Thus while some 'adjustments' to the Maoist Revolution were officially sanctioned, the 'counter-revolution' did not proceed to the stage of allowing democratic choice in government. The 'emperor' demanded total obedience and brooked no challenge to his authority. He had to display ruthless strength or be seen to have surrendered the mandate of heaven.

Over the 84-year period from 1912 to 1996, many features of Chinese society were subjected to revolutionary change. The power of the landlords, and the feudal system through which they had dominated society, had been broken forever. Some traditional practices, however, survived. Perhaps, in total, China was 'a world so changed' as Mao had predicted, but the changes were not as encompassing as he had sought and expected.

MAJOR EVENTS INVOLVING CHINA SINCE THE DEATH OF MAO ZEDONG

1976 Deaths of Zhou Enlai and Mao Zedong

1978 Treaty of Peace and Friendship with Japan
Deng outlined a programme for reform and opening to the West

1979 Resumption of full diplomatic relations with USA
A new investment law was passed, allowing foreign investors to become part-owners of Chinese business enterprises

1980 Hua Guofeng resigned his post as premier, and was replaced by Zhao Ziyang (a protege of Deng Xiaoping)

1982 The office of chairman was discontinued, as a means of breaking all links with the Maoist era
The new constitution forbade the development of 'personality cults'

1986 Student demonstrations demanding reforms led to hardline communists claiming that 'bourgeois liberalisation' was proceeding too quickly

1989 The funeral for a liberal-minded official became the occasion for massive student demonstrations in favour of democratic reforms in Beijing, Shanghai and other cities. On 3–4 June the Tienanmen Square massacre occurred: troops used force to disperse demonstrators. Deng Xiaoping commended the troops 'for suppressing counter-revolutionaries trying to overthrow the CCP'.

1995 Jiang Zemin, the new general secretary of the CCP, in an address to mark the fiftieth anniversary of Japan's defeat in World War II, committed the government of the People's Republic to continuing the economic reforms of Deng Ziaoping

chapter twelve

Revolution in Cuba

Onwards Cubans!
Let Cuba give you a prize for heroism.
For we are soldiers going to free the country
   Cleansing with fire
Which will destroy this infernal plague
Of bad governments and insatiable tyrants
Who have plunged Cuba into evil.
   The Cuban people
Drowned in grief feels itself wounded
And has decided
To pursue without respite a solution
Which will serve as an example
To those who don't have pity
And we risk, resolved
For this cause to give our life:
'Long live the Revolution!'

   'Hymn of 26 July' (as adopted by the *Fidelistas*)

On 1 January 1959 a small military force, led by Fidel Castro, took over the government of the Caribbean island of Cuba after years of guerrilla warfare against what appeared to be insurmountable odds. As had been the case in China in the period 1945–49, much of this success was due to the erosion of support for the dictator in power. Units of the army had deserted to the guerrilla force in large numbers because the rebels had won the 'victory of the minds'—their cause had ensured for them the people's support.

Since the dissolution of the Spanish and Portuguese empires in the early nineteenth century, armed seizures of power had been commonplace in Latin (or Hispanic) America. The attainment of power in Cuba by the *Fidelistas* (the followers of Fidel Castro) was significantly different, however, from all the previous examples. For this was not a case of one military leader displacing another. It was a people's movement, promising not just a change in the exercise of power, but a true revolution in the sense of building a new society on principles of justice and fairness for all. Although definite socialist policies only emerged after the consolidation of power, the Cuban Revolution is now generally regarded as the first socialist revolution in the Western hemisphere.

Theme Questions

➤ Are there factors in the history of Cuba that serve to explain the uniqueness of the Cuban Revolution?

➤ Although Cuba was not a colony at the time, did anti-colonial objectives play a significant part in the emotional climate of the Revolution?

➤ Did the Cuban Revolution fulfil the Marxian prediction on the nature and course of social Revolution?

I CUBA: FROM COLONY TO MILITARY DICTATORSHIP

The island of Cuba was discovered (in the sense of being brought into the sphere of knowledge of the Europeans) during the first voyage of Christopher Columbus in 1492. The native inhabitants (Caribs) were termed 'Indians' by the Spanish, in the belief that Cuba and the nearby islands were adjacent to India, one of the proposed destinations of Columbus's westward voyage from Spain.

Spanish occupation and conquest of Cuba began in 1511, and Cuba quickly became established as the base from which the Spaniards explored and conquered the adjacent mainland. From Cuba, expeditions departed for Mexico, the Mississippi Valley and Florida. Cuba's chief city and port, Havana, rapidly grew into the naval base and administrative centre for Hispanic America. An agricultural economy developed in Cuba, for the purpose of provisioning both the growing colonial occupation force and the ships that serviced the Spanish colonial empire. Plantations for the production of the commercial crops of sugar and tobacco were also established.

The native people, ravaged by European diseases and repressive Spanish actions, declined in numbers. They did not willingly accept work as plantation labourers, so from 1522 the Spanish began the importation of African slaves to work the plantations. Today there are no identifiable remnants of the original 'Indian' inhabitants. About 75 per cent of the population is classed as being of Spanish descent, 13 per cent are descendants of the African slaves, and 12 per cent are of mixed race.

The Fight for Independence

As the virtual headquarters of the Spanish Empire in the Americas, Cuba suffered many attacks from Spain's colonial rivals—Britain, France and Holland. In the late eighteenth century, however, the economic success of the colony led to an influx of Spanish-speaking immigrants from Spain itself and from other Spanish colonies in Central and South America.

When the major Spanish colonies on the Central and South American mainlands achieved independence from Spain in the early nineteenth century, Cuba remained relatively stable under Spanish rule. Some recognition of the right of the Cubans to participate in decisions of government was made in 1810, when they were given the right to elect deputies to the mother country parliament, the *Cortes*. This was a right that had been denied to the British-ruled colonists in North America prior to the 1776 Revolution.

Discontent and restiveness developed in Cuba as the mother country failed to permit the growth of self-government. In 1837 Spanish rule became more repressive with the withdrawal of the right to send representatives to the Cortes and the introduction of rule by special laws—in effect, arbitrary rule by the governor.

By the 1850s powerful US trading interests had established contacts in Cuba, and from this time forward the Americans consistently encouraged the Cubans to seek independence from Spain. A war for independence broke out in 1868, now known as the Ten Years' War. After large-scale loss of life, Spain triumphed, but the legacy of bitterness was never erased. Spain tried to heal the breach with comprehensive government reforms, an amnesty for political opponents, the abolition of slavery, and the restoration of direct representation for Cuba in the Cortes.

Unfulfilled promises and undiminished hatreds ultimately sparked off another war in 1895. The rebels proclaimed a republic, and Spain sent 200 000 troops to suppress the uprising. After three years of bitter fighting the USA entered the war against Spain (this became known as the Spanish–American War of 1895, from which the USA acquired possession of the Philippines) and brought it to a rapid conclusion.

By the Treaty of Paris, December 1898, Spain handed Cuba over to the USA in trust for its inhabitants. In its declaration of war the USA had disclaimed any intention of controlling the island permanently. It was committed to making self-government possible for the Cubans.

Spanish rule ended officially on 1 January 1899. US military rule functioned from that date until 20 May 1902, and the USA is credited with considerable achievements in public works, education and sanitation in that time. The independent Cuban republic was established in 1902. Cuba was the last of the former Spanish colonies in South America to attain its independence.

The Continuing American Influence

Cuban independence, however, was conditional rather than absolute. Within the constitution establishing the new republic was a set of provisions known as the Platt Amendment, insisted upon by the USA. By the Platt Amendment Cuba undertook, inter alia, to lease naval bases to the USA and to permit the USA to intervene in Cuban affairs if this was necessary to preserve Cuban independence or to ensure the maintenance of a government capable of protecting life and property.

At the time, the Platt Amendment could be interpreted as a welcome guarantee of protection—a means of ensuring that Cuban independence would not be subverted by external forces. Over the years, however, it became apparent to critics and opponents of the USA that it was a formula for continued American dominance of the Cuban economy. It was later claimed that although Cuba had ceased to be a Spanish colony, it became instead an economic colony of the USA.

Over the decades between 1902 and 1959 the administration of Cuba was frequently disrupted by uprisings and military seizures of power. After the establishment of the republic in 1902, the US acquired a naval base at Guantanamo, and strengthened the Cuban sugar industry by making provision for the acceptance of a quota of Cuban sugar into the US market. From this time the major influence on the Cuban economy was US investment in the sugar industry and the dependence of that industry on the US market.

In 1906 the Cuban administration collapsed under rebellion from within, and another period of US administration followed (1906–09). The republic was inaugurated a second time in 1909. Three presidencies spanned the period 1909–25, but corruption in government was widespread, resulting in further US intervention on several occasions. Some vestiges of democracy were evident, however, not least in the holding of elections.

General Gerardo Machado, elected president in 1925, established a dictatorship in 1928, resorting to a rule of terror and suspension of freedom of speech and assembly. In 1933 a general strike and fervent anti-Machado activity forced him to flee the island. From Machado's departure in 1933 until the *Fidelista* seizure of power in 1959, Cuba had several presidents, but most of them were installed or deposed by a former army sergeant, Fulgencio Batista, who gained effective control of the armed forces at the time of the downfall of Machado. Batista assumed the presidency himself from 1940 to 1944, and again from 1952 to 1959.

The military-based regimes sponsored or led by Batista represented the entrenched pro-American political élite. The wealth of the leaders was directly linked to American investments. Batista held what were regarded as 'window-dressing' elections, but opposition groups disputed the election results and organised a campaign of disobedience and sabotage. From December 1956 civil war raged as an armed force of guerrillas led by Fidel Castro and 'Che' Guevara assaulted the Batista regime, promising a reformed society and a more equitable distribution of wealth.

II THE VICTORY OF THE FIDELISTAS

The victorious leader of the **guerrilla** band that deposed Fulgencio Batista was brought to the world's attention as a bearded revolutionary dressed in shapeless army fatigues—a style of dress he maintained for decades after his victory. Fidel Castro, for all his wildness of appearance, was a well-educated man, having attended Roman Catholic schools and receiving a law

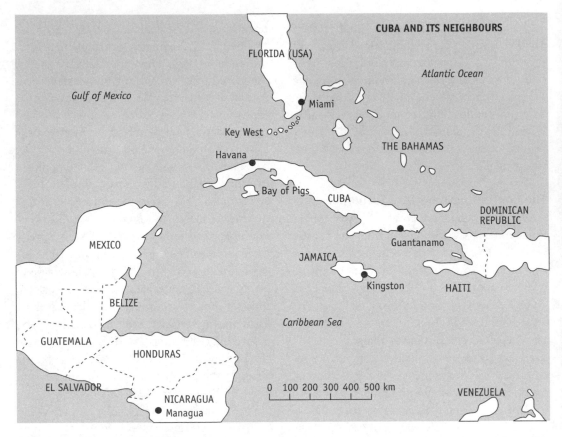

MAP 12.1 Cuba and its neighbours

The central position of Cuba in the Caribbean region is shown on this map. Key West, the nearest US territory to Cuba, is less than 200 km away. The *Fidelistas* trained for their invasion of Batista's Cuba in nearby Mexico. The victory of the *Sandinistas* in Nicaragua in 1979 was in many ways similar to the *Fidelista* victory in Cuba in 1959. The USA still has the use of the naval base at Guantanamo, an arrangement that dates from the Spanish-American War of 1898.

degree from Havana University in 1950. He was only thirty-two years of age when he and his followers, the *Fidelistas*, gained control of Cuba on 1 January 1959.

During his student days Castro had become active in protest against the corruption and inefficiency of the Batista regime. On 26 July 1953, with his brother Raul and other anti-Batista zealots, he led an unsuccessful armed assault on the Moncada Barracks. It was a desperate flamboyant act, and the Castros were incredibly lucky to survive. From this foolhardy attempt to depose Batista the *Fidelistas* acquired an identity—they called themselves the '26 July Movement'—and a legend for bravery in action.

In 1955 Fidel Castro and his brother were released from prison as part of a general amnesty for political prisoners proclaimed by Batista. At this stage there had been no indications that Castro was or could be anything more to the Batista regime than a minor trouble-maker. The Castros retreated to Mexico in the hope of recruiting a revolutionary invasion force. There they met up with the other great personality of the early Cuban Revolution, a man who for a time became the symbol of pro-socialist revolution throughout the Americas—'Che' (which means 'buddy' or 'chum') Guevara.

Born in 1928 (one year later than Fidel), Guevara was an Argentinian, qualified as a doctor but dedicated to what he saw as the cause of anti-imperialism and socialist revolution. He particularly abhorred militarist rule of the type he had experienced in Argentina under Juan Peron, even though Peron had claimed to be a friend of the poor workers. Guevara regarded most of the governing cliques of Latin America as capitalist oligarchies working in association with US 'dollar imperialism'. By the time he met up with the Castros in Mexico, he had visited many South American countries, making contacts with pro-socialist revolutionary groups. Guevara assumed a position of great influence within the movement as both a brilliant tactician in guerrilla warfare and a teacher of socialist ideology. He educated the *Fidelistas* both militarily and politically.

In December 1956 the Castros, Guevara and eighty followers returned to Cuba from Mexico, dedicated to the seemingly hopeless task of deposing Batista by force. They had trained themselves for guerrilla warfare, and, retreating to the Sierra Maestra mountains, revived the 26 July Movement, recruited followers, and educated the Cuban people to expect a true social revolution rather than simply the replacement of one regime by another.

After two years of warfare, with their support growing every week, the *Fidelistas* totally undermined the Batista regime. On 1 January 1959, Batista having fled into exile, the guerrillas seized government. Cuba had been liberated, but the question remained: could Castro and his followers sustain a true social revolution?

III CAUSES OF AND STAGES IN THE CUBAN REVOLUTION

The Castroist Revolution was significantly different from the other major modern revolutions and, in fact, was something of a surprise to observers in the rest of the world. Many of the factors regarded as 'necessary conditions' for a revolution were not apparent. There was no intellectual ferment for a reformed society; the existing regime had not been destabilised by involvement in an external war (as was the case in the French, Bolshevik and Chinese revolutions);

and although the poor were discontented and miserable, there weren't masses of totally desperate people on the verge of rebellion.

The Cuban Revolution was primarily a revolution against several key grievances, and, secondly, a revolution in favour of a democratic system (which in the long run was not delivered).

Resentment of the cruel and repressive Batista militarist regime was inextricably linked with a revulsion for the extent to which US investment dominated the Cuban economy. Although many Cubans prospered as a result of the American business interests, the majority of the population were shut out of the opportunities to share in the benefits derived from the US-dominated sugar and tourism industries. The US government supported the Batista regime and its predecessors almost solely on the criterion of the degree of co-operation with US business interests. In this way the USA provided the key revolutionary element of 'the external enemy', against which emotional animosity could be directed.

Finally, the *Fidelistas* had Fidel Castro himself, providing the immeasurably fervent and courageous leadership that was indispensable to the success of such an apparently impossible venture.

Stages in the Revolution

After the *Fidelistas'* successful expulsion of Batista, their revolution expanded beyond the seizure of power into a genuine social revolution that transformed Cuba. As it did so, it acquired socialist and 'world communist' characteristics, but these developed as the Revolution proceeded, rather than influencing it from the beginning. Commentators on the Cuban Revolution often say that communism was not a cause of the Revolution, but rather a result.

In the period preceding their attainment of government, from 1953 to 1959, the *Fidelistas* were primarily a group of zealous nationalists following a charismatic leader, dedicated to the task of overthrowing a military dictator and a regime that subordinated the people of Cuba to the capitalist interests of the USA. Their motto,

SOURCE 12.1
Fidel Castro claims 'History will absolve me', October 1953

HISTORICAL CONTEXT: As a young man of twenty-six years, Fidel Castro led an attack on the Moncada Barracks, in southern Cuba, on 26 July 1953—an attempt to spark off an insurrection against the military dictatorship of Fulgencio Batista. This foolhardy attack provided the revolutionary cause with its 'legendary deed of heroism', and from this occasion there emerged the 'Hymn of 26 July' and the movement's original name: the 26 July Movement.

The attack was foiled, and many of the rebels were executed. Castro, however, was brought to trial and (as a qualified lawyer) was surprisingly permitted to speak in his own defence. The event, on 16 October 1953, later became famous because of the long and impassioned speech made by Castro in his defence. As there were only twelve persons present, and as there was a nation-wide censorship in operation, the contents of the speech were neither recorded nor published at the time.

From this situation and trial (in which he was sentenced to nineteen years imprisonment), Castro was later able to produce the most famous document and the most effective item of propaganda for the Cuban Revolution. Known by the title derived from its rousing last sentence ('History will absolve me'), the published version is a reconstruction (and no doubt an expansion) of the original. In its published form it would take close to four hours to deliver as a speech.

Source: **R.E. Bonachea and N.P. Valdes (eds), *Selected Works of Fidel Castro*, Vol. I, *Revolutionary Struggle, 1947–58*, The MIT Press, Cambridge, Massachusetts, 1972, pp. 217–221 passim**

It is well known that in England during the seventeenth century two kings, Charles I and James II, were dethroned for acts of despotism. These events coincided with the birth of liberal political philosophy, which was the ideological foundation for a new social class then struggling to break the bonds of feudalism. Against the tyrannies based on divine right, the new philosophy upheld the principle of the social contract and of the consent of the governed, and constituted the foundation of the English Revolution of 1688 and the American and French revolutions of 1775 and 1789. These great events opened up the liberation process of the Spanish colonies in America—the last link being Cuba.

. . . The right to rebel against tyranny was consecrated definitively at that time, and was converted into an essential postulate of political freedom.

. . . How was the Prosecutor to justify Batista's right to power, when he obtained it against the will of the people, violating by treason and by force the laws of the Republic? How was he to qualify as legitimate a regime of blood, oppression, and ignominy? How was he to call a government revolutionary, when it was composed of the most reactionary men, ideas, and methods of our public life?

. . . We were taught that October 10 and February 24 are glorious dates of patriotic rejoicing because they were the dates on which the Cubans rebelled against the yoke of infamous tyrannies. We were taught to love and defend the beautiful flag of the lone star, and to sing every afternoon a hymn whose verses say that to live in chains is to live in disgrace and abject submission, and that to die for the fatherland is to live. We learned all that and we shall not ever forget it, even though today in our fatherland men are being killed and jailed for putting into practice the ideas they were taught from the cradle. We were born in a free country which was left to us by our fathers, and we would rather the island sink into the sea than consent to be anyone's slave.

. . . I conclude my defense, but I shall not end it as all lawyers for the defense do, asking for acquittal of the defendant. I cannot ask for acquittal when my companions are already suffering in the ignominious prison on the Isle of Pines. Send me there that I may share their fate. It is conceivable that honest men should be dead or in prison when the president is a criminal and a thief!

. . . As for me, I know that jail will be as hard as it has ever been for anyone, filled with threats, with vileness, and cowardly brutality; but I do not fear this, as I do not fear the fury of the miserable tyrant who snuffed out the life of seventy brothers of mine.

Condemn me, it does not matter. History will absolve me!

QUESTIONS

1 The links between the revolutions of the modern era are evident in these excerpts. What would Castro be hoping to achieve by his references to the American and French revolutions?

2 What did Castro mean by claiming that Batista's regime was 'reactionary' rather than 'revolutionary'?

3 Compare the conclusion of this speech with that of the speech in Source 3.1. In what ways are the conditions similar?

Patria o Muerte (Fatherland or Death), revealed their emphasis. Their first song of revolution, the 'Hymn of 26 July' promised freedom from 'bad governments' and 'insatiable tyranny', but made no promises of a socialist character. They were operating outside the world communist movement and its bureaucracy, and although Guevara was attempting to educate them to socialist objectives, their focus was upon victory through guerrilla warfare.

After the *Fidelistas'* seizure of power in 1959, Che Guevara issued his famous statement that the Cuban Revolution appeared to contradict one of Lenin's maxims in that it was initially simply a liberation movement, that is, not at that stage driven by a comprehensive ideological framework. Guevara claimed that the theories for a reformed society could be worked out in practice once liberation had been attained.

It was in this second phase, 1959–62, that Castro and Guevara (who for a time was virtually second-in-command) launched into a policy of pragmatic socialism. The immediate practical tasks were redistributing land ownership and building a more equitable society, to be attained through education and social reforms. The rural revolutionaries, whose primary aim had been the overthrow of Batista, now merged with the more politically conscious urban workers in the *Organizaciones Revolutionarias Integradas* (Integrated Revolutionary Organisations), dedicated to building a new society.

After the failure of the April 1961 US-backed counter-revolutionary invasion at the Bay of Pigs, Castro used the May Day celebration of that year to proclaim Cuba a socialist nation and to abolish elections. Cuba had become a one-party State, and Castro had broken one of his most prominent revolutionary promises—the proposed introduction of democratic elections.

The third stage (1962–65) was characterised by the deliberate and well-publicised adoption of Marxian socialist ideology as a national policy for development. The Revolution had now acquired its theory and the leaders their sense of conviction. In a speech at Havana on 1 May 1966, Castro made this claim: 'Today, after seven years, during which it has been necessary to remake everything, we no longer have the old capitalist and bourgeois state. No! We now have the new socialist state!'

From 1966, Castro moved to another stage: the 'true communist' stage of adopting a one-party structure and of encouraging world revolution by offering Cuban troops to help communist revolutionary movements in other nations. Castro had earlier operated within the 26 July Movement aimed at liberation. Now he developed the *Partido Communista de Cuba*, and attempted to export the revolution.

Sect. IV

The Social Revolution

Castro's immediate objectives in his early years were the elimination of American control of the economy, the nationalisation of manufacturing industries, redistribution of land ownership to the people, and the improvement of the health and education facilities for all citizens. To

The inspirational Cuban revolutionary leader, Fidel Castro, was extremely effective in convincing his followers that the Cuban Revolution was a cause worthy of their devotion. Castro always appeared in a guerrilla fighter's uniform and was likely to deliver lengthy speeches of up to four hours, angrily denouncing US imperialism and US sponsorship of attacks by anti-Castro Cuban exiles.

pursue these goals, the new Cuban government, in 1960, expropriated all US investments without the payment of compensation, resulting in an intense spirit of animosity towards the Castro regime in the USA.

The large plantations were subdivided, and the land was redistributed for the use and benefit of the people. Farms of 67 hectares were established for food production, plantations of 1 340 hectares for sugar and rice, and less productive land assigned to use as cattle ranches. Seventy per cent of the cultivable land was worked by 1 400 co-operatives. An attempt was made to achieve rapid industrialisation in the hope of diversifying the economy and making Cuba less reliant on its two major export crops, sugar and tobacco.

Despite the spirit of urgency and the climate of enthusiasm, the achievements of the early years of the Cuban social revolution were disappointing. The USA, antagonised by the nationalisation of American investments, reduced the Cuban sugar quota in 1960, and in 1961 declared a total trade embargo on Cuba, to be sustained until compensation was paid. Later, in 1972, the US Foreign Claims Commission certified claims by US citizens for compensation payments totalling US $1 500 million (in 1972 values). Twenty-five years later (1996) the trade embargo was still in force, with the compensation claims still being supported by the US Congress.

Denied the traditional American market, the Cuban sugar industry faltered. The new industrialisation ventures also failed, due to lack of expertise and shortage of markets.

In 1961 the USSR stepped into the breach, accepting Cuban sugar for the Russian market, and granting Cuba a huge development loan at the very low interest rate of 2.5 per cent. Thus began a very close association with the USSR that was to lead to extreme tension in Cuba's relations with USA.

After the difficulties of the first few years,

Che Guevara explains that the Cuban Revolution began purely as a liberation movement, and that the theory for the reconstruction of society emerged later, 1960

HISTORICAL CONTEXT: Guevara, a committed Marxist, felt obliged to explain that the Cuban Revolution could serve the Marxist cause even though it appeared not to have followed the predicted course. He here virtually claims that temporarily hidden historical forces were at work in the Cuban Revolution to ensure that because the liberators were 'firm' in their objective (that is, liberation), it was virtually inevitable that they would become instruments of social reform after attaining power.

Source: **C. Guevara, 'Notes for the Study of the Ideology of the Cuban Revolution', in** *Verde Olivo*, **the magazine of the Cuban armed forces, 8 October 1960**

This is a unique revolution which some people maintain contradicts one of the most orthodox premises of the revolutionary movement, expressed by Lenin: 'Without a revolutionary theory there is no revolutionary movement.' It would be suitable to say that revolutionary theory, as the expression of a

social truth, surpasses any declaration of it; that is to say, even if the theory is not known, the revolution can succeed if historical reality is interpreted correctly and if the forces involved are utilised correctly . . .

The principal actors of this revolution had no coherent theoretical criteria; but it cannot be said that they were ignorant of the various concepts of history, society, economics, and revolution which are being discussed in the world today.

Profound knowledge of reality, a close relationship with the people, the firmness of the liberator's objective, and the practical revolutionary experience gave to those leaders the chance to form a more complete theoretical concept.

QUESTIONS

1 To what theory is Guevara referring in his words 'when historical reality is interpreted correctly' (see Chapter 5)?

2 Which supposed quality is (according to Guevara) going to ensure that the *Fidelistas* will develop a theory for social revolution?

---

many of the objectives of the proposed social and economic revolution were attained. Improved health services were established, and higher standards of living were achieved. Illiteracy was drastically reduced. The pre-Revolutionary rate of illiteracy was about 25 per cent, but by 1970 this had been reduced to 4 per cent. Most children were now expected to complete their primary education (which had not been the case before the Revolution), and adult education for illiterates was also provided in the early years of the Revolution. Secondary schools trebled from 1960–70, industrial colleges increased enrolments from 6 000 to 30 000, and university enrolments doubled. Agricultural research stations were established to ensure the advancement of Cuban agriculture.

The expectation of immediate plenitude was not fulfilled. For most of the 1960s the Cubans

still endured a fairly austere way of life. Conditions improved during the 1970s, with the Cuban people assured of standards of living higher than most of the other peoples of Central and South America.

The Moral Revolution

Castro found that if the socialist ideals of redistribution of wealth were to be achieved, the people had to be educated to productivity and co-operation in sharing. Castro acknowledged that Cubans were at first deluded into thinking that socialism would simply redistribute the existing wealth, as if it was 'sitting in shop windows waiting to be handed out'. He exhorted his people to realise that they had to work to generate wealth.

The encouragement of a co-operative approach to production was a major emphasis

SOURCE 12.3
At the United Nations General Assembly Fidel Castro proclaims the achievements of the social revolution in Cuba, 1960

HISTORICAL CONTEXT: By September 1960 Castro was being subjected to severe criticism for his action in expropriating all foreign properties in Cuba without compensation. At the world forum of the UN General Assembly he was able to imply that the benefits brought to the people of Cuba outweighed the apparent injustice of the expropriations.

Source: F. Castro, in a speech to the General Assembly of the United Nations, 26 September 1960

What did the Revolution find when it came to power in Cuba? . . . First of all, the Revolution found that 600 000 able Cubans were unemployed as many, proportionately, as were unemployed in the United States at the time of the great depression . . . Three million out of a population of somewhat over six million did not have electric lights and did not enjoy the advantages and comforts of electricity. Three and a half million out of a total of slightly more than six million lived in huts, shacks, and slums, without the slightest sanitary facilities. In the cities, rents took almost one third of family incomes . . . Thirty seven and one half per cent of our population was illiterate; seventy per cent of the rural children had no teachers . . .

. . . eighty five per cent of the small farmers were paying rents which came to almost thirty per cent of their income for the use of land, while one and one half per cent of the landowners controlled forty six per cent of the total land area of the nation.

. . . Public utilities, electricity, and telephone services all belonged to United States monopolies. A major portion of the banking business, of the importing business, and the oil refineries, the greater part of the sugar production, the best land in Cuba, and the most important industries in all fields belonged to American companies.

QUESTION
1 What 'right' is Castro (by implication) claiming in this address (refer to Source 3.3)?

---

in the moral revolution. A widely used slogan was 'The Road to Communism is to create wealth through *conciencia*'—a key word, the most repeated word in the language of the Cuban Revolution, meaning an amalgam of conscientiousness, commitment and consensus. The implication was that the old capitalist order was based on greed and selfishness, but in the new society people must work harmoniously for the common good. Abundance would flow from co-operative effort, and with it a humane lifestyle characterised by a sense of concern for one's fellow human beings.

IV THE EXTERNAL ENEMY AND THE COUNTER-REVOLUTION

As had been the case with many other revolutionary movements, the Castro-led regime derived great strength from the emotional effect of an external threat. Batista's hated regime had reflected many of the worst aspects of capitalism. The system by which all economic power had passed into the hands of a privileged élite, while the masses endured deprivation and poverty, could be directly linked with Cuba's dependence on US investment and the US market within the system of international capitalism.

The apparent evils of capitalism could be seen to be practised by the USA, which had virtually treated Cuba as an economic colony. The sugar crop, upon which Cuba's prosperity was so dependent, had been tightly controlled by a monopolistic structure linked to the American sugar quota. This system guaranteed profits for Cuban sugar interests, both growers (predominantly members of the pro-Batista oligarchy) and the refiners and exporters

SOURCE 12.4

Castro stresses that the people of a socialist society cannot simply expect wealth to be 'distributed', 1969

HISTORICAL CONTEXT: As was the case in many socialist revolutions, Castro discovered that it was not easy to achieve the successful application of the Marxist maxim 'from each according to his ability, to each according to his need'. He discovered that he needed to educate his people to the need to work to create wealth, and expressed his faith in the willingness of the people to rise to this challenge.

Source: **F. Castro, in a speech on 2 January 1969, the tenth anniversary of the triumph of the rebellion**

. . . The mirage of class society, of capitalist society, of full store windows, created for the masses the illusory idea that all that was necessary was to break the glass and distribute the riches. But the mirage was based on misery, on unemployment and under- *employment. And now the masses understand that riches must be created.*

At the beginning, our production did not grow— it decreased. And what we produced was in conditions of misery, sickness, hunger, evictions, dismissals. Cane was cut by hand, 15, 16, 17 hours a day. These bad conditions changed before we had the new machines, the new knowledge. From too much work, some substituted too little. Production went down to 3.8 million tonnes of sugar. But now it has changed . . . In Cuba, production in 1970 will be double that in 1958.

QUESTION

What fundamental problem associated with setting up a socialist society is highlighted in this extract from Castro's speech?

SOURCE 12.5

Castro claims that the Cuban Revolution has moral strength in its search for a 'higher society', 1968

HISTORICAL CONTEXT: To signal his commitment to the prolonged task of achieving a social revolution based on a new set of moral values, Castro sought to contrast the selfish individualistic values espoused by capitalism with the spirit of co-operation valued under communism. He claimed that he would never give up his faith in the ability of humankind to adopt this 'higher value' of co-operation, or what he called *conciencia*.

Source: **F. Castro, in a speech on 13 March 1968**

We cannot encourage or even permit selfish attitudes among men if we don't want them to be guided by the *instinct of selfishness, by the wolf, by the beast instinct . . . The concept of socialism and communism, the concept of a higher society, implies a man devoid of those feelings; a man who has overcome such instinct at any cost, placing, above everything, his sense of solidarity and brotherhood among men . . . If we are going to fail because we believe in man's ability, in his ability to improve, then we will fail; but we will never renounce our faith in mankind.*

QUESTION

How does this excerpt help to explain the success achieved by Castro and his Fidelistas?

(predominantly American or American-financed). But the mass of Cuban wage-earners and small farmers had been firmly excluded from a share in the benefits that flowed from Cuba's most productive enterprise.

The first emphasis in the Revolution was therefore upon the redress of the ill-effects of capitalism through the nationalisation of industries and the confiscation of American investments. Emotional tirades against US 'dollar imperialism' naturally enough brought American retaliation. The USA imposed a trade embargo on Cuban exports in 1961, and broke off diplomatic relations later in the same year. Castro and Guevara meanwhile indicated their intention to encourage the extension of the anti-capitalist revolution to the Dominican Republic, Venezuela, Bolivia and other neighbouring nations.

Alarmed by this threat to the stability of Hispanic America, the US Central Intelligence Agency moved to encourage a counter-revolution. In April 1961 a US-sponsored armed force of 1 400 anti-Castro Cuban exiles landed at Playa Giron (the Bay of Pigs) in an attempt to depose Castro. Despite CIA backing and American-supplied air support, the Bay of Pigs expedition proved to be a fiasco. Castro supporters rallied quickly to defeat the attempted invasion, taking 1 113 prisoners. The Americans had gravely under-estimated the degree of support enjoyed by Castro.

On the other hand, the event proved to be an enormous boost to Castro. The overt actions of the 'capitalist enemy' virtually validated the proclamation of Cuba as a socialist republic in the following month (May 1961). Castro was also able to combine his socialist policies with nationalism. He promoted the first few years of his new regime as a desperate struggle to restore the tarnished national honour of Cuba. The motto 'Fatherland or Death', used so successfully against Batista, was now applied to the external enemy, USA, and its capitalist associates. Che Guevara strenuously promoted the notion of a war against 'the enemy', by which he meant all the capitalist-aligned nations of Latin America,

as well as the USA. These were portrayed as the forces of counter-revolution, to be resisted through extreme effort and dedication.

In the emotional climate of animosity and suspicion that was a product of the Cold War tensions of the 1960s, the socialist-aligned Cubans naturally turned for help to the Union of Soviet Socialist Republics. The Soviets not only agreed to purchase the Cuban sugar crop but also granted Cuba a huge development loan at the low interest rate of 2.5 per cent (see above). Although Castro insisted that Cuba was a 'non-aligned' nation (an ally of neither the USSR or the USA), his trade connection with the USSR rapidly expanded into a military association that almost precipitated a third world war.

Because the Bay of Pigs invasion had been US-sponsored, Castro was arguably justified in seeking means of defending Cuba against another attack. It was natural, therefore, to turn to the USSR for military aid. Nikita Khrushchev, the Soviet leader, supplied Cuba with weapons and rockets, but among the latter were intermediate-range ballistic missiles capable of reaching any city in the USA—and they were stationed only 160 kilometres from American territory.

President Kennedy of the USA claimed that the presence of Russian missiles in Cuba destroyed the delicate balance of world security and could not be tolerated. He demanded the removal of the missiles, and took the additional risk in October 1962 of ordering the US navy to intercept Russian ships supplying Cuba, thus bringing the world to the brink of war. Eventually both sides backed away from the conflict; the USSR undertook to remove the missiles, but after insisting that the USA promise not to interfere with Castro's regime.

Both sides, of course, claimed victory, but for the Fidelistas it was a great emotional triumph. A small nation of 8 million people had defied their giant neighbour and former capitalist master, and won their point that they should be secure from US-sponsored attack. The USA moreover, had been forced to accept the presence of a communist (and therefore an unco-operative) State on its borders. This situation was what the USSR had refused to accept when Hungary attempted to dissociate itself from the Soviet satellite network in 1956.

Animosity towards the USA remained a basic feature of the Cuban Revolution for two decades after the initial missile crisis. Cuba's intensified association with the USSR, firstly as a market for sugar and a source of loans, later as a supplier of oil, exacerbated the tensions. Cuba joined COMECON (Council for Mutual Economic Assistance), the USSR-sponsored economic organisation, in 1972, and in 1976 it was announced that the Soviets would supply Cuba with a nuclear power plant.

Despite these developments, the Carter administration in 1977 lifted travel restrictions on Americans wishing to visit Cuba, and there were signs that a relaxation of animosity between the two nations could follow. This tentative move towards better relations was drastically reversed in 1979 when, after it was revealed that a Soviet combat brigade was stationed in Cuba, President Carter announced that, as a counter-measure, the USA would maintain a full-time military task force in the Caribbean and renew air surveillance of Cuba.

V EXPORTING THE REVOLUTION

The presence of the Argentinian Guevara within the *Fidelista* movement, and the broad anti-capitalist and anti-imperialist sentiments in the revolutionary proclamations, ensured that the revolutionary impulse would flow to other Latin American nations.

Once Castro was established in power, and committed to a state of economic dependence on the USSR, he turned his formidable energies to the advocacy of world communism. As did Mao Zedong in China, Castro stressed that true revolutionaries would not just wait for change to occur, but rather would seek it by action.

Castro deliberately cited his success in Cuba as a model for others to follow. In an address on 30 August 1966, he claimed that Cuba was the only nation at that time 'building socialism in Latin America', and the only nation that had 'freed itself completely from imperialism'. He went on to claim that other nations would follow Cuba's example:—that 'We are the banner and the banner will never be lowered.'

Che Guevara made the policy of 'exporting the revolution' his special interest, and quickly became the focal point for pro-socialist revolutionary movements in the region. It was while he was organising revolutionary insurrection in Bolivia that he met his death in 1967.

Cuban sponsorship of insurrection brought retaliation. In 1964 the OAS (Organisation of American States) voted to impose economic sanctions on Cuba. This brought further problems to Castro, for it meant he was denied supplies of oil from his neighbour, Venezuela, and had to turn to the USSR for oil supplies, increasing his dependence on that great power.

Attempts to foster left-wing revolutions in Latin America frequently brought the opposite effect. Salvador Allende, a Marxian socialist, was elected president of Chile in 1970 and embarked on a policy of extensive socialist reforms and nationalisation of industries, including the takeover of some US firms, for which no compensation was paid. As had been the case with Castro, Allende soon discovered that trade barriers were erected against Chile by capitalist countries. Like Castro, Allende turned to the USSR for help. By 1972 widespread middle-class disquiet concerning the trends of events under Allende led to a crisis of insecurity. In September 1973 the Chilean military staged a coup d'état, Allende was deposed, and Chile fell under extreme right-wing military rule, with General Pinochet as president. A militarist right-wing government also established control over Argentina. In both instances fear of the communist threat to property ownership had led to support for quasi-fascist anti-communist movements.

The Cuban prototype helped to generate a second socialist–communist state in Latin

In the early years of the Cuban Revolution, the Argentinian-born Ernesto ('Che') Guevara was Fidel Castro's major supporter as both a source of revolutionary proclamations and as an expert on guerrilla warfare. After the victory of the *Fidelistas*, he was for a time the second most influential person in the Cuban Revolutionary government. Here he is seen (centre) arriving in Beijing as leader of a Cuban Economic Delegation visiting China in November 1960.

America when, in 1979, the Batista-style Somoza family dictatorship in Nicaragua was deposed by the *Sandinistas*, guerrilla fighters of the *Fidelista* type. The parallels with the Cuban situation were strong: the *Sandinistas* derived their name from a charismatic guerrilla leader, Auguste Sandino, who, like Castro, had fought to liberate his people from élitist and military rule and from US economic dominance. Although he had been killed in 1934, the Sandino mystique had survived in the *Sandinista* movement, which in turn drew strength from the *Fidelista* example.

More significant than the 'export' of the revolution to other parts of Latin America was the Cuban involvement in Africa. In July 1974, after a revolution in Portugal had deposed a long-established right-wing government, the new Portuguese administration announced its intention of granting self-government to the Portuguese overseas colonies. A struggle for power between pro-socialist and pro-Western groups erupted in the colonies. In Portuguese Angola, for example, the Popular Movement for the Liberation of Angola (MPLA) adopted a Marxist policy and openly sought support from the USSR. Direct military aid for the Marxist socialist cause arrived in the form of some 7 000 Cuban troops, which assured the MPLA of victory.

The injection of Cuban troops into the African continent elicited vigorous protests from the USA and other Western powers, which branded the Cubans as 'surrogate Soviets', and interpreted the move as a dangerous intensification of **Cold War** tensions. Undeterred, the

Castro regime expanded its involvement in African affairs by sending troops to Malawi, Mozambique, Guinea, Cameroon, Ethiopia and Gabon. In March 1976 Castro visited many of the African nations to whom he was supplying military support. He stressed that the Cuban aid was a contribution to the communist world revolution for the liberation of exploited peoples from the dominance of capitalist imperialist practice. By the end of 1976, it was estimated that Cuba was sustaining over 20 000 troops in Africa; by 1978 there were somewhere between 34 000 and 50 000.

These activities by the Cubans brought them criticism from 'middle-power', non-aligned nations. At the conference of non-aligned nations at Belgrade in July 1978, which Cuba still claimed a right to attend, Cuba was called to account by Egypt and some other nations for its involvement in African affairs. In 1979, at a similar conference, Cuba was again accused (by

Yugoslavia) of having stepped outside the guidelines of non-alignment and non-interference.

Castro's policy of exporting the revolution had brought world-wide attention to a relatively small nation, and had publicised that aspect of the Cuban Revolution on which he had concentrated since the late 1960s—the promotion of the concept of world revolution.

VI THE OUTCOMES AND THE SIGNIFICANCE OF THE CUBAN REVOLUTION

The Uniqueness of the *Fidelistas'* success

As the first socialist revolution in the western hemisphere, the Cuban Revolution has been deeply analysed. Some commentators claim it is the first true communist revolution on the Marxist pattern because it was a genuine uprising

An enthusiastic rally of *Fidelistas*. Fidel Castro was cheered and feted by this huge rally of his supporters in Havana at the time of the unsuccessful US-sponsored attack on the Castro regime (in the notorious Bay of Pigs invasion) in 1961. The guerrilla-fighter ethos of the *Fidelistas* is clearly portrayed in the details of this photograph. What are these details?

by an exploited proletariat against capitalist overlords, and unlike the Russian, Chinese, Yugoslavian and most of the other revolutions claiming to be communist, there was no direct connection between the event and its supporters' involvement in either of the two world wars. Moreover, unlike Algeria, Vietnam or Indonesia, in which similar revolutions against capitalist dominance had occurred, Cuba was not a colony at the time of the Revolution.

Even this simple claim has to be modified. Cuba was highly urbanised, with more than 50 per cent of its population resident in urban areas. At first glance it might be assumed that a true city-based proletarian uprising on the Marxist plan had occurred. This was not so—the bulk of the fighting was done by rural workers. It was true, however, that many of the *Fidelistas* were landless wage-earners, working on the plantations, and could be defined as a type of proletariat.

Castro's achievement was different from that of the Bolsheviks in Russia in that in the attainment of the victory he was dependent almost entirely on his own charismatic leadership and the mystique associated with the 26 July Movement. There was no significant communist party organisation or party bureaucracy associated with the victory. Castro was to make use of a party structure after he attained power, but even then he chose to preserve his rural leadership image. It was symptomatic of this emphasis that he never gave up wearing the jungle fatigue uniform of the fighting *Fidelistas*, even after nearly forty years in power.

Castro's supporters stressed that his revolution was based on discovery of principles through action rather than theory, and by faith in will-power rather than in doctrinal blueprints. Castro liked to stress that the *Fidelistas* were acting outside all interests in the existing order, were primarily concerned with the restoration of Cuba's national honour, and were non-bureaucratic in style. 'The school of war', Fidel told farm workers in 1967, 'taught us how men [sic] can . . . accomplish many tasks when they apply themselves in a practical way . . . a small

nucleus of combatants developed into an army . . . and won the war without bureaucracy . . . And war taught us what man can do when he dedicates himself to working with enthusiasm, interest, and common sense'.

Although the Cuban Revolution was not launched by an intellectual élite on the Bolshevik pattern, in another sense it was very close to the Marxist model. It can be claimed that it was the first genuine revolution in a capitalist country staged without the impetus of an external war. The pre-Castro Cuban economy was capitalist in function, and most of the problems associated with uneven distribution of wealth stemmed from this fact. Many of the workers, both urban and rural, were wage-earners, and thus part of (or victims of) the capitalist system. There were virtually no elements of a feudal system remaining; there were very few subsistence peasants or land workers working leasehold or 'grace and favour' farms. This is not to say that poverty and misery were not widespread. Thousands of rural workers received wages for only part of the year according to the sugar season, and eked out a precarious existence otherwise. As wage-earners, however, they were proletarians rather than peasants, owing no feudal loyalties.

In some other nations that experienced revolutions, the ruling classes were bolstered by a social base of long-established feudal practice, which tended to give their rule a type of 'legitimacy'. Workers in this relationship found it hard to regard their former masters as being deposed. The sustained resistance by the counter-revolutionary White Russians to the Bolshevik takeover, and the amount of loyalty the White Russians attracted, is an example. No such apparently legitimate ruling class existed in Cuba. The profit-making enterprises were either US-owned or US-dominated. The ruling cliques were kept in power by a brutal militarist regime which enjoyed no popular sense of legitimacy and, despite its enormous military supremacy on paper, was ripe for overthrow by a vigorous nationalist movement.

Important too to the character of the

Revolution was that there was virtually no 'Indian problem' in Cuba. Cruelty, neglect and indifference to the original inhabitants on the part of the early Spanish colonists had resulted in their virtual disappearance as an identifiable ethnic group. All Cubans, white, black or of mixed race, were in 1959 essentially the descendants of immigrants. There was no native class able to 'claim' the Revolution on the grounds that they had been dispossessed by the later arrivals.

The absence of a sense of partnership between the Roman Catholic Church and the pre-Castro governments was another factor in their failure to attain legitimacy. The militarist regimes had neglected the Church, which neither supported the existing administration nor greatly influenced the masses. It had lost its influence as a conservative force. Cuba was thus capitalist and secular, and devoid of a sense of national loyalty to the existing system. The loyalty and the emotional commitment of the people were readily won over to the forces of revolution, which offered an alternative system of control. The politically conscious workers talked about anti-capitalism and anti-imperialism, and looked forward to a socialist society. The *Fidelistas* offered the leadership to make this possible.

When the victory came, the Castro administration quickly got on with the practical tasks of building a socialist society. It can be claimed that the new government more profoundly transformed the social structure than was the case in any other socialist revolution. In the first thirty years of the Castro regime scarcely any aspect of the old economic and social order remained intact in Cuba because of the virtual elimination of private ownership in the systems of production and distribution and the establishment of a centrally planned, publicly owned and managed economy. The total break with the US market aided this transformation.

Another distinguishing factor in the Castroist Revolution was that as Cuba had ceased to be a colony as far back as 1895, there was no 'mother country' from which military power could be brought to bear to counter the Revolution. Examples of this process include the French and Dutch obstruction of the nationalist revolutions in Vietnam and Indonesia respectively in the immediate post-World War II decade, and the British attempt to stop the American Revolution of 1776. Although there was no oppressive mother country to resist, there was, however, a former economic master to be despised.

The Revolution as a Leader of the Decolonisation Movement

The Cuban animosity towards the USA was virulent and severe. It was further intensified when the American-sponsored Bay of Pigs invasion of 1961 appeared to indicate that the USA would stop at nothing to overthrow the Castro regime. American interference (some would say bungled interference) served to ensure that the menace of American **neo-imperialism** remained a target against which the Revolution could be focused. Cubans saw themselves as an embattled society, striving to fulfil a noble cause against an evil opponent, which was guilty in their eyes of having persistently interfered in Cuban internal affairs in the profit-making interests of its own citizens.

The Cuban Revolution thus exerted great influence in the post-World War II era of decolonisation in that it provided a striking example of a successful revolution against **neo-colonialism**. A small nation had successfully defied the capitalist giant, providing an encouragement for other ex-colonies still enmeshed in the servitude of economic dependence that characterised the 'neo-colonialist' trap. For a few decades the small nation of Cuba assumed the ideological leadership of the **Third World**.

The Cuban Revolution additionally set an example to anti-imperialist movements in its young leadership and its display of success through guerrilla warfare. Castro was only thirty-two years of age in 1959. He and his even younger supporters became symbols of the power of youth to displace established authority figures, thus providing a role model for members of socialist movements in many of the newly emerging nations. Similarly, the success of Castro's guerrilla warfare tactics encouraged other revolutionary movements. Virtually all revolutions of the modern era have involved the use of violence. Castro's success, after taking on all the strength of a modern military government with (at first) only a tiny force of irregular volunteers, was inspirational to his imitators.

Balance Sheet: Failed Promises and Acknowledged Achievements

If a critic set out to compile a list of Castroist promises not kept, it could be noted that there have been no free elections, no tolerance of other political parties, and no opportunities for truly free expressions of opinion in the media. Cuban newspapers and radio stations are State-controlled and are prohibited from 'attacking the revolution'. Dissidents have been gaoled, as occurred under Batista. This is virtually the same practice of prohibiting opposition that led many dissenters to the guillotine in the French Revolution. There is also no independent judiciary. Most of these features of a democracy were fervently called for in Castro's 'History will absolve me' speech of 1953, but were never delivered. Through these denials of basic freedoms the Castro regime itself has acquired all the characteristics of a **totalitarian state**.

Supporters of Castro (who are still numerous among the older generations) refer with fervent pride to 'the achievements of the revolution', and list these as: the successful land reforms; the attainment of full employment in the years of the economic partnership with the USSR; the provision of education for all children and adults; and the creation of a very successful health and hospital system. Cholera and dysentery, common problems in Latin America, have been eliminated. Surgical care is available for all citizens. The overall standard of living is much higher than it was in pre-Castro days.

Finally, it must be noted that the Castroist Revolution has been unusual in that stability of leadership has prevailed. Although Castro at first attempted to operate behind the scenes, he

assumed the presidency in December 1976. Nor was this a one-man dictatorship; an elected National Assembly functioned from July 1976, albeit without opposition parties. Unlike the Stalin versus Trotsky quarrel in the USSR, or the Deng Xiaoping versus Gang of Four disagreements in China, the Cuban leadership of the Castro brothers—Fidel and Raul—has remained effective and unchallenged for almost forty years. After all those years, moreover, the leaders still wear the uniform of the guerrilla movement, serving always to remind their people and the watching world that they were, first and foremost, nationalist revolutionaries whose slogan was *Patria o Muerte*, and that they came to power without dependence on a bureaucratic party structure.

VII MODIFICATIONS TO THE CUBAN REVOLUTION: 1969–96

For thirty years the Cuban Revolution was cited by supporters of communist ideology as a model for communist-oriented reforms in Latin America. However, when the Eastern European communist regimes collapsed in 1989, and the USSR itself disintegrated in 1991, the Cuban government lost its support base, its subsidies and its markets. Castro and his supporters were virtually isolated in an uncooperative world.

Production of sugar, the nation's major export crop, plummeted drastically. Secondary industries also reduced their production levels because of lack of overseas markets. Export totals diminished to 30 per cent of the level enjoyed in the days of the Soviet subsidies. The people found that life became exceedingly miserable, bedevilled by shortages of most consumer goods. Fuel was in short supply. Rationing was introduced, even for basic food items. Thousands of Cubans (30 000 in 1994 alone) attempted to flee the country, striving to reach the USA. Castro did not attempt to prevent this, regarding it as one way of solving food shortages, and tacitly approving

Source 12.1

the departure of people who were not true supporters of the Revolution.

A possible solution to Cuba's problems lay in the lifting of the US trade embargo. If this were done, so the theory ran, US investments would reinvigorate the tourist trade and other industries. The US Congress, however, remained adamant that the compensation payments for all the confiscations of US property back in 1959 were still to be paid. The US government further argued that US companies would sue any companies from other nations if they acquired Cuban-based properties that had been under American ownership before the Revolution. This served to discourage other nations from investing in Cuba.

The United Nations General Assembly in October 1994 attempted to influence the USA by voting 101 to 2 (the USA and Israel) to have the embargo lifted. The USA held its position despite this level of disapproval, stressing that to lift the embargo would amount to 'legitimising' the Castro regime. Thus there is little chance that the USA will change its policy until there are major constitutional reforms in Cuba and Castro steps down or dies.

In 1993 Castro nevertheless contrived to attract US capital into Cuba by authorising the use of the American dollar in trade transactions. This made it easy for the approximately 2 million Cuban exiles in the USA to send money to relatives in Cuba, and for the latter, in turn, to be able to purchase items on world markets in American currency.

The most difficult step for Castro to make, however, was to admit that his form of communism (in which private enterprise was virtually forbidden, and citizens could not employ other citizens) had to be modified. In 1993 he made the great ideological leap and listed 135 occupations in which citizens were permitted to 'work for themselves'. By 1995, 170 000 Cubans held licences to operate in this manner. It was hoped that the incentives these people could now identify would generate an attitude of mind different from that prevalent under the pure communist system, in which each individual expected that 'the State would provide'.

In 1995 Castro announced another nineteen new fields in which self-employment was permitted. He maintained a prohibition on university-trained professionals accepting any employment other than that of working for the government, on the grounds that their publicly-funded education obliged them to return the benefit through community service.

In September 1995 Castro took another major step towards partnership with capitalism by inviting foreign investors to become full owners of businesses in Cuba. (Prior to 1995, foreign investors were accepted only as minority partners in joint ventures with the Cuban government.) The major restriction on this means of expanding foreign investment was the denial of access by foreigners to 'strategic' businesses connected with national security, defence, education and public health. The foreign firms were also prohibited from hiring Cuban workers of their own choice. Rather, they received workers allocated by State-managed employment agencies. The communist ethos that the State controls the individual was thus sustained.

As an additional incentive to foreign investors, Castro guaranteed that foreign-owned properties will not be expropriated without compensation (as had happened to the American companies in 1959). Ironically, this assurance reintensified the US insistence on the trade embargo which is specifically designed to elicit the long-delayed compensation for the 1959 expropriations.

With a 1995 population of 11 million, and with a high potential for both tourism and agricultural produce, Cuba could regain a reasonable measure of prosperity within a few years if the economic reforms succeed. Foreign investment could help the workers by creating thousands of jobs and injecting new currency into the spending cycle, but Castro's insistence that Cuba remain a communist society has delayed this process.

In 1995 Fidel Castro was still only sixty-seven years of age and apparently in good health. He continued to insist that, despite the

In 1995 Fidel Castro asserted his place in the ranks of the world's leaders by attending the fiftieth anniversary celebrations of the United Nations Organisation, thirty-six years after his attainment of power in Cuba. In a surprising adjustment to his long-established image, he appeared in a lounge suit instead of in his army fatigues. In this photograph he is pictured conversing with Boris Yeltsin, president of Russia, ironically one of the major influences in the dismantlement of the USSR and the consequent cancellation of the favourable trade relations Cuba once enjoyed with the Soviet bloc countries.

openings for a measure of capitalist enterprise, he was, like the Pragmatist leaders of Communist China, still managing a communist society. In March 1995, in an address to the party faithful, he said: 'we are not going to create a capitalist society . . . here revolutionaries are in power . . .

this is a government of workers for workers'.

It was evident in 1995 that millions of younger people, well informed of the standards of consumer goods and luxury items available in the USA and South American nations, were dissatisfied with the Castro regime. They particularly resented the restrictions on freedom of expression, and the terms of imprisonment that punish outspoken dissenters. Many called themselves 'slaves' of the system, and demanded greater freedoms.

Among the older generations a deep pool of respect and admiration for Fidel Castro survives. They are proud that the *Fidelistas* freed the nation from the foreigners who owned the hotels, banks, fuel companies, casinos and sugar plantations, and who exploited the poor and weak. They remember when poor people were denied education and did not have access to hospitals and health care. They remember the relatively good days when the Soviet subsidies ensured that the communist system appeared to be able to provide a reasonable standard of living for all.

IMPORTANT EVENTS IN THE CUBAN REVOLUTION 1898–93

1898 Cuba won independence from Spain after the Spanish–American War. Declared a protectorate of the USA.

1901 Platt Amendment attached to the Cuban constitution gave the USA the 'right to intervene' to ensure stable government in Cuba

1906–09 Second US intervention

1917–22 Third US intervention

1934–40 Fulgencio Batista (an army sergeant) controlled Cuba through puppet governments

1940–44 Batista officially held power as president

1952 After permitting two civilian presidencies, Batista again took power as president

1953 Fidel Castro led an insurrection against the Batista government at the Moncada Barracks. At his trial Castro made the later famous speech entitled 'History will absolve me'.

1955 Castro and some of his followers were released from prison, and went into exile in Mexico

1956 The *Fidelistas* returned to invade Cuba, and set up a base in the Sierra Maestra mountains in southern Cuba

1959 After three years of conflict, the *Fidelistas* achieved effective control of Cuba. Batista fled into exile. Castro assumed the office of premier under Dr Manuel Urrutia as president.

1960 Castro expropriated all US-owned businesses in Cuba, beginning with sugar mills and oil refineries

In retaliation, the USA cut Cuban sugar imports, depriving Cuba of its single largest market for its single largest product

Castro concluded trade agreements with the USSR and Communist China, and received a massive loan from the USSR

1961 The USA imposed a total trade embargo on Cuba

The American CIA supported an invasion of Cuba by Cuban exiles in an attempt to depose Castro. This was the infamous Bay of Pigs episode, which failed in its objective but brought US–Cuban relations to breaking point.

1962 Castro agreed to the placement of Soviet ballistic missiles in Cuba. This in turn led to a US naval blockade on Cuba and the US demand that the USSR remove the missiles. This crisis almost triggered off World War III. Eventually the USSR agreed to remove the missiles provided the USA promised not to sponsor any further attacks on the Castro regime.

1963 After the missile crisis, Castro continued to stage his planned social revolution. All private property was expropriated, and the government introduced communist-style reforms aimed at ending unemployment, creating a free public education system and an effective public health programme. Dissenters, however, were repressed and imprisoned. The earlier promise of freedom of expression was not fulfilled.

1972 The US Foreign Claims Settlement Commission certified claims by US companies for compensation of expropriated property amounting to US $1 500 million

1993 Castro responded to the difficulties his economy had encountered through the collapse of the USSR and the ending of Soviet subsidies by reintroducing private enterprise in specified industries and occupations

---

chapter thirteen

Revolutions Reviewed

Common to all revolutions is a stated desire to build an improved society. Equally common to all such attempts is a degree of 'shortfall' between the hope and the attainment. Basic also to most revolutions is a striving for a group identity—as a nation liberated from the intrusions and interferences of other nations, or as a society released from burdens imposed by an anachronistic and exploitative authority.

The topics selected for the earlier chapters of this book have addressed only some of the major revolutions of the modern world. It is interesting to observe that 'fashions change' in terms of what events are called revolutions and which revolutions are recommended for study. The Fascist and Nazi seizures of power in the 1920s and 1930s in Italy and Germany respectively were often called revolutions at the time, but are seldom so described today. Other events undergoing redefinition are the **anti-colonial** revolutions of the post-World War II period and the associated nationalist revolutions in many nations—Indonesia and Vietnam being but two examples of particular relevance to Australian students. Even the momentous events which culminated in the attainment of independence by India and Pakistan, it could be argued, might qualify to be called revolutions.

Historians seldom claim that 'History repeats itself'. They do, however, look for similarities or parallels in historical events, and attempt to ascertain whether or not certain causative factors are 'necessary conditions' preceding an event. They likewise seek parallels in terms of outcomes or repercussions.

Theme Questions

➤ Is it possible to identify some common features that were operative in the societies in which major modern political and social revolutions have occurred?

➤ Are there obvious reasons for the fact that in some societies major changes occurred peacefully whilst, in other societies, they appeared to require the impetus of violent change?

➤ Is there an identifiable sequence of events characteristic of most political revolutions of modern times?

I REBELLION OR REVOLUTION?

The features that distinguish a rebellion from a revolution have been outlined in Chapter Two. In a rebellion a new ruling group may emerge, but the basic characteristics of the society may not have changed. In a revolution, however, the administrative organisation and social structures are drastically altered, or at least the intention exists to have them altered. A rebellion, if it succeeds, can therefore be seen as a process of overthrowing and replacing a ruling group; a revolution is a process of overthrowing a ruling group and then attempting to build a new and different society.

Successfully staged revolutions are usually dependent upon a great sense of discontent, possibly bordering on desperation, among the general population, together with a policy or promise of a reformed society, provided by an educated group. Mass support for change is thus one factor in success; the other is a sense of belief in and commitment to a new ideology, together with the leadership and organisation this belief generates. Intellectual leaders, usually influenced by foreign teachings or example, are basic to successful revolutions. This can be observed in the French, Russian, Chinese and Cuban revolutions.

It is sometimes claimed that the populace will rise to support a revolution when people's misery and desperation is so extreme that they 'have nothing to lose but their chains', to use Marx's expression. It would seem, however, that other elements are necessary: the expectation of success associated with the promise of better conditions, and a 'breaking point' created by a crisis.

The French, Russian and Chinese masses all endured incredible hardships for decades, with only occasional protests and uprisings. The revolutions came when some concessions had already been granted, and a crisis offered the opportunity to demand more. In all three instances a 'window-dressing' parliament or assembly had been convened, but had not been given real power. In all three instances also, a crisis of financial extremity, war or dynastic inheritance added another factor of instability.

If a study is made of several revolutions, a student may be able to identify several common 'causes' of revolutions. A word of caution is appropriate at this point, however, because it can be easily assumed that because certain events did occur before a revolution, they were indispensable influences in the creation of the revolution. While these events may have made the revolution more likely, they are not necessarily essential conditions for revolution.

Successful revolutions can, however, usually be associated with three basic conditions. Firstly, the 'project'—the proposed formula for a reorganisation of society—must be well understood and *believed in* by the potential leaders of the revolution. Zeal is indispensable to success. The project need not be a detailed plan for rebuilding (the *Fidelistas* of Cuba, for example, had no such plan), but the basic intention to *achieve* reform must unify the revolutionaries. Secondly, the project must have visible *relevance* to large numbers of people. The revolutionaries must 'win over' the mass of the populace either before their seizure of power or very shortly after it. Thirdly, the outgoing regime must have surrendered its 'right to rule' and, with it, the loyalty of a significant proportion of the people. The 'old order' must be losing social control, perhaps through being weak, corrupt or viciously cruel, or from a depletion of the repressive forces which previously made revolution unattainable. A repressive army, for example, is useless protection for a tyrannical ruler if the bulk of the personnel are ready to desert to the opposition.

II CAUSES OF REVOLUTION AND COUNTER-REVOLUTION IN MODERN TIMES

Before any revolution can be so acclaimed, the very idea of a revolution must exist and must be regarded by a significant number of the people as attainable. It is significant that the word itself is used in the English-speaking world only for events of relatively modern times. One of the most significant upheavals in British history— some would say the greatest—was the execution of King Charles I as an accused traitor and tyrant, and the eleven years of non-monarchical rule that followed under Oliver Cromwell as

Lord Protector of 'the Commonwealth' (1649–60). Yet this series of events is still usually referred to as the 'Civil War', or sometimes the 'Great Rebellion', but not as a revolution, largely because Cromwell ruled as a 'substitute monarch' (being offered the crown himself).

For most of recorded history humankind believed that the authority to rule came from God. In some societies, ancient Egypt for example, the rulers themselves were acclaimed as gods. This belief was the basis of the feudal system that functioned throughout Europe and Britain. In British terms, it was called the divine right of kings. In China a similar concept was expressed in the idea that the emperors ruled by a mandate of heaven.

The patience of God or the gods, however, was a variable factor in this belief. In some societies 'divine right' meant that the monarch could do no wrong. In other societies a provision applied: if the divinely appointed ruler proved to be delinquent or corrupt in performing his office, he could be challenged, and if necessary deposed. In Chinese society it was thought that if the emperor was forfeiting the mandate of heaven, certain signs and portents (floods, earthquakes and the like) would indicate this and rebellion would be thus encouraged.

In some European societies the nobility assumed the right to 'manage' the monarch and place limits upon his power. One such contract was the English Magna Carta (Great Charter) of 1215, by which King John recognised and defined certain rights of the barons, clergy and freemen of the realm.

The application of the principle that a community's leaders could reject the authority of a monarch was demonstrated on the occasion of the secession of the United Netherlands from Spanish rule in July 1581. In their statement justifying separation, the Dutch leaders claimed that Phillip II of Spain was no longer fit to govern them. Similarly, the leaders of the parliamentary forces in the English civil wars of 1642–49 justified their execution of King Charles I by accusing him of being a traitor and a tyrant, guilty of misgoverning the people and

causing loss of life in the wars. One of their spokesmen, William Goffe, claimed that the king's misuse of power had acted 'against the Lord's cause and people in these poor nations'.

Such denials and rejections of authority were the precursors of similar claims in the American and French revolutions. This principle is also encapsulated in the saying: 'when governments become traitors, honest men become revolutionaries'.

It is noteworthy that the word 'revolution' was introduced into common usage in the English language for the so-called Glorious Revolution of 1688–89, when King James II was deposed and forced into exile, and his daughter Mary, together with her husband, William of Orange (a Dutch principality), were installed on the British throne as joint monarchs. This exchange of monarchs was a remarkably peaceful affair, characterised by a lack of bloodshed or violence (hence the term 'glorious'), but significant in that the newly constituted monarchy of Britain was clearly validated by the will of parliament rather than by divine right. Thus was instituted a **constitutional monarchy**, a model that other nations in time also sought to adopt.

The Will of the People

With the advent of the modern era there emerged the additional revolutionary factor known as the 'general will' or 'the will of the people'. American colonists, justifying their revolution against British rule, stressed that governments must derive 'their just powers from the consent of the governed', and that if a government becomes 'destructive to these ends it is the right of the people to alter or abolish it'.

In France this concept developed even greater potency in the widespread acceptance of the argument made by Jean-Jacques Rousseau that 'the general will . . . is the source of the laws . . . for all members of the State'. The theory of revolution had acquired the power of the masses, as was vividly demonstrated in the Jacobin phase of the French Revolution.

In 1791 Thomas Paine, writing in defence

SOURCE 13.1

Leaders of a Dutch separatist movement claim that if a prince becomes a tyrant, he can be deposed, 1581

HISTORICAL CONTEXT: The region now known as Holland, or the Netherlands, was in the sixteenth century part of the territories ruled by the King of Spain. As most of the Dutch people had converted to Protestantism, and the Spanish king, Philip II, was insistent on the enforcement of Roman Catholic religious practice, several leaders of the Dutch provinces decided, in 1579, to proclaim the secession of what they called the 'United Netherlands' from Spain. This was effectively an identical situation to that which occurred when the American colonies proclaimed their independence from Britain in 1776. It could therefore be called the 'Dutch Revolution'.

The justification for secession, issued by the Dutch leaders in 1581, provides an early example of the claim that a revolution against a tyrannical ruler is justifiable.

Source: **Leaders of the Dutch secessionist movement, quoted in C.V. Wedgwood,** *William the Silent: William of Nassau, Prince of Orange 1533–1584*, **Jonathon**

Cape, London, 1944, p. 224

. . . A prince is constituted by God to be ruler of a people, to defend them from oppression and violence, as the shepherd his sheep; and whereas God did not create the people slaves to their prince, to obey his commands, whether right or wrong, but rather the prince for the sake of the subjects, to love and support them as a father his children, or a shepherd his flock . . . and when he does not behave thus but . . . oppresses them, seeking opportunities to infringe their ancient customs, exacting from them slavish compliance, then he is no longer a prince but a tyrant, and they may not only disallow his authority, but legally proceed to the choice of another prince for their defence.

QUESTIONS

1 This statement offers a surprising variation on the principle of the divine right of monarchs. What is said to be God's intention?

2 Why do the authors stress that they can 'legally' proceed to choose another prince?

3 What is the Chinese equivalent of this situation?

---

of the American and French revolutions, added an ingredient to revolutionary theory by stating that: 'What we now see in the world, from the Revolutions of America and France, are a renovation of the natural order of things, a system of principles as universal as truth and the existence of man, and combining moral with political happiness and national prosperity.' All potential revolutions gained authenticity if they could activate this claim to be applying 'universal principles' and seeking the 'natural order'.

In the mid-nineteenth century, with the publication of *The Communist Manifesto* (1848) and the subsequent writings of Karl Marx and Friedrich Engels, the theory of revolution gained two additional elements: a theory of inevitability and a prediction of permanence.

Marx claimed that the revolution to overthrow the capitalist system was certain to come: 'its (capitalism's) fall, and the victory, of the proletariat are equally inevitable', he claimed.

Marx's argument continued with the prediction that because the sequence of conflicts between rival classes, which had ranged over centuries, would end (according to the Marxian predictions) with the establishment of a classless society, the socialist-communist revolution would be *permanent*. The reformed society that would be built after the proletarian seizure of power would ensure an even distribution of wealth and the elimination of suffering and exploitation.

Marxian theories on the nature of revolution came under question and challenge, however, at the time of the successful seizure of power by the Bolsheviks in Russia in 1917. This event was clearly neither a manifestation of the 'general will' of the people nor an application of the Marxian theory of the inevitable uprising of the proletariat. Although Marxian theory was applied in later years to explain the Bolshevik Revolution, at the time it was not a spontaneous uprising of the working-class masses. Rather, it was a seizure of power through quasi-military tactics by a small, determined group. Lenin did, of course, seek the support of the proletariat, and through the use of slogans such as 'all power to the soviets' made the Revolution appear to be a genuine working-class uprising.

Despite the fact that the events of the October–November 1917 Russian Revolution did not quite fit the Marxian pattern, it was a spectacular and earth-shaking event which succeeded in inducing the 'tremblings' in the European property-owning classes that Marx had predicted. It provided an impulse for other socialist revolutions around the globe, and was used to establish the Marxist-Leninist theory of revolution as both a means of destroying old regimes and a formula for creating a reformed and egalitarian society on a permanent basis.

Right-wing Revolutions

Whenever a major reform of society is proposed or launched, people previously advantaged feel threatened. Lenin's and Stalin's successes in Russia and the USSR elicited opposition throughout Europe. Many millions of people, particularly property-owners and practising Christians, feared and opposed Marxist–Leninist communism. Right-wing movements emerged to counter the Leninist threat, and where they succeeded in forming a government, their seizure of power could also logically be called revolutions. Although the term is not

---

SOURCE 13.2
An Australian university professor tells school pupils that the Nazi seizure of power in Germany is a 'first-class revolution', 1933

HISTORICAL CONTEXT: From the time of the successful Bolshevik Revolution in 1917, fear prevailed among the property-owning and Christian sectors of Western societies. They envisaged that if a communist revolution occurred in their country, their property and even their lives would be at risk. From 1922 onwards there was widespread tacit approval of the political achievements of the Fascist leader, Benito Mussolini, in Italy. The Fascist movement was specifically devoted to countering the appeal of communism.

When the Nazi Party came to power in Germany in early 1933, those opposed to the communist ideology welcomed the event, anticipating that the Nazi Party would also act as a counterforce to communism. The Australian history professor quoted here regarded the Nazi takeover as a 'revolution'.

Source: Sydney Morning Herald, **Sydney, 22 April 1933**
. . . Professor A.H. Charteris, speaking yesterday afternoon to pupils of Fort Street Boys' High School (Sydney) on conditions in Germany, said that the boys would be able to tell their grandchildren that they had lived through a first-class revolution and a most extraordinary one. 'The ease with which the revolution went through surprised even the Nazis themselves,' Professor Charteris said. Hitler, however, was 'not in the same street' as Mussolini.

QUESTIONS
1 Why might Professor Charteris have used the term 'first-class revolution'?
2 Does the professor appear to approve or disapprove of the event? Why?
3 What reasons might you advance to explain why the professor regarded Hitler as not being 'in the same street' as Mussolini?

often applied to Fascist Italy or Nazi Germany today, both these movements were often referred to as 'revolutions' at the time.

Both Mussolini and Hitler made extensive use of the myth of a revolutionary movement. Mussolini organised his seizure of power in the so-called 'March on Rome', in which very few people actually marched. Hitler created a myth around the unsuccessful Munich *putsch* of 1923, from which the brown-shirt movement derived and fostered a mystique associated with a group of revered martyrs. Hitler's book, *Mein Kampf* (My Struggle), was also revolutionary in emphasis. His struggle, as he portrayed it, was to redress the wrongs imposed upon Germany by the victors of World War I, and to find the *Lebensraum* (living space) for the superior Aryan race—another myth.

Revolutions Based on Self-determination

During World War I the president of the USA, Woodrow Wilson, sponsored a proposal for a peace settlement. One of the key principles he advocated was the right of every nation 'to determine its own institutions'. Implied in this general principle, and then specifically detailed in many of the 'Fourteen Points' in relation to existing colonial territories and parts of the former Habsburg, Ottoman and Russian empires, was the right of a distinct ethnic group to form its own nation. In one sense this was a restatement of the basis on which the United States of America had itself claimed its nationhood; it was not a new idea. Nevertheless, this principle of 'self-determination' was reactivated at the time of the 1919 peace conferences, and in the following years became the basis for numerous nationalist revolutions around the world.

Even while World War I was still raging, the Irish people staged a rebellion (the Easter Rising of 1916) against British rule—one of the earliest of the twentieth-century wars of national self-determination. Ireland's subsequent achievement of independence in 1922 was unusual in that it was the only example of secession from a victor of the First World War. The word 'revolution' was not used to describe this event,

although had it occurred in the 1980s it might well have been so described.

During the nineteenth century there had been many examples of wars and rebellions leading to the establishment of new national identities. Greece and Belgium are examples. Italy and Germany also witnessed struggles for unification, generally welcomed at the time by other nations. Yet, strangely enough, these were seldom called revolutions, despite the fact that the earlier American and French revolutions were similar movements for national unity. The Italian and German unification movements did not, however, involve breaking away from an empire, or the forced abdication of a monarch. By the 1870s the emphasis in the use of the term 'revolution' referred to social change rather than military effort.

In the peace settlements after World War I, several new nations—Poland, Czechoslovakia and Yugoslavia among them—were created. In theory each of these three nations was a homeland for an ethnic group previously disadvantaged by having been locked into a large dynastic empire. Each, on paper, was a shining example of the just application of the principle of self-determination. In 1996, some seventy-six years after the creation of these nations, not one of them remains as it was in 1919. Poland's frontiers were drastically changed again after World War II, and the other two nations have fragmented into smaller units as a result of ethnic rivalries and hatreds.

The births of these new nations were not called revolutions at the time, but they opened the way to the acknowledgment of 'national self-determination' as a type of revolution involving the reshaping of society and the creation of a new community. Accordingly, the post-World War II examples of national groups seeking self-determination have often been called revolutions. The Indonesian battle for independence against Dutch colonialism and the Vietnamese nationalist war against French domination are examples. These events fulfilled many of the acknowledged characteristics of a revolution in that they involved the overthrow of the existing order by popular movements, and promised a rebuilt, equitable, just society.

Guerrilla Warfare in Modern Revolutions

The post-1945 era brought to prominence another component of the theory of revolution: the utilisation of guerrilla ('little war') warfare. The concept originated with the Spanish groups opposing Napoleon in 1808, but did not play a significant part in the Russian Revolution. It achieved significance in China, however, when the forces led by Mao Zedong adopted guerrilla tactics to harass both the Guomindang and the Japanese. Mao fused the technique of guerrilla war with the ideology of Marxism, and published a book on the subject. The Vietnamese similarly adopted guerrilla techniques as an integral part of their revolution. Vo Nguyen Giap, a prominent lieutenant of Ho Chi Minh, published *People's War, People's Army*, a justification of the technique.

In 1958–59 the success of Fidel Castro's followers in using guerrilla warfare to depose an apparently entrenched military dictatorship greatly boosted the status of this path to revolution. In 1961 Che Guevara's *La Guerra de Guerrillas*, an infectiously zealous text of guerrilla tactics, further added to the legend, providing in effect a 'handbook' for insurgency methods. Castro and Guevera thus built up what amounted to a tradition of guerrilla warfare, and promoted it in other Latin American and African nations through their practice of 'exporting the revolution'.

Counter-revolution

One of the laws of physics is 'that for every action there is an equal and opposite reaction'. In this sense 'reaction' means 'counter-action'. In every major revolution of modern times a similar effect is observable in what is called the 'counter-revolution'. During the French Revolution the counter-revolution was so effective that for prolonged periods large areas of France were acting in total defiance of the Parisian-based government. In the case of the Bolshevik Revolution, it could be argued that while the

first counter-revolution was extinguished in the Civil War of 1918–21, the truly effective counter-revolution did not occur until 1991, when the USSR was disbanded. In this instance the rejection of communist ideology and practices came from within the prevailing bureaucracy. Boris Yeltsin and his supporters, who dissolved the Communist Party and introduced a market-driven economy, were themselves former officials of the party.

The events in China demonstrated that the labels of 'revolution' and 'counter-revolution' are very subjective. What may be regarded as a counter-revolution from one point of view may well be regarded as the true revolution from another. Thus in China the Guomindang-led Nationalist Revolution of 1911–37 was hailed by their supporters as the true revolution— achieving the termination of the Manchu Dynasty and the introduction of reform policies to create a modern state. The campaigns waged by the Mao Zedong-led Communist Party were seen by the Guomindang as a counter-revolution. With the victory of the Communist Party in 1949 the official position changed: the Communist victory and administration now constituted 'the Revolution'. The year 1949 was permanently identified as the 'year of liberation'.

Subsequent events in China generated further complications in the matter of perceptions of counter-revolution. The modernisation policy sponsored by Deng Xiaoping and his fellow Pragmatists, with its emphasis on trade with capitalist nations and the free operation of market forces, was such a drastic departure from the policies and practices of Mao Zedong that dedicated Maoists could readily label it as a counter-revolution. But this policy had been sponsored from within the Communist Party, and had been accompanied by renewed lip-service pronouncements of continued commitment to communism.

Deng Xiaoping on the other hand used the term 'counter-revolution' to condemn the student-led demands for democratic political practices that resulted in the massacre in and around Tienanmen Square in May 1989. On

Map 4.2

9 June 1989 Deng publicly praised the work of the People's Liberation Army in suppressing 'counter-revolutionaries attempting to overthrow the CCP'. This vividly demonstrated that what is or is not a counter-revolution largely depends on the frame of reference of the commentator.

In the instance of Cuba, the scale and effectiveness of a potential counter-revolution has varied greatly. So popular was the *Fidelistas'* victory (and so unpopular was the deposed Batista regime) that for the first two years after Castro's victory there was little evidence of a counter-revolutionary movement. By 1961, however, a significant number of victims of Castro's property expropriations had gathered in the southern states of the USA. Encouraged, financed and supported by the US Central Intelligence Agency, a force of 1 200 of these Cuban exiles landed in southern Cuba in April 1961 with the long-term objective of deposing Castro. They expected to gather support from anti-Castro elements on the island, but such support was not forthcoming and the attempt to initiate a counter-revolution failed.

In the 1990s thousands of Cubans fled the country because of economic hardship. In terms of the sheer size of the exiled Cuban community, mostly based in the USA, the potential for a counter-revolutionary force existed. However, some of the other elements necessary for the mounting of a revolution—such as an intellectual leadership promoting a new ideology and a viable alternative government—did not emerge. Meanwhile, Castro himself was gradually altering the nature of the economic management of Cuba, permitting some foreign investment and encouraging some market forces. As a result, the likelihood of counter-revolution was reduced.

III OBSTACLES TO REVOLUTION

In a society in which the constitutional processes exist for the people to vote for a change in government, and to select from political parties offering alternative policies, revolution is unlikely because it is not necessary. The British and Australian multi-party election systems are examples of this opportunity to effect changes by evolution rather than revolution, although it is significant to remember that even in Britain it was necessary to stage a political revolution (that of 1688) to establish a constitutional monarchy as a step towards the later implementation of multi-party democracy.

For the thousands of years in which the feudal system operated, as well as in most modern authoritarian societies, it was not easy for discontented masses to launch a revolution. The governing power usually could thwart any attempt to use force to destroy its authority, most notably by using its own army and police force. Simple opposition or dissatisfaction with the existing regime was not enough to bring about a change in government, particularly if the right to vote had not been awarded to the masses. Poverty, oppression and the denial of what are now regarded as basic human rights will not necessarily produce a revolution.

An authoritarian society can adopt many policies to obstruct the likely emergence of revolutionary initiative. Ignorance among the masses can be one of the safeguards against the spread of propaganda, so if the education policy is one which prevents the growth of a literate and thinking working class, change in society is made unlikely. Severe censorship laws, combined with extreme indoctrination programmmes, can further enforce this barrier to revolution. The effects of such inhibiting elements could be observed in Tsarist Russia and in both Manchu China and Maoist China.

Fear and terror—the use of secret police, imprisonment without trial, execution of troublemakers—is the proven way of combating groups plotting the overthrow of a dictator. Such tactics, however, can produce a counter-action in the form of assassination attempts launched against the ruling classes by the dissidents.

Distracting the masses from the defects of the administration can also be effective. National emergencies involving war against an 'aggressive neighbour' and grandiose national festivals or religious celebrations may be generated for this purpose. When the very existence of the nation appears to be under threat from an external enemy, extreme demands can be placed upon the people to remain loyal. Dissidents can then be labelled as 'traitors', and summarily imprisoned or executed. This feature can be observed in the French, Bolshevik, Chinese and Cuban revolutions.

In theory, an impending revolution can also be avoided if the reforms the people most desire are in fact given, thus making a revolution unnecessary and preserving the existing social order. In practice—again observable in several of the cases named above—it is when some reforms are conceded that the demand for more becomes intense, and the likelihood of a rebellion preceding a revolution correspondingly increases.

While the key groups—the military officers, government officials, public servants and property-owners—remain united in loyalty to the regime, dissatisfaction alone will not produce revolution. The defection of some of these groups, usually as a result of the successful promotion of a new ideology by an intellectual class, is necessary before a revolution can be successful.

In many instances a key factor is the introduction to a society of new ideas from foreign sources. The French soldiers returning from helping the infant USA in the War of Independence, and the Russian troops who journeyed right across Europe to Paris in the war against Napoleon are two examples of this. In the long run, however, as Mao Zedong was reported as saying, 'power grows out of the barrel of a gun'. A revolution will not occur in an authoritarian society until the opponents of the regime acquire military strength and a supportive populace, usually aided, in the period of extreme crisis, by troops deserting from the defeated government.

IV AN IDENTIFIABLE SEQUENCE OF EVENTS?

There are three major phases in most political revolutions: (a) a process of decay; leading to (b) violent action and sudden change; followed by (c) recovery and rebuilding. Further examination of these phases in historical cases can, perhaps, lead to the identification of the following more detailed sequence of events:

1 A run-down in the efficiency of the old regime, and a loss of faith in it, even among the groups which are in favour of, and benefit from, its policies.

2 A wavering in the resolution of the governing dynasty or ruling group, often accompanied by indications of a sense of 'guilt' about past events and existing policies.

3 Educated leaders of the society expose the weaknesses and the lack of justification of the regime, and propose a 'better society' based on radically different ideologies.

4 Token efforts at reform are attempted but achieve little. The projected reforms alarm the former supporters of the regime, who therefore consider seizing power themselves. On the other hand, the reformers are also not satisfied. These concessions on the part of the old regime are usually offered too late to counter the move towards revolution, and are in fact possibly a signal to the revolutionaries to proceed to violent action.

5 With perhaps the added factor of an economic or military crisis, a 'paralysis of government' may occur, in which the old government virtually ceases to function.

6 The revolution (in the sense of the actual seizure of executive functions) now occurs, usually involving violence, but sometimes with little force necessary because even the bureaucracy (and perhaps the army) of the old regime is ready to accept change.

7 Moderate reformers may attempt to govern, but the various factions that previously acted in unison to overthrow the old regime now begin to quarrel among themselves, resulting in different groups claiming the right to govern. This may lead to further disorder, and perhaps civil war. The condition of order and stability, desired by the masses, is not attained.

8 External aggression may now also become

a factor. Neighbouring nations or regimes, sympathetic to the old regime, may attempt to interfere in order to suppress a movement that could endanger them.

9 The 'external threat' aids the more extreme groups leading the revolution, who can now whip up enthusiasm and repress dissenting groups with the assertion that those who do not co-operate are 'traitors' to the revolution. The threat of invasion can justify the continued exercise of power by the extremists, who will therefore sustain the 'war scare' as long as possible. This phase is very evident in both the French and Russian revolutions. One of the groups which opposed the former regime emerges as the new governing authority; other parties are suppressed.

10 An outgrowth of the 'war scare' phase is often a 'terror' phase, in which former ruling classes are accused of aiding the external enemies of the revolution. Purges and trials of 'traitors to the revolution' were common to the French, Russian and Chinese revolutions, in all of which the availability of scapegoats for the pent-up anger of the masses was an important factor in the consolidation of the revolution.

11 A return to less extreme leadership may ensue. This could perhaps be delayed for several decades, as in the case of the USSR, where Stalin sustained extremely repressive features of the phase described above for about thirty years. Under the more moderate leadership, the prestige and status of the founders of the revolution may be maintained, but compromises may be reached between surviving features of the old order and basic elements of the new ideology. This phase was observable under Mikhail Gorbachev in the USSR and Deng Xiaoping in Communist China. Social stability is sought, and reconciliation (or detente) is negotiated with the external enemies.

12 The attempts to achieve a social and cultural revolution are now resumed, and social order is enforced despite the major readjust-ments being effected to both the original revolutionary theory and the practical management of the economy. This phase is especially observable in Communist China and Castroist Cuba in the 1990s.

V ELEMENTS OF CONTINUITY IN REVOLUTIONISED SOCIETIES

After the installation of a revolutionary regime, it can usually be observed that, despite strenuous efforts by the office-holders of the new regime, some features of the 'discredited' society will survive or re-emerge. In the USSR, for example, decades of campaigning against 'bourgeois' practices did not prevent the ultimate reintroduction of incentive payments for factory managers and their staff. Russia under Communist rule was still characterised by a centralised bureaucracy and a privileged class, as in Tsarist times, except that the new privileged class were technocrats and party officials rather than a landowning aristocracy. The masses did not attain a means of 'changing the government', even though this was one of the initial aims of the revolutionaries.

Similarly, in China one official interpretation of life, the Confucian tradition, was replaced by another, the Leninist–Maoist ideology; and one set of powerful sponsors of the official ideology, the mandarin class, was replaced by another, the party officials. Mao Zedong displaced the old orthodoxy with a new orthodoxy, the 'thoughts of Chairman Mao'.

In Cuba the administration of Fidel Castro, although fulfilling many of its promises in the fields of social welfare and health services, turned out to be just as intolerant of expressions of dissent as the Batista regime it deposed. Castro even defined and prohibited such dissent as an act of 'attacking the revolution'.

Looking further back, to the French Revolution, we can also see that one autocrat, Louis XVI, was in time replaced by another, Napoleon Bonaparte. The French nation has at times of crisis sought additional versions of the 'grand ruler' as with Napoleon III (1852–70), Boulanger in the 1880s, and Charles de Gaulle in the period 1959–69.

In a study of revolutions we should also examine societies that have undergone gradual change without violent revolution. There are, on reflection, only a few such examples. Even Britain, which is often cited as a model of a society achieving a gradual ordered progression from an absolute monarchy to rule by a democratically elected parliament, endured the violence of a civil war in the seventeenth century on the issue of the powers of the monarchy. Similarly, the USA, born out of a revolution against rule by a distant parliament, and established as a classless society of 'free men', endured another 'revolution' (in the American Civil War of 1861–65) before this concept was applied to all men, and later women, regardless of colour.

Australia and New Zealand are two examples of nations in which the elected government has never been overthrown in a political revolution. Possible reasons are the existence, since the early days of European settlement, of a democratic system of changing the government and the scale of education given to the people. Perhaps the working classes of any given society must be adequately educated in order to perceive the advantages of evolutionary change, and to be patient enough to wait for that rather than to resort to violence. In the case of Australia and New Zealand, however, the need for revolution has never existed in the ways we have observed in pre-revolutionary France, Russia, China or Vietnam.

Common to all revolutions is a stated desire to build an improved society. Equally common to all such attempts is a degree of 'shortfall' between the hope and the attainment. Basic also to most revolutions is a striving for a group identity as a nation liberated from the intrusions and interferences of other nations, or as a society released from burdens imposed by an anachronistic and exploitative authority.

glossary

anarchism or anarchist socialism: A form of socialism based on the belief that since any form of centralised government is a type of tyranny, human society would be better off if there was no central government ([Gk] *a*, without; *narkhos*, a ruler).

anti-clerical: Opposed to the influence of the Church in society.

anti-colonialism: A term applied to the belief that nations should not exercise colonial control over other nations or groups of people; it also describes the movement that grew to oppose such colonial rule.

anti-Semitic: An emotional bias against Jewish peoples.

antithesis: An opposing force or counterforce.

aristocracy: The people of the most powerful or privileged class (usually a landowning class), exercising political power ([Gk] *aristos*, best; *kratia*, rule). In most modern revolutionary movements a major objective was the reduction of the power of the aristocracy and a redistribution of power among other classes.

atheist: A person having no belief in the existence of God ([Gk] *a*, not; *theos*, a god).

authoritarian rule: A form of government in which the people are expected to accept the 'natural' authority of their superiors, or one dominant figure, and obey without ques-

tion. In many nations the emphasis on loyalty to the nation has led to this condition.

autocratic rule: Absolute government exercised by one person (an autocrat).

balance of power: The policy by which a great power places itself in theoretical or real opposition to another great power or group of powers. In this way no one nation becomes so powerful that it threatens all its neighbours. Britain applied this policy in its relations with other European nations for most of the nineteenth century.

Bolsheviks: The name given to members of the majority group in the Russian Social Democratic Party in the early twentieth century. The Bolsheviks overthrew the provisional government in Russia in November 1917, and their leader, Lenin, became virtual ruler of Russia. The Bolsheviks claimed to follow the teachings of Karl Marx, and were classed as communists.

bourgeoisie: The investing and commercial class of the towns, sometimes called the middle class because their activities are those of 'middle men'—between the primary producers and the consumers. By their acquisition of wealth they also became the 'middle' class between the aristocracy and the peasants. The word 'bourgeoisie' is of

French origin ([Fr] *burgus*, town) and means 'men of the towns'. It was this 'middle class' that most effectively challenged the long-standing power of the aristocracy in the nineteenth century.

bureaucracy: The group of salary-earning, permanent office-holders who administer policies. In the case of a government, the bureaucracy is made up of civil servants, who are not elected by the people but who may exert great influence on day to day matters concerning the rights of citizens.

capital goods: Productive resources (for example, factory machinery) applied to the function of producing other goods.

capitalism: The economic system in which the investment of capital in search of profit is the main incentive to production, and in which the operation of the 'laws' of supply and demand determines the selling prices of products.

capitalist roader: The label used by the Chinese Communist Party to criticise and condemn persons who appeared to be abandoning communism and taking the 'capitalist road'.

Celestial Kingdom: An English version of an expression used by the Chinese Manchu emperors to describe their domain. 'Celestial' means 'elevated' or 'heavenly'.

chauvinism: An emotional and unreasonable belief in the superiority of one's nation or group. The term 'male chauvinism' is an example of its application. The term is derived from a French nationalist, Chauvin, a veteran of the Napoleonic Wars.

coalition: A joining together of two or more political parties as a means of forming a government. The link is temporary, and the parties do not merge into one single party.

Cold War: The state of political and military tension between the pro-capitalist world, led by the USA, and the pro-communist world, led by the USSR, from 1945 till 1991. Both sides built up enormous military capacities in anticipation of a major war.

collective security: By banding together, nations can take collective action to protect each nation in the group from attack by an aggressor. This policy of collective security was attempted through the League of Nations and, in a different way, is one of the aims of the United Nations Organisation.

collectivism: Another form of socialism, encompassing the belief that all members of society would be better off if they worked collectively.

Cominform: An abbreviation of Communist Information Bureau, established in 1947 to disseminate propaganda and to co-ordinate the activities of communist parties in numerous countries. It was dissolved in 1956.

Comintern: An abbreviation of Communist International, an association of communist parties in countries all over the world, set up in Moscow in 1919 and dissolved in 1943.

command economy: An economy in which a central planning body (the government or one of its agencies) makes the major decisions about what is to be produced and by whom. This is in direct contrast to a market economy.

communism: The belief that it is possible to have a classless society, characterised by community ownership of the factors of production, the attainment of which is the aim of Marxian socialists. Communists oppose the capitalist system. In the theoretically ideal classless society the community would own the factors of production and private ownership of profit-making resources would be discontinued.

conservatism: The belief and the policy that the major features of society and societal relationships should either be retained or changed very gradually.

constitutional government: A form of government in which procedures regarding the roles of the legislature, judiciary and executive are defined in a constitution intended to safeguard the rights of the people. The constitution may be formally written down (as in Australia) or it may have evolved in practice (as in Great Britain).

constitutional monarchy: A monarchy in which the power of the monarch is very limited, and in which a set of regulations, usually devised by a parliament, defines the extent of that power or authority.

coup d'état: A 'blow to the State'. In a coup d'état an organised group makes a sudden forceful move to seize control of the government.

cultural revolution: An extreme change brought about in the life patterns, values and modes of communication within a society, usually as a consequence of a political revolution in which a new system of government has been established, with markedly different professed priorities from those of the previous regime. *see also* Great Proletarian Cultural Revolution

demagogue: A political leader who appeals directly to the people ([Gk]: *demos*, people) in the search for popularity and power. The tactics of a demagogue usually involve the making of extravagant promises and the arousing of fears and prejudices through oratory (sometimes called rabble-rousing).

democracy: Government with the consent of the people ([Gk] *demos*, people). Democracy is a political system in which the government (theoretically or in practice) is controlled by the people, either directly or through elected representatives. The key question to be asked is: 'Can the will of the people be used to change the government?' In modern Western democracies representatives are elected to a legislature (governing assembly or parliament), by or from which an executive is appointed, and both the legislature and the executive are responsible (or answerable) to the people.

demokratizatsiya: One of the policies of Mikhail Gorbachev, general secretary of the Russian Communist Party and president of the USSR in the late 1980s. It was a commitment to democratising the system of government within the USSR, thereby diminishing the influence and power of the party.

despotic: Tyrannical, dictatorial.

dialectical materialism: The theory (advanced by Karl Marx) that the major features of society are determined by the material conditions (the dominant 'mode of production'), and that major historical changes in class relationships are effected through conflict between opposing material forces or systems of production.

duma, Duma: The elected town councils introduced in Russia by Tsar Alexander II, with functions similar to those of the *zemstva* in the rural districts. When Tsar Nicholas II called a national parliament in 1905, he named it the Duma.

dynastic empire: The governing of an empire made up of territory conquered and ruled by a dynasty or royal family, for example, the Habsburgs of the Austro–Hungarian Empire, the Hohenzollerns of Prussia, and the Romanoffs of Tsarist Russia. Dynastic rule usually ensured that democratic forms of government were denied, or only slowly permitted to develop.

emigrés: Exiles, in particular, persons who left France during the revolutionary upheavals and were consequently branded as 'traitors'.

entrepreneur: An economic 'enterpriser'; one who invests capital in a business venture with the aim of making a profit.

exploitation: The practice of taking advantage of other persons or countries unfairly for one's own profit. Nineteenth-century capitalist factory owners, for example, could be said to have exploited their wage-earners. Most imperialist powers exploited the peoples of their colonies.

extra-territorial rights: Rights claimed and exercised in China by intruding imperial powers, by which segments of Chinese cities were set aside as 'concessions' to nations such as France and Britain. In these concessions Chinese laws did not apply. 'Extra' means 'outside'; the nationals of the intruding power were outside Chinese law.

Fabian Socialists: A group of socialists who believed in achieving socialism by gradual rather than revolutionary means. The name was derived from a Roman general, Quintus Fabius Maximus, who wore down the invading Carthaginians by gradual tactics. The Fabian Socialists aimed to achieve socialism by winning democratic elections and gaining a majority in parliament.

factors of production: A term used in Marxist theory for the wealth-producing forces (land, labour and capital) in society. According to socialist principles, the factors of production should be owned by society as a whole, and the wealth produced equitably distributed instead of passing to the capitalist investors.

fascism: A form of government based on opposition to communism and the protection of private property ownership; characterised by one-party rule, suppression of opposition, control of the media, and military aggrandisement. The emphasis in fascist States was on the unity of the nation, in contrast to the communist prediction of class conflict.

feudal system, feudalism: A system of government whereby under a form of contract the people pay 'fees' (in the form of goods, labour or service) to a 'lord', king or warrior chieftain in return for permission to work the land and for protection in time of war.

franchise: ([Fr] *franc*, free) The right to perform a function or exercise a privilege; in the political sense, the right to vote in elections. *see also* suffrage

Four Freedoms: The widely promoted objectives of the Allied powers during World War II—freedom of speech, freedom of religion, freedom from want, and freedom from fear.

***glasnost*:** A Russian word meaning 'openness', used by Mikhail Gorbachev, General Secretary of the Communist Party, in 1986 to launch his policy of freedom of expression.

Great Proletarian Cultural Revolution: The mass movement in Communist China (*circa* 1965–69) in which, under the leadership of Mao Zedong, young people were organised into Red Guards in order to destroy the power of the bureaucracy and to revitalise the revolution of society.

guerrilla: The word is of Spanish origin and means 'little war'. A guerrilla fighter does not operate in the conventional way; instead of fighting in large, formally organised units, guerrillas fight irregularly, in small units or even singly. They often employ 'hit and run' techniques, using the countryside as a sanctuary and sometimes enjoying the support of local people.

Habsburgs: The royal family of Austria, rulers of the Austro–Hungarian Empire, descendants of the German count, Rudolf of Habsburg, who was the Holy Roman Emperor from 1273 to 1279. The Habsburgs ruled in Vienna until 1918. Charles, Emperor of Austria and King of Hungary, went into exile at the end of World War I.

hegemony: Leadership, or domination, of several nations by one nation.

hereditary monarch: A monarch who inherits the throne from a parent or an ancestor, and claims it by right.

hierarchy: A graded system of administration whereby authority is ranked, as on a ladder. The name is derived from the levels of authority in the administration of the early Christian Church ([Gk] *hierarkhes—hieros*, sacred; *arkhos*, ruler).

historicism: The belief that certain 'forces' operate in History, or that patterns repeat themselves in historical events.

humanitarian: Concerned with the welfare of fellow human beings regardless of class or race.

ideologies: Systems of belief in ways of organising society. Socialism and capitalism are examples of ideologies.

imperialism: The belief and practice that a strong society has the right and the duty (in terms of 'bringing civilisation' or 'salvation') to a weaker society by incorporating it in an empire. A conquest of one society by another.

industrialisation: The process whereby a

society's productive effort shifts from predominantly primary production in rural areas and domestic industry to secondary production in industrial cities. The change occurs when capital becomes available to either private or government enterprise for investment in manufacturing industries.

insurgency: An uprising against an established government, frequently used in the period 1945–75 in the term 'communist insurgencies'.

internationalism: The belief and practice that several nations can act together in a community of interest, for example, in the League of Nations. Another meaning is the expectation that the people of several nations can act co-operatively for an ideal that transcends national loyalties, for example, in the Marxian socialist ideal of loyalty to an international 'brotherhood' of the proletariat.

investment: The application of wealth to the purpose of seeking more wealth, either by putting the money to work to manufacture goods to sell at a profit, or by using the money to provide a service for which a charge can be made (even the loan of money to another person, with interest charged, is an investment).

jingoism: The aggressive and belligerent form of nationalism. The term is derived from the British music hall song: *We don't want to fight, but by Jingo, if we do, we've got the ships, we've got the men, we've got the money too.*

kulaks: Wealthier farmers in the USSR, many of whom had prospered during the New Economic Policy period, 1921–28. By 1928 Stalin had decided to 'liquidate' them as a class. A number joined the new collective farms; others who resisted were killed or imprisoned.

laissez-faire: 'Let things be'; the economic policy of allowing trade and commerce to function with as few government-imposed restrictions as possible.

legislative powers: The powers, possessed by a government, but usually exercised by a parliament, for the making of laws.

left-wing: A political term that means tending towards socialist policies. The term originated during the French Revolution, when the most radical groups (those wanting most extreme change) sat on the left side of the National Assembly.

liberal–capitalist state: A nation in which the liberal principle that the government should ensure the freedom and security of the individual is associated with the provision of opportunities for capitalist enterprise.

liberalism: An ideology that advocates liberty for the individual, particularly from excessive government restrictions. The liberals of the nineteenth century wanted freedom from the controls imposed by absolute monarchies, and particularly wanted 'free enterprise' in commerce. They favoured the parliamentary system of government based on a property franchise as the best means of assuring the protection of individual liberties. Many nations were founded in the nineteenth and twentieth centuries on this principle.

mandate of heaven: The Chinese version of 'divine right', based on the belief that the emperor had been given the responsibility of command by heavenly authority.

manhood suffrage: The right of all adult males to vote in the election of parliamentary representatives. *see also* franchise *and* suffrage

market economy: An economic system in which the government does not interfere in the pricing of goods and services. In theory the 'laws' of supply and demand operate, through competition, to set price levels. This contrasts with the command economy.

Marxian socialism: The ideology, based on the predictions of Karl Marx, that the capitalist system will be overthrown by a revolution led by the proletariat. This will result in a new economic system (communism), in which the resources of production will be owned by the community rather than by private capitalists. Marx claimed that, in industrialised societies, this proletarian seizure of power was inevitable. He said that with the achievement of true communism, economic classes would eventually fade away and there would be a classless society.

medieval period or times: The Middle Ages—that period of time between the fall of the Roman Empire (*circa* AD 500) and the Renaissance (*circa* AD 1500).

mercantilism: An economic policy based on the belief that the wealth of the world is static, and that a nation can best secure both its wealth and its power by acquiring a 'closed empire'. This would ensure that all vital products were available within the empire, and dependence on foreign powers would be cut to a minimum.

middle class: *see* bourgeoisie

Middle Kingdom: The Chinese term for China, based on the belief that it lay in the centre of the world, and that the people of the outer lands were 'barbarians'.

mixed economy: An economy in which there is a considerable amount of government planning but in which aspects of a market economy still function to a significant degree. *see also* command economy

monopoly capitalism: The extreme condition of capitalism in which competition no longer functions adequately because one nation or one company controls the supply of a product.

nationalisation: The process by which a government takes over the ownership of an industry previously owned by private shareholders.

nationalism: The belief that a group of people of common language and culture have a right to form a separate nation and govern themselves; the act of seeking to achieve this condition.

neo–colonialism, neo–imperialism: Imperialism in a new guise; no longer as a form of direct rule but through economic or cultural controls.

Ottoman: The name of the dynasty ruling the Turkish Empire from *circa* 1300 until 1922.

parlements: Literally, these were 'speaking assemblies', which functioned in pre-Revolutionary France. As the aristocracy was the only class authorised to express an opinion on the workings of the monarchy, the *parlements* were composed solely of aristocrats, who passed their official positions on to their heirs. The *parlements* of Paris and the major provincial cities had the duty of registering and, if they chose, protesting against royal decrees. They were not, however, parliaments in the English sense. When the Estates-General was called in 1789, the *parlements* ceased to function.

parochial: Local-minded; concerned only with the issues of the parish. Thus a parochial attitude is one in which the larger interests of the province, State, or nation are seen to be less important than local interests.

paternalistic: 'Fatherly' in attitude. A paternalistic government limits the freedom of the people by making most of their decisions for them.

patriotism: Love of, and willingness to defend, one's country. This is perhaps a longer-standing emotion than nationalism, which has a wider meaning.

perestroika: A Russian word meaning 'restructuring', which came into general use in 1986, after Mikhail Gorbachev, General Secretary of the Communist Party of the USSR, used it to describe the reform programme he proposed to introduce to Soviet economic and social practices.

planned economy: *see* command economy

plebiscite: A direct vote by the people of a defined area on a vital matter, often related to frontiers or the constitution.

political tutelage: The process by which, in theory, the Chinese people would be taught by the Guomindang to participate (eventually) in democratic practices.

pragmatic, the Pragmatists: The policy of emphasising practical considerations ('getting things done') rather than ideals or principles; the group of Chinese leaders who succeeded Mao Zedong and who proposed this policy instead of rigid adherence to Maoist–Marxist philosophy.

proletariat: The urban working class, who depend on the sale of their skill and labour to earn wages.

provisional government: A temporary government, entrusted with power pending the formation of a permanent government.

puppet regimes: Governments having the appearance of independence but which are heavily or totally influenced by an outside power.

radical: Wanting extreme change in the existing political or social system.

reactionary: An adjective to describe a person or group which opposes or reacts (acts against) proposals for political or social change.

representative government: A form of government in which the legislative power is entrusted to elected representatives. This, however, is not necessarily a democratic form of government, because the franchise may be severely limited.

republican government: That form of government in which the head of state holds office by election rather than inheritance.

responsible government: The form of government in which the executive (the prime minister and cabinet) is responsible (answerable) to the parliament, and must have the continued support of a majority in the parliament to stay in office.

revisionist: (a) A political leader seeking a 'revision' of the peace treaties of 1919 on the grounds of their basic injustice; or (b) a person acknowledging a need to 'revise' the theories of Marx and Lenin regarding the pathway to world communism.

revolution: A series of political or social changes that result in drastic alterations to the previously observed practices. In instances such as the Agrarian or Industrial revolutions, this means that the people's daily routines, work patterns, and relationships with other members of society are irrevocably changed. In the instance of a political revolution, the previously dominant regime is overthrown and repudiated, and a new system of government, professing new principles and objectives, is installed. In the years following the installation of the new government, a revolution in the culture of the community may also occur (*see* cultural revolution). The metaphor of the 'turn about' in standards implies something revolving 180 degrees to a position opposite to that formerly operative.

right-wing: A general term used to describe groups that oppose radical change. In the twentieth century, 'right-wing' is often used to describe groups opposed to communist or socialist ideas (seen by them as 'left-wing').

Risorgimento: An Italian word meaning 'resurrection'. The word is used to describe the movement for Italian unity in the nineteenth century.

Romanoff: The ruling dynasty (royal family) of Russia from 1613 to 1917. The last Romanoff tsar was Nicholas II, murdered in July 1918.

secularism: A belief that material things are of more significance than spiritual or religious concerns; a rejection of religion.

self-determination: The right of an identifiable group of people to determine (decide) for themselves their form of government and the nation to which they wish to belong.

sinologist: An expert on Chinese history ([Gk] *Sinai*: China).

socialism: A belief that there should be social ownership of the factors of production (instead of private ownership), and that this would eliminate poverty and ensure an equal distribution of wealth.

social ownership: Ownership of the factors of production by society as a whole rather than by profit-seeking individuals, the profits being shared amongst all members of the community; communal ownership. *see* communism

soviets: A Russian word which means 'councils' or 'committees', used to describe the councils of workers' representatives formed in the Russian cities before the 1917 Revolution. The Bolsheviks included the word in the title of their new nation, the USSR or Union of Soviet Socialist Republics.

suffrage: The right to vote in elections for parliamentary representatives. Manhood suffrage is the right of all adult males to vote; universal suffrage is the right of all adults to vote.

surplus value: A term devised by Marx to refer to the value added to raw materials by workers' labour and skill, but retained by the capitalist owner as profit instead of being distributed among the workers as wages.

syndicalism: A belief among trade unionists that if all workers acted together to deny their productive labour, the State would be forced to grant economic and social reforms.

tariff: A levy or tax imposed on an imported product, usually to increase its sale price. This protects home-produced goods, which can be sold more cheaply than the imported goods. Without the tariff, the foreign product could undersell the local product. Tariffs also provide the government with revenue.

Teutonic peoples: People of Germanic race and culture, including German-speaking Austrians.

Third World nations: A term used from the 1950s until the early 1990s to describe the nations (usually of Africa, Asia and Latin America) which were not aligned with either the capitalist or communist power blocs. The term usually also implied that the nations were poor and under-developed.

tithe: A tax paid to the Church (usually one-tenth of income), widely applied in the Middle Ages and occasionally in modern times.

totalitarian State: A nation in which a dictatorial government demands the total devotion of the people to the service of the State, and in which individual rights are suppressed.

trade unions: Organisations of working people (craftsmen or wage-earners) which emerged in Britain during the nineteenth century, and later spread to countries all over the world. By joining together as a united group, workers were able to enter into 'collective bargaining' with their employers. In this way they could offer their collective co-operation in return for fair wages and safe conditions. If these were not granted, the trade union could instruct its members to go on strike (withdraw their labour). This could threaten the capitalist employers with economic failure.

tributary State: A State which pays 'tribute' (in allegiance and possibly taxes) to a dominant neighbouring State.

tsar: The emperor of Russia, sometimes spelt czar ([L] *caesar*).

unequal treaties: The term used to describe the treaties imposed upon China and Japan by Western powers in the nineteenth century. Because of the military superiority of the Western powers, China and Japan had to accept humiliating conditions in which they were not treated as equals.

urbanisation: The process whereby the population of a country or region becomes concentrated in cities.

vassalage: The condition of being a 'vassal'— a person or a nation owing allegiance to a superior authority.

welfare State: A State in which the welfare of the people is not left to chance or financial success, but is provided for in government policies. The wealth of the community is redistributed by taxing the rich and aiding the poor through welfare benefits.

world revolution: The event, anticipated by adherents of Marxian socialism, in which the proletariat all over the world will overthrow capitalist governments. In theory, a world community of people devoted to socialist principles would then emerge.

xenophobia: A hatred or fear of foreigners or foreign powers.

zemstvo **(plural** *zemstva***):** Elected provincial or district councils set up in Russia in January 1864 as part of Tsar Alexander II's reform programme.

index